The great favourite

MANCHESTER
1824

Manchester University Press

STUDIES IN EARLY MODERN
EUROPEAN HISTORY

This series aims to publish
challenging and innovative research in all areas
of early modern continental history.
The editors are committed to encouraging work
that engages with current historiographical
debates, adopts an interdisciplinary
approach, or makes an original contribution
to our understanding of the period.

SERIES EDITORS
Joseph Bergin, William G. Naphy, Penny Roberts and Paolo Rossi

The great favourite

The Duke of Lerma and the court
and government of Philip III of Spain,
1598–1621

PATRICK WILLIAMS

Manchester University Press
Manchester and New York

distributed exclusively in the USA by Palgrave

Published by Manchester University Press
Oxford Road, Manchester M13 9NR, UK
and Room 400, 175 Fifth Avenue, New York, NY 10010, USA
www.manchesteruniversitypress.co.uk

Distributed in the United States exclusively by
Palgrave Macmillan, 175 Fifth Avenue,
New York, NY 10010, USA

Distributed in Canada exclusively by
UBC Press, University of British Columbia, 2029 West Mall,
Vancouver, BC, Canada V6T 1Z2

British Library Cataloguing-in-Publication Data is available

Library of Congress Cataloging-in-Publication Data is available

ISBN 978 0 7190 8141 5 paperback

First published by Manchester University Press in hardback 2006

This paperback edition first published 2010

Printed by Lightning Source

For
Phillip, Michael, Katherine, Russell

Contents

List of tables

Acknowledgements

It is a pleasure to acknowledge the debts incurred in the writing of this book. John Lynch supervised the doctorate from which this study has grown and most generously supported me with encouragement and guidance without ever asking when it would be finished; I am enduringly obliged to him. Joseph Bergin commissioned the book and guided it to publication with calm generosity and patience; I hope that he has some idea of what his support has meant to me.

It was my good fortune to begin my study of Lerma in the enervating company of Geoffrey Parker and the late Albert Lovett; great scholars, a joyous time! Henry Kamen brought me back to Lerma after I had strayed from him, and I thank him for doing so. Pauline Croft, Ronald Cueto, Bernardo García García, Dámaso de Lario, Santiago Martínez Hernández, Rob Stradling, Tony Thompson, Richard Trewinnard, Lorraine White and Phillip Williams have discussed Lerma with endless patience and good humour while Xanthe Brookes, David Davies and Nigel Glendinning have expertly guided me through the catalogues of Lerma's collections of paintings. Special thanks, as always, to John W. Tobias and Helmut Koenigsberger. The Rev. Brian Scantlebury and the late Rev. George Talbot patiently answered many questions about theological and canonical matters. P. Palomares Ibañez O. P. shared his rich knowledge of the monastery-church of *San Pablo* in Valladolid with me while P. Jesús Castilla Fuente, parish priest of *San Pedro* in Lerma, allowed me free rein to explore Lerma's great cathedral-church.

I am deeply indebted to the kindness and expertise of innumerable archivists, especially those who have guided me in the incomparable archive of Simancas. In Simancas, too, Anunción and the Álvarez Sánchez family have welcomed me to the splendours of the *Casa Curro* with great warmth and cheerfulness. Doña Lucía Feijóo guided me patiently through the prodigious holdings of the Lerma archive in Toledo. The British Academy and the Leverhulme Foundation provided generous support for work in Spain.

At Portsmouth, thanks to Elizabeth Clifford, Aurea Sánchez-Martín, Julie Weller and the library staff who have been patient and generous with their time and expertise. At Manchester University Press, Jonathan Bevan and Alison Welsby guided the book to production with exemplary diligence and good humour. George Pitcher was an indefatigable copy-editor who patiently guided me through a myriad of technical problems and Angela Brennan enthusiastically made light of the final corrections (and the composition of the index). Thanks, too, to the anonymous Readers who commented so helpfully on the manuscript.

The book is dedicated to my children, who have grown up with 'The Duke' as a member of their family. For my adored Margaret, there is another book; hopefully it will not take quite as long as this one has done.

Note on Spanish-language documents

The spellings (including written accents) of all Spanish-language texts – particularly those of the sixteenth and seventeenth centuries – have been shown throughout as in the original documents adduced as sources, thus reflecting the not-then-standardized language usages as well as the dialects and practices of the various regions / states of the Iberian peninsula and beyond.

List of abbreviations

ACA	Archivo de la Corona de Aragón, Barcelona	
	CA	*Consejo de Aragón*
*ACC	*Actas de las Cortes de Castilla*	
ADL	*Archivo del Duque de Lerma,* Toledo	
AEA	*Archivo Español de Arte*	
AGI	Archivo de Indias, Seville	
	IG	*Indiferente General*
AGS	Archivo General de Simancas, Valladolid	
	BBS	*Bulas y Breves Sueltas*
	CC	*Consejo de Castilla, Cámara de Castilla*
	CG Inv. 24	*Contadurías Generales, Inventario 24*
	CJH	*Consejos y Juntas de Hacienda*
	CMC	*Contaduría Mayor de Cuentas*
	CSR	*Casas y Sitios Reales*
	DGT	*Dirección General del Tesoro*
	E	*Estado*
	GA	*Guerra Antigua*
	K	*[French series of papers of Council of State]*
	PR	*Patronato Real*
	QC	*Quitaciones de Corte*
AHM	Archivo Municipal de Madrid	
	LA	*Libros de Actas*
AHN	Archivo Histórico Nacional, Madrid	
	C	*Consejos*
	Inq	*Inquisición*
	LP	*Libros de Plaza*
	OM	*Órdenes Militar*
	Os	*Osuna*
AHPM	Archivo Histórico de Protocolos Notariales de Madrid	
AHR	*American Historical Review*	
AIEM	*Anales del Instituto de Estudios Madrileños*	
AMV	Archivo Municipal de Valladolid	
	LA	*Libros de Actas*
ASV	Archivo Secreto de Vaticano, Rome	
BBMP	*Boletín de la Biblioteca Menéndez Pelayo*	
BHS	*Bulletin of Hispanic Studies*	

BIHR   *Bulletin of the Institute of Historical Research*
BL   British Library (Section of Manuscripts)
    Add   *Additional*
    Eg   *Egerton*
    Sl   *Sloane*
    St   *Stowe*
BN   Biblioteca Nacional, Madrid (*Sección de Manuscritos*)
BRAH   *Boletín de la Real Academia de Historia*
CIH   *Cuadernos de Investigaciones Históricas*
Cnta   *Consulta*
*CODOIN   *Colección de documentos inéditos para la Historia de España*
CSP   Calendar of State Papers
    D   Domestic
    F   Foreign
    V   Venetian
*DHEE   *Diccionario de Historia Eclesiástica de España*
    IEF   Instituto Enríque Flóres
DIHE   *Documentos inéditos para la historia de España*
Econ. Hist. Review   Economic History Review
EHQ   *European History Quarterly*
EHR   *English Historical Review*
ESR   *European Studies Review* (subsequently, *European History Quarterly*)
Gaçetas y Nuevas   G. Gascón de Torquemada, *Gaçetas y Nuevas*
HH   Hatfield House
    CP   Cecil Papers
HMC   Historical Manuscripts Commission
    Salisb   Salisbury Papers
    Trum   Trumbull Papers
IH   *Investigaciones históricas*
IEM   *Instituto de Estudios Madrileños*
JCL   Junta de Castilla y León
NA   National Archive, London
    SP   State Papers, Spain
RABM   *Revista de Archivos Bibliotecas y Museos*
RAH   Real Academia de la Historia, Madrid
Relaciones   Luis Cabrera de Córdoba, *Relaciones de las cosas sucedidas en la corte de España desde 1599 hasta 1614*
RB   Real Biblioteca, Palacio Real, Madrid
SECCFC   Sociedad Estatal para la Conmemoración de los Centenarios de Felipe II y Carlos V

* For full reference, see bibliography

Glossary

adelantado	governor of a frontier province responsible for civil and criminal case/s; an honorary dignity by the late sixteenth century; *adelantamiento*, province ruled by *adelantado*
alcabala	sales tax of 10 per cent on goods sold in Castile
alcaide	castellan of a castle or strongpoint; *alcaidía,* office of the *alcaide*
alcalde de casa y corte	judge responsible for ordinary jurisdiction at the court and within five leagues
alcázar	royal palace
alférez mayor	chief ensign bearer
almadraba	tunny fishery
arbitrio	proposal for political or economic improvement; *arbitrista,* proposer of *arbitrio*
asiento	a loan, generally to the crown
auto	decree of judgement in civil, criminal or religious case; *auto de fé,* public ceremony of the Inquisition in which verdicts were read and sentences carried out; *auto de posesión* act of taking possession of an office
aya	governess of a child
ayuda de cámara	servant who helps *camarero* in the King's chamber
ayuda de costa	aid to expenses, normally in addition to a royal salary
bailía	unit of jurisdiction in Crown of Aragón
bienes	possessions or goods on which monetary value can be set; *bienes libres,* those *bienes* which can be freely disposed of within system of *mayorazgo*
caballería	cavalry; *caballerizo mayor,* Master of the King's Horse
caballero	gentleman
Cámara de Castilla	Chamber of the Council of Castile dealing with royal patronage, established in reform of Council in 1588
Cámara y Estado de Castilla	Secretariat of the Council of Castile responsible for management of crown's estates, established in 1588
camarera mayor	Lady Chamberlain (masc., *camarero mayor*) in charge of royal quarters; *camarería mayor,* office of *camarero mayor*
cancillería	judicial tribunal (Kingdom of Castile being divided between those of Granada and Valladolid)
capa y espada	a councillor drawn from ranks of nobility

capellán mayor	chief chaplain (of the King)
capitán general	captain-general; *de la caballería de España*, of the Cavalry of Spain
capitulación	marriage agreement
carrera real	royal road
casa	Royal household; *de Aragón*, of Aragon, *de Borgoña*, of Burgundy; *de Castilla*, of Castile
Casa de Campo	royal hunting lodge on western outskirts of Madrid, adjacent to royal palace
casa de la moneda	royal mint
Casa de la Ribera	palace and grounds 'on the riverbank' (of Valladolid)
casa profesa	religious house for Society of Jesus
casa y corte	royal court, residence of monarch
cédula	royal decree, having the force of law
censo	loan or mortgage
chantre	director of choral music in cathedral or collegial church
clientela	informal network of people owing loyalty to a patron, usually at court
comedia	theatrical story, normally of common life, carrying a moral content
Comendador Mayor de Castilla	senior commander in military order of Santiago, responsible for province of Castile and presiding over chapter of the order
Comisario General de la Cruzada	Chief Commissioner of the Crusade, *de facto* President of the Council of the Crusade (a tax granted to the King of Spain by the Pope)
comuneros	rebellion of the towns of Castile, 1520-21
con palío	a formal royal entrance into a town or city in which the monarch is covered by a canopy or pallium; normally signifying the monarch's first visit to a town or city during his reign
concordia	a legally binding agreement
consignaciones	monies assigned to bankers against specified crown revenues
consuegro/a	relationship enjoyed by parents of a married couple
consulta	document in which a council advises the King
Contador	accountant; *de mercedes*, of grants of the royal grace; *de sueldo*, of salaries
Contaduría Mayor de Cuentas	Chief accounting office
contino	person serving as guard to the monarch
convento	convent or monastery
copero mayor	Chief cup-bearer (to the King of Castile)
corregidor	governor of city or province for the King
cortes	meeting of representatives of kingdom summoned by monarch to advise him and to approve taxation; *corts*, of Catalonia
criado	servant

Cristo Yacente	artistic representation of the dead Christ
Descalzas Reales	convent for barefoot Franciscans in Madrid, founded by Juana, sister of Philip II
desempeño	redemption of royal rents pledged to bankers
empresa de Inglaterra	fleet (or *armada*) sent against England, 1588
encabezamiento	commutation of *alcabala* tax
Encarnación	Augustinian convent of 'The Incarnation', founded by Queen Margaret, 1611
encomienda	endowment of a rent in a Military Order
Escribanía de sacas y cosas vedadas, diezmos y aduanas	office assessing and collecting taxation from import and export dues on Andalusian coast
escribano	public notary
escudo	coin or family shield
estado	landed estate of a lord
etiquetas	rules governing public ceremonial, particularly those involving royal households
fanega	amount of wheat grown in an area 576 metres square
fiesta	public celebrations or entertainments
fiscal	crown lawyer (the office of *fiscalía*)
fray	friar
galeote	lesser galley, with 16-20 oars per side
general de la mar	an admiral serving as the King's eyes in a royal fleet
gentilhombre de la cámara	gentleman of the King's chamber
grande	grandee; *grandeza*, the rank of grandee
hechura	person attaching himself (or herself) to the service of a lord; a henchman
hijodalgo	a nobleman pledged to serve a lord (or monarch)
hombres de negocios	bankers or money-lenders
huerta	a garden; or a house with its own gardens attached
infante	prince (fem., *infanta*)
jornada	royal journey
juegos de caña	tilting on horseback
Junta	meeting of royal ministers, often informal *de Fábricas y Armadas*, of shipbuilding; *de Gobierno*, of Government, established by Philip II to guide Philip III at beginning of reign; *de Hacienda*, of Finance; *de Obras y Bosques*, of palaces and hunting lodges; *de Provisiones*, of provisions; *de Reformación*, of Reform; *del Desempeño Real*, of redemption of royal rents
juro	government bond
Justicia	leading law officer of Aragón; or secretaryship of Council of Castile responsible for judicial affairs, established in 1588

lermista	follower or henchman of the duke of Lerma
Licenciado	lawyer's title
limosnero mayor	dispenser-in-chief of royal charity to poor
limpieza de sangre	bloodline free of Jewish or Moorish ancestry
lliur	One pound (Valencian)
lugar	a small settlement, defined as having 'any population' or 'a small population'
maestrazgo	grand mastership
maestre de campo general	Field-marshal (of Army of Flanders)
maestresscuela	director of ecclesiastical and liturgical studies in cathedral or collegial church
maestro	educational tutor
maravedí	unit coinage of account
mayorazgo	entail to which eldest son succeeds
mayordomo mayor	chief of royal household
medio general	terms of settlement with royal bankers after a suspension of payments by the crown
merced	grant from royal grace
millones	grant from Cortes of Castile for specified period; in millions of ducats
monasterio	an enclosed convent or monastery
moneda forera	money paid to the crown every seven years
Monteros de Espinosa	officers of king's household who were charged with ensuring the security of the King's palace, particularly at night
moriscos	Moorish converts to Christianity
nómina	payroll identifying individuals who were entitled to salary
oidor	judge or councillor
ordenanzas	laws or decrees
padrino/a	godfather/mother
pagador	paymaster
parecer	opinion or recommendation made by councillor
parentela	kinship network
pasadizo	passageway
pasquín	polemical or satirical writing
Patronato Real de la Iglesia	Secretaryship of the Church, Council of Castile, established in 1588
Patronazgo	patronage
Pax Hispánica	'The Spanish Peace' (sc., the period 1610-18, after the assassination of Henry IV)
peage y leuda	toll
plaza	public square; *plaza mayor*, chief square of town or city; *plaza ducal*, square in front of a ducal palace (sc. in Lerma); *plaza de armas*, parade ground

presidio	frontier post/garrison
privado	royal favourite; *privanza*, exercise of office of *privado*
prueba	proof accepted for noble status or purity of blood
regidor	town councillor
repartimiento	allocation to individual towns or cities of responsibility for tax of the *millones*, 1611
reputación	reputation (of the King)
rey prudente	the Prudent King (sc., Philip II)
salmas de trigo	measurement of wheat
servicio	tax voted by Cortes
servicios ordinarios y extraordinarios	the ordinary and extraordinary taxes voted by the Cortes of Castile
sumiller de corps	Groom of the Stole (to the King)
Superintendente de hacienda de Flándes	Superintendent of financial affairs in the loyalist provinces of Low Countries
Suprema, la	the Council of the Inquisition
tierra	landed estate
título	nobleman who is not a grandee; generally, a count or marquis
toisón de oro	(Order of) Golden Fleece
tribuna	private window or bench in a church, giving privileged access to divine services
valido	royal favourite; *valimiento*, exercise of position of *valido*
vecino	householder
veedor	purchase of victuals
vellón	copper money of Castile
vicechanciller	vicechancellor; *de Aragón*, President of Council of Aragón
villas de behetría	Castilian towns having right to choose their lord
visita	judicial investigation; *visitador*, examining judge

Sources: Real Academía de Historia, *Diccionario de Autoridades*, 3 vols., Madrid, 1726-37 and Sebastián de Covarrubias Horozco, *Tesoro de la lengua castellana o española*, 2 vols., Madrid, 1611.

The Duke of Lerma and the house of Sandoval
1. Grandparents, parents and siblings

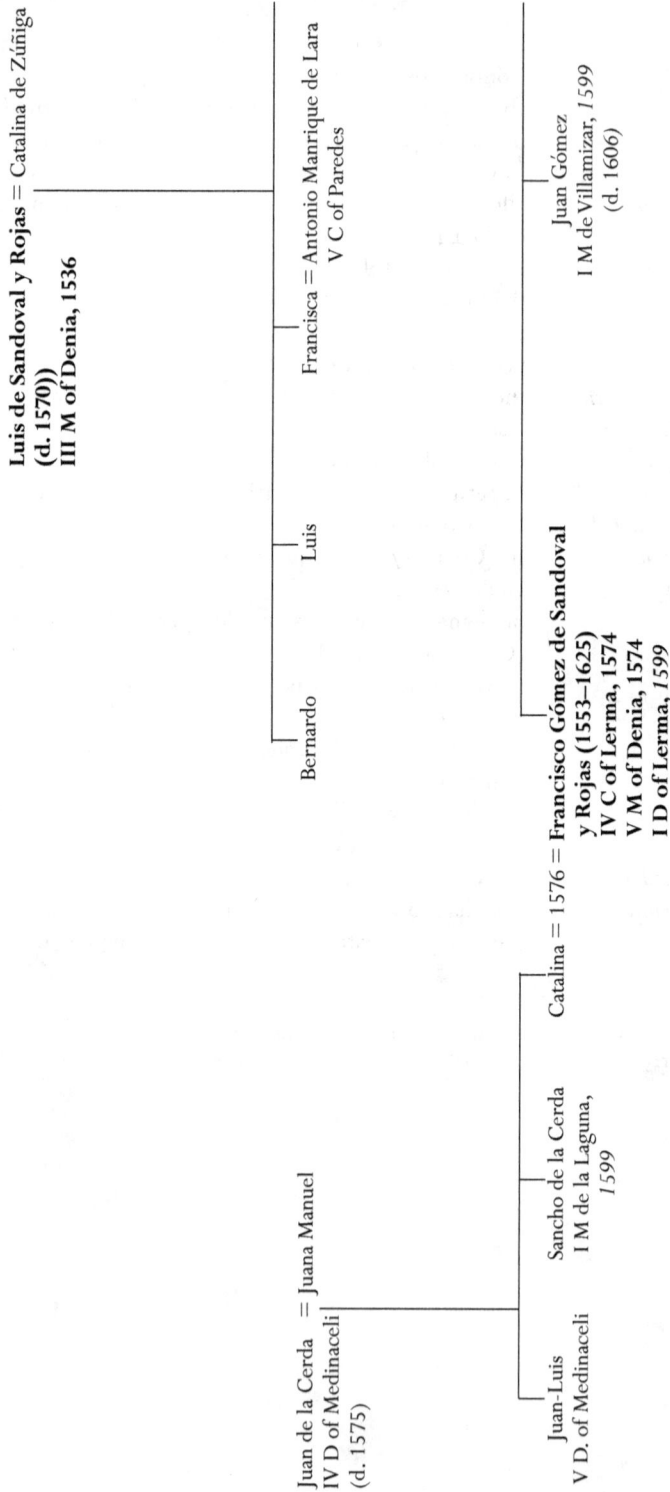

Luis de Sandoval y Rojas
(d. 1570))
III M of Denia, 1536 = Catalina de Zúñiga

Bernardo

Luis

Francisca = Antonio Manrique de Lara
V C of Paredes

Juan-Luis
V D. of Medinaceli
(d. 1575)

Juan de la Cerda = Juana Manuel
IV D of Medinaceli

Sancho de la Cerda
I M de la Laguna,
1599

Catalina = 1576 = **Francisco Gómez de Sandoval**
y Rojas (1553–1625)
IV C of Lerma, 1574
V M of Denia, 1574
I D of Lerma, *1599*

Juan Gómez
I M de Villamizar, *1599*
(d. 1606)

in **bold**, the head of the family; in *italics*, the date of titles endowed by Philip III

The Duke of Lerma and the house of Sandoval

1. Grandparents, parents and siblings, *continued*

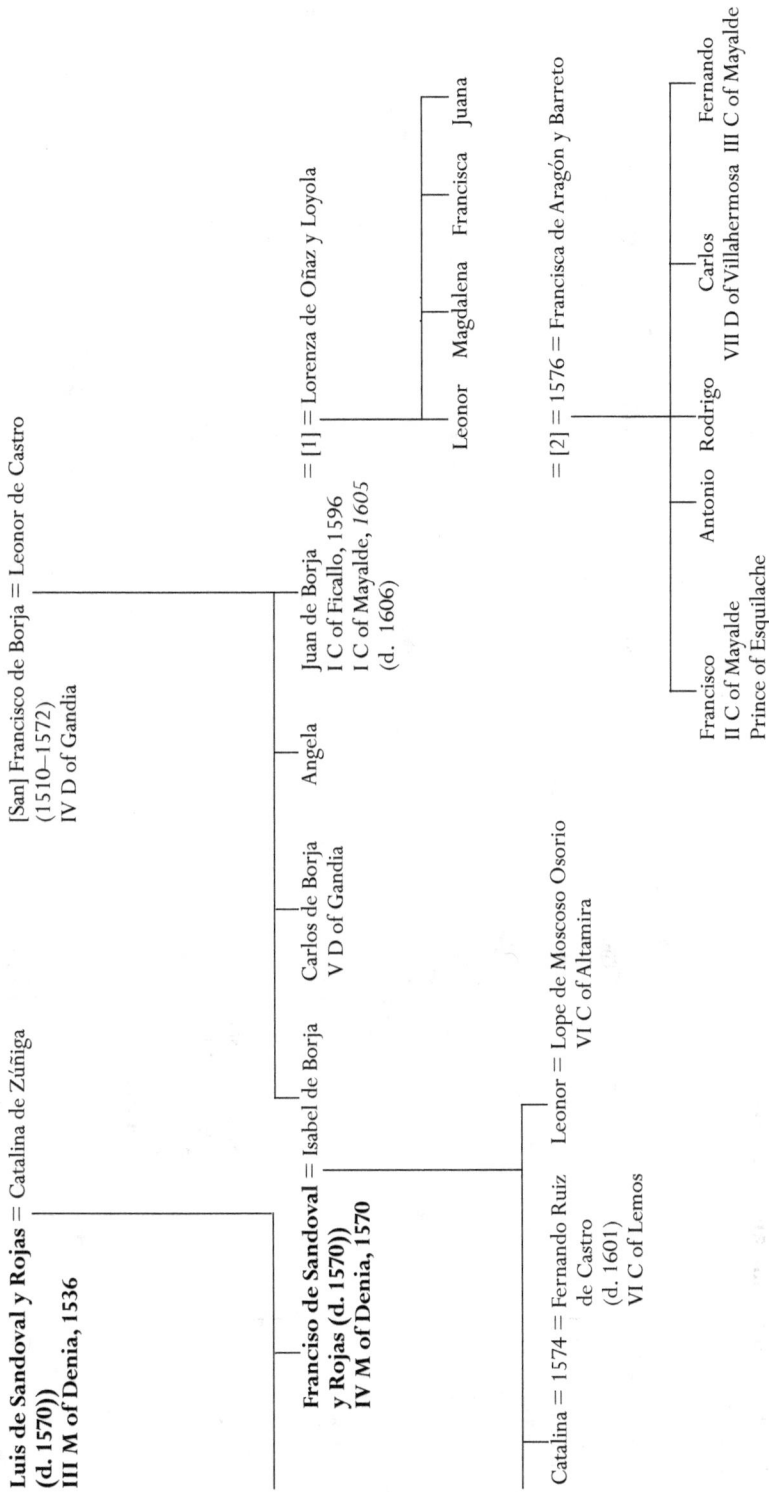

Luis de Sandoval y Rojas = Catalina de Zúñiga
(d. 1570))
III M of Denia, 1536

[San] Francisco de Borja = Leonor de Castro
(1510–1572))
IV D of Gandia

Franciso de Sandoval = Isabel de Borja
y Rojas (d. 1570))
IV M of Denia, 1570

Carlos de Borja
V D of Gandia

Angela

Juan de Borja
I C of Ficallo, 1596
I C of Mayalde, *1605*
(d. 1606)

= [1] = Lorenza de Oñaz y Loyola

Leonor   Magdalena   Francisca   Juana

= [2] = 1576 = Francisca de Aragón y Barreto

Francisco
II C of Mayalde
Prince of Esquilache

Antonio   Rodrigo

Carlos
VII D of Villahermosa

Fernando
III C of Mayalde

Catalina = 1574 = Fernando Ruiz
de Castro
(d. 1601)
VI C of Lemos

Leonor = Lope de Moscoso Osorio
VI C of Altamira

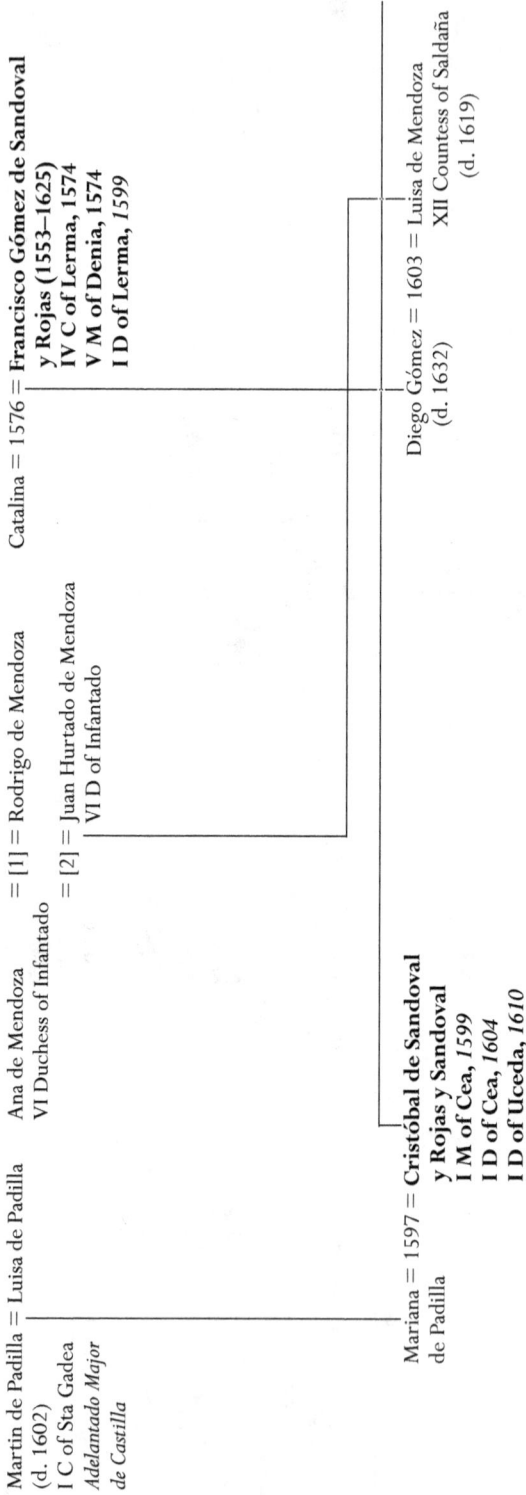

The Duke of Lerma and the house of Sandoval

2. Children

Martín de Padilla = Luisa de Padilla
(d. 1602)
I C of Sta Gadea
*Adelantado Major
de Castilla*

Ana de Mendoza
VI Duchess of Infantado

= [1] = Rodrigo de Mendoza

= [2] = Juan Hurtado de Mendoza
VI D of Infantado

Catalina = 1576 = **Francisco Gómez de Sandoval
y Rojas (1553–1625)
IV C of Lerma, 1574
V M of Denia, 1574
I D of Lerma, *1599***

Mariana = 1597 = **Cristóbal de Sandoval
y Rojas y Sandoval
I M of Cea, *1599*
I D of Cea, *1604*
I D of Uceda, *1610***

de Padilla

Diego Gómez = 1603 = Luisa de Mendoza
(d. 1632)   XII Countess of Saldaña
                     (d. 1619)

The Duke of Lerma and the house of Sandoval

2. Children. *continued*

Catalina = 1576 = **Francisco Gómez de Sandoval y Rojas (1553–1625)**
IV C of Lerma, 1574
V M of Denia, 1574
I D of Lerma, 1599

Catalina = 1574 = Fernández Ruiz de Castro
(d. 1601)
VI C of Lemos, 1599

Juan de Zúñiga
VI C of Miranda
I D of Peñaranda, *1608*
(d. 1608)

= María de Zúñiga

Alonso Pérez de Guzmán
(1549–1615)
VII D of Medina Sidonia, 1615

= Ana de Silva y Mendoza

Catalina = 1598 = Pedro Fernández de Castro
VII C of Lemos, 1599

Juana = 1598 = Manuel Pérez de Guzmán
(1579–1636)
VI C of Niebla
[VIII D of Medina Sidonia, 1615]

Francisca = 1603 = Diego López de Zúñiga
Avellaneda
VII C of Miranda, 1608
II D of Peñaranda, 1608

The Duke of Lerma and the house of Sandoval

3. Children and grandchildren

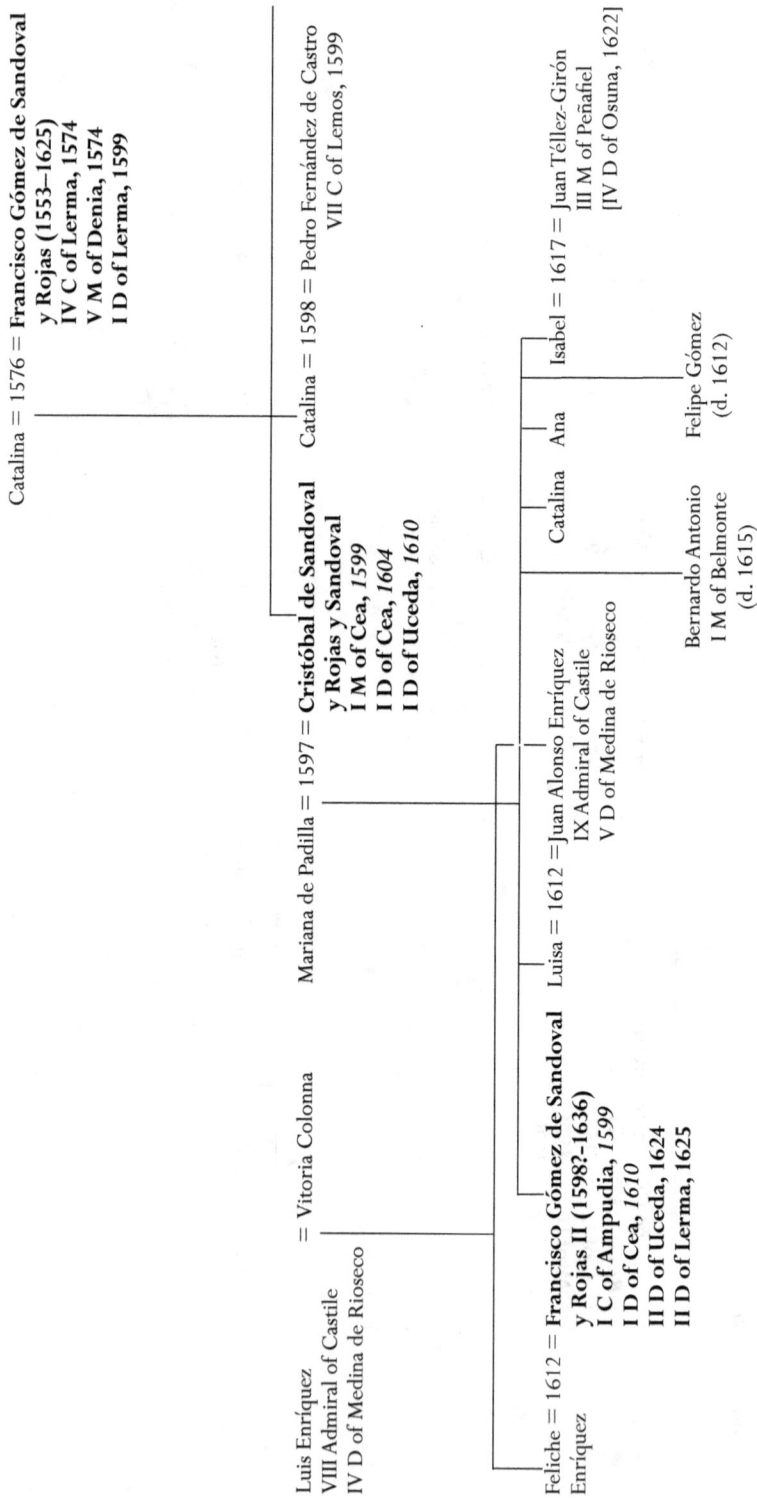

Catalina = 1576 = **Francisco Gómez de Sandoval
y Rojas (1553–1625)
IV C of Lerma, 1574
V M of Denia, 1574
I D of Lerma, 1599**

Catalina = 1598 = Pedro Fernández de Castro
VII C of Lemos, 1599

Isabel = 1617 = Juan Téllez-Girón
III M of Peñafiel
[IV D of Osuna, 1622]

Ana

Felipe Gómez
(d. 1612)

Catalina

Bernardo Antonio
I M of Belmonte
(d. 1615)

Mariana de Padilla = 1597 = **Cristóbal de Sandoval
y Rojas y Sandoval
I M of Cea, 1599
I D of Cea, 1604
I D of Uceda, 1610**

Luisa = 1612 = Juan Alonso Enríquez
IX Admiral of Castile
V D of Medina de Rioseco

Luis Enríquez
VIII Admiral of Castile
IV D of Medina de Rioseco

= Vitoria Colonna

Feliche = 1612 = **Francisco Gómez de Sandoval
Enríquez   y Rojas II (1598?–1636)
I C of Ampudia, 1599
I D of Cea, 1610
II D of Uceda, 1624
II D of Lerma, 1625**

The Duke of Lerma and the house of Sandoval

3. Children and grandchildren, *continued*

Catalina = 1576 = **Francisco Gómez de Sandoval
y Rojas (1553–1625)
IV C of Lerma, 1574
V M of Denia, 1574
I D of Lerma, 1599**

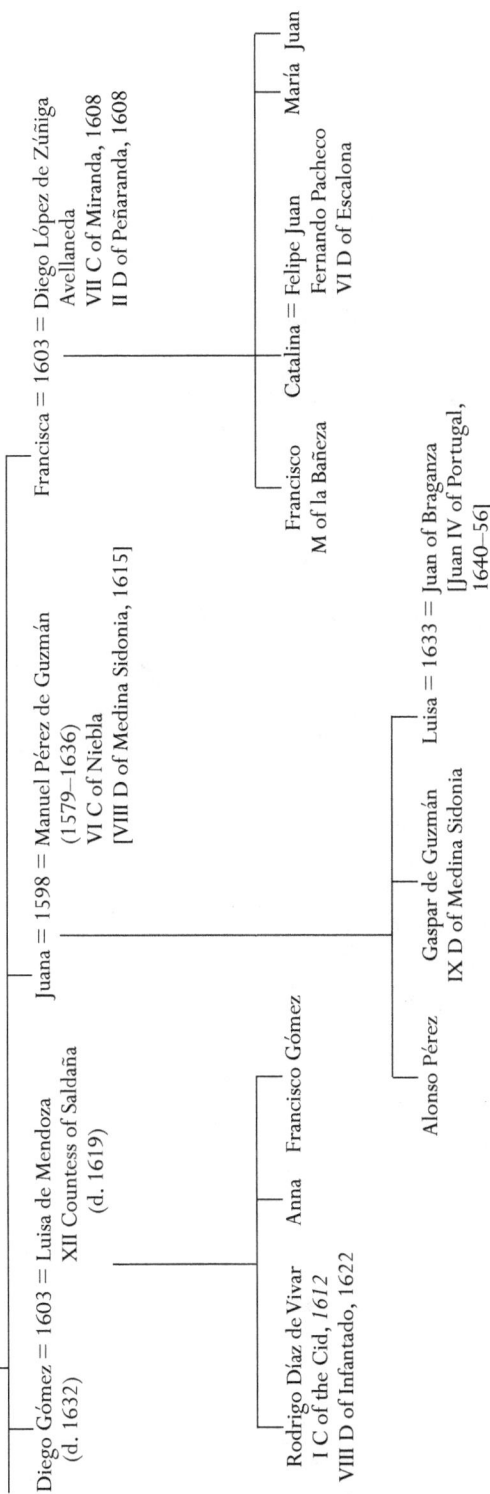

Diego Gómez = 1603 = Luisa de Mendoza
(d. 1632)   XII Countess of Saldaña
           (d. 1619)

Rodrigo Díaz de Vivar   Anna   Francisco Gómez
I C of the Cid, *1612*
VIII D of Infantado, 1622

Juana = 1598 = Manuel Pérez de Guzmán
           (1579–1636)
           VI C of Niebla
           [VIII D of Medina Sidonia, 1615]

Alonso Pérez

Gaspar de Guzmán
IX D of Medina Sidonia

Luisa = 1633 = Juan of Braganza
        [Juan IV of Portugal,
        1640–56]

Francisca = 1603 = Diego López de Zúñiga
            Avellaneda
            VII C of Miranda, 1608
            II D of Peñaranda, 1608

Francisco
M of la Bañeza

Catalina = Felipe Juan
        Fernando Pacheco
        VI D of Escalona

María   Juan

Introduction

Valladolid, Pentecost Sunday, 29 May 1605:
'Protector generall and Advocate of all the world'.[1]

On Pentecost Sunday 1605, don Francisco Gómez de Sandoval y Rojas, fifth marquis of Denia and first duke of Lerma, carried the infant heir to the thrones of the Spanish monarchy in procession to his christening in Lerma's own monastery-church of *San Pablo* in Valladolid. The day was a joyous celebration of the endurance of the Habsburg dynasty in Spain but it had also been chosen to celebrate the close relationship that the Spanish crown enjoyed with the Roman Catholic Church, for Pentecost Sunday was celebrated in the Roman canon as the day on which the Church itself had been founded. This neatly rounded out the profound symbolism that attached to the fact that the heir to the throne had been born on Good Friday, the day of the crucifixion of Jesus. In fine, the days of the child's birth and baptism emphasised and celebrated both the unique sacrality of Spanish kingship and the close identification of the Spanish crown with the House of Habsburg.

This was the second time that Lerma had performed this service for King Philip III and Queen Margaret in *San Pablo*, for in 1601 he had carried the couple's first-born child, Anne, to her baptism there. Because girls could succeed to the thrones of Spain, Anne was in 1601 the heir-presumptive to her father and her baptism had been marked by joyous festivities.[2] However, the birth of a male child made the royal dynasty immeasurably more secure and therefore justified more resonant celebrations: Lerma very consciously took advantage of the opportunity provided by the baptism to emphasise his own pre-eminence in Court, Church and State.

Lerma was fifty-two years of age, nearly twice as old as the King, who was twenty-eight. He had served as a courtier in Philip's household while he was Prince and by the time that Philip succeeded to the throne on 13 September 1598 had won his fullest confidence. Accordingly, in the very first moments of his reign Philip had solemnly declared his trust in Lerma (who was then the Marquis of Denia) and within a few days he then ordered that all of the governmental councils through which Spain was governed should obey Lerma's commands as if they were his own.[3] Philip had taken Denia as his favourite (*valido* or *privado*) and had formally vested in him at the very outset of his reign what amounted to the comptrollership of the affairs of the monarchy. It was this pre-eminence that Lerma now displayed to everyone who observed the ceremonies on Pentecost Sunday.

The position of *valido* was certainly not new. Indeed the greatest of previous Spanish *validos,* don Álvaro de Luna, had exercised the role (*'valimiento'*) as recently as the fifteenth century. But don Álvaro had lived in comparatively simple times and was, indeed, merely the *valido* of the King of Castile. Lerma was the *valido* of a king whose writ extended across the whole of the Iberian peninsula, much of Europe and the western Mediterranean and across the great oceans of the world into the Americas and the Far East. Moreover, so complete was Lerma's power that he became the prototype for many of the great favourite-ministers of the European seventeenth century; for example, in Spain he was followed by the Count-Duke of Olivares, in England by the Duke of Buckingham and in France by the two great cardinal-ministers, Richelieu and Mazarin.[4] Lerma's appointment as *valido* in September 1598 therefore inaugurated what has been referred to as 'the European phenomenon' of government by favourites. This era, during which young or weak kings seemed to be governed by favourites who dominated court and government, endured in many of the western European monarchies throughout the first two-thirds of the seventeenth century. This study will suggest not only that Lerma was the first of the great favourites of the seventeenth century but that he has claims to be considered as the most typical, perhaps even the greatest, of them, the benchmark against which they should be measured. Certainly, this was how one English courtier and writer viewed him; as late as 1668 Sir Robert Howard published a play about Lerma which he entitled *The Great Favourite.*[5]

Lerma had been born in 1553 in the royal palace in the small town of Tordesillas, 21 kilometres to the south-west of Valladolid and had grown up to regard Valladolid as his native city. In 1601 he engineered the removal of the royal court to Valladolid from Madrid and during the five years that the court resided in the city he exercised a unique degree of control over it: these were the years of the plenitude of his power. It was appropriate, therefore, that he should have controlled both of the buildings used in the baptismal ceremony of 1605. The procession had begun in the royal palace on the south side of the *Plaza de San Pablo*, which Lerma had owned until he sold it to the King in 1602. In gratitude, Philip conferred the governorship of the palace on Lerma in perpetuity, thereby allowing him to maintain his control of it (and to live in it free of charge) even though he no longer bore any financial responsibility for it.

The monastery-church of *San Pablo* faced the royal palace across the *plaza*. Lerma was currently rebuilding the church at enormous expense so that it could serve as the mausoleum for himself and the members of his family, past, present and future. In doing so, he was deliberately – and perhaps daringly – making allusion to the great monastery-palace of San Lorenzo del Escorial which Philip II had completed as the pantheon of the royal family as recently as 1584: a historian of Valladolid has rightly referred to *San Pablo* as 'the Escorial of the favourite'.[6] For the baptismal procession, Lerma had linked the palace with the church by creating a temporary passageway (*pasadizo*) in the form of an elevated corridor which had windows so that the procession could be seen by the public milling below. So determined had he been to ensure that the complex of *San Pablo,* the royal palace and the elevated walkway were completed for the baptism that Lerma had six hundred men working day and night to finish them. The reason for this urgency now became evident, for Lerma halted at every window to show the infant to the populace, who cheered joyously.[7] And of course, everyone who saw the Prince also saw Lerma, the King's *valido*, the comptroller of the affairs of the monarchy.

Among his innumerable dignities, Lerma was patron of the Castilian province of the Order of St Dominic, and it happened that 600 reverend fathers of the Order were celebrating their chapter in *San Pablo* in the week of the christening. Lerma ensured that the infant was baptised in the font which had been used for the christening of St Dominic himself in *c.*1172. His influence was also surely evident in the third of the names chosen for the child – Philip Victor Dominic: Philip, after his father and grandfather; Victor, after his godfather Victor Amadeus, Prince of Savoy; and Dominic, after the patron saint of the church in which he was baptised. The heir to the thrones of Spain – King Philip IV as he became in 1621 – was named in part for the church of the Duke of Lerma.

As he controlled the buildings used for the ceremonies, so Lerma played the decisive role in choosing many of the people who held the leading positions in the royal households. For instance, his two sisters supervised the preparation of the prince for his baptism; Leonor, Countess of Altamira, as his Governess (*aya*), dressed him for the ceremony while Catalina, dowager Countess of Lemos, as Lady Chamberlain (*camarera mayor*) of the Queen, had supervised the birth of the child and now escorted him to the baptismal font.

At the entrance to *San Pablo*, Lerma, Catalina and the prince were welcomed by the celebrant of the baptism, the Duke's great-uncle, Bernardo de Sandoval y Rojas, Cardinal-Archbishop of Toledo and Primate of Spain. Bernardo's elevation to the primatial see in 1599 had been one of the first manifestations of Lerma's extraordinary power. At the Cardinal's side, as a co-celebrant, stood Dr Juan Bautista de Acevedo, formerly tutor to Lerma's children and now Bishop of Valladolid and Inquisitor General. Between them, the Cardinal-Primate and the Bishop-Inquisitor General held the commanding offices of the Spanish Church; through them, Lerma knew what was happening at every level of the Church.

The secular ceremonies that accompanied the baptism were overseen by don Juan de Zúñiga, sixth count of Miranda and President of the Council of Castile. Like Cardinal Sandoval y Rojas, Miranda had been appointed to office in 1599 in Lerma's seizure of the levers of power and – again like the Cardinal – he took advantage of his new eminence to repay Lerma's patronage: year after year, in legal judgement after judgement, Miranda led the Council of Castile in granting privileges, powers and incomes to Lerma. He was well rewarded: as recently as 1603, Miranda's heir, Diego López, had married Lerma's third daughter, Francisca, and when Miranda retired from the presidency in 1608 he became the first non-Sandoval to be raised to the dukedom by Philip III, as Duke of Peñaranda del Duero. When he died a few months later, Diego López became the second duke of Peñaranda – and Francisca became the first of two of Lerma's daughters to become duchesses.[8]

The authority of the state was focussed around thirteen councils, and supporters and relatives of Lerma held key positions in most of them, particularly in the presidencies and the offices which controlled patronage. Lerma had also appointed trusted followers to the secretaryships of the King and Queen while the King's confessor, fray Diego de Mardones, had been Lerma's own confessor until the Duke had handed him on to the King in 1604. Almost every man or woman of significance in court, state and Church seemed in 1605 to owe his or her position to the Duke of Lerma, to be answerable to him almost as much as they were to the King himself.

In 1605 there were 160 or so aristocratic families in Spain, and they competed with each other to serve the crown and to win the rewards that flowed from service.[9] An elite group of thirty-five families held the rank of *grandeza* or grandeeship, recognising that they had royal blood and therefore stood in close proximity to the royal family. Even the grandees had to accommodate themselves to Lerma, acknowledging that he occupied the space between the King and themselves; indeed, as an ambassador put it in 1607 there was 'as much distance between him and the other Grandees, as there is between the King and him'.[10] Some of the grandee families had, like Miranda's, already connected themselves to the Sandovals by marriage – the Duke of Medina Sidonia and the Count of Lemos in 1598 and the Duke of Infantado in 1603. Others competed between themselves to do so.

The nobility who did not hold *grandeza* were known as *títulos,* the titled nobility. Their families aspired to win *grandeza,* and Lerma was constantly besieged by men who were seeking his support so that they could attain the great honour. He almost invariably refused to intercede for them with the King for he understood well enough that in keeping nobles desperate to win *grandeza* he maintained his hold over them.

It happened that two days before the baptism an English delegation led by Charles Howard, Earl of Nottingham, arrived in Valladolid to ratify the Treaty of London which in 1604 had brought the long war between England and Spain to an end. Lerma took advantage of the Earl's presence in Valladolid to propose a radical shift in Anglo-Spanish relations: in an orchard in the grounds of his riverside palace, he suggested to Nottingham (who had commanded the fleet that defeated the 'Spanish Armada' in 1588) that Spain and England should work towards a marital alliance to bind their new friendship. The prospect of winning a Spanish Match so beguiled King James I of England that for twenty years he made it a lynch-pin of his foreign policy to win a Spanish bride for a son. The celebrations of 1605 therefore left their mark upon international affairs for the best part of a generation.

Nottingham and his men stayed in Valladolid until 18 June. These were weeks of ceaseless celebration as the old enemies competed with each other in the ostentation of their display and in the carelessness of their spending in a series of courtly and manly celebrations – in the running of bulls; in tilting and equestrian tournaments; in eating and drinking, dancing, exchanging presents, and so on. The festivities were celebrated, too, with elegant masques and theatrical productions that became the measure of the new age of courtly elegance and splendour. Indeed, the conjuncture of the celebrations for the birth of the heir to the thrones of Spain with those for the end of a war which had been fought in Europe and in the Atlantic was helping to give birth to what a contemporary described as 'a new style of greatness' at court, to the establishment of the baroque court.[11] This new court, characterised by the ostentation with which wealth and power were flaunted, came into being with the new century (and with the end of the devastating wars that had marked the second half of the old century). In this court, men were measured by the extravagance of their display and by their spending on secular, religious and cultural affairs. Lerma played the primary role in the creation of this court in Spain, and in doing so helped to re-establish the cultural reputation of that court in Europe.

At the accession of Philip III, Lerma and his family had been desperately poor. The extent of his poverty can most conveniently be evidenced by looking at the estimates of aristocratic income that contemporaries so loved compiling (Appendix I).[12] A list drawn up in about 1595 by Pedro Núñez de Salcedo listed 118 aristocratic families with a total rent-roll of 4,272,000 ducats and an average income of 34,732 ducats. The Marquis of Denia's income was estimated to be 20,000 ducats and placed him in fifty-eighth position, exactly half-way down the list. He was the poorest of the grandees and his income was only one-eighth or so of that of the Duke of Medina Sidonia (170,000 ducats). Medina Sidonia's family had reigned supreme on these lists for nearly eighty years now, but within ten years of the accession of Philip III Denia had acquired so much landed wealth that he had overtaken him. A list drawn up in 1616 valued Denia's annual income (he was now the Duke of Lerma) at 300,000 ducats while that of Medina Sidonia had only reached 200,000. There was some slight exaggeration in the figure for Lerma's income but little in what happened next: in the years after his retirement from court in 1618 his income collapsed so substantially that by 1620 he had fallen to second place, with 165,000 ducats against Medina Sidonia's 170,000. He was still richer than all his other aristocratic colleagues but he was no longer mega-rich, no longer in a category all of his own, as he had been after the first decade of the reign of Philip III. Moreover, the government of Philip IV inflicted penalties upon Lerma that further diminished his income, and in doing so further emphasised the connection between royal favour and ministerial wealth that had characterised Lerma's exercise of the *valimiento* (Appendix I) Denia's use of the royal favour to enhance his wealth (and that of his family) through the exploitation of the King's favour had no serious parallel in Spanish history and can perhaps only be compared in seventeenth-century Europe with the example of Cardinal Mazarin in France. Joseph Bergin has described Mazarin as 'the most successful predator of the entire ancien régime': the present study will suggest that Lerma should at least be considered as a contender for the title.[13]

This is the more true because the impoverishment of the Sandoval family had been so profound and had endured for so long. This poverty was created by the confiscation by the crown of the family's lands and titles in 1436 and 1476. When he became *valido* Lerma was determined to recover his family's ancestral lands and to win compensation from the crown for the injuries that it had inflicted upon his forebears and upon the enduring reputation of his family. He did so with measured tread, systematically using his influence over Philip III to take revenge on the crown for the wrongs that it had done his family a century and more before he was born.

It was a truism that the favour of kings could be lost as quickly as it was won and Lerma knew full well just how precarious favour at court could be. Indeed, the lesson was not far to seek in Valladolid, for Álvaro de Luna had been beheaded in 1453 in the city's *plaza mayor*, a few minutes walk from the church of *San Pablo*. In more recent years, favourites in England and France – the Earl of Essex (1601) and Marshal Birón (1602) – had also gone to the block after rebelling against their monarchs in their fury at losing favour to rivals. Lerma was far too wise to risk sharing their fate and did everything he could to assuage the resentment that his peers and rivals felt at his pre-eminence by allowing them to reap (or at least to hope to reap) the benefits of the royal grace by working through him. Lerma became – as the observer of 1598 noted with prescience – the 'Protector generall and Advocate of all the world', the man who interceded for his peers with the King, the facilitator who could (as appeared) arrange whatever use of the royal grace that he wished. Accordingly, most of the men in the upper reaches of the court sought to accommodate themselves to Lerma rather than to oppose him. Indeed, so overwhelming did Lerma's power become that it often seemed as if his was the only power-grouping at court and that all power-relationships worked through him. In reality, however, there was always opposition to him in court, government and Church, but in the days of his pomp it tended to be obscured by the overwhelming lustre of his power. But as his power declined and then collapsed, opposition became correspondingly more visible – and more potent.

It is unlikely that in 1598 Lerma had expected his good fortune to last more than a few years. However, as he realised that his power could endure, that his position could be bolstered and reinforced rather than ebbing away, he switched to a strategy of breathtaking audacity, to ensuring the continuation in power not just of himself but of his family. At the core of Lerma's use of power by 1605, defining and crystallising it, was his determination to pass the *valimiento* on to his eldest son, Cristóbal, so that he in turn could ensure that the gains that Lerma had made were not lost or confiscated in the next generation.

Lerma had taken the first step to securing his family's hold on favour in 1604 by having the King raise Cristóbal to the dukedom of Cea. In 1609–10 Philip endowed a third dukedom upon the family – that of Uceda – and so the Sandovals became the first family in Spanish history in which father, son and grandson were all dukes.[14] As the patriarch of what was now beyond compare the greatest aristocratic family in Spain, Lerma did not see himself as an individual so much as the guardian of a legacy who was obliged to honour his forebears and to advance his successors. The sense of dynasty – of the endurance of his multigenerational family – lay at the heart of Lerma's political and courtly ambitions and was fundamental to his perception of self. In this, he was truly a representative of his caste and a progenitor of the great minister-favourites of the seventeenth century.[15]

Transmitting power to his son would also enable Lerma to fulfil his deepest personal ambition by retiring into religious life to devote his last years to a preparation for a Christian death. It has often been observed that Lerma secured a cardinalate in 1617–18 only to save himself in his political decline. This is not true: Lerma's religiosity was genuine and profound, and the acquisition of the cardinalate was the logical culmination of the drive that informed the whole of his life.[16] While it was certainly characteristic of him that he became a cardinal before he became a priest – rank, after all, was everything to him – it was also undeniable that he had yearned throughout his adulthood to enter religious life. When he did so, in 1617–18, it was as the *fulfilment* of his dearest wish, the climax of his career rather than an escape from it. Lerma was a brilliant, scheming courtier who took greed and self-advancement to a new level in Spanish politics. But he was also a deeply committed Roman Catholic. We cannot understand him unless we appreciate that his piety was at least as important to him as his secular and familial ambitions. In truth, they were all of a piece: Lerma did not distinguish between them and neither should we.

It was central to Lerma's exercise of power that he displayed his power and wealth, that he demonstrated that he was at once a good and faithful servant of his king and the most commanding figure at court – that he stood at all the major entrances to what John Adamson has eloquently termed 'the foyers of power'.[17] In 1598 he had been appointed as Philip's *caballerizo mayor* (Master of the Horse) and he gave expression to the prestige that this office conferred upon him by riding his magnificent white Neapolitan stallion in many of the secular celebrations that were associated with the baptism – in processions, jousting tournaments and the like. He rode his great horse the more proudly because in 1603 he had been named as *capitán general de la caballería de España* (Captain General of the Cavalry of Spain) and so was entitled to pre-eminence among Spain's military commanders. In 1603 Peter Paul Rubens visited the court and Lerma had him paint an equestrian portrait of him to celebrate the duality of his two great offices (and also, perhaps, to mark Lerma's fiftieth birthday in that year). It was a daring choice of subject, for the equestrian portrait was traditionally a royal *genre*. However, the dangerous brilliance of Rubens's portrait further legitimised Lerma's prestige and status at court; the painting was a stunning success and it remains the finest portrait of Lerma. It also reminds us that in these early years of the reign Lerma saw himself as a soldier, seeking military glory for himself and his king (see front cover).[18]

The commission that Lerma gave to Rubens was part of a wider strategy, for he became the most influential lay patron of the arts in Spain in his generation. Indeed, he was one of the major collectors of paintings in the seventeenth century.[19] Lerma was also the greatest builder of his age, and in his building programme – definitively studied by Luis Cervera Vera – we can follow the development of his ambitions for himself and his family. Nowhere was Lerma more measured and more calculating than in his building programme: truly, he wrote his autobiography in stone.[20] Moreover, the exquisite gardens which he incorporated into many of his buildings also mark him out as a significant figure in the history of gardening while the bull-rings that he created in four of his palaces have earned him a niche in the annals of that most Spanish of popular cultures, the bull-fight. More substantively still, perhaps, Lerma was a cultivated patron of literature; many of the greatest members of Spain's golden generation of writers – among them Miguel de Cervantes, Felix Lope de Vega and Luis de Góngora – had good reason to appreciate the duke's generosity. So, too, did some of the finest musicians of the age. In matters public, familial and artistic, Lerma operated on the grandest of scales, and in doing so he had influence well beyond Spain, helping to lay down the benchmark for the aristocrat of early seventeenth-century Europe, as a man who was completely at ease in the affairs of the world, the soul and the arts.[21]

Lerma was imaginative and subtle in his use of power, insistently demonstrating that he was a patron who could reward his followers and punish those who opposed him. He always endeavoured to avoid antagonising his peers and rivals, soothing their anger and enticing them into accepting his hegemony. A gambler in private life, Lerma normally eschewed risks in politics. However, when he failed to reach an accommodation with his opponents he could be ruthless with them and could indeed pursue vendettas against the greatest men (and women) in the land: the men who felt his anger most bitterly and most enduringly boasted the titles of Constable of Castile and Admiral of Aragon. Both men conspired with others to overthrow Lerma and he responded by harrying them over many years, twice sending the Constable on missions abroad and having the Admiral arrested and imprisoned for years in harsh conditions in Spain.

There was, however, a risk in sending powerful personalities to key positions abroad, for in doing so Lerma provided them with the opportunity to make political initiatives of their own. The Constable of Castile was not politically astute enough to do so, but in the later years of his *valimiento* Lerma found it increasingly difficult to control powerful proconsuls in strategically important positions away from Spain as they pursued policies that were at variance with his own. The loss of prestige that he subsequently suffered contributed significantly to the decline in the confidence that the King held in him.

While Lerma displayed and wielded power with clear-sighted purpose he also disguised his use of it with powerful effectiveness: anonymity and obfuscation were as fundamental to his exercise of power as was display.[22] Lerma was acutely conscious of the dangers of committing himself to a political programme, and therefore made few public statements and wrote few letters or statements on policy matters, aware that these might surface to be used against him in the future. He allowed the Council of State to exercise a much-expanded role in policymaking, both to relieve the burden that he carried and because he and Philip genuinely valued the advice of the seasoned diplomats and soldiers who sat on the Council. However, aware that the views of councillors were recorded in writing, Lerma attended the council only rarely. While he was therefore careful, as in May–June 1605, to take centre stage at moments when he could earn great applause and prestige, he was wary of associating himself too closely with the policies of the government that he dominated. Certainly, he was determined not to leave written evidence of his involvement in policymaking that could be used against him in the future – a characteristic that has not always commended him to historians.

At the heart of Lerma's *valimiento*, therefore, was the paradox – public display, a man at the heart of events as the diligent servant of the King and the commanding figure at court: political reticence, a man who let his views be known either alone in the presence of the King or obliquely in public, or indirectly through clients whom he could subsequently disown if he needed to do so. Lerma intended to make the important decisions himself while distancing himself – sometimes even literally so – from the formulation of controversial or unpopular decisions.[23] This had profound importance for the development of the governmental councils. The reign of Philip III witnessed a substantial advance in the professionalisation of conciliar government as the King and Lerma allowed the authority of the councils to expand so that they could share responsibility in policymaking. In this regard, as in others, the changes that came about during the reign endured throughout the seventeenth century.[24]

The government of Philip III was much more belligerent than has often been supposed, and it took its lead from the King.[25] Lerma faithfully encouraged Philip in his warlike ambitions. Philip had made the peace with England only reluctantly in 1604, but he welcomed the opportunity that the peace had created to concentrate his resources on the conflict with the Dutch rebels which had entered its fourth decade as he ascended the throne; indeed, he proclaimed that he would wage a war of 'blood and iron' on his rebellious subjects.[26] In the summer of 1605, the commander of the Army of Flanders, Ambrosio Spínola, was beginning a campaign in the Low Countries that would rank among the most imaginative and successful of all Spain's campaigns there. The status that Spínola won with his brilliant military successes allowed him to become the first – and indubitably the greatest – of the proconsuls whose exercise of power away from Spain enabled them to influence policymaking in Madrid.

Military glory was, however, expensive. The wars of the early years of the reign were financed in part by record grants from three of the four major representative assemblies of Spain – from the Catalan *corts* in 1599, the Castilian *cortes* in 1601 and the Valencian *cortes* in 1604. Lerma claimed the credit for these grants, and in raising so consistently the tax-yield of the different parts of Spain he demonstrated to Philip his abilities as a minister and his political acumen. In particular, the taxpayers of Castile contributed more to the expenditures of a government that was nominally at peace than they had done towards one that had fought wars across Europe and the world. The resentment which they felt about this fuelled opposition in the Cortes of Castile (and elsewhere) to the crown's policies, and the later years of Philip III's reign were dominated by debates within and beyond government about the burdens being imposed on the people of Castile. This criticism, too, helped to undermine Lerma, the minister who had been instrumental in creating new levels of taxation.

If in 1605 Lerma stood at the height of his power, changes were taking place at court and across the face of the Hispanic world which had serious implications for his exercise of power and perhaps even for his continuance in office. The birth of the heir of Philip III slowly helped to bring to the King maturity and, with it, a determination that his son would not be dominated by the Sandovals as he had been. Philip III began, therefore, to face the quandary of how to avoid having the Sandoval primacy extended into the reign of his son exactly as Lerma began to place his son in power so that he could eventually retire from involvement at the centre of affairs. In the spring of 1605 the King of Spain and his *valido* were embarking, slowly and imperceptibly, on courses that would bring them to a parting of the ways. Their relationship came to be bound up with and defined by – and then fractured by – their ambitions for their eldest sons.

Their relationship became bound up, too, with the dynastic ambitions of the querulous and charismatic Duke of Savoy. Charles-Emmanuel had married Catalina Micaela, the second daughter of Philip II, in 1585 and by 1598 had hopes that one of their ten children would succeed to the Spanish thrones.[27] The births of Anne and Philip Victor Dominic put an end to that ambition. Undaunted, Charles-Emmanuel sought a throne for his family elsewhere. He allied with Henry IV in 1609–10 to attack the power of Spain and her Austrian Habsburg cousins, and when Henry's death in 1610 left him isolated he refused to reconcile himself to Spain but became instead the most fractious, the most determined and the most resourceful of the enemies of Philip III. Paradoxically, while Charles-Emmanuel confronted Spanish power and encouraged Europe to follow him in doing so his son Philibert-Emmanuel was living at court in Spain. Philibert insinuated himself into the favour of the King, and Lerma became anxious that he would compete with Uceda for the succession to the *valimiento*. In consequence, Lerma developed a venomous hatred for the Duke of Savoy and his son. In doing so, he overstepped a key mark, for Philip III would not allow even his beloved *valido* to measure himself against a prince of the blood.

In the years to 1605 Lerma had rewritten the political rulebook, but thereafter he became subject to the most inexorable of all the laws of politics – that the man who stood at the centre of events was himself vulnerable to them. Already by the early summer of 1605 it was evident that the experiment of having the court in Valladolid was failing badly and by the time of the royal christening Lerma was making plans to move the court back to Madrid. Once again, he was ahead of the game.

But not for long. Late in 1605 events threatened to move out of his control. The peace with England was placed under severe stress when in November Guy Fawkes and his colleagues attempted to blow up the house of Parliament with James I and his ministers inside, including many of the men who had celebrated the making of peace in Valladolid. Even more importantly, a day or so after Fawkes's arrest, the loss of four treasure galleons in a ferocious storm in the Caribbean meant that the crown did not receive any American silver during 1605 and for most of 1606. The crisis that developed as a result of this disaster seriously undermined Lerma and had profoundly important implications for European politics. As the crisis began to unravel in the later months of 1606, Lerma struggled to maintain his pre-eminence at court. In 1607, Philip III was forced to declare a 'state bankruptcy' and in 1609 to make a humiliating truce for twelve years with his rebels in the United Provinces. Suddenly, dramatically, Lerma had to confront failure at home and abroad; he was no longer invulnerable. But – brilliantly if not always elegantly – he survived until he was ready to leave court of his own volition in 1617–18. At that point the King dismissed him, unwilling to let it be known that his *valido* was abandoning him and leaving court voluntarily.

This book is a study of how Lerma acquired and used power, how he displayed it and disguised it, how he profited from it and endeavoured to protect its benefits, and how ultimately he tried to strip himself of power while retaining the advantages and status that it brought for himself and his family.

NOTES
1 Quotation from untitled document of 1598–99 listing the councillors of State of Philip II and Philip III, NA SP 94/6, fol. 170. On the baptism: *Relaciones*, pp. 238–58; T. Pinheiro da Veiga, *Fastigiana: vida cotidiana en la corte de Valladolid*, Valladolid, 1989 reprint, pp. 43-171; Anon., *Relación de lo sucedido en la ciudad de Valladolid desde el punto del felicísimo nacimiento del príncipe don Felipe Dominico Víctor nuestro señor hasta que se acabaron las demostraciones de alegría que por él se hicieron*, ed. N. Alonso Cortés, Valladolid, 1916; Robert Tresswell, 'A RELATION Of such Things as were observed to happen in the Journey of THE RIGHT HONOURABLE CHARLES, EARL OF NOTTINGHAM, Lord High Admiral of England', *Harleian Miscellany*, ii (London, 1809), pp. 535–66.
2 'Relación de la orde(n) que se tuuo en el bautismo de la ... primogenita del ... Rey don Felipe III ... en Valladolid', Valladolid, 1602.
3 Lerma's power has been the subject of a profoundly well-researched study by Bernardo José García García, *La Pax Hispánica. Política exterior del Duque de Lerma*, Leuven, 1996. On Lerma's relationship with Philip III and the *valimiento*, the innovative study by Antonio Feros, *Kingship and Favoritism in the Spain of Philip III, 1598–1621*, Cambridge, UK, 2000; an expanded edition, *El Duque de Lerma. Realeza y favoritismo en la España de Felipe III*, Madrid, 2002. On the *valimiento* in Spain, Francisco Tomás y Valiente, *Los validos en la monarquía Española del siglo XVII (Estudio Institucional)*, Madrid, 1963. Court politics in the reign are the subject of a

superlative study by Santiago Martínez Hernández, *El marqués de Velada y la corte en los reinados de Felipe II y Felipe III. Nobleza cortesana y cultura política en la España del Siglo de Oro*, JCL, 2004. See also my articles, cited in the bibliography.

4 Gaspar de Guzmán, Count-Duke of Olivares, favourite of Philip IV (1621/2–1643); George Villiers, Duke of Buckingham served James I and Charles I (1616–28); Cardinal Armand Jean du Plessis de Richelieu was favourite-minister of Louis XIII (1616–42) and Cardinal Jules Mazarin of Louis XIV (1643–61, with two interruptions during which he was exiled from power). On favourites and European courts, A. G. Dickens (ed.), *The Courts of Europe. Politics, Patronage and Royalty 1400–1800*, London, 1977 and J. H. Elliott and L. W. B. Brockliss (eds.), *The World of the Favourite*, New Haven, 1999 and J. Adamson (ed.), *The Princely Courts of Europe 1500–1750. Ritual, Politics and Culture under the* Ancien Régime *1500–1750*, London, 1999.

5 Sir Robert Howard, *The Great Favourite, or, The Duke of Lerma*, in the Savoy, 1668.

6 J. Martín González, *La arquitectura doméstica del Renacimiento en Valladolid*, Valladolid, 1948, pp. 178–9; see also, A. Bustamante García, *La arquitectura clasicista del foco vallisoletano (1560–1641)*, Valladolid, 1983, p. 417.

7 '*Relación de lo sucedido en la ciudad de Valladolid ...*', p. 53; *Relaciones*, p. 246 and Pinheiro da Veiga, *Fastigiana*, p. 94.

8 Juana became duchess of Medina Sidonia in 1615. Catalina was already Countess of Lemos.

9 I. A. A. Thompson, 'The Nobility in Spain, 1600–1800', in H. M. Scott (ed.), *The European Nobilities in the Seventeenth and Eighteenth Centuries*, 2 vols., London, 1994–95, vol. i, *Western Europe*, pp. 174–236; M. J. Rodríguez-Salgado, 'Honour and profit in the Court of Philip II of Spain', in M. Aymard and M. Romani (eds.), *La Cour comme institution économique*, Paris, 1998, pp. 67–86.

10 Charles Cornwallis, 'A Discourse upon the Present Stayte of Spaine', BL Add 29,853, fol. 160, copy; there are several printed versions of this tract, but none are as full as this manuscript version.

11 Below, p. 59. On the Spanish court, G. Redworth and F. Checa, 'The Courts of the Spanish Habsburgs 1500–1700', in Adamson (ed.), *Princely Courts*, pp. 43-65.

12 These lists have significant faults – they tend to rely heavily upon each other and so perpetuate errors – but they are on the whole suprisingly accurate. They are used as the basis for Appendix I; see below, pp. 270–2.

13 J. Bergin, *Cardinal Richelieu. Power and the Pursuit of Wealth*, New Haven, 1985, p. 5.

14 On this title, below, pp. 158–9.

15 See J. Bergin, *The Rise of Richelieu*, New Haven, especially, chapter 1 'Family Traditions', pp. 12–49.

16 See my 'Lerma, 1618: Dismissal or Retirement?', *EHQ*, 19, no. 3, July 1989, pp. 307–32. On an English parallel, J. M. Sutton, 'The Retiring Patron. William Cecil and the Cultivation of Retirement, 1590–1598', in P. Croft (ed.), *Patronage, Culture and Power. The Early Cecils*, New Haven, 2002, pp. 159–79.

17 'The Making of the Ancien-Régime Court 1500–1700', in Adamson (ed.), *Princely Courts of Europe*, p. 17.

18 Below, pp. 88–9.

19 J. Brown, *The Golden Age of Spanish Painting*, New Haven, 1991, p. 55.

20 See especially Cervera Vera's *El conjunto palacial de la villa de Lerma*, 2-vol. reprint, Lerma, 1996 of 1 vol. original, Madrid 1967; Cervera's magnificent work has been little known to historians but is indispensable to any study of Lerma. Cervera Vera has supplemented it with studies of Lerma's individual buildings in Lerma; together, they constitute one of the great achievements of modern historical scholarship: see the bibliography.

21 On his patronage of the arts, see below, pp. 88–9, 98–9, 229. On a great English patron, Robert Cecil, who had many of the same ambitions as Lerma, Pauline Croft's brilliant 'Introduction', in Croft (ed.), *Patronage, Culture and Power*, pp. ix–xxi.

22 On Lerma's 'art of seeming', L. von Ranke, *The Ottoman and Spanish Empires in the Sixteenth and Seventeenth Centuries*, London, 1848, p. 51.

23 Lawrence Brockliss observed that 'Minister-favourites were clearly Janus-faced: to the outside world they appeared as demi-gods; in the royal closet they were humble and contrite servants', 'The Anatomy of the Minister-Favourite', in Elliott and Brockliss (eds.), *The World of the Favourite*, pp. 279–309, at p. 290.

24 I am developing these arguments in a study of conciliar government in Habsburg Spain.

25 See my 'Philip III and the Restoration of Spanish Government, 1598–1603', *EHR*, 83, no. 349, October 1973, pp. 751–69, at p. 756.

26 On the Dutch Revolt, the seminal works of Geoffrey Parker, *The Dutch Revolt*, London, 2002 and *The Army of Flanders and the Spanish Road 1567–1659. The Logistics of Spanish Victory and Defeat in the Low Countries' Wars*, 2nd edn, Cambridge, 2004.

27 There is a vivid characterisation of Charles-Emmanuel in A. Bombín Pérez's splendid study,

1

The Sandoval family and
the crown of Castile

The Sandoval family 1412–1574: Deprivation and recovery

The status of the Sandoval family was established by Diego Gómez de Sandoval (1385–1454), fifth-grandfather of Francisco Gómez. Diego Gómez was the leading soldier of the *infante* Ferdinand, uncle of King John II of Castile (1406–54) and he played the decisive role in securing the crown of Aragon for Ferdinand when in 1412 he defeated Ferdinand's chief rival, the Count of Urgell, at the battle of Perpignan (27 February). Diego Gómez's reward was immediate and it was significant of the priorities that informed his life that he chose to take it in Castile rather than in Aragon: on 18 July 1412, less than three weeks after the Compromise of Caspe (28 June) settled the Aragonese throne on him, Ferdinand founded the entail (*mayorazgo*) of Lerma for Diego Gómez, with the town of Lerma at its head.[1]

The *mayorazgo* was the central instrument of Castilian landholding. It was a royal title to land which ensured that the family estate became inalienable, passing from one generation to the next, normally from father to eldest son.[2] The holder of a *mayorazgo* could settle small sums from his 'free goods' (*bienes libres*) on his younger sons and give dowries to his daughters but he could not alienate the entailed property itself from the ownership of the family; a modern historian has likened the *mayorazgo* to a tree from which each generation could enjoy the fruits while being unable to alter the tree.[3] Unfortunately, this meant that a family could not tap into its assets to acquire capital and therefore had often to find cash by borrowing against its revenues. Accordingly, many Castilian noble families built up huge debts while possessing great landed wealth.[4]

For the Sandoval family, the *mayorazgo* of 1412 meant that it had reached the stage from which it could build, generation after generation, upon the success of Diego Gómez. Twenty-nine kilometres south of Burgos on the main north-south road of Castile (the '*carrera real*', the royal road), Lerma was a town of military and commercial importance. Its strong walls and castle had allowed it to play an important role in the war of reconquest against the Moors in the later eleventh century. It had taken advantage of its position on the *carrera real* to develop a variety of trading functions while the countryside around it produced grains, wines, fruits and light woods, and provided good grazing for livestock and rivers for fishing. By the end of the fifteenth century it had a population of about one thousand people.

Diego Gómez's loyalty to the crown earned him a series of further advancements and he systematically built up his landholdings in Old Castile. He fought for Ferdinand in Sicily and as a reward was presented with the Castilian town of Saldaña (3 July 1415). In 1419, Diego Gómez was raised to the rank of grandee (*'grande'*) in recognition of his standing and – enduringly – that of his family at the highest level of Castilian society.[5] On 14 September 1419 he was given permission to establish a second *mayorazgo* which was based upon the town of Cea (which he had bought) while his brother Pedro García was given the *mayorazgo* of the town of Ampudia. At some time shortly thereafter, in circumstances that are unknown, the *mayorazgo* of Ampudia passed into the hands of Diego Gómez. One last possession came to him when he was presented with the town of Portillo (21 September 1423). All of these towns were of economic importance but their real significance was seigneurial and military; Lerma, Saldaña, Cea, Ampudia and Portillo all had strong castles. Diego Gómez therefore became, in the years 1412–23, a landholder and a baron of substantial importance in Old Castile, and his new eminence was confirmed when on 11 April 1426 he was raised to the titled aristocracy, as Count of Castrojériz. He was known as the Count of Castro. The title was almost certainly given to him to mark his marriage to doña Beatriz de Avellaneda (10 March 1426), and in her marriage portion Beatriz brought Diego Gómez the towns of Gumiel de Mercado and six small *lugares* near it on the River Esgueva.[6]

Events now turned against the new Count of Castro as the 'Aragonese' faction in Castile to which he belonged was eclipsed by the 'Castilian' party led by Álvaro de Luna. In 1436 Diego Gómez was forced to flee to Aragon. In doing so, he saved his life but lost his life's work: his possessions in Castile were confiscated by the crown. He retained the title of Count of Castro but it was now an empty dignity, despoiled of its landholdings in Castile. However – crucially for the future of his family – he retained his status as a grandee.[7] As compensation for his devastating loss of land, Ferdinand's successor, Alfonso the Magnanimous (1416–58), granted Diego Gómez the town of Denia on the coast of Valencia and its dependent village of Javea (8 March 1431). However, Diego Gómez had no intention of settling down in Valencia and when a rebellion against John II broke out among Castilian nobles he allied himself with the dissidents. In 1439, after the rebels had captured Valladolid, Diego Gómez secured the promise from John II that his Castilian properties would be restored to him. The King broke his word. Diego Gómez lived until 1454 but even in death he was exiled from his own territories, being interred in his wife's town of Aguilar.[8]

Although his life had ended in political failure, Diego Gómez had laid the foundations for a noble dynasty for he had been successful in the main familial duties of an aristocrat: he had lived long, married well and produced enough male children to secure the succession and enough females to form political alliances – he was seventy when he died, and of his six children four were boys. His heirs proved to be as fecund as his wife and himself; the next four generations (1454–1570) produced twenty-one children, nine of whom were boys, and on average the head of the family lived for just over a quarter of a century after succeeding to the title. Diego Gómez also mapped out the area of the family's landed interests – the swathe of land confined within a quarter-circle south from Valladolid, to Cea, Burgos and Aranda de Duero formed the heartland of its estates. The properties in the east continued to be of subsidiary importance and because they were held under a separate *mayorazgo* were perhaps even destined to remain separate from the main holdings.

Diego Gómez left another legacy to his successors: a king-maker who had fallen from power when he had lost the favour of a king, his bitter experience persuaded the family that it must commit itself firmly to the holder of the crown of Castile. His son Ferdinand (II count of Castro, 1454–74) pledged his support to Henry IV of Castile (1454–74) and in return was promised that the towns of Lerma, Cea and Gumiel de Mercado and the places over which they held jurisdictional rights would be restored to him. But once again, a king broke his word: only Cea was returned to the family.

Henry IV reneged on his agreement with the Count of Castro exactly as his own half-sister, Isabella, challenged for the succession to his throne.[9] It cost him Castro's support. Isabella married Ferdinand, the heir to the throne of Aragon, in Valladolid on 18 October 1469, and on 4 December agreed to hand over to Castro the royal taxes from the lands that had been confiscated from Diego Gómez. Isabella also pledged that she would in time return the estates to the Sandovals. However, she then broke her word in order to secure the support of the greatest family in the land, the Mendozas: in 1476 Isabella confiscated the countship of Castrojériz from Diego Gómez's grandson and namesake and conferred it upon Ruy Díaz de Mendoza, a member of the Infantado branch of the Mendoza clan. Diego Gómez II was left without a title, and his landed possessions were now confined to Denia and Javea.[10]

In 1479 Isabella duly won the civil war and her husband succeeded to the throne of Aragon; the kingdoms of Castile and Aragon were united in the persons of their monarchs if not in strict legal theory. 'Spain' had in a very real sense come into being under the dual monarchy. Diego Gómez II had the political acumen to realise that Isabella's power would endure and redoubled his support for her. He led a troop of his servants and supporters in the war against the Moslem kingdom of Granada. His loyalty was rewarded in 1484 when Isabella conferred the marquisate of Denia upon him and presented the countship of Lerma to his eldest son, Luis. Isabella also returned the towns of Lerma and Gumiel de Mercado to the family.[11] After a break of eight years, the Sandovals again ranked as titled aristocracy in Castile and had begun to restore their standing in the kingdom. However, the fact that the Valencian lands carried the senior of the two titles served once again to emphasise that the family had secondary standing among the Castilian aristocracy.

Denia was a town of greater and more varied importance than Lerma. On land, it was the capital of a small but fertile area, rich in citrus fruits, wines, olives, almonds and sugar. As a seaport, it was second in importance within the kingdom of Valencia only to the capital city. Situated at the southern end of the Bay of Valencia, it was the chief port for trade with the Balearic Islands. As a natural vantage-point – the name 'Denia' means 'watch-tower of the morning' – the town had the responsibility for organising the defence of the south-eastern coast of Spain against corsairs. Accordingly, its castle was one of the most important on the coast. However, these defensive functions conferred major responsibilities upon the Marquis and committed him to substantial expenditures.[12] Diego Gómez II enjoyed the marquisate until he died in 1502, when he was succeeded by his son Bernardo (II marquis, 1502–36). It fell to Bernardo to consolidate the relationship of the Sandoval family with the crown at a time of profoundly important historical development.

Queen Isabella died in 1504 and the throne of Castile passed to the eldest of her four daughters, Juana. The new queen's mental health was already fragile and she lost her precarious hold on sanity when she was widowed in 1506 and the succession passed in practice to her six-year-old son Charles of Habsburg, who became co-ruler with her. When Ferdinand died in 1516 Charles succeeded to the throne of Aragon and therefore united in his person the thrones of Castile and Aragon, becoming the first monarch to rule over the whole of Spain. In September 1517 Charles arrived in Spain to claim his inheritances; he ruled now as King Charles I. In 1518 he appointed the Marquis of Denia as guardian of Queen Juana in her place of safety, the royal palace at Tordesillas.[13] The Sandovals were to remain in Tordesillas for forty years as the guardians of the tragic queen, cut adrift from mainstream political life at court.

An even greater title came to Charles when in 1519 he was elected Holy Roman Emperor, and in May 1520 he left Spain to claim the imperial throne (and with it, the title of 'Charles V' by which he is known to history). His contemptuous departure from Castile united many sections of society against him and became the catalyst for a great rebellion (the 'revolt of the *comuneros*', 1520–21) which rapidly assumed the characteristics of a nationalist rebellion against foreign rule. In protecting Juana – and in preventing her from becoming the talisman for the revolt – the Marquis of Denia was caught at the eye of the storm.

Embarrassingly, Bernardo was taken unaware by a sudden attack on Tordesillas and Juana was seized from his control. He raised an army and recovered both Juana and Tordesillas. He further earned Charles's gratitude by commanding some of his own troops at the battle of Villalar which crushed the *comuneros* revolt (23 April 1521).[14] Charles showed his appreciation by appointing him as *alcaide* of the palace in perpetuity, but in doing so he confirmed that Bernardo and his family were to remain indefinitely in Tordesillas, far from the royal court.[15]

In the crisis of 1520 Charles secured the support of leading families in Castile by designating twenty of them as 'grandees of Spain', replacing the *grandeza de Castilla* which had hitherto distinguished the social élite. He thereby bound these families to the destiny of the house of Habsburg and in doing so laid down one of the enduring characteristics of Spanish society, creating a social and political élite that survived even longer than his own dynasty. The new grandees had the right of direct access to the king and could expect to be informed personally by him of great affairs of state; indeed, the monarch addressed them as 'cousin' in acknowledgement of their having royal blood and afforded them the privileges of wearing their hats in his presence and of carrying his coffin when he died.[16] Five families – the Acuña, Aragón, Córdoba, Zúñiga and Manrique – were recognised in 1520 in two of their lines, and so in all twenty-five families were given *grandeza*. In appreciation of their service in guarding Juana, Charles included the Sandovals among the new grandees. However, because they held their marquisate in the Crown of Aragon they remained even now recognisably inferior to their Castilian colleagues. And they remained poor: with an income of about 10,000 ducats, the Sandovals occupied twenty-eighth place in the list of aristocratic incomes (see Appendix I).

When Charles returned to Spain in July 1522, he came as Holy Roman Emperor and, effectively, as an absolute monarch in Castile. Moreover, he came back as the ruler of a second empire, for while he had been in northern Europe Hernán Cortés had conquered Mexico for Castile, re-christening it as 'New Spain'. Charles V now ruled more of the earth than any European had ever done. In backing Charles in these defining years in Spain's historical development, the Sandovals had secured their future.

Bernardo died in 1536, and although Charles had real affection for his son Luis (III marquis of Denia, 1536–70), he insisted that he remain in Tordesillas as Juana's guardian.[17] Moreover, Charles gave Luis no significant

Table 1 The grandees named in 1520

1 Crown of Castile	Dukes (10)	Alba, Arcos, Alburquerque, Béjar, Cardona, Frías, Infantado, Medinaceli, Medina Sidonia, Nájera
	Marquises (4)	Aguilar de Campoo, Astorga, Priego, Villena
	Counts (6)	Benavente, Cabra, Lemos, Melgar, Miranda, Urueña
2 Crown of Aragon	Dukes (3)	Gandía, Segorbe, Villahermosa
	Marquis (1)	Denia
3 Kingdom of Navarre	Constable (1)	Lerín

Source: Listed by F. Fernández de Béthencourt, *Historia genealógica y heráldica de la Monarquía española, Casa Real, y Grandes de España*, 10 vols., Madrid, 1897–1920, at the front of each volume.

increase in his wealth and by 1540 the income of the marquisate amounted to only 14,000 ducats, placing Luis thirty-fifth among seventy-eight heads of noble families (Appendix I). Charles did, however, allow Luis to make two marital alliances with the families of fellow-grandees. Luis married Catalina de Zúñiga y Cárdenas, the eldest daughter of the third count of Miranda, and Francisco, Luis's second son, married Isabella, daughter of Francisco de Borja, IV duke of Gandía. The Miranda lands lay to the north of Burgos while those of Gandía were adjacent to Denia; the marriages therefore consolidated the local influence of the Sandoval family in its two spheres of interest and provided further alliances at court. In 1537 Charles also allowed Luis to incorporate the marquisate of Denia into the Castilian *mayorazgo* as an entail for a younger son; on 3 January 1549 Luis signed it over to his grandson Francisco in anticipation of his marriage to Isabella. Francisco and Isabella lived in Tordesillas, and it was there in 1553 that their first child, Francisco Gómez, the future Duke of Lerma, was born.[18]

Juana died in 1555. Her death freed Charles to abdicate all of his thrones except the imperial title and to retreat into the Jeronimite monastery of Yuste in Extremadura to prepare for his own death. Juana's death also liberated the Sandovals from their bondage in Tordesillas, allowing them to move to court to compete for royal favour with their peers on equal terms. In 1566, Francisco Gómez was introduced into the household of the heir to the throne, Don Carlos. He therefore became the first member of his family to grow up as a political insider, and he remained at court for fifty-two years until he was dismissed as *valido* in 1618.

Luis died in 1570 and since his eldest son, Bernardo, had predeceased him, the title passed to Francisco and the estates of Lerma and Denia were now united in the one *mayorazgo*. Francisco was named by Philip II in 1568 as one of the gentlemen of the chamber charged with the hazardous duty of guarding Don Carlos, who had become alarmingly violent and unstable and was now under house arrest after threatening to kill the King. When the misshapen prince died

after a life of enveloping trauma he was cradled in the arms of the Marquis of
Denia (24 July 1568).[19] However, Denia remained poor; shortly after Don
Carlos's death, he was forced to beg the king for an *encomienda* in the order of
Santiago 'because his need is so great'. He was given the *encomienda* of Parac-
uellos but it made little difference to his impoverishment. When Francisco
died on 21 March 1574 the King had to pay the arrears of his salary as captain
of arms to help with his burial expenses.[20] The Sandovals had yet to learn how
to serve the crown and make a profit.

Francisco Gómez de Sandoval y Rojas, fifth Marquis of Denia (1574–99)

The Archbishop of Seville and the General of the Society of Jesus

The new Marquis of Denia had not been particularly close to either of his
parents. He was an affectionate man who was enduringly loyal to those whom
he loved but among his many surviving statements of love for his relatives none
refer to his mother and father. Indeed, he barely knew his mother, for Isabella
died in 1558 when he was five years of age.[21] In time, he paid his father's debts
but he erected no monument to him as he did for those relatives whose memory
was important to him. He was, however, genuinely close to his sisters Catalina
and Leonor and to his brother Juan Gómez, and they to him; the children of
the fourth marquis of Denia retained deep affection for each other throughout
their lives.

The suspicion that Denia found his father to be inadequate is bolstered by
the love that he showered on two other male relatives, both of whom rose to high
distinction in the Church, his great-uncle Cristóbal de Rojas (1502–80) and his
maternal grandfather, Francisco de Borja (1510–72). Cristóbal was the illegitimate son of Bernardo, II marquis of Denia. He held a succession of bishoprics
and actively supported the work of Teresa of Ávila in reforming the Carmelite
order of nuns in Spain; indeed, in a celebrated gesture, Cristóbal once publicly
knelt before Teresa in homage to her saintliness. His career reached its peak with
his appointment as archbishop of Seville in 1571, and until his death in 1580 he
also assumed many of the functions of Primate of Spain during the imprisonment on charges of heresy of Bartolomé de Carranza, Archbishop of Toledo;
during those last nine years of his life, therefore, Cristóbal was in practice the
senior churchman in Spain. He gave a great deal of moral and financial support
to Francisco Gómez. He also introduced him to a young Cordoban poet, Luis
de Góngora, who became a life-long friend (and eulogist). When Cristóbal
died Francisco Gómez was genuinely desolate. In time, he honoured Cristóbal's
memory by paying his debts and by commissioning a splendid alabaster statue

of him for the great church that he built in Lerma (the town in which Cristóbal
had been born). He interred Cristóbal under the high altar, and paid even more
intimate homage to him by naming his first-born son after him.[22]

On his maternal side, Francisco Gómez was a Borja. He was thus descended
from the most infamous of all the popes, Alexander VI (1492–1503). As far as
is known he never referred to the fact. The Spanish Borjas, as if to compensate
for their ancestry, became famously devout and provided the Catholic Church
with a succession of bishops, priests and nuns. The most distinguished of them
was Francisco de Borja, IV duke of Gandía. In 1550, four years after being
widowed, Francisco renounced his dukedom in his son's favour so that he could
enter the religious life. In the following year he was ordained a priest and in
1554 was received into the Society of Jesus. He did not, however, abandon his
connections with the court: he administered the last rites to Queen Juana and
was said to have been one of the first two people to have known in advance of
Charles V's decision to abdicate. He preached the sermon on Charles's death
and served as one of his testamentaries. He acted for a time as a tutor to Prince
Philip.[23] Throughout his life, Francisco moved effortlessly between the highest
levels of court and Church and he surely provided Francisco Gómez with the
perfect example of how to reconcile courtly influence with private spiritual
development. Moreover, since Francisco Gómez's paternal grandfather Luis,
III marquis of Denia, also chose to end his days in a monastery (although he did
not renounce his title), it therefore happened that before Francisco Gómez left
his infancy both of his grandfathers had voluntarily abandoned public life to end
their days in religious devotion. In time he followed their example.

Francisco de Borja was particularly close to Prince Philip's sister Juana,
late queen of Portugal, and under his guidance Juana developed such a deep
commitment to the Society of Jesus that she was allowed to become the only
female member of the Society in its history. When Juana founded her splendid
Carmelite convent of the *Descalzas Reales* in the heart of Madrid in 1557 the first
nuns to enter it were brought from Borja's convent of Santa Clara in Gandía.
From Francisco de Borja, as from Cristóbal de Rojas, Francisco Gómez inherited an enduring reverence for the reformed Carmelites.

Borja rose to be General of the Society of Jesus in 1565 and at the time
of his death was even spoken of – somewhat optimistically, it must be acknowledged – as a candidate for elevation to the papacy itself. The grandeur and
simplicity of his life had the most profound effect upon Francisco Gómez; in his
testament in 1617 he expressly acknowledged that '... I and all my descendants
have the obligation to give infinite thanks to God our Lord because among the
other favours that He has done me and them is to have given me as grandfather and them as forebear, Father Francisco de Borja ...'.[24] In 1617, Francisco
Gómez had his grandfather's corpse brought back to Spain from Rome and

began to build a splendid church in which to house it. He also instituted the process that led to Francisco's canonisation in 1671. He was, moreover, always unwavering in his support of the papacy, a characteristic that he probably inherited from his Jesuit grandfather. So deep was the influence of Francisco de Borja and Cristóbal de Rojas upon him that he attempted to follow them into the religious life, and although he was twice frustrated in his attempts to join the Society of Jesus (1572 and 1621) he did contrive to renounce the secular world in 1617–18 and to enjoy a cardinalate in his last years.[25]

The religiosity of Francisco Gómez was profound and sincere and it was coloured by the lives of Cristóbal de Rojas and Francisco de Borja. He inherited from them a deep commitment to the principles and practices of the Roman Catholic Church of the Counter-Reformation and a devotion to the new orders of the reformed Carmelites and the Jesuits. He was thus a very modern Roman Catholic. But he remained – always – a son of Old Castile, and he therefore had a particular devotion to the greatest saint that the kingdom had produced, St Dominic of Guzmán (c. 1172–1221), who had been born at Caleruega, only thirty kilometres south-east of Lerma; throughout his life, Francisco Gómez had the most unwavering devotion to the Dominicans. However, like many Spanish Catholics, he balanced his commitment to the stern Dominicans with one to the gentle Franciscans. When he came into the *valimiento* he patronised all four religious orders – the Dominicans and Franciscans, the discalced Carmelites and the Jesuits – with unstinting generosity. He built magnificent churches and houses for them and he acknowledged his own deep spirituality by using his political influence to press the papacy to beatify Teresa of Ávila and Francisco de Borja. It was, indeed, the return of his grandfather's body to Spain in 1617 which provided him with the occasion to leave court in direct emulation of him.

Estates and income: 'The poor grandee'

As fundamental to the formation of the Marquis of Denia's character as his religiosity was the impoverishment that had marked and demeaned his family during the sixteenth century. A list of aristocratic incomes dating from 1578 (four years after he inherited the title) listed 105 families, with an average income of 26,519 ducats; the marquisate of Denia was worth a mere 14,000. The Marquis ranked sixty-fourth on the list and twenty-third among the thirty-six marquises. He was the poorest of the grandees, of whom there were now thirty-seven. His family's income remained fixed stubbornly at the level that it had enjoyed in the 1540s: in a period of dramatic population growth and of high inflation, the Sandovals' income had not kept pace with that of their aristocratic colleagues, most of whom had seen their rents increase by at least 50 per cent during the middle third of the sixteenth century (see Appendix I).

Table 2 The population of Lerma and its dependent territories, 1541–91

	1541	1591
Lerma	1368	1125
Avellanosa del Muñó	99	81
Villalmanzo	661	616
Santillán	31	29
Villoviado	184	238
Ruyales del Agua	243	180
Revilla-Cabriada	261	265
Quintanilla de la Mata	225	346
Torrecilla del Montet	–	40
	3072	2920

Source: 1541, 'Vecindario de Castilla', AGS CG 768, fol. 33v, 'la villa de Lerma con t[ie]rra'; 1591, AGS DGT Inv. 24, 'Provincia de Burgos'. I have converted from *vecinos* at a quotient of 4.5.

Moreover, precisely as Francisco Gómez entered upon his inheritance, the towns and cities of the Duero Basin of Old Castile had begun to feel the effects of Philip II's wars in northern Europe. The population of the town of Lerma declined by about 20 per cent in the half century to 1591 but a slight growth in the population of its dependent *lugares* maintained the overall population of the Marquis's Castilian possessions at about the level that they had in 1541. About 3,000 people lived on the *estado de Lerma*.

As the capital of a rich agricultural area, Valladolid was better able than many of its neighbours to resist the impact of the wars; by 1591 it had a population of 40,000 and was the largest city in Old Castile, the true capital of the region. By contrast, proud Burgos – nominally the capital city of Old Castile – entered into vertiginous decline; the 18,000 people who had lived there in 1571 had declined to only 11,947 twenty years later.[26] Accordingly, it was to Valladolid that Denia turned his ambitions: indeed, to be the leading nobleman in Valladolid lay at the very heart of those ambitions.

The Marquis's eastern lands supported about 4,000 inhabitants at the time of his accession.[27] They, too, were experiencing economic difficulties as the growth of privateering (both Christian and Islamic) in the western Mediterranean threatened the security of the south-eastern coast of Spain. However, when Philip II commissioned a report in 1575 on the coastal defences of the kingdom of Valencia he was advised that the crown would have to pay for the strengthening of the castle of Denia because the Marquis did not have the resources to do so himself.[28] Philip marked Denia's succession to the marquisate by conferring upon him the titular command of a company of the Guards of Castile, but this was worth a paltry 667 ducats a year and made no significant difference to his impoverishment (26 September 1574).[29]

Determined to demonstrate his worth to the King, on 4 June 1575 the Marquis wrote to Philip asking to be allowed to contract for the maintenance of four of the twenty-four galleys of the Squadron of Spain (which operated out of Denia) for four years. He acknowledged his lack of experience in naval matters but professed himself confident that with good advisers he would be able to serve as the Captain General of the galleys. His uncle Cristóbal and the Genoese banker Agustín Spinola would stand surety for him. The grounds on which his hopes were rejected are not known but may be readily guessed at.[30]

In November 1576 Denia married Catalina de la Cerda, the youngest of the seven children of Juan de la Cerda, IV duke of Medinaceli. Since both her parents were dead the negotiations for the marriage were conducted by her brother Sancho. The fortunes of the de la Cerda were in decline: the family had ranked fifth among the Castilian aristocracy at the beginning of the sixteenth century but had now fallen to twenty-eighth (see Appendix I). However, they were still appreciably richer than the Sandovals, and if it is probable that Sancho only countenanced the match because the Sandovals were grandees there may well have been a more pressing reason for his giving assent – the first child of the marriage, Cristóbal, was born only five months after the wedding, on 18 April 1577. Certainly, for the Marquis the marriage was a lucrative one: Catalina brought a dowry of 29,467 ducats and jewels and valuables worth 8,454 ducats.[31] The marriage came to be a genuine love-match, and Catalina presented Francisco Gómez with five children, all of whom lived to adulthood. Cristóbal was followed by Diego Gómez and by three daughters, Catalina, Juana and Francisca.[32] The Marquis proved to be a devoted husband and father, gentle and loving: the members of his family were deeply committed to each other and as the children grew up the bonds between them strengthened.

Loving the family may have been, but it remained desperately poor by the standards of the senior aristocracy and the Marquis did what he could to win advancement at court. For instance, on 1 May 1578 he was present at the baptism of Prince Philip, the fourth son of Philip II's marriage to Anne of Austria.[33] Attendance at such events required that he maintain suitable style and surround himself with servants whose appearance and number reflected his status. Since he could not do this, he began now to throw himself repeatedly on the mercy of the King, begging for favours so that he could maintain his family and attend court with dignity. In May 1579 he wrote to Philip that 'most certainly I do not know a man who finds himself in greater poverty' than himself. It availed him nothing.[34]

In 1580 Denia was among the nobles whom Philip II ordered to lead a company of guards to accompany him on his invasion of Portugal. Before his departure, Denia undertook two important transactions in his eastern lands and it is probable that at least the first of these was to help him to pay for his expenses on the journey. He was already committed to repaying a mortgage (*censo*) of 12,000 ducats on his rents in Denia and Javea to the towns themselves, and on 1 March 1580 he added a further 4,000 ducats to the debt, ceding all the rents of the marquisate to the two town councils until the full amount was repaid. Six years into his tenure of his marquisate, Denia no longer controlled the financial management of his eastern lands.

Despite this, he was able six months later, on 21 September, to pay 51,000 ducats for the purchase of the village of Vergel, which had a population of about 350 people and was six kilometres south of Denia and slightly inland from the coast. Vergel had no real economic significance but its purchase was probably of great symbolic and emotional importance to the Marquis for it represented the first of his acquisitions of landed property. He was not able to produce any of the money himself: 26,000 ducats came as a gift from his great-uncle Cristóbal and a further 14,000 from Catalina's dowry. The remainder was raised by taking out yet another *censo*, which committed him to annual repayments of 2,067 ducats. Since Vergel brought in only 2,500 or so ducats annually, the Marquis was left with around 433 ducats of income from the town, a derisory return on such an investment. Philip II gave him permission to sell some of his Castilian property to raise the money but because the lands involved had *censos* assigned on them it proved difficult for him to do so.[35] The Marquis was falling deeper into debt and to little immediate purpose for his services in Portugal secured him honours rather than resources: in Lisbon, Philip appointed him as a gentleman of his chamber and named him as a *trece* of the military order of Santiago.[36] No doubt his command of the guards was symbolic for he had no military experience but at least he had demonstrated his loyalty to his king and played a part, however nominal, in the greatest triumph of Philip's reign, the acquisition of Portugal and its empire.

In the autumn of 1580 the Archbishop of Seville died. Denia sank into despair at the loss of his beloved patron, and in writing yet another begging letter to Philip II he probably revealed more of himself than he intended. He prefaced his plea by claiming that Catalina had recently been in some danger in childbed – giving birth to the daughter who was named after her – while he had been so ill that he was unable even to write in his own hand to the King; in fact, he always found it difficult to write letters. He expressed his confidence that Philip would not allow his family and himself to 'perish with hunger'. As far as is known, the letter produced no results.[37]

Ever more despairing, in 1583 Denia appealed for support to the royal confessor, fray Diego de Chaves, and to convince him of his hardship set out a detailed account of his financial position. He had a total income now of 12,160 ducats: 9,493 ducats (78 per cent) were in Castile and 2,667 (22 per cent) in Valencia. However, in Castile he had to meet *censo* payments of 7,280 ducats and administrative costs of 1,200 ducats; he therefore only enjoyed 1,013 ducats of free income (8.3 per cent). In Valencia he had a mere 400 ducats of free income after his repayments for the *censos* held by the town councils of Denia and Javea. He also received 1,500 ducats a year from the position of gentleman of the chamber and 667 ducats as captain of the Guards. He was committed to paying 2,600 ducats a year on government bonds (*juros*) and owed cash debts of 11,000–12,000 ducats. He implored fray Diego to represent the depths of his need to the King, insisting that he did not have enough money to feed his family, much less to maintain its social standing:

> I do not have even a *real* with which to live or indeed which can be used for anything other than ... the purchase of food. Because I am a servant of His Majesty and my wife and myself are children of servants of great antiquity ... it will be necessary if his Majesty (may God protect him) does not help us that we place the very bed in which we sleep into the hands of a Justice and take ourselves off to a charitable home because we are weary of repeatedly begging our friends and supporters for the wherewithal with which to eat. We are asking for nothing more than the means to sustain ourselves as people who have been honoured in the service of His Majesty ...[38]

It was a deeply humiliating letter for a grandee to write, and Denia turned once again to Philip II, begging for some charity so that he and his family could preserve their dignity.[39] His self-abasement yielded no reward and when in 1584 he was ordered to accompany the King and his court to the meeting of the *cortes* of Aragon at Monzón he addressed himself again to Philip, insisting that 'I have nothing to help me other than the clemency and greatness of Your Majesty ...'.[40] The King remained deaf to his pleas.

Denia also sought help from some of Philip's senior servants. In 1584 he twice presented himself at the office of Juan Delgado, Secretary of the Council of War, but was told that Delgado was not receiving visitors.[41] He had more success with the 'arch-secretary' Mateo Vázquez, who assured Philip that he had 'rarely seen' such poverty as Denia's in a man of his rank.[42] Denia was among those who pledged their fealty to Prince Philip when on 11 November 1584 he was sworn in as heir to the throne of Castile.[43] It may have been through Vázquez's intercession that on 19 January 1585 Denia was included among the men who were charged with the education of Prince Philip, who was seven years old.[44]

The Marquis then accompanied the court on the royal progress to Monzón where the Prince took the oaths to the three states of the Crown of Aragon. It was a dangerous and expensive journey: the court was away from Madrid for fourteen months (January 1585–March 1586) and some ninety courtiers died in Monzón when plague ravaged the town.[45] It was perhaps as a reward for his service on the journey that in 1590 Denia was given the *encomienda* of Reyna

Table 3 The rentable value of the Sandoval estates in 1598 (in ducats)

Total income	Kingdom	Income	Estates	Percentage of total
8,027	Castile	3,067	Lerma estate	19
		3,200	Cea estate	20
		1,760	Gumiel de Mercado	11
8,000	Valencia		Denia, Javea, Vergel	50
16,027				

Source: 'Relación de las rentas y hazienda', ADL 54, no. 9, no fol.

in the Order of Santiago. He accepted it, as Vázquez reported to Philip, 'with much humility'.[46]

The Marquis had much reason to be humble. No evidence survives about his expenditure on the *jornada de Aragón* but it is likely that these months destroyed the last vestiges of his solvency, for immediately on his return he was taken to court in the Chancellery of Valladolid by his Castilian creditors. He suffered the most profound humiliation of his life when control of his Castilian lands and properties was taken away from him; he was assigned 4,000 ducats a year to maintain himself and his family and the remainder of his income was embargoed to meet his debts.[47] It was a poignant token of his impoverishment that in 1588 his *camarero* had to leave his service because the Marquis could not afford to pay his salary.[48] Even Philip II could not ignore such penury in a grandee and in 1589 he conferred the *encomienda* of Mérida, worth 2,267 ducats annually, upon Denia.[49]

Welcome though this was, it could not substantially improve Denia's circumstances and he now took the only means available to him to escape from the bondage imposed by his creditors. In 1589 he placed the management of his estates into the hands of a professional moneylender, taking out an *asiento* with Sebastián Pascual, a crown banker of Medina del Campo, to cover the whole of his income in Castile and Valencia for the eleven years from 1590 until 1600. Denia gave Pascual legal authority to administer the Castilian estates together with the interest and rents in the eastern lands, the rents of such *encomiendas* as he and his heir might enjoy, his income as Captain of the Guards and any increase in his income that might come about before 1600. In return, Pascual agreed to pay 15,773 ducats annually to cover the Marquis's expenses, a total of 173,500 ducats.[50]

When Philip II died, Denia had an income from his estates of 16,027 ducats, and it was divided equally between his properties in Castile and Valencia (see table 3).

The Marquis's Castilian revenues had decreased by one-sixth since 1583 and he had *censos* of 5,409 ducats charged against them. In the east, his *censos* cost 4,566 ducats per year and he had to spend a further 2,000 ducats on protecting his concession on the right to fish tunny (*almadrabas*). His unavoidable expenses therefore came to 11,975 ducats, which left him with a free income of 4,078 ducats together with the 2,267 ducats from the *encomienda* of Mérida. To maintain himself and his family he had a total of 6,345 ducats. On such an income he had no possibility of paying off any of his debts or of redeeming the *censos*. Much less had he the means with which to maintain the status of a grandee. When Philip II died the Marquis of Denia needed new sources of income – and he needed them quickly.

NOTES

1 'FVNDACIÓN [DEL Mayorazgo de la villa de Lerma, su jurisdición, señorio, y vassallage, pechos, y derechos, por el señor Rey de Aragón D. Fernando, en 18 de Iulio del año de 1412]', ADL 12, fol. 2; A. López de Haro, *Nobiliario genealógico de los reyes y titvlos de España*, 2 vols., Madrid, 1622, i, pp. 156–61. On the Sandoval family, Prudencio de Sandoval, *Chrónica del inclito Emperador de España, don Alonso VII*, Madrid, 1600, pp. 187–252; M. de Viciana, *Crónica de la inclita y coronada ciudad de Valencia*, ed. S. García Martínez, Valencia, 1972, 2 vols., ii, pp. 147–8 and Gaspar Escolano, *Decada primera de la historia de ...Valencia*, Valencia 1972 reprint of 1611 edition, 6 vols., vi, pp. 162–3.

2 B. Clavero, *Mayorazgo. Propiedad feudal en Castilla (1369–1836)*, Madrid 1974, pp. 33–5. Some important studies of aristocratic families: I. Atienza Hernández, *Aristocracía, poder y riqueza en la España moderna. La Casa de Osuna, siglos XV–XIX*, Madrid, 1987; M. del Pilar García Pinacho (ed.), *Los Álvarez de Toledo. Nobleza viva*, JCL, 1998. See also, Helen Nader, 'Noble Income in Sixteenth-Century Castile. The Case of the Marquises of Mondéjar, 1480–1580' EHR, 1977, no. 30, pp. 411–28 and J. R. L. Highfield, 'The De la Cerda, the Pimentel and the So-called "Price Revolution"', EHR, 1972, 87, pp. 495–512.

3 Thompson, 'The Nobility in Spain', pp. 195–6.

4 Rodríguez-Salgado, 'Honour and profit in the court of Philip II of Spain', p. 79. See also, Charles Jago, 'The Influence of Debt on the Relations between Crown and Aristocracy in Seventeenth-century Castile, *Econ. Hist. Review*, 26, 1973, pp. 218–36 and Jago, 'The "Crisis of the Aristocracy" in Seventeenth-Century Castile', *Past and Present*, 84, 1979, pp. 60–90.

5 Sandoval, *Chrónica de ... Alonso VII*, fol. 214. On *grandeza*, below, pp. 19–20.

6 'FVNDACIÓN DEL MAYOrazgo de las villas de Ampudia, y Villacidaler, su jurisdición, señorío, y vassallage, pechos y derechos, por el señor Rey Don Iuan el Segundo, en 14 de Setiembre del año de 1419', appended to 'FVNDACIÓN DEL Mayorazgo de la villa de Lerma', ADL 12, fol. 23.

7 Cervera Vera, *El conjunto palacial*, i, 188 and Roque Chabas, *Historia de la ciudad de Denia*, 3 parts, Denia, 1874–6, iii, pp. 56–64. See also L. Suárez Fernández, *Historia de España. Edad Media*, Madrid, 1970, pp. 531–42. On the 'Lands of the Recompense', below, pp. 68–9, 141–2.

8 Viciana, *Crónica de ... Valencia*, ii, pp. 145–6; López de Haro, *Nobiliario*, i, pp. 156–62.

9 Henry's designated heir was his daughter Juana but it was widely believed that Juana's father was not the King but one of his nobles, don Beltrán de la Cueva, Duke of Alburquerque. Isabella, the daughter of Juan II's second wife, Isabella of Portugal, claimed the succession for herself.

10 Cardinal-Duke of Lerma, 'Descripción e imbentario de las Rentas Vienes, y hazienda del Cardenal Duque de Lerma, en conformidad de lo que S[u] M[agestad] que Dios Guarde, manda por su decreto Real ...', Valladolid, 27 March 1622 [hereafter 'Imbentario'], ADL 43, fol. 4, a copy. A summary of another copy, A. Domínguez Ortíz, *La sociedad española en el siglo VII*, 2 vols., Madrid 1963–70, pp. 363–6.

11 Sandoval, *Chrónica de ... Alonso VII*, pp. 232–3; López de Haro, *Nobiliario*, i, p. 162.

12 Viciana, *Crónica de … Valencia*, ii, pp. 144–6; J. F. O'Callaghan, *A History of Medieval Spain*, Ithaca, NY, 1975, pp. 133, 134, 196, 220, 296, 297.

13 Bethany Aram, *La reina Juana. Gobierno, piedad y dinastía*, Madrid, 2001, pp. 206–7; and Charles V to Denia, Barcelona, 14 Jan. 1520, printed by M. Fernández Álvarez, *Corpus Documental de Carlos V*, 4 vols., Salamanca, 1973–81, i, pp. 82–3.

14 Joseph Pérez, *La revolución de las comunidades de Castilla (1520–1521)*, 3rd edn., Madrid, 1977, pp. 314–15.

15 López de Haro, *Nobiliario*, i, p. 164. See also, Aram, *La reina Juana*, pp. 195–240.

16 Thompson, 'The Nobility in Spain', pp. 192–3. On the grandees, J. H. Elliott, 'Philip IV of Spain, Prisoner of Ceremony', in A. G. Dickens (ed.), *Courts of Europe*, pp. 169–89, at 173–4.

17 Pedro Girón, *Crónica del emperador Carlos V*, ed. J. Sánchez Montes, Madrid, 1964, p. 64; Aram, *La reina Juana*, p. 236.

18 Cervera Vera, *El conjunto palacial*, i, pp. 176–7, 197, n. 39; Pérez, *La Revolución de las comunidades de Castilla*, pp. 38, 68, 207; Chabas, *Denia*, iii, p. 114.

19 L. P. Gachard, *Don Carlos y Felipe II*, Madrid, 1984, pp. 66–8.

20 Denia to Philip II, 1570–2, BL Add Mss, 28,337, fol. 35; on salary as captain of arms, 'Imbentario', ADL 43, fol. 24v; Luis de Salazar y Castro, *Los Comendadores de la Orden de Santiago*, Madrid, 1949, i, p. 272.

21 Fernández de Béthencourt, *Historia genealógica*, iv, pp. 123–4.

22 Teresa de Ávila, *Obras completas*, eds. E. de la Madre de Dios and O. Steggink, Madrid, 1962, pp. 564, 714, 916. On Cristóbal's career, Sandoval, *Chrónica de … don Alonso VII*, pp. 240–3 and G. González Dávila, *Teatro eclesiástico de las yglesias metropolitanas y catedrales de los reinos de las dos Castillas*, 4 vols., Madrid, 1645–1700, ii, pp. 96–7; L. Cervera Vera, *La iglesia colegial de San Pedro en Lerma*, Burgos, 1981, pp. 18, 52–7.

23 Cándido de Dalmases, *Padre Francisco de Borja*, Madrid, 1983; W. Stirling-Maxwell, *The Cloister Life of the Emperor Charles V*, London, 1891, pp. 117–27, 245–8, 395, 445–50.

24 'Testamento' of the Duke of Lerma, included at pp. 2–34v in 'AVTOS QVE SE HIZIERON PARA ABRIR el testamento del Excel[entísimo] señor Cardenal Duque de Lerma', Madrid, 12 June 1617, ADL 12, a printed copy. On this document, below, pp. 221–6.

25 F. Cereceda, 'La vocación jesuítica del duque de Lerma', *Razon y Fé*, 605, Jun. 1948, pp. 512–23; and J. M. Palomares Ibáñez, *El patronato del Duque de Lerma sobre el convento de San Pablo de Valladolid*, Valladolid, 1970, p. 22; Williams, 'Lerma, 1618. Dismissal or Retirement?'.

26 B. Bennassar, *Valladolid en el siglo de oro. Una ciudad de Castilla y su entorno agrario en el siglo XVI*, Valladolid: 1983 reprint of *Valladolid au siècle d'or. Une ville de Castille et sa campagne au XVI siècle*, Paris, 1967, pp. 98, 326–8.

27 See above, pp. 28–9.

28 Vespasiano Gonzaga to Philip II, Valencia, 30 Sep. 1575, AGS GA 79, fol. 102.

29 Lerma, 'Imbentario', ADL 43, fols. 24–24v; summary of Denia to Philip II, undated (1574–75), BL Mss Add 28, 339, fol. 356.

30 Denia to Philip II, Madrid, 4 Jun. 1575, AGS GA 80, fol. 195; a summary of Denia's proposition, with further details, same to same, 18 Jun. 1575, ibid. 175, fol. 23.

31 Fernández de Béthencourt, *Historia genealógica*, v, pp. 256–7; on birth of Cristóbal, Sandoval, *Chrónica de … Alonso VIII*, p. 240 and Chabas, *Denia*, iii, p. 121 (who records that Cristóbal was baptised in Denia on 28 April).

32 Catalina was born in 1580 and Diego Gómez in 1587, but the dates of birth of Juana and Francisca are not known.

33 Luis Cabrera de Córdoba, *Historia de Filipe Segundo, Rey de España*, reprinted by Junta de Castilla y León (JCL), 3 vols., Salamanca, 1998, eds. J. Martínez Millán and C. Javier de Carlos Morales.

34 Denia to Philip II, Madrid, 28 May 1579, BL Add 28, 341, fol. 352.

35 Lerma, 'Imbentario', ADL 43, fols. 12–12v; Denia to fray Diego de Chaves, (Madrid ?),

8 Jun. 1583, BL Add 28, 344, fols. 122–3; Chabas, *Denia*, iii, pp. 121–2, 125 n. 1 and 205. See also, Bernardo García García, 'Los marqueses de Denia en la corte de Felipe II. Linaje, servicio y virtud', in J. Martínez Millán (ed.), *Felipe II (1598–1998). Europa dividida. La Monarquía Católica de Felipe II. Actas del Congreso Internacional*, 4 vols., Madrid, 1998, ii, pp. 305–31.

36 'Imbentario ...', ADL 43, fol. 23b.

37 Denia to Philip II, Cigales, 20 Sep. 1580, BL Add 28, 342, fol. 127.

38 Same to fray Diego de Chaves, Madrid?, 8 Jun. 1583, BL Add 28, 344, fols. 122–3.

39 Same to Philip II, Madrid, 23 Sep. 1583, ibid., fol. 250.

40 Same to same, El Pardo, 20 Oct. 1584, ibid. 28, 345, fol. 211.

41 Same to Delgado, Aranjuez, 24 April 1584, AGS GA 161, fol. 152.

42 Vázquez de Leca to Philip II, El Pardo, 12 Jan. 1585, printed in C. Riba García, *Correspondencia privada de Felipe II con su secretario Mateo Vázquez de Léca 1567–1591*, Madrid, 1959, p. 351. See also, Feros, *Kingship and Favoritism*, pp. 38–9.

43 Anon., 'Juramento del Principe D. Felipe', 1584, printed by José Simon Diaz, *Relaciones breves de actos públicos celebrados en Madrid de 1541 a 1650*, IEM, Madrid, 1982, pp. 20–9.

44 'Imbentario...', ADL 43, fol. 15.

45 Enrique Cock, 'Anales del año ochenta y cinco ...', in J. García Mercadal (ed.), *Viajes de extranjeros por España y Portugal*, 3 vols., Madrid, 1952, i, pp. 1295–1412.

46 San Lorenzo, 18 Jun. 1589, BL Add 28,374, fol. 274.

47 Anon., 'Relación de las rentas y hazienda que el Cardenal Duque mi s[eño]r Tenia y gocaua en fin del año de 1598 Y de las que su Ex[celenci]a acrecentó en su estado y mayorazgo desde el d[ich]o año hasta el de 1625 que falleció es en esta Manera' (hereafter, 'Relación de las rentas y hazienda'), no date, ADL 54, no. 9, no fol.

48 Mendoza, *camarero* of the Marquis of Denia, to Mateo Vázquez, San Lorenzo, 9 April 1588, BL Add Mss 28,347, fol. 358.

49 Luis de Salazar y Castro, *Los Comendadores de la Orden de Santiago*, Madrid, 1949, p. 602.

50 'Assiento que por 11 años hizo el S[eño]r d[o]n franc[isc]o de Rojas Marqués de Denia con Sebastian Pasqual', Madrid, 13 Dec. 1589, ADL 49, no. 13, no fol. On the 1590s in Castile, James Casey, 'Spain. A Failed Transition', in Peter Clark (ed.) *The European Crisis of the 1590s*, London, 1985, pp. 209–28.

2

The accession of Philip III

The legacy of Philip II

Philip II left a failed foreign policy and a broken exchequer to his son. During his last decade he fought three major wars simultaneously – against the rebels in the Low Countries who had been in revolt against his authority since the late 1560s; against the English who had been at open, if undeclared, war with him from 1585; and against Henry of Navarre, a protestant who in 1588 had succeeded to the throne of France as Henry IV. These wars were ruinously expensive, and in 1596 Philip was forced to suspend payments to his bankers for the fourth time.[1]

In the early summer of 1598 Philip took a series of major initiatives to provide a manageable inheritance for his son in foreign affairs. He reaffirmed Spain's dynastic solidarity with the Austrian branch of the Habsburg family by agreeing that young Philip would marry Margaret, the thirteen year-old daughter of the Archduke Charles of Styria, while Isabella was betrothed to the Archduke Albert, brother of the Emperor Rudolf II. Neither Rudolf nor any of his four brothers had children and Philip II calculated that his son's marriage might bring the imperial title back to the Spanish royal family and restore the dual monarchy of Charles V.[2]

In the first week of May 1598 Philip II restricted the military commitments that his son would have to maintain by making two settlements in foreign affairs. On 2 May, he brought his war with Henry of Navarre to an end at the Peace of Vervins, tacitly acknowledging the failure of his policy by recognising his great rival as the legitimate king of France, Henry IV.[3] Four days later, he ceded direct control over the Low Countries to Isabella and Albert, endowing the parts of the county of Burgundy that were still ruled by Spain upon Isabella as her dowry; the conduct of the war against the rebels in the Low Countries would be devolved upon his daughter and son-in-law.[4]

The settlements of May 1598 were bitterly resented among the Spanish military élite. The Count of Fuentes, kinsman of the Duke of Alba, spoke for many in declaring of the Peace of Vervins that 'we are ashamed of it; and it was concluded by those who don't understand the use of arms'.[5] The alienation of direct control over the conduct of the war in the Low Countries proved even harder for these men to accept: it was in this war that many of them had learned their craft and they regarded Philip's decision to hand over control for the future conduct of the war to his daughter and son-in-law as a dereliction of his kingly duty.[6] Philip II's settlements of May 1598 therefore created a very clear danger that divisions would arise between his son's ministers and his generals.

Government: ministers, councils and *juntas*

In the first half of the 1580s, Philip II made major state visits to Portugal (December 1580–February 1583) and to Aragon (January 1585–March 1586). During these long absences from his capital, the King necessarily developed close working relationships with the small group of ministers who travelled with him and in consequence these men acquired quasi-ministerial status. Moreover, during both *jornadas*, Philip became so seriously ill that he nearly died. He never recovered his full vigour after 1586 and the last dozen years of his life were marked by a progressive deterioration in his physical condition. His debility, together with the growing complexity of the crises with which he had to deal, further accentuated the importance of his group of trusted close advisers.[7]

The inner coterie was balanced between noblemen, professional administrators and churchmen and was a surprisingly cosmopolitan group. Three were nobles: Gómez Dávila y Toledo, second marquis of Velada, a Castilian; Diego de Cabrera y Bobadilla, third count of Chinchón, an Aragonese; and Juan de Zúñiga, an untitled younger son of a Catalan noble family. Another three men had made their careers as secretaries of state – Mateo Vázquez de Leca, an Andalusian; Cristovão de Moura, a Portuguese, and Juan de Idiáquez, who was of Basque ancestry (although he had been born in Madrid). Two churchmen, both of whom were Castilians, also played important roles when confessional matters were involved in policymaking – fray Diego de Chaves, confessor of the king, and García de Loaisa, archbishop-elect of Toledo.[8]

Chinchón and Velada belonged to the service aristocracy. Neither of them was a grandee and their titles were relatively modern, dating from 1520 and 1557. Chinchón's income of 30,000 ranked him forty-third on the list of incomes in 1595 while Velada had only 10,000 and ranked one-hundredth. By personality and temperament they were very different; Chinchón was aggressive and vindictive and lived in a cocoon of hostility that he created around himself while Velada was a self-effacing courtier who skilfully served the King without creating enemies.[9]

Juan de Zúñiga held no title but was a close friend of Philip II and until his death in 1586 played a prominent role in the inner circle. So, too, did Mateo Vázquez de Leca, who died in 1591. The deaths of the two men led to the further concentration of power in the hands of Velada, Chinchón, Moura and Idiáquez, and in September 1593 Philip brought the Archduke Albert of Austria to court to direct their work. Philip had real affection for Albert, who had proved himself to be uniquely loyal among his senior male relatives, and trusted him to co-ordinate the work of his ministers for him.[10] The body on which these ministers worked soon became known as the 'Junta of the Night' in recognition both of the hour at which it conducted business and of the secrecy that surrounded its conduct of affairs. Albert served until 1595, when Philip II appointed him as Governor of the Low Countries. Thereafter, the four surviving ministers continued to work as a group, and as the political and financial crises of the 1590s developed – and as Philip II's physical decline entered its terminal phase – they gathered power to themselves. It was to these men that Philip II looked to control and guide his son in the early years of his reign.

The most important of them were Moura and Idiáquez. They had come to prominence at the end of the 1570s and served Philip as senior secretaries for the remainder of his reign. Both had progressed to councillorships of State, Moura in 1587 and Idiáquez in 1594. Moura had become Philip's senior adviser on Portuguese affairs and had masterminded the takeover of his own country by Philip in 1580. As Philip became weaker he leaned increasingly on Moura, for whom he had real affection. Idiáquez was a member of one of the major secretarial dynasties of the sixteenth century and by the middle of the 1580s had become Philip's chief adviser on foreign affairs, particularly those in northern Europe. Both were enormously hard-working ministers, but both remained true to their roots: Moura, a courtier and foreigner; Idiáquez, an administrator and a political insider. There was, too, a difference in their psychological resilience: Moura was pliable but weak; Idiáquez was malleable but resilient.

Philip had as a matter of principle rigorously excluded the grandees and the very richest aristocrats from important positions at the heart of his government. Nine of the twelve aristocrats who according to the calculations of Núñez de Salcedo in 1595 had incomes of over 100,000 ducats were dukes (Medina Sidonia, Osuna, Medina de Rioseco, Alba, Infantado, Cardona, Alcalá, Escalona and Sessa), two were marquises (Priego and del Valle de Oaxaca) and only one was a count (Benavente). Only two of these men held substantive governmental posts when Philip II died and both were serving away from Madrid: the Duke of Medina Sidonia was co-ordinating the crown's naval activities in Andalusia while the Count of Benavente was appointed as Viceroy of Valencia in the last weeks of Philip's life. None of the twelve appears to have sat on the Council of State in the 1590s and none held conciliar presidencies.

The kings of Spain governed their realms through a system of advisory councils, most of which had been founded in the years 1480–1525. At their head stood the Council of State, which had been established in 1523 to advise the king on major affairs of war and diplomacy. The Council of War had developed as a junior body that was loosely attached to the Council of State; it was responsible for organising the waging of war on land and sea. Both councils were composed of nobles; as a general rule, the councillors of State were senior noblemen who had served abroad in viceroyalties and captaincies-general and embassies while the councillors of War had earned their livings as military commanders and provisioners and were therefore socially junior to the councillors of State. Both councillorships were unpaid; the honour of serving the king was deemed to be reward enough. The two councils did not have presidents; in theory the king presided, but in practice this happened only on the rarest of occasions. They were also distinct from the professional councils in that they were not subject to *ordenanzas* which governed their practices and procedures.

The professional councils may for convenience be divided into two groups. Seven were responsible for individual states within the monarchy: Castile (1480), Aragon (1494), Indies (1523), Navarre (1525), Italy (1559), Portugal (1582) and Flanders (1588). Another four were responsible for areas of government: the Inquisition (1481) dealt with matters involving purity of faith and was the only professional council to have authority over the whole of Spain; Military Orders (1494) administered the lands of the Orders of Santiago, Calatrava and Alcántara; Finance (1523) managed the revenues of the crown of Castile, and Crusade (1568) controlled the tax after which it was named.

Philip II valued his councils and made a consistent effort to modernise them. He created new councils for Crusade, Portugal and Flanders. He also brought about a major restructuring of the Council of Castile in 1588 by establishing a separate chamber within it (the *Cámara de Castilla*) to deal with matters of patronage in Church and State – and carried out a long-overdue reform of the Council of Finance in 1593. Unfortunately, both latter reforms fell by the wayside – that of the Council of Castile because of weaknesses in the presidency and that of Finance when the financial collapse of the 1590s made it imperative for Philip and his inner circle to take over responsibility for financial matters. Philip II was more successful in giving extra weight to the councils of State and War. By the time of the Armada campaign in 1588 he was allowing the Council of State to develop a substantive role in government but he remained determined that the Council would not become a regularly-functioning part of the governmental apparatus; he still did not convene it on a regular basis and its membership was ill-defined (save that the most senior aristocrats were in practice excluded from attending). Philip also extended the authority of the Council of War during the crises of his last decade.[11]

The key figure in the development of the professional councils was the president. He nominated men to serve as councillors and officers and then exercised discipline over them. The holders of the two greatest presidencies – those of Castile and Inquisition – ranked among the leading men in the land. The Council of Castile was the primary judicial bench in the kingdom and its president was therefore the senior judge in Castile. Since the Council also supervised appointments to most major offices in Church and State in Castile, its president had enormous powers of patronage at his disposal. The Inquisitor-General was responsible for maintaining religious orthodoxy throughout Spain (and by the later 1570s in the Indies) and he had at his command the only truly national institution in the country. He too had great powers of patronage and supervised a nationwide police force of *familiares*.

During the last two decades of his reign Philip II extended the use of *juntas* by creating bodies to deal with major areas of policy – the organisation of the 'Invincible Armada'; the provisioning of armies and fleets; the protection of frontiers; the crisis in Aragon in 1591–92, the negotiations with the Cortes of Castile for taxes in the 1590s, and so on. The usefulness of *juntas* to Philip II was precisely that they were more flexible than councils and could be more easily controlled and directed; they did not have *ordenanzas* defining who should sit on them, how often they should be convened and what matters they were entitled to deal with.

This, however, did not mean – as has sometimes been suggested – that Philip II used *juntas* to replace councils. In the fulminating crises of the 1580s and 1590s government underwent a series of parallel and interdependent developments and a complex set of interacting relationships developed between king, councils and the *juntas* and the inner circle of ministers. Underpinning all of them were the secretaries of state. The secretaries were no longer the great figures they had been in the earlier sixteenth century but more of them were now needed to cope with the growing volume of work; at the beginning of Philip's reign only six secretaries were employed by the central councils but by 1598 there were twenty-six.[12] Most of the growth came about in the last decade of the reign as offices were multiplied to cope with the increasing volume of business and as it became necessary for the secretaries to become specialists in the areas for which they were responsible. In 1586, for example, the secretaryship of War was separated into offices for Land and for Sea.[13] Until 1588, the Council of Castile had only one secretaryship, for the '*Cámara y Estado de Castilla*'; in the restructuring of the council in that year a second office was added for the Church (*Patronato Real de la Iglesia*) and in 1592 a third, for judicial affairs (*Justicia*). Similar changes were taking place in other councils, and in the last years of Philip II's reign the conciliar secretariat expanded substantially. The cost rose commensurately: in 1579 the salaries of the secretaries who were paid on the conciliar *nomina* amounted to 10,120,740 *maravedis*, but by 1598 it had risen to 25,132,545 *maravedis*.[14] During the last decade of Philip II's reign the government of Spain had become much bigger and more complex, and it had become more difficult to manage.

Prince, courtiers and ministers

The prince who inherited these problems of policy and government had been born in 1578, the third son of Philip II and Anne of Austria. The King and his wife were doubly related to each other – as cousins and as uncle and niece – and Philip III was the only one of their four children who lived more than seven years. Like his siblings, young Philip was physically weak and his childhood – and indeed his whole life – was marked by the frequency and suddenness with which illnesses took hold of him.[15] His psychological development may well have been further arrested by the death of his mother in 1580. The dowager Empress María, sister of the King, took over the role of mother, but she was severe and remote and seems to have been little compensation to him for the loss of his mother.[16]

Philip became the heir to the thrones of Spain in 1582 on the death of Diego Felix, the third of his elder brothers.[17] In the years 1583–86 he became the first prince to be sworn in by each of the kingdoms of Iberia – Portugal (in absentia), 1583; Castile, 1584; the three states of the Kingdom of Aragon, 1585; and Navarre, 1586.[18] After he had taken the oath to the kingdom of Castile a household was established for him (19 January 1585).[19] Juan de Zúñiga took the leading positions, as *mayordomo mayor* and *ayo* while fray García de Loaisa was appointed as *maestro* and *limosnero mayor*, charged with educating the Prince in moral and political matters. After Zúñiga's death in November 1586 Philip persuaded the Marquis of Velada to take on the position of *ayo* and to supervise his son's education and instruct him in his civic and governmental obligations (August 1587). The King rounded out his son's household in 1589 when he named Moura as his *sumiller de corps*: he and Velada would play the dominant roles in the household.

The Prince's introduction to government was measured. In 1593 he made his first formal appearance in public and in the same year the senior members of the King's inner circle were convened as the *Junta de Gobierno* to supervise his education – Albert, Moura, Idiáquez, Chinchón and Velada. The Prince showed himself impatient at having to work under the guidance of these men.[20] On 9 July 1596 he began to preside over meetings of the Council of State so that he could familiarise itself with the business of the Council and learn how to work with its members. Not until May 1597 could Philip II bring himself to agree to hand over to his son the responsibility for signing despatches in his name.[21] Even now he continued to sign documents himself; his last monogram on a *consulta* of the Council of War was dated 13 September 1597, exactly one year before his death.[22]

Two perceptive descriptions survive of the heir at this time. In 1595 Francisco Vendramin, the Venetian ambassador, penned a portrait in which he described the Prince as a calm young man who was intent on emulating the qualities of his father, to whom he was deeply obedient. Vendramin noted that although the Prince took rather more pleasure in the hunt than he did in the affairs of government he still spent one hour a day with the Council of State. The Ambassador observed that young Philip was not particularly intelligent but that he greatly enjoyed the study of mathematics and – an exaggeration, this – spoke several languages with some fluency.[23] On 20 October 1596, García de Loaisa sent the King an assessment of the Prince's progress on behalf of his tutors – himself, Diego de Yepes, the Prince's confessor; Moura, Velada and Idiáquez. This report also described a deeply religious young man who was completely obedient to his father. It glossed over the doubts that the tutors clearly entertained as to the Prince's intellectual shortcomings and noted that he was very correct in dealing with people but that he had not yet acquired the gravity that went with kingship, although he knew how to disguise his feelings.[24] Moura and García de Loaisa would soon learn just how true that was.

The Marquis of Denia was not appointed to the Prince's household, but as a gentleman of the King's chamber he had access to the Prince and was able to insinuate himself into the affections of the impressionable young man.[25] By the middle of the 1590s the members of the *Junta de Gobierno* were becoming anxious about the influence that he was exercising over the heir. They encouraged Philip II to send Denia away from the capital, and the King appointed him as Viceroy and Captain-General of the Kingdom of Valencia. He left Madrid on 7 June 1595. He kept in contact with the Prince through his brother Juan, who had been appointed as young Philip's *caballerizo*, and through his friend Alonso Muriel de Valdivielso, who was named as an *ayuda de cámara*.[26]

Denia was reasonably successful as viceroy, taking initiatives to deal with the problems created by the unsettled *morisco* minority on land and by pirates and corsairs on sea.[27] Unfortunately, he was severely embarrassed by the financial demands that his position placed upon him. He received a monthly allowance of fifty ducats from his great-uncle, Bernardo, bishop of Pamplona, but this was of only token importance to him.[28] However, the manifest intimacy of his relationship to the heir now drew others to support him. In 1595, Martín de Padilla, the elderly Count of Santa Gadea and *Adelantado Mayor* of

Castile – a crusty old sailor not known for the sensitivity of his political judgement – negotiated a marriage between his daughter Mariana and Denia's heir,
Cristóbal. Mariana brought a dowry of 75,000 ducats.[29] It is probable that in
his penury the Marquis availed himself of some of this but there is no evidence
on the matter.

Denia's most pressing need was to return to court to maintain his influence over the heir to the throne. He begged Philip II to allow him to come
to Madrid on grounds of ill-health, 'the doctors having told him that in order
to convalesce it would be necessary for him to have some absence from this
kingdom'. In December 1596, the King gave him licence to return briefly to
the capital. He did so, returning to Valencia on 23 February 1597. He continued
to complain about the effect of the Mediterranean climate on his health and
Philip II gave way, releasing him from his servitude: on 7 November 1597 the
Marquis returned to Madrid.[30]

He renewed his relationship with the Prince by giving him some money.
When the King heard of this he rebuked his son and, perhaps in a fit of pique,
conferred the *encomienda* of Hornachos in the Order of Santiago upon Denia
(19 May 1598). The *encomienda* was of only moderate value and Philip II may
have presented it to Denia to satisfy any claims he had on the royal grace and to
prevent his son feeling under any obligation to reward him.[31] Philip balanced
this by driving home Moura's importance to his son's future by allowing young
Philip to serve as godfather at the marriage of Moura's daughter Beatriz to
don Perafan de Rivera, duke of Alcalá (23 April).[32] To further counterbalance
Denia's influence over his son, Philip nominated García de Loaisa to the
archbishopric of Toledo and named the Dominican Gaspar de Córdoba as young
Philip's confessor.[33] The struggle for influence over the heir and his household
had begun in earnest.

The household of the heir

The household of the Spanish monarch had two distinct parts which reflected
the fusion of Castilian and Burgundian dynasties and cultures that had come
about under Charles V – the *Casa y Corte de Castilla* which was the household of
the kings of Castile, and the *Casa de Borgoña* or Burgundian household, which
Charles V imposed upon his son in 1548.[34] The *Casa de Castilla* combined service
to the king with some responsibilities towards the queen while the *Casa de
Borgoña* was devoted exclusively to the king's service. Both households were
governed by *etiquetas* which could be modified at will by the monarch.

Philip II took advantage of this prerogative in 1562 to simplify the structure
of his court by consolidating the pre-eminence of the *Casa de Borgoña* over the

Casa de Castilla. Each *casa* was led by a *mayordomo mayor* or Lord High Steward, who was responsible for managing the royal palace, and the two posts were now merged so that one *mayordomo mayor* operated jointly in both households. The same arrangement was instituted in the Queen's household, and so henceforth she also had only one *mayordomo mayor*. The *mayordomos mayores* assumed sole responsibility for housing, feeding and clothing the king and queen and for arranging the accommodation of their servants and courtiers. They attended the king and queen at all public events within the palace and supervised their meals. The King's *mayordomo mayor* had precedence over all household officers everywhere in the palace except in the king's private chambers, where the *camarero mayor* (Lord Chamberlain) held sway. He made the seating arrangements for the royal chapel, and even if he was not a grandee had precedence over the grandees in the chapel. He maintained discipline over the staff of the royal palace and organised the accommodation for visitors to the court.

In the *Casa de Castilla* the monarch's day was organised by the *camarero mayor* while in the *Casa de Borgoña* the *sumiller de corps* (Groom of the Stole) carried out the same function. These offices were both retained in 1562 and therefore continued to operate in parallel to each other. While the King's *mayordomo mayor* did his work in public, his *camarero mayor* performed his duties in private in the presence of the king. Accordingly, his office carried more overt political significance. The *camarero mayor* slept in the king's chamber or immediately adjacent to it and was responsible for waking and dressing the king in the morning and for supervising his undressing at night. He handed the towel to the king when he washed. The *sumiller de corps* had comparable responsibilities within the chambers but – and it was a crucially important distinction – the *camarero mayor* had seniority over him since the offices of the *Casa de Castilla* office had precedence over those of the *Casa de Borgoña* whenever there was overlap between them.

The *caballerizo mayor* or Master of the Horse operated jointly for both *casas*. In strict theory, his responsibilities seemed routine enough, for he controlled the royal stables and helped the king to dress to ride and to mount his horse. In practice, however, he was responsible for the safety and comfort of the king's person when he was on horseback or outside the palace. In practice, therefore, he had the enormous privilege of controlling the King's appearances in front of his subjects, and was therefore himself always highly visible on public occasions outside the palace, for he was in the closest proximity to the King in every appearance that he made in his capital city, be it courtly, religious or familial. He rode his horse ahead of the King and was entitled to join him in the royal carriage when that was appropriate. Nor were his responsibilities confined to the capital city; whenever the king travelled away from the capital it was the *caballerizo mayor* who organized every detail of the journey, even down to ordering the candles by which the road was lit at night. When the king made formal entry into a town or city for the first time, the *caballerizo mayor* carried the royal sword on his shoulders. In the unlikely event of the king going to war, he would carry the standard. The *caballerizo mayor* therefore had status in court and beyond it. Indeed, he even had one significant role within the confines of the royal palace, for no one was allowed to ride on horseback within the palace without his permission. When he could not perform his duties in person, his deputy, the *primer caballerizo*, served in his place. The role of the *caballerizo mayor* was therefore of fundamental importance in all public ceremonies and events outside the royal palace, and if the prestige that accrued to him was not reward enough he was also entitled to receive one bottle of wine every day of the year. It may reasonably be assumed that the wine was of the finest quality.[35]

The death of Philip II, 13 September 1598

At the end of July 1598 Philip II travelled to the Escorial to die. He spent the last six weeks of his life in bed in his tiny chamber overlooking the high altar, in dreadful agony which he endured with stoic heroism.[36] He continued to insist that his son make the fullest use of his senior ministers. On 5 August he urged young Philip to be guided by the *junta de gobierno* and commended the archbishop-elect of Toledo to him, noting that 'I have placed him in this dignity so that he can serve my son'.[37] On 15 August he appointed Denia as his son's *caballerizo mayor*.[38] At last, the Marquis had reached the heart of influence at court. On the following day, Philip II attempted to further counter Denia's role at court when in a document that was signed with a movingly feeble monogram, he again commended García de Loaisa to his son and charged young Philip to retain his councillors of State 'all the time that they live and have health and strength to continue'. The Marquis of Velada had served as *mayordomo mayor* of the Prince, and Philip II now appointed Moura as his son's *camarero mayor*, Juan de Idiáquez as Margaret's *caballerizo mayor* and Juana de Velasco, Duchess of Gandía, as her *camarera mayor*.[39] Although the new king would have the right to choose his own officers for these positions it was extremely unlikely that he would presume to undo his father's dying wishes. In practice, therefore, Philip III and his wife – and the Marquis of Denia – would be surrounded by a group of experienced and powerful personalities: Philip II had effectively circumscribed his son's freedom to choose the senior figures in his own household when he became king.

Philip II now presented his son with his instructions. In them, he pointedly defined a good minister as one who sought to bolster the king's authority rather than his own and urged Philip not to abandon the responsibilities of government to anyone. He gave his blessing to his two children as they kissed his hands, and, with tears in their eyes, they bade him farewell. García de Loaisa read the Passion of St John to the King and the Prior of the Escorial intoned the Commendation of the Soul to God. Philip's last words, uttered in breathless agony, affirmed that he died as a Catholic in obedience to the Roman Church. It was about 5.00 a.m. on Sunday 13 September 1598.[40]

The succession passed to the new king without need of human intervention: not since 1379 had a coronation of a monarch taken place in Castile.[41] Philip III immediately confessed and received communion. He then withdrew into an antechamber with the Marquis of Denia, and when they returned he announced that the Marquis held his fullest confidence and that he had appointed him to a councillorship of State.[42]

King and *valido*: 'All the affairs of state and war'

Because the king of Spain was the agent of God on earth an unbridgeable distance separated him from even the closest of his kinsmen and the greatest of his subjects.[43] It was therefore a stunning break with the traditions of Spanish monarchy when during the first week of his reign Philip III sent an order to the councils instructing them to obey Denia's commands as if they were his own. Unfortunately, the document has not survived.[44] However, in 1612 Philip issued a decree to the councils which alluded to and restated this order, and in it he underscored the nature of his relationship with his favourite, who was now the Duke of Lerma:

> Since I have known the Duke of Lerma, I have seen him serve the king my father and lord, who is in heaven, and myself with such satisfaction on the part of both of us that I have found myself to be daily more satisfied with the good account that he gives of everything that I entrust to him. Because of this, and because of the help that he gives me with the weight of affairs, I order you to fulfil all that the duke tells and orders you to do ... *and although it has been understood thus since I succeeded to these kingdoms*, I have ordered and encharge it now.[45]

Denia's relationship with Philip developed over the years, but underscoring it was the enduring dependence of the King upon him, and his eagerness to lavish rewards upon the Marquis in gratitude for his guidance in affairs of state. It was doubtless at Denia's insistence that Philip insistently made the connection between service and reward explicit in documents that he issued to Denia. Certainly, the Marquis was always assiduous in ensuring that the favours given him by Philip were formally and legally justified and he fastidiously preserved in his family archives the papers in which the King had conferred his favours and privileges upon him.

When in May 1599 Philip allowed the Marquis the right to levy tolls on goods passing through the town of Denia he observed that he made the grant 'for the Marquis's good service to me and because he deserves it'.[46] Six months later, Philip recorded in the title by which he raised Denia to the dukedom that he was honouring him on account of the services that his forebears had made to the crown and 'those which you have made to me and which you make daily'. He added that because of these services Lerma was 'very worthy of the many great favours that we make you'.[47] In August 1600, Philip agreed to the city of Valladolid's request to appoint Lerma as a *regidor* of Valladolid 'because of the great and important services that the Duke of Lerma ... has rendered to me in continuing the [services] that his forebears always made to the kings my predecessors'.[48]

The fullest statement of Philip III's dependence upon Lerma dates from 1603 and exists only as a copy: it was almost certainly presented to Lerma with his office of *capitán general de la caballería de España*. It justified the awards that Philip and his father had given to Lerma in recognition of his services and those of his forebears to the crown, and Philip observed that he intended to reward those services 'so that it will serve as a great example for others and [encourage] an increase in virtue'. He noted in a measured phrase that an ancestor of Lerma, Ruy Gutiérrez de Sandoval, had been a favourite of the *infante* Don John ('he was very favoured'): in doing so he consciously justified Lerma's role as his own favourite. He proceeded to lend himself – and the authority of the crown – to a reinvention of tradition in which the Sandovals had played decisive roles at most of the key events in the creation of the kingdom of Castile: at the conquest of Toledo (1085); the battle of Las Navas de Tolosa, which in 1212 had opened up Andalusia for reconquest by the Christian north; the capture of the great cities of Córdoba (1236) and Seville (1248). The services of Diego Gómez were itemised in admiring detail. Not only had he won the crown of Aragon for Ferdinand but his loyalty to the *infantes* proved to be 'the cause for the Crown of Aragon and the kingdoms adjacent to it being possessed by our progenitors and ourselves'. His successors had emulated his example in wars in Sicily, the conquest of Granada, the expulsion of the French from Catalonia and of course in the crushing of the revolt of the *comuneros*.

Naturally, even Diego Gómez's services were dwarfed by those of Lerma. Philip declared that it was precisely because his illustrious father had valued Lerma so highly that he had allowed him to be educated with Don Carlos and appointed to a succession of honoured positions in court and government – as a gentleman of his chamber, Viceroy and Captain General of Valencia and as *caballerizo mayor* to himself as prince. Moreover, Philip observed that both he and his father had 'committed and do commit to your providence and faithfulness all the affairs of state and war'.[49] Put this way, the grant of the *valimiento* to

Lerma appeared to be almost an obligation, satisfying the honour of the crown by rewarding the unparalleled services that it had received from him.[50]

Philip was prepared to acknowledge this obligation to reward Lerma even in his dealings with the sovereign pontiff. In 1605, for instance, when he invited Pope Clement VIII to accede to the duke's request that the church of *San Pedro* in Lerma be raised to collegial status, he ensured that the Pope understood the importance that he attached to the matter by adding a postscript *in his own hand*: 'I hold it for certain that Your Holiness will be pleased to grant this grace because of how well the Duke of Lerma serves me and because I greatly desire it '.[51] The Pope agreed to the request.

In legal documents, too, Philip affirmed his deep trust in Lerma. When he approved in 1607 the testamentary agreements that Lerma had made with his heir (and which had already been authorised by the Council of Castile) he expressly acknowledged that he wished to reward

> the services that you continuously render to us, through your work in govern-ment, in the preservation of our state and our royal crown, in such serious matters of war and peace, to my great satisfaction and pleasure and to the detri-ment of your own health. You carry [these duties] out with extraordinary care and dedication. It is right that we satisfy your needs and look to your require-ments, and especially to those which concern the protection, succession and defence of your inheritance and status, so that the memory of [your services] may live on and be perpetuated, and so that those who succeed you may retain the same level of authority and dignity ... so that by your example, they and others may be encouraged to serve and to be worthy of these and other even greater rewards and favours. [52]

At the turn of 1609–10, Philip conferred the dukedom of Uceda upon Lerma's eldest son and recorded that he did so because of 'the many great and pleasing services which the Duke of Lerma, your father, and you, the Duke of Uceda, his son, have performed and continue to perform for our royal person'.[53] In May 1615 Philip agreed to allow Lerma to arm a squadron of galleys to protect the eastern coasts because 'the Duke always demonstrates the zeal that he has for the affairs of my service'.[54] A few months later when he issued his instructions for Lerma to accompany Anne to the frontier on her journey into France after her marriage to Louis XIII he expressly recorded

> the great confidence that I have of your person, and the great zeal which you employ in matters of my service, and the good account that you have always given me and continue to give of the weight of business that at my command you undertake, and in which I find myself greatly satisfied...[55]

Philip even allowed Lerma to share in the quasi-sacramental functions of kingship: when on Maundy Thursday 1609, the King washed the feet of twelve poor men, Lerma poured the water over the feet while the papal nuncio then dried them.[56]

Philip acknowledged his dependence upon the duke in more personal ways, allowing him to perform services for himself and members of his family that carried deeply important symbolism. In 1601 and in 1611, Philip allowed Lerma to be the senior testamentary after himself to his wife's will and testament even though he held no position in Margaret's household,[57] and in 1619 and again in 1621 he named Lerma as one of his own testamentaries even though the Duke had left court in 1618. More extraordinary still, in his very last hours, Philip summoned Lerma to court so that he could comfort him at his death. He thereby ended his reign exactly as he had begun it, with an explicit demonstration of his profound dependence upon his *valido*.[58]

The only letters which have survived between Philip III and Lerma date from 1617, by which time Lerma had made it evident that he was leaving court. Philip signed his letters to Lerma as his 'friend' but we must remember that by 1617 the relationship between king and *valido* was in its climactic phase; in signing himself in this way Philip was carefully assuring Lerma of his continued affection even though both of them recognised that the duke was about to leave court.[59] Their personal relationship reached its climax in friendship as their courtly relationship came to its end.

Philip also allowed himself on occasions to relax very ostentatiously with Lerma. In 1599 in the city of Valencia he rode with Lerma and the Count of Benavente, the Viceroy of the Kingdom, in masks in a nocturnal adventure. On the joyous entry which his wife made to Madrid later in the year Philip once again exchanged intimate pleasantries with Denia while both wore masks. That Philip could allow himself to be seen (and recognised) in masks was a radical break from the reserved kingship of his forebears.[60] Philip further breached the traditions of monarchy when in 1599 in the ceremonies in Valencia cathedral that ratified his marriage, he astonished the court by embracing his *valido*.[61] In January 1608 Philip went even further with the most remarkable single affirmation that he ever made in public of the uniqueness of his relationship with Lerma; at the swearing of fealty to his son as heir to the throne of Castile he greeted Lerma in a way which formally distinguished him from the other grandees:

> he behaved differently with the Duke of Lerma than he did with the others. When the Duke presented himself, the King stood up [from his throne], took a step and, very lovingly, embraced him and gave him his hand to kiss. The same [was done] by the Queen.[62]

Philip's greeting was extraordinarily suggestive, for in the absence of a coronation the swearing of the oath to the heir was the most solemn and important of all royal ceremonies in Castile: no one present could have misunderstood the significance of the distinction that the King had made between Lerma and the other grandees.[63] In 1615, when Lerma agreed to accompany Anne to the French border after her marriage, Philip again embraced Lerma and avowed that (as Lerma recorded) 'I am very confident that you will relieve me of this burden with the authority and display that I desire'.[64] When Lerma used his declining health to escape the responsibility for accompanying Anne to the border, Philip accepted his excuse: 'and because the Duke was unable to under- take this journey without notable risk of his life on account of some fevers that he was suffering from, and because it was necessary that the journey should not be delayed and the health of the Duke should be preserved as is so necessary for the affairs of my service'.[65]

Philip allowed important events to take place on days that had special significance for Lerma and he even gave names to two of his children which acknowledged the intimacy of his relationship with the Duke: in 1605, as we have seen, Philip named his heir in part for the church of the Duke in which he had been baptised (Philip Victor Dominic), and in 1610 when a daughter was born to him in the palace in Lerma he named her Margarita Francisca, for her mother and for the duke in whose city the child had been born. When Anne left Burgos cathedral in 1615 after her marriage by proxy to Louis XIII, she passed under the banners not just of Spain and France but of the house of Sandoval; it was an extraordinarily ambitious statement by Lerma about the unique impor- tance of his family.[66]

Lerma was always discreet in his written references to his relationship with the King, portraying himself as Philip's diligent servant and minister. The first expression of his ambitions for the king came when in November 1598 he wrote to Juan de Borja that 'I am always working ... because the number of people who come to me cannot be believed, and I spend most of the day listening to them'.[67] He was fastidious in ensuring that he maintained a high public profile as the servant of the King rather than as his master. In July 1599 he wrote that 'His Majesty has to be the most loved and respected king that has ever been seen, for these are the two points in which good govern- ment consists'.[68] Philip was duly impressed, as Lerma intended that he should be. His *valido* was his dutiful and trusted servant, never his master. In his few surviving letters to Philip, Lerma signed himself as 'the most humble slave of your Majesty'.[69] But in reality Lerma was (at least until 1613; perhaps even until 1615) the master in the relationship between the two men.

The Marquis of Denia, 13 September 1598

It has been observed that the personal development of the Marquis of Denia was marked by the effects upon him of the poverty and deep religiosity that characterised his family. A third characteristic may also be adduced – the effect that living at court from his early childhood had upon him. Santiago Martínez Hernández has demonstrated that as a young man Denia joined a noble Academy in Madrid in which, in the company of his peers – men who would be his allies and rivals for future influence at court – he learned how a man should conduct himself at court.[70] Certainly, he instinctively observed the first law of courtly politics, 'to remain in his place, to sew up his mouth'.[71] Unlike other great favourites – Olivares and Richelieu chief among them – Denia was not a theorist. Indeed, he was disdainful of men who spoke too much (or too freely). Above all, he was a practical man who came to understand all the resonances of royal majesty and of serving at court. Most especially, he knew how to reach accommodations with his peers and to avoid making enemies of those with whom he had to work.

Like so many other Spaniards in the later sixteenth century, Denia found that the enormous personality of Philip II dominated his political and courtly perspectives. It seems certain that the Marquis learned from the King how to manage a court, and it is probable that it was on his journeys with the royal household in 1580 and 1585 that he began to acquire a deep understanding of how a court operated on the road, and how indeed it could be influenced and controlled while it was itinerant. Moreover, since Denia lived at court while the monastery-palace of the Escorial was being built and then put into full use, he must have developed an appreciation of how buildings could express and amplify the exercise of power while also serving the needs of the multigenerational family. He certainly noted the significance of Philip II's incomparable collection of pictures and understood the uses – personal, familial and political – to which such collections could be put.

While, however, Denia was impressed – overwhelmed, perhaps – by Philip II's personality and achievements, in common with most of his contemporaries he recognised that a new order was coming into being with the end of the king's reign. There can be little doubt that he recognised that Philip II's policies had failed, both in war and in peace. In all probability, too, he appreciated that the methods of government employed by the king in the last decade of his reign were not adequate to the challenges facing the state, that a small clique of ministers simply could not cope with the enormous problems created by the new warfare of the 1590s. Certainly, too, as a leading nobleman he had reason to hope that the aristocracy could once again play a major role in government after Philip II died.

Little evidence has survived of Denia's taste in these last years of Philip II's reign. He seems to have been a typical aristocrat, distinguished only by his extreme poverty. He was present at most of the major courtly celebrations in the capital in the 1590s and it may be presumed that he had developed those tastes for display and for the enjoyment of the pleasures of food and drink that distinguished him when he became wealthy enough to indulge them. Certainly, the letters that he wrote to Philip II and his ministers reveal that the melancholy that marked his character was already in evidence; he was easily dispirited and disposed to self-pity. As to his private pastimes: he gambled at cards, but he does not seem to have done so to excess and had no significant debts arising from this. Probably, too, he had already developed that need to retreat periodically from the stress of life at court into his private houses and to seek solitude in his gardens, to revive himself in solitude and in the pleasures that he took in the natural world. His sins were few. He liked and admired women and understood the political roles that they could usefully occupy but he did not dally sexually with them. He was utterly faithful to a wife whom he came to adore and was selflessly devoted to his children.

Denia had surrounded himself with a cabinet of advisers who counselled him and provided him with moral support. At the head of the group were three senior male relatives – Bernardo de Rojas y Sandoval, his great-uncle and bishop of Jaén; Juan de Borja, his cousin; and the Count of Miranda, his first cousin – and his sister Catalina, Countess of Lemos. Bernardo de Rojas and Miranda were a few years older than Denia, born in 1546 and 1541 respectively, while Borja was twenty years older (1533). The three men were broadly experienced in Church and State and by 1598 Denia had developed a deep respect for their knowledge and judgement. Bernardo's career had received its first impetus from the patronage of Archbishop Cristóbal de Rojas, who had appointed him as a canon of Seville cathedral (1574). He had then enjoyed a reasonably successful ecclesiastical career, serving in bishoprics of middling importance – Ciudad Rodrigo (1585), Pamplona (1588) and Jaén (1596). Bernardo's relations with Denia were deeply affectionate, based upon mutual admiration and respect. However, perhaps because they trusted each other so deeply, the two men were prone to have angry disagreements but they were always quickly reconciled, recognising the paramountcy of family. It was indeed in tribute to his great-nephew that Bernardo reversed the order of his own name (to Bernardo de Sandoval y Rojas) to emphasise that he was a relative of Denia's.

Juan de Borja and the Count of Miranda were widely knowledgeable about foreign affairs. Borja was the second son of Francisco de Borja, and had served Philip II as an extraordinary ambassador to Portugal (1569) and then as ambassador to the Emperor (1576). In 1581 he had become *mayordomo mayor* to Philip II's sister, the Empress María. Miranda had served as a soldier under

Don John in Italy and had then been appointed to the viceroyalties of Catalonia (1585–86) and Naples (1586–95).

Denia attached great importance to the advice of two female relatives, his wife and his sister, both of whom were named Catalina. The two women could not have been more different. Denia's wife was the model of aristocratic discretion, having no distinct public persona other than as his wife, while his sister, Countess of Lemos, was proverbially indiscreet, arrogant and overbearing, given to melodrama. As it happened, the Countess was absent from court in the years 1599–1603 and returned as the Duchess died; she immediately assumed a dramatic and central role in court politics that proved to have profound implications for her brother and indeed even for the royal family.[72]

During the 1580s and 1590s, Denia also attached to himself a number of men whom he came to know in the city of Valladolid. Two of these men served him well enough to place their sons into important positions in his service. Francisco Calderón had served under the Duke of Parma in the Low Countries and on his return to Valladolid became a town councillor. A brusque and efficient man, Francisco looked after Denia's interests in the city of Valladolid, and the Marquis took his son Rodrigo on as a page in the later 1580s. At the same time, as we have seen, Sebastián Pascual, a merchant banker of Medina del Campo, salvaged Denia's financial position, and it was probably in gratitude for his services that Denia took his son Juan into his service as a financial adviser.

A number of men whom Denia came to know in Valladolid in the 1580s and 1590s may be characterised as close personal friends: Diego Sarmiento de Acuña, Diego de Covarrubias, Juan Bautista de Tassis, Agustín Álvarez de Toledo and Pedro Messía de Tovar. To them should be added Alonso Muriel de Valdivielso, who had acted as Denia's private secretary, and became very close to him. Denia also developed close ties with many of the members of the *Chancellería* of Valladolid, and several of the men who served as *oidores* in the 1590s were advanced to governmental office when he became *valido*. A number of professional administrators formed close personal relationships with the Marquis, chief among them Pedro Franqueza, who had served in the Council of Aragon since the 1560s.

Four household servants of Denia's became sufficiently trusted by him to be raised to the status of confidants and advisers: Dr Juan Bautista de Acevedo and his brother Fernando had served as tutors to the Marquis's children; Tomás de Ángulo, as his treasurer, and Juan de Ciriza, as his secretary. All formed attachments to Denia that lasted for decades. Juan de Ciriza also brought his younger brother Tristán into the Marquis's service.

These different groups of men were bound to Denia by ties of blood or interest and it is remarkable how many of them retained a deep personal affection for him. Very few men (or women) broke with him on personal or political grounds and even those who were dismissed from office (or whom he did not protect as they would have wished) generally did not turn against him. Certainly, they learned from him and some of them survived him to serve a regime that was hostile to everything that he stood for.

When Philip II died, the Marquis of Denia did not stand out in any way from his colleagues, save that he had conquered the will of the heir to the throne. He was a typical courtier, defined by his rank and station. Nothing about him attracted attention. He had never espoused any particular policies and he had certainly never fallen out with anyone at court. He was to all intents and purposes just another grandee-courtier, notable only for his poverty. Nothing in his past suggested that he was a leader, much less an innovator. Certainly, no one could have suspected when Philip II died not only that the Marquis of Denia would change the ways in which the court worked but also that he would transform the very nature of monarchy itself. But so complete was his under-standing of the court that he was now able to reshape it to his own purposes while convincing the King and his fellow-aristocrats that he was doing so in their interests.

NOTES

1 On the financial legacy of Philip II, I. A. A. Thompson's classic study, *War and Government in Habsburg Spain, 1560–1620*, London, 1976: see 'Table A. The Finances of Castile', p. 288. See also, Williams, *Philip II*, Basingstoke, 2001, pp. 228–55.

2 R. J. W. Evans, *Rudolf II and his World. A Study in Intellectual History 1576–1612*, Oxford, 1973, pp. 43–83.

3 I. A. A. Thompson, 'L'audit de la guerre et de la paix. Avant et après Vervins', in Jean-François Labourdette et al. (eds.), *Le Traité de Vervins*, Paris, 2000, pp. 391–413.

4 'Condiciones de la renunciación que hizó el rey don Felipe Segundo, de los Estados de Flándes en la infanta doña Isabel su hija', Madrid, 6 May 1598, CODOIN, xlii, pp. 218–22. On 'the Archdukes', W. Thomas and Luc Duerloo (eds.), *Albert and Isabella 1598–1621*, Brussels, 1998.

5 *CSPV*, ix, 19 Jul. 1598, no. 711, p. 332.

6 See García García, *La Pax Hispánica*, pp. 27–30. An English translation of García's brilliant book is urgently needed, for it is central to our understanding of Philip III's foreign policy.

7 A. W. Lovett, *Philip II and Mateo Vázquez de Leca. The Government of Spain 1572–1592*, Geneva, 1977, pp. 201–10; on the government of Philip II, J. Martínez Millán (ed.), *La corte de Felipe II*, Madrid, 1994. On the decline of Philip II, G. Parker, *The Grand Strategy of Philip II*, New Haven, 1998, pp. 269–80.

8 S. Fernández Conti, *Los consejos de estado y guerra de la monarquía hispana en tiempos de Felipe II 1548–1598*, Valladolid, *JCL*, 1998, pp. 185–233 and J. F. Baltar Rodríguez, *Las juntas de gobierno en la monarquía hispánica (siglos XVI–XVII)*, Madrid, 1998, pp. 43–55.

9 On their appointments and their friendship ('eran intimos amigos'), G. González Dávila, *Historia de la vida ... de ... don Felipe III*, published in P. Salazar de Mendoza, *Monarquía de España*, Madrid, 1770–71, pp. 14–18. On Moura and Idiáquez, Thomas Contarini, 'Relación de la estancia en España' (1593), in García Mercadal, *Viajes de extranjeros*, i, pp. 1457–8; On Moura, A. Danvila y Burguero, *Diplomáticos españoles. Don Cristóbal de Moura*, Madrid, 1900; on Idiáquez, J. A. Álvarez y Baena, *Hijos de Madrid. Diccionario Histórico*, 4 vols., Madrid, 1789: reprint, Madrid, 1973, iii, pp. 133–5 and F. Pérez Mínguez, *D. Juan de Idiáquez, embajador y consejero de Felipe II*, San Sebastian, 1934–35; on Chinchón, S. Fernández Conti, 'La nobleza cortesana. Don Diego de Cabrera y Bobadilla, Tercer Conde de Chinchón', in Martínez

Millán (ed.), *La Corte de Felipe II*, pp. 229–70. On Velada, this volume, pp. 33–4, 37, 57, 123–4, 153, 167, 203, 217.

10 M. J. Rodríguez-Salgado, 'Honour and Profit in the Court of Philip II of Spain', p. 221.

11 In recent years, substantial advances have been made on the study of councils. On Castile, Ignacio Ezquerra Revilla, *El consejo real de Castilla bajo Felipe II. Grupos de poder y luchas faccionales*, Madrid, 2000, especially, pp. 227–63; on Finance, C. J. de Carlos Morales, *El Consejo de Hacienda de Castilla, 1523–1602, JCL*, 1996, pp. 159–73; on State and War, Fernández Conti, *Los consejos de estado y guerra*, pp. 185–233.

12 These figures derive from the *Nóminas de los consejos*, AGS CG 886–9; the documentation deals with the councils of State, War, Castile, Finance, Indies, Orders and all royal secretaries.

13 I. A. A. Thompson, 'The Armada and Administrative Reform. The Spanish Council of War in the Reign of Philip II', *EHR*, 82, 1967, pp. 712–14.

14 *Nómina de los consejos*, 1579, 1598, AGS CG 887.

15 *CSPV* viii, 18 Aug. 1587, no. 567, pp. 305–6.

16 The role of women at court has been the subject of a vibrant study by M. S. Sánchez, *The Empress, the Queen, and the Nun. Women and Power at the Court of Philip III of Spain*, Baltimore, 1998, pp. 85–9, 120–2, 157–63.

17 Two other brothers had previously been sworn in as heir to the throne of Castile, but Carlos Lorenzo had died in 1575 and Fernando in 1578.

18 Anon., *'Nacimiento y successos (por mayor) Del Rey don Phelipe tercero y de su muerte que fue a 31 de março de 1621'*, BL Add 10,236, fols. 138–43.

19 The following is based upon Martínez Hernández, *El Marqués de Velada*, pp. 245–357. There are important analyses of Philip III's education in Feros, *Kingship and Favoritism*, pp. 15–31 and García García, *La Pax Hispánica*, pp. 3–15.

20 M. J. del Río Barredo, *Madrid. Urbs Regia. La capital ceremonial de la Monarquía Católica*, Madrid, 2000, pp. 80–1.

21 'Auiendo su Mag[esta]d resuelto por Justas consideraciones q[ue] de aquí adelante el Principe n[uest]ro s[eño]r firme todos los despachos que el solía firmar ...', Hieronymo Gassol to Juan de Ibarra, San Lorenzo, 6 May 1597, AGI IG 868, no fol.

22 Williams, 'Philip III and the Restoration of Spanish Government', p. 755.

23 Francesco Vendramin, 'Relación del viaje' (1595), in García Mercadal (ed.), *Viajes de extranjeros*, i, p. 1488.

24 Cabrera de Córdoba, *Felipe Segundo*, iv, p. 200–1; Report printed by González Dávila, *Teatro de las Grandezas de ... Madrid*, pp. 43–6. See García García, *La Pax Hispánica*, pp. 8–10.

25 Matías de Novoa, *Historia de Felipe III, Rey de España*, CODOIN, Madrid, 1874, lx–lxi, lx, p. 31.

26 Lerma, 'Imbentario', ADL 53, fol. 25; S. García Martínez, *Bandolerismo, piratería y control de Moriscos en Valencia durante el reinado de Felipe II*, Valencia, 1977, pp. 89, 95.

27 On this, see the forthcoming study on the *moriscos* by Phillip Williams.

28 Lerma, 'Imbentario', ADL 53, fols. 24–7.

29 Cervera Vera, *El conjunto palacial*, i, p. 183.

30 Lerma, 'Imbentario', ADL 53, fols. 25v–26.

31 Salazar y Castro, *Comendadores de ... Santiago*, p. 630.

32 J. de Quintana, *A la muy antigua, noble y coronada villa de Madrid. Historia de su antigüedad, nobleza y grandeza*, Madrid, 1629, p. 363, and del Río Barredo, *Madrid, Urbs Regia*, p. 81.

33 'Imbentario', ADL 53, fols. 23v–24; González Dávila, *Felipe III*, p. 25; appointment of Córdoba, Moura to Gerónimo Gassol, Madrid, 6 Jul. 1597, BL Mss Add 28,379, fol. 20.

34 The following paragraphs are informed by my discussions with Drs Richard Trewinnard and Santiago Martínez Hernández. I am much obliged to Dr Trewinnard for permission to use his unpublished PhD thesis, 'The Household of the Spanish Monarch. Structure, Cost and Personnel 1606–65', University of Wales, Cardiff, 1991. A contemporary description of court offices, González Dávila, *Teatro de las Grandezas de ... Madrid*, pp. 313–35.

35 Anon., 'Las preheminencias que tiene el Cauallerizo maior del Rey', no date (late Philip II), RAH K-58, fols. 164–7. González Dávila, *Teatro de las Grandezas de ... Madrid*, pp. 316–17; see also del Río Barredo, *Madrid, Urbs Regia*, p. 125 and 132. Religious affairs within the palace came under the purview of the *capellán mayor* in the *Casa de Castilla* and the *limosnero mayor* in the *Casa de Borgoña*; both offices were retained in the reorganisation of 1562.

36 Javier Varela, *La muerte del Rey. El ceremonial funerario de la monarquía española (1500–1885)*, Madrid, 1990, pp. 39–44 and C. M. N. Eire, *From Madrid to Purgatory.The Art and Craft of Dying in Sixteenth-century Spain*, Cambridge, UK, 1995, pp. 255–368.

37 'Advertimientos' of Philip II, San Lorenzo, 5 Aug. 1598, AGS PR 29, fol. 37, a copy.

38 Denia's appointment, 'Imbentario', ADL 53, fol. 24, which records that the offices of *sumiller de corps* and *caballerizo mayor* brought a joint income of 10,000 ducats. See also, Feros, *Kingship and Favoritism*, p. 47; also Jonathan Brown and J. H. Elliott, *A Palace for a King:The Buen Retiro and the Court of Philip IV*, New Haven, 1980, p. 16; and G. Redworth and F. Checa, 'The Courts of the Spanish Habsburgs', in J. Adamson (ed.), *The Princely Courts of Europe 1500–1750*, London, 1999, pp. 47–51.

39 Codicil to Testament of Philip II, San Lorenzo, 16 Aug. 1598, AGS PR 29, fol. 38.

40 González Dávila, *Teatro de las Grandezas de ... Madrid*, pp. 46–8; Anon, 'A Briefe and Trve Declaration of the Sicknesse, Last Wordes and Death of the KING OF SPAINE, Philip,The Second That Name' (Madrid, 1599), *Harleian Miscellany*, ii, (London, 1809), pp. 284–7.

41 Redworth and Checa, 'The Courts of the Spanish Habsburgs', p. 56.

42 Denia to Juan de Borja (?) (San Lorenzo), 13 Sep. and 27 Nov. 1598, BL Add 28,422, fols. 4 and 17; González Dávila, *Felipe III*, pp. 29–32; *CSPV*, ix, 14 Sep. 1598, no. 738, p. 344, and Carlos Seco Serrano, 'Los comienzos de la privanza de Lerma según los embajadores florentinos', *BRAH*, 144, 1959, pp. 75–101, at p. 81.

43 On this, see Feros, *Kingship and Favoritism*, especially the suggestive chapter on 'The power of the king', pp. 71–90. See also Ruth Mackay, *The Limits of Royal Authority. Resistance and Obedience in Seventeenth-century Castile*, Cambridge, 1999.

44 On the beginning of the reign, below, pp. 54–6.

45 Printed by F. Tomas Valiente, *Los validos en la monarquía española del siglo XVII*, Madrid, 1963. p. 161; copies, AGS CJH 371 (511), fol. 75 (from which the date is taken) and AGS E 2023, no fol.; my italics.

46 *Cntas.Vicecanciller* Covarrubias, 15 Feb. and 5 May 1599, ACA CA 652, fols. 54/1and 54/5.

47 'TITVLO DE DVQUE DE Lerma, y mayoragzo fundado del, y de otros bienes, por el señor Rey D[on] Felipe Tercero, en 11 de Noviembre del año de 1599', ADL 12, no fol., a printed copy, quotation at fols. 4–4v.

48 Copy of *cédula*, Valladolid, 13 Aug. 1600, AMV LA 23, fol. 130v; see below, p. 69.

49 Anon., 'Relación de los servicios prestados por los Duques de Lerma à los Reyes de España', BN Mss 11260, no. 6, copy. Phrases within the document are recognisably similar to (and sometimes identical with) phrases used in documents in the documentation in the Archivo de los Duques de Lerma, notably the title to the dukedom of Lerma in 1599.

50 Certainly, this was how it came to be viewed by the Sandoval family; see 'Petición que se dió en el consexo, por el Duq[ue] mi s[eño]r, Adelantado Mayor, sobre el pleyto de las m[e]r[ce]d[e]s de su abuelo', no date (1626?), ADL 25, no. 32, fol. 6b (second foliation, which begins after fol. 22b of original document).

51 L. Cervera Vera, *La iglesia colegial de San Pedro*, p. 127, n. 29.

52 *Cédula*, Madrid, 17 Sep. 1607, printed in 'Testamento', ADL 12, at pp. 9b–11.

53 *Cédula*, Madrid, 16 Feb. 1610, ADL 12, no. 16, fols. 4–13, at fol. 5b.

54 *Cnta* St. 14 May 1615, AGS E 1945, no fol.

55 *Cédula* to Lerma, Lerma 23 Sep. 1615, printed by Novoa, *Historia de Felipe III*, lx, pp. 537–41, quotation at pp. 537–8.

56 Anon., 'Viaje del rey Felipe III a Lerma en abril de 1610', RAH G-31, fol. 1.

57 See below, pp. 82, 169, 246–7.

58 Below, pp. 246–7.

59 See below, pp. 226–7; see Williams, 'Lerma, 1618. Retirement or Dismissal?', pp. 319–20, and for a different perspective, Feros, *Kingship and Favoritism*, pp. 115–25.
60 *Relaciones*, p. 8. Philip II had relaxed informally with courtiers; see Henry Kamen, *Philip of Spain*, New Haven, 1997, pp. 55, 76 and 97. However, royal practice had become much more formal since the beginning of Philip II's reign.
61 *Relaciones*, p. 11.
62 Anon., '*Relación verdadera, en que se contiene todas las ceremonias y demás actos que passaron en la jura que se hizo al Serenissimo Principe nuestro señor don Phelipe quarto*', printed in Simon Díaz, *Relaciones breves de ... Madrid*, at p. 55.
63 María José del Río Barredo observed that 'los rituales de acesión al trono suelen ser considerados los más importantes del ceremonial regio por lo que se piensa declaran sobre el origen del poder, las relaciones entre gobernantes y gobernados, y en último término, la constitución política de un Estado', *Madrid, Urbs Regia*, p. 23. See also, María Cristina Sánchez Alonso, 'Juramentos de príncipes herederos en Madrid (1561–98) in Fernando Checa (ed.), *El real alcázar de Madrid. Dos siglos de arquitectura y coleccionismo en la corte de los reyes de España*, Madrid, 1994, pp. 29–41.
64 'Petición que se dio en el consexo', ADL 25, no. 32, fols. 7–7b. No other source exists for this.
65 'Instrucción del Rey al Duque de Uzeda para que por enfermedad de su padre execute el viage y las entregas', Miranda de Ebro, 28 Oct. 1615, RAH G-29, fols. 39b–40.
66 See below, pp. 199–200.
67 Denia to Juan de Borja, El Pardo, 27 Nov. 1598, BL Add Mss, 28,422, fol. 17.
68 Same to same, Barcelona, 5 July 1599, ibid., fol. 74.
69 For a different view, Feros, *Kingship and Favoritism*, pp. 233–46.
70 Martínez Hernández, *El Marqués de Velada*, pp. 65–124.
71 This was the advice given by Juan de Ovando to Mateo Vázquez de Leca, cited by A. W. Lovett, 'A Cardinal's Papers. The Rise of Mateo Vázquez de Leca', *EHR*, 88, 1973, pp. 241–61, at p. 244.
72 See below pp. 90–1.

3

The establishment of the *valimiento*, 1598–1601

The seizure of power, September 1598–January 1599

From the moment that Philip II was laid to rest the Marquis of Denia controlled politics at court with an accomplished ease that belied his inexperience in government. Within a week he secured councillorships of State for his two most senior and trusted lay advisers – the Count of Miranda on 13 September and Juan de Borja a few days later – and had Philip issue the momentous order to the councils to follow Denia's orders as if they were his own.[1] On 15 September, his brother Juan was appointed as *primer caballerizo* to help him to organise the *caballería* and within days Juan Bautista de Tassis was named as a gentleman of the King's Chamber. When the royal households settled into their new accommodation in Madrid on 15–16 September 1598 Denia was allocated rooms in the Alcázar while his wife was given the Queen's room in San Jerónimo.[2] On 29 September, Alonso Muriel de Valdivielso was appointed as a royal secretary.[3]

The Marquis also strengthened his financial position. When news arrived at court that two corsair ships had been captured in the Mediterranean, Philip promised Denia 40,000 ducats from the value of their cargoes (29 October). A fortnight later (12 November) Philip conferred upon Denia the first and the most lucrative of the municipal offices that he was to hold during his *valimiento*, the *escribanía de sacas y cosas vedadas, diezmos y aduanas* of the city of Seville and its dependent places. This extraordinary office levied import taxes along the whole of the coast of Spain from the Portuguese border to Cartagena and was worth 9,000 ducats annually in rent (capital value: 173,000 ducats).[4] In two months, Denia had more than doubled his annual income, to over 35,000 ducats.

However, while Philip gave the strongest endorsement to Denia and his *hechuras* he also demonstrated within the very first days of his reign that he was determined to receive the widest range of information and advice from his councils. On 20 September he convened a meeting of the Council of State and ordered that he was henceforth to be 'consulted' after every meeting of the Council.[5] The *junta de gobierno* gave way to the Council of State, which in a flurry of activity was now convened at least on every second or third day. By the end of October virtually every man of distinction had either attended the council itself or exercised the right that councillors of State enjoyed to attend the Council of War – Moura and Idiáquez; the dukes of Nájera and Medina Sidonia; the counts of Fuensalida, Miranda, Fuentes, Chinchón; Denia himself; the *Adelantado Mayor* of Castile; Rodrigo Vázquez de Arce, President of the Council of Castile; Juan de Borja and Pedro de Velasco.[6]

The senior aristocracy were excited by the prospect of playing a role in government after enduring decades of hostility from Philip II. The *Adelantado* grandiosely declared that the world 'would see what the Spanish were worth now that they have a free hand and are no longer subject to a single brain that thought it knew all that could be known and treated everyone else as a blockhead'.[7] The *Adelantado* was now a relative of Denia's by marriage and his outburst may have been more carefully calculated than at first appeared, a device to encourage the belligerent patriotism that was bursting forth at the beginning of the new reign.

It was indeed the King himself who set the tone. When Philip attended the Council of State for the first time, he instructed his councillors that they were to pursue military victories with all vigour.[8] On 22 September he approved the plan of the Archduke Albert of Austria to invade the territory of the United Provinces and a month later ordered that all Dutch ships in Iberian ports were to be seized.[9] Among those who noted with admiration the King's determination to reassert the power of Spain was Luis Valle de la Cerda, a professional administrator, who wrote that in the first forty days of his reign Philip had shown a dedication to the pursuit of military victories that inspired love in his supporters and fear in his opponents.[10]

To provide him with his great victory, Philip turned to his Council of War. In 1597–98 only four men had attended the council – Moura and Idiáquez as councillors of State and Juan de Acuña Vela and Pedro de Padilla as councillors of War proper. Within weeks, Philip transformed the Council by appointing to it four distinguished soldiers – Bernardino de Velasco, Luis Enríquez, Francisco de Valencia and don Francisco de Bobadilla, Count of Puñonrostro. Philip also dissuaded Acuña Vela from retiring. These five men formed the nucleus of the Council of War for many years and the council was now convened about twice as regularly as it had been during Philip II's last years, and its average attendance also virtually doubled.[11] Early in 1599 Robert Cecil, Queen Elizabeth's Secretary of State, received a report that 'the Council of War of 12 persons sits five times a week, and since 13 September [1598], when the old King died, all the old martial men are sent for, and soldiers are training'.[12] In all but name, it was a new council that was advising Philip III on his quest for a great victory and from these first weeks of the reign it began to set a newly belligerent tone at the heart of government.

Denia demonstrated his new eminence by bringing about great marriages for two of his daughters in the first eight weeks of the reign. On 6 November, he agreed that Catalina should marry her cousin Pedro Fernández de Castro, son of Fernando Ruiz de Castro, VI count of Lemos and Denia's sister Catalina. The Lemos title dated back to 1457 but the family was not especially wealthy, ranking only twentieth in the list of aristocratic incomes in 1595 (see Appendix I). When the marriage agreement was signed on 10 January 1599 the Marquis was confident enough of his financial resources to undertake to provide a dowry of 70,000 ducats.[13] Even more indicative of his new power was the demonstration that he gave to the court of his mastery of the royal grace: on 18 January 1600 the bridegroom's father was appointed to the richest office in the gift of the crown, the viceroyalty of Naples.[14]

On 18 November 1598, the Marquis concluded an even greater marriage when Juana married Manuel Pérez de Guzmán, heir to the Duke of Medina Sidonia. That the richest aristocrat in Spain should have married his heir to Denia's daughter was striking recognition of the Marquis's new status at court but even more significant of that status was that the King broke his mourning for his father to honour the bride and groom by eating with them and then by accompanying them on their triumphal ride through Madrid back to Medina Sidonia's palace.[15] Moreover, like the Count of Lemos, Medina Sidonia received a spectacular favour from the King: the debts of about 100,000 ducats that he owed the crown were written off as a present to his new daughter-in-law.[16] No secret was made of this: Denia was again demonstrating to all at court that his influence with the King enabled him to dispense the privileges and resources of the monarchy to those whom he favoured, or whose support he sought.

Philip made his formal entrance into Madrid on Sunday 8 November. However, because he was in mourning, he entered his capital city with restrained grandeur. By contrast, Denia was uninhibited in his enjoyment of the occasion; as the royal procession made its way to the church of *San Jerónimo el Real* it halted outside the Marquis's town house (which was known as the '*huerta*' or garden) and the gentlemen who were to accompany the King formed two columns: Denia rode at the head of one column as *caballerizo mayor* while his brother Juan, as *primer caballerizo*, led the other column. After the kissing of hands, Denia led the procession to the church of Santa María where García de Loaisa and other senior churchmen formally welcomed Philip to his capital; García had to confront the pre-eminence of Denia's power.[17]

Denia now moved decisively to emphasise the new realities at court. He personally informed Moura that he was dismissed as *camarero mayor* of the King and was to leave court immediately to serve as Viceroy and Captain General of Portugal, an appointment which would take him away from Madrid for three years. The Marquis must have relished the task, revenging himself upon the man who had been instrumental in exiling him to Valencia only five years earlier. Don Cristóbal's humiliation was disguised by his elevation to the grandeeship – a singular honour for a foreigner – and by the right that he was given to choose a Portuguese title. He took the marquisate of Castel Rodrigo. Juan de Borja replaced him as the senior member of the Council of Portugal and was given the countship of Ficallo in Portugal for his lifetime.[18] Denia confirmed his triumph by taking the oath as Philip's *sumiller de corps* on 18 December. He now controlled the private household of the King, and the *sumillería* and the *caballeríza mayor* together brought him 10,000 ducats of annual salary. He did not bother to take Moura's post of *camarero mayor*, which was left vacant.[19] The only senior post in the King's household that he did not now control was that of *mayordomo mayor*, which was left in the hands of Velada.

Denia now turned on three other senior servants of Philip II: the Duke of Medina Sidonia, García de Loaisa and Pedro Portocarrero, the Inquisitor-General. He had his wife Catalina create a melodramatic scene with the Duchess of Medina Sidonia that provoked her husband into taking her back to San Lúcar 'to forget the court': Medina Sidonia, the richest nobleman in the land, would not cast a shadow over Denia's lustre at court.[20] García de Loaisa had his lodgings taken from him in an unsubtle hint that he was to be exiled from court. He died on 22 February, leaving the archbishopric of Toledo – the primatial see – vacant. His death gave rise to much moralising: some ascribed it to a broken heart while others noted the significance of his enmity to Denia.[21] Pedro Portocarrero, the Inquisitor-General, brought about his own disgrace in November 1598 by appointing a man of notoriously doubtful purity of blood to a councillorship of Inquisition. In gravely embarrassing the King at the beginning of his reign, Portocarrero obligingly ended his own career; it remained only to work out the details of how his dismissal would be managed.[22]

Increasingly confident, in December Denia advanced four of his *hechuras* to key governmental positions: Pedro Messía de Tovar and Juan Pascual were appointed as Treasurers-General, Iñigo Ibáñez de Santa Cruz as a royal secretary and Lic. Pedro de Tapia as *fiscal* or crown lawyer of the Council of Castile.[23] The significance of these appointments would shortly become apparent.

By the end of 1598 the extent of Denia's new power was alarming observers at court. On 4 January 1599, Philip II's biographer, Luis Cabrera de Córdoba, began keeping a log with a view to writing a history of the new reign and he observed that 'the position as favourite that the Marquis of Denia has had with his Majesty since he inherited is increasing by the day without anyone knowing of a comparable favourite because the favours that are given him are so extraordinary'.[24]

The royal marriage journey, January–October 1599

The arrangements for the marriage of the new king were already well advanced when Philip II died. As it happened, the Archduke Albert left Brussels on the day of Philip II's death and Margaret departed from Graz on 30 September. Albert represented Philip III when on 15 November, in Ferrara, Pope Clement VIII celebrated the new king's marriage to Margaret. Three days later she began the journey to Genoa, from whence she would embark for Barcelona.[25]

The Cortes of Castile voted the grants to celebrate the royal marriage on 21 January 1599 and thereby freed Philip to travel to Barcelona to meet and marry his bride. Philip took note of the request from the procurators that he return quickly to Castile and left Madrid on the same day.[26] He was away for nine months. Denia gave a subtle but powerful demonstration of his new power at court when it was announced that the ratification of the royal marriages would take place not in Barcelona but in Valencia. In taking the King to his own estates in Valencia – and in isolating him there – Denia would develop his influence over him.[27]

Philip began now to shower his grace on men whose company he required on his great *jornada*. He created five noble titles before the *jornada* began, chief among them the marquisate of la Laguna de Camero-Viejo for Denia's brother-in-law Sancho de la Cerda. Philip also disposed of commanderships in the Military Orders with such liberality that it was remarked that he had given more of these away in the first few months of his reign than his father had done in a decade.[28] The 'inflation of honours' that would characterise Philip's reign – and the seventeenth century as a whole – began with powerful emphasis in the first weeks of 1599.[29] Almost as an afterthought, a mere three hours before he left Madrid, Philip conferred councillorships of State on four senior men to compel them to accompany him.[30]

As *caballerizo mayor*, Denia assumed responsibility for the management of the journey and he began now to make the first full use of the range of powers available to him. He gave control of the financial arrangements for the *jornada* to three of the *hechuras* who had been promoted to key offices in December 1598. The Treasurers-General, Pedro Messía de Tovar and Juan Pascual, were made responsible for the collection and disbursement of the cash used on the journey while Alonso Muriel de Valdivielso witnessed and signed the majority of the royal decrees authorising payments.[31] In addition, Denia's *camarero mayor* Juan de la Serna was allowed to authorise payments of expenses for the royal households. Through these *hechuras*, Denia bought coaches and horses for the royal *caballerías*, clothes, jewels and gifts for the King and his family. The cost of the journey has not yet been fully tabulated but it reputedly came to about one million ducats.[32] The expenditures of the fortnight after 13 April might be used to demonstrate the unbridled extravagance that distinguished the King's expenditure in these months; during these two weeks alone Muriel de Valdivielso signed orders for the payment of 99,888 ducats – 37,888 ducats for Margaret's servants (13 April), 40,000 ducats for carriages and horses (24 April) and 22,000 ducats for the costs of Margaret's household (26 April).[33]

In addition to his little coterie of advisers, Denia used two senior administrators to assist him when the court entered the Crown of Aragon – Diego de Covarrubias, the new *vicecanciller* of the Council of Aragon, and Pedro Franqueza, who had until 1597 been secretary of the Council for Valencian affairs. Covarrubias was a trusted friend of Denia's and, as *vicecanciller*, he now assumed seniority among the crown's servants while the King was in the Kingdom of Aragon. During the *jornada* he dutifully served Lerma in a number of ways, political and seigneurial. Franqueza had spent thirty-five years in the service of the Council of Aragon and was incomparably more knowledgeable about the affairs of the kingdom of Aragon than any other servant of the crown. He now placed that knowledge at Denia's disposal. But even more importantly, he was given a wide swathe of responsibilities for conciliar affairs; he acted as secretary of the Council of State during the *jornada*, and he also conducted a great deal of work on the papers of other councils and *juntas*. He made himself so indispensable to Denia that by the time the court returned to Madrid he had become in practice the most influential professional administrator in the government.

The royal households spent three weeks on the road before they reached the coast. They then stayed in Denia for five days. For the first time, the Marquis acted as host to his monarch and he entertained him with such vibrant extravagance that Gil González Dávila wrote of 'a new style of greatness' coming into being during these days.[34] Certainly, the Marquis was exultant at the success of his efforts; he wrote to the Marquis of Poza, President of the Council of Finance, that he had provided 'the best hospitality that a vassal has ever provided to his king' and proudly boasted that the town of Denia had shown itself to be 'among the most honoured places that there are in Spain'.[35] Denia was now consciously creating an image for himself as the comptroller of the affairs of the monarchy and of the court, and when Philip entered the city of Valencia on 19 February for the first major 'joyous entry' of his reign, Denia carried the sword of state.

Margaret disembarked at Vinaroz on 28 March and on the following day Denia led a glittering cohort of *caballeros* to greet her.[36] Philip accompanied them and in the contrived fashion of the day observed his bride for two hours, ostensibly without her knowledge. King and *valido* were captivated by Margaret: Denia shortly professed that she was 'beautiful and most intelligent'.[37] Philip promptly declared that official mourning for his father was to cease so that he could throw himself into the celebrations.

The court stayed in the city of Valencia until 4 May, and during these long and joyous weeks of almost unceasing celebrations the 'new style of greatness' was fully developed. The coincidence of the celebrations of the royal marriages with the beginning of the King's reign – and also with the celebrations of Carnival, Holy Week and Easter – provided the opportunity for the court to throw itself into a joyous and uninhibited round of celebrations – of joyous entries and ceremonial processions; of musical concerts, theatrical productions and poetry competitions, firework displays, mock battles on land and sea and even of displays of flower arrangements. Lope de Vega was among the writers who accompanied the court, and his allegorical *auto*, *Las Bodas del Alma con el Amor divino* was produced in a public square in Valencia. In organising these celebrations, the Marquis of Denia displayed to King and court the range of his power and of his cultural interests.[38] He did so again later in the summer when the court spent a month in Denia itself, and the *fiestas* in Valencia and Denia in the summer of 1599 became a point of reference in the development of court culture. Elizabeth Wright, a literary historian, has described them as 'epoch-making' in their expression of courtly power,[39] while Norman Shergold, a historian of the Spanish stage, has defined them as marking 'the beginning of a new royal interest in the drama which enabled the court theatre of the seventeenth century to be created.'[40]

On 18 April Denia was the guiding figure when the ratification of the two marriages was celebrated in the cathedral of Valencia; a eulogist described him as 'noble, discreet, generous and prudent' and observed, tellingly, that the name of Sandoval was now 'important for all the world'.[41]

Denia rounded out his control of the court by launching a subtle attack on one of the senior servants of Philip II. On 17 March he had forwarded a paper to Diego de Covarrubias, as *vicecanciller* of the Council of Aragon, in which fifteen charges were laid against the Count of Chinchón over his conduct as Treasurer General of the Crown of Aragon. The charges alleged that the Count had abused his power for 'his private purposes'. No evidence survives of any decisions taken in the case but it is likely that, in bringing the allegations against Chinchón to the notice of the King, Denia had done quite enough to neutralise his influence with the King: certainly, the abrasive Count remained curiously tranquil during the next months.[42]

Denia now seized control of the commanding officers of Church and State for his senior supporters. Negotiations to raise Bernardo de Sandoval y Rojas to the primatial see had certainly been under way for some months and it happened that the papal bull appointing him was issued in Rome on the day after the wedding.[43] Denia's plans to seize the presidency of the Council of Castile for the Count of Miranda can be dated to the end of January; as Bernardo

García has demonstrated, on 28 January 1599, fray Diego de Yepes, who had been confessor of Philip II, wrote to Denia making serious allegations about the conduct of Rodrigo Vázquez de Arce, President of the Council of Castile, and the members of his household. Sensationally, Yepes even accused the austere president of having had numerous dalliances with ladies of the night.[44] Denia dutifully passed the allegations on to the King. Early in May, Philip wrote to Vázquez de Arce informing him that he wished to have Miranda as his President of the Council of Castile and inviting him to suggest how his own departure from office should be announced.[45] At the same time, Gaspar de Córdoba, the King's confessor, wrote to the President giving him the reasons for his dismissal, and although these were not officially made public Denia was careful to circulate the paper.[46] The King's confessor was now Denia's man.

Miranda was presented with his title to office in Barcelona on 25 May.[47] A bluff man of action, he had no experience qualifying him for the senior judicial position in the country, which normally went to lawyers or bishops. Moreover, he had gone somewhat to seed in recent years: he had carried a war-wound for twenty years and had become corpulent and inert. However, Denia had need of a loyal and complaisant President of the Council of Castile and over the years to his retirement in 1608 Miranda insistently fulfilled his *consuegro's* expectations of him.[48]

Denia also moved against Juan Alonso Pimentel, eighth count of Benavente. As Viceroy of Valencia, Benavente was in a position to compete with Denia for Philip's attention while the King was in the east. However, it is probable that once again Denia was planning far ahead; Benavente was the richest nobleman in the city of Valladolid and therefore a rival of Denia's within the city, and in undermining his reputation with the King, Denia was almost certainly beginning to prepare for the time when the court would move to Valladolid.[49] On 9 May, Diego de Covarrubias and fray Gaspar de Córdoba, both of whom were accommodating themselves without apparent effort to the demands that Denia was making of them, sat to judge an anonymous allegation that Benavente had exploited his office for financial advantage. They found that he had kept 1,600 ducats from the sale of confiscated goods and suggested that more serious charges might well have been brought against him. Benavente was not apparently allowed to defend himself; indeed, he may not even have known of the allegations against him.[50] Benavente was a relaxed, rather languid, personality but he was not a forgiving man and he knew how to pursue a vendetta: the treatment that he received at Denia's hands in 1599 marked the beginning of a feud that he pursued until he died in 1621.[51]

While the wedding celebrations had been taking place in Valencia and Denia, representatives of the principality of Catalonia had begun to meet in the *corts* at Barcelona. The *corts* dragged on until 6 July but then voted a *servicio* of

1,100,000 *lliures* that was twice as large as any grant that it had previously made to the crown. Once again, Denia used his *hechuras* to control the money; Muriel de Valdivielso passed 136,000 ducats to de la Serna to pay for provisions for the royal households.[52] The *corts* also promised the Queen a gift of 100,000 ducats, and presented Denia with 10,000 and his *hechuras* with smaller amounts. Philip reciprocated with a generous grant of titles.[53] The *corts* were generally considered to have been a success but the greatest act of royal generosity was never made public: Philip presented the remaining 200,000 ducats from the down-payment of the *servicio* to Denia.[54]

Philip stayed in Barcelona for a week after the closing of the *corts* and on 13 July left for Madrid, taking the road to Zaragoza, the capital of Aragon. However, when he learned that the plague was spreading on the road he decided to return to the city of Valencia. He spent only two days there before sailing down to Denia, leaving all but a few courtiers and administrators in Valencia.[55] When the Council of State was informed of the extent of the damage that the plague was inflicting upon the kingdom of Castile, it again advised Philip to stay in the east.[56] Philip was only too happy to do so and settled down in Denia; he stayed there for a month (24 July–24 August).

These weeks were filled with a riot of entertainment for the King, but unlike those which had so enthralled Philip in the city of Valencia in the early summer, these were not public events in which the whole court was involved; Denia organised a series of masques, theatrical productions, dances, jousts and tournaments in his own town to which he invited the guests. He was again enraptured by the beauty of what he was accomplishing and he wrote to Juan de Borja that he was 'radiantly happy' and boasted that 'there is no such *fiesta* in the world'.[57] It was no doubt at Denia's insistence that Lope de Vega put his formidable pen to work to publish a poem which celebrated the *Fiestas de Denia*.[58]

Philip dragged himself away from Denia on 24 August and headed for Zaragoza, where he spent eleven days (11–22 September). He sought to end the bitterness that had been engendered by the revolt of Aragon in 1590–91 by ordering that the four heads of executed traitors be removed from their pikes on the city's bridge and a few days before he entered the city he issued a general pardon to all who had been involved in the tumult.[59] Philip refused to hold a meeting of the Cortes of Aragon but promised that he would return shortly to do so, and to encourage him to keep his promise the kingdom gave Philip 100,000 ducats and his wife a further 10,000 *escudos*. Denia and his associates were presented with 10,000 ducats.[60] Philip moved on to Medinaceli, where he spent four days as a guest of the duke, uncle of Denia's wife. He then travelled around Madrid to the Escorial. Only when Denia was satisfied that the plague had died out in the capital did Philip travel into the city.[61]

The royal journey to the east was brought to a magnificent conclusion when the Queen made her joyous entry into the capital on 24 October. The city corporation prepared a splendid reception for the royal couple; leading artists decorated the streets and created triumphal arches under which Philip and Margaret passed, and the city gave itself over to a week of extravagant celebrations.[62] A new court had come into being; led by a young king it was joyous, extravagant and determined to celebrate its greatness in public. But it was also bankrupt, and it was an appropriate comment on the state of the royal finances that in November the coinage of Castile was debased. Spain had throughout the sixteenth century maintained the integrity of its coinage, but one month before the century ended the new King broke with tradition by issuing debased coinage.[63]

Duke of Lerma, 11 November 1599

The *jornada* of 1599 had set the pattern for the relationship between king and *valido*. For nine months Denia had controlled access to the King and decided upon his movements. He had shown him much of his new kingdom and had supervised the circumstances under which he had seen, met and married his bride. He had also demonstrated to Philip how great the services to the crown of his own family had been: the point would have been made repeatedly in Denia, Gandía and Medinaceli. In the formal entrances 'con palio' that Philip had made into his towns and cities, Denia insistently emphasised his own pre-eminence at court by carrying the ceremonial sword – at Játiva, Valencia, Barcelona, Teruel, Zaragoza, Calatayud and Madrid.[64]

The Marquis's finances were transformed during the *jornada*. He received cash grants (or the promise of them) to the value of 216,000 ducats: 200,000 given to him by the King from the *servicio* of the *corts* of Catalonia; 10,000 ducats given directly by the *corts* and 6,000 as a gift from the Kingdom of Aragon. Doubtless, too, he had received many casual grants and gifts of which no record has survived.[65] His annual income had increased by 24,000 ducats, to about 60,000 ducats. One week into the journey, on 4 February, Philip granted Denia the right to provide armed galleys as protection for his tunny-fishing concession on the Valencian coast. This award was worth around 5,000 ducats annually and was vested in his *mayorazgo*.[66] At the end of February Philip presented Denia with the small town of Purroy in Aragon, confiscated after the rebellion of 1591; it was valued at only 500 ducats annually. Much more substantially, on 3 April Philip gave him the *escribanías* of Alicante and Orihuela; these offices entitled Denia to levy charges for the taking of oaths and to administer import taxes in fifty towns and villages, and brought him 3,500 ducats a year.[67] A month later, Philip readily agreed to a strong recommendation by *vicecanciller* Covarrubias that Denia be given the right to charge tolls (*'peage y leuda'*) on goods travelling through his marquisate; this was worth 1,000 ducats annually.[68] At an unknown date during the *jornada*, again after consulting with the Council of Aragon, Philip conferred on Denia the right to produce salt in his marquisate to preserve the tunny of the *almadrabas*; this brought him about 2,000 ducats annually (capital value: 10,000 ducats).[69] When news arrived at court of the death of don Pedro López de Ayala, Count of Fuensalida, Philip gave the position of *Comendador Mayor de Castilla* to Denia (3 September). Fuensalida had been a trusted confidant of Philip II and his *encomienda* was the senior dignity in the Castilian province of the Order of Santiago; it was appropriate that it now passed to Denia as the leading servant of the new king. It had the further advantage of bringing Denia 12,000 ducats per annum.[70]

As soon as the court returned to Madrid, Denia consolidated his authority in government by securing major promotions for two of his most senior advisers. On 9 October Juan de Borja was appointed to a councillorship of State of Portugal (even though he was not himself Portuguese) and a few days later the Cardinal of Toledo was named as a councillor of State.[71] Borja repaid Denia with devoted service over many years, but the Cardinal of Toledo made a more practical and immediate acknowledgement of his obligation, and it was one which his great-nephew deeply appreciated: on 1 November (as Denia bluntly put it in 1622) 'on being promoted to the archbishopric of Toledo, he assigned 20,000 ducats per annum to us for the redemption of [the debts] of our house'.[72] Denia enjoyed the award until the cardinal's death at the end of 1618 and derived 380,000 ducats from it. His verifiable annual income from his rents now reached 79,027 ducats, taking him into fourteenth place on the table of aristocratic incomes: one year into the reign, he had virtually quintupled his income (see Appendix III).

No record survives of Denia's expenditure on the *jornada* but it is likely that he had spent even more than he had acquired. In 1622, when he was defending his conduct during his *valimiento*, he claimed to have spent well over 300,000 ducats on the *jornada* of 1599. He even suggested that because the Indies' treasure fleet had arrived later than expected he had borne the chief costs of the journey. There was doubtless some exaggeration in his claims – and in 1622 he had real need to defend his conduct – but the justification that he put forward for the exercise of his *valimiento* was revealing of his priorities and values:

> We took the greatest care to conduct affairs with the solemnity and greatness that became celebrated, not only in Spain but among foreign nations. We provided very expensive clothing and jewels for our own person and that of the Duchess, our beloved wife and for our sons and daughters and our servants. We

had lavish costumes made, both for the day of the weddings and for the journey on the road. We paid for the preparation of great banquets. The cost of all of this was very great because the (treasure) fleet was detained for longer than had been expected and I had to pay the expenses. When on behalf of the King, our lord, I went to welcome the Queen, our lady, I was accompanied by sixty gentlemen, all dressed in red velvet bordered with silver. In addition to the aids to expenses that were given to me, I spent more than 300,000 ducats on the expenses of the journey and on hospitality.

He did not make it clear how he had come by these huge amounts.[73]

The greatest reward was yet to come. On 11 November, in the Pardo palace, Philip raised Denia to the dukedom of Lerma. He also endowed him with the marquisate of Cea with permission to pass it on to his eldest son to use with immediate effect and conferred the countship of Ampudia on Francisco Gómez II, the eldest son of the new Marquis of Cea.[74] Only eight dukedoms had been created in the years 1508–98, the most recent of them being that of Pastrana in 1572.[75] No new possessions were granted with the three titles; the Castilian possessions of the new dukedom consisted of the marquisate of Cea and the towns of Ampudia, Gumiel de Mercado and Ventosilla and their *tierras* while the marquisate of Denia was subsumed into the dukedom.

The awards made on 11 November had multiple significance. For Philip himself, 11 November carried the most evocative importance, for it had been on that day in 1584 that he had received the fealty of his subjects in Castile and had been proclaimed as their next king. For the new Duke of Lerma, the award had the most enduring personal importance in that it raised him to the highest levels of Spanish society. It had even more powerful symbolism for his family. As far as is known, no family had ever before received three titles on the same day; much less, had any family been honoured in three generations on one day: Philip was therefore distinguishing the Sandoval family from all others in his realms. Moreover, in restoring Cea and Ampudia, Philip was expressly making good to the family the wrongs done them by successive monarchs in the fifteenth and sixteenth centuries.

Even this unexampled multiple grant did not exhaust Philip's generosity to the Sandoval family, for on 29 December he granted the marquisate of Villamizar to Denia's brother, Juan Gómez. Villamizar was only a dozen kilometres away from Cea, and so the two estates rounded each other out.[76] With Sancho de la Cerda's marquisate of la Laguna, this was the fifth noble title conferred on Lerma and his immediate *parentela* during 1599. The fears that Cabrera de Córdoba had hinted at a year earlier were now substantively validated: there could no longer be any doubt that the age of the *valimiento* had returned to Spain, that the royal benevolence was being focused on the needs and ambitions of one man and his family, its allies and supporters.

Lerma now drove this lesson home by seizing control of the Queen's household. Once again, he used the King's confessor in a courtly intrigue, ordering Gaspar de Córdoba to inform the Duchess of Gandía that the King wished her to retire as *camarera mayor* of the Queen so that the office could be given to Denia's wife (4 December). The brusque dismissal of the Duchess was fiercely resented: Cabrera de Córdoba noted that 'the whole court has shown its sympathy at her dismissal'. The Duchess was the sister of the Constable of Castile, and among the members of her *parentela* who ostentatiously accompanied her out of the palace were the Marchioness of Camarasa, the Countess of Monterrey and the Count of Alva de Liste.[77] Denia also appears to have moved against Enrique de Guzmán, V Count of Alba de Liste, *mayordomo mayor* of the Queen; in October 1599, Alva de Liste stormed out of the palace because Denia had made an appointment which infringed upon his rights as *mayordomo mayor* of the Queen.[78] But as always, Lerma sought reconciliation with opponents or with people who might oppose him; he had dispensed with the services of Cristóbal de Moura and the Duchess of Gandía – two of the four people who had been placed in major offices by Philip II to circumscribe Denia's influence over Philip III – but on 12 December 1599, Juan de Idiáquez was sworn in as President of the Council of Military Orders. Don Juan would add his authoritative voice to the support of Lerma and his regime.[79] Supremely confident of his power, Lerma now prepared for the greatest coup of his career, the removal of the court to Valladolid.

Court and capital: preparations for the removal to Valladolid, 1600

Philip II had chosen Madrid as his capital city in 1561, and had begun the construction of the great monastery-palace of San Lorenzo at the village of the Escorial 50 kilometres away in 1563. By the time that the Escorial was completed in 1584, Philip had the 'courtly complex' that was fundamental to his kingship; no fewer than seventeen royal palaces and hunting lodges lay within 60 kilometres of Madrid. Chief among them were the extensive hunting grounds in the *Casa de Campo* to the west of Madrid and his hunting-lodges and palaces of the Pardo, the Escorial and the 'Woods of Segovia', each of which provided him with places of recreation within a few hours' ride of his capital city. Philip also owned an elegant palace at Aranjuez which was renowned for the beauty of its gardens.[80]

Madrid had the essential buildings and spaces for a royal capital. The royal palace – the Alcázar – was a converted fortress, and if it was functional rather than elegant it provided the wide range of accommodation needed to house the King and a court of some 2,500 people.[81] The city's *plaza mayor* was somewhat derelict but could be used for courtly and religious celebrations (and for executions). Curiously, Madrid did not have a cathedral and the church of Santa María was used for some royal services while the crown's convents and monasteries in the city served for baptisms and weddings.

The population of Madrid had grown from about 16,000 in 1561 to some 83,000 (perhaps as many as 90,000) at the end of Philip II's reign. However, the king's nobles had not taken to the city with any enthusiasm; only about thirty-five aristocratic families owned palaces there when Philip III succeeded to the throne.[82] By contrast, the religious orders had established sixteen religious houses in Madrid between 1561 and 1598; the influence of the regular clergy was therefore felt throughout the city. The city's growth had, however, been bought at the expense of the health of a sizeable part of its population: in the years 1595–1600 it lost 18–22 per cent of its people every year, a total of nearly one-tenth of its population after the new arrivals were accounted for: the city was living a continuous subsistence crisis, and as Philip II lay dying his ministers feared that food shortages might lead to food riots in the capital.[83]

It was, therefore, not entirely unreasonable that doubts should be expressed at the beginning of Philip III's reign about the suitability of the city as the capital of the monarchy. In the first two years of his reign Philip confirmed some of these uncertainties by his reluctance to spend much time in Madrid; having been away from his capital for nine months in 1599, he then spent a total of another eight months away in 1600.

The King stayed for a month in Toledo in the spring. If he had entertained any idea that Toledo might once again serve as a capital he would have been disabused by the poverty that made it impossible for the once-proud city to mount a reception worthy of his visit.[84] Philip returned to Madrid on 15 April 1600 so that he and his ministers could put pressure on the procurators of the Cortes of Castile to agree to provide a new grant of the *millones*. On 22 April the procurators agreed to provide Philip with 18,000,000 ducats over six years. The eighteen '*millones*' was twice as much as the Cortes had voted in 1590 (8,000,000 ducats over six years) and enabled the crown to budget for a regular income from this source alone of 3,000,000 ducats annually. As part of the negotiations for the grant, Lerma seems to have renounced the *escribanía de sacas* of the south-western coast into the King's hands; at this time, Philip gave him rents in Portugal worth 9,200 ducats annually, and it is likely that he did so as compensation for his renunciation of the great *escribanía* in Seville.[85]

The procurators could not commit their cities to the agreement and Philip made brief visits to Segovia (6–12 June), Ávila (15–22 June) and Salamanca (25 June–1 July) to encourage the city councils to validate the agreement. Lerma carried the ceremonial sword when the King entered *con palio*. King and duke then relaxed in two towns which did not have votes in the Cortes: Medina del Campo (2–8 July) and Tordesillas (12–19 July) before entering Valladolid (which was of course represented in the Cortes) on 19 July.[86] They stayed there for six weeks.

These were decisive weeks for the development of Lerma's *valimiento*. He was able to demonstrate to Philip that Valladolid's walls could be used to restrict entry: orders were issued in July to the *corregidor* that (as was reported) 'no one, of whatever quality, should be allowed to enter into the city if they did not carry a licence from the Duke of Lerma or from the Count of Miranda'. Guards were placed on the city walls and the instruction was observed to the letter.[87] Valladolid was secure.

As preparation for the removal of the court to Valladolid, Lerma also very provocatively embroiled himself in 1600 in a dispute with one of the leading noblemen of the city, the Marquis of Camarasa. He appealed to the Council of Castile on behalf of the Cardinal of Toledo in his dispute with Camarasa over the right of nomination to the *adelantamiento* of Cazorla. Control over the *adelantamiento*, which lay in the mountains of Granada, had been contested for fifty years by the marquises of Camarasa and the archbishops of Toledo. However, the lawsuit which now ensued over Cazorla was the occasion rather than the cause of a feud between Lerma and Camarasa, and at its centre lay Camarasa's great palace in the *Plaza de San Pablo*: it was the finest palace in the city and Lerma coveted it for himself. He would force Camarasa to sell him his palace by threatening to take the *adelantamiento* of Cazorla from his family.[88]

The Sandoval family already had a long-standing feud with the Enríquez family who were dukes of Medina de Rioseco and Admirals of Castile; the families had developed an intense rivalry with each other in the household of Juana *la Loca* in Tordesillas. The Enríquez family was nominally the third-richest in Spain but by 1600 it was heavily in debt and Lerma took advantage of its vulnerability to propose a marriage between the new Admiral (Juan Alonso Enríquez de Córdoba, who was an infant) and his own granddaughter, Luisa, the eldest daughter of his heir. In the circumstances, the agreement was soon made and was subsequently extended to a double marriage in 1612.[89] The Enríquez family were then doubly bound to the Sandovals.

During 1600 Lerma entered legal pleas in the Chancellery of Valladolid and in the Council of Castile to begin the recovery of some of his family's ancestral lands and incomes. In doing so, he consciously built upon the King's decision to return some of the lands confiscated from Diego Gómez I to him in his ducal grant of 1599. He also prepared for the removal of the court to Valladolid. He started with Ampudia, winning from the Chancellery the recognition of his right to incorporate the *alcabalas* and *tercias* of the town into his *mayorazgo*; these were worth about 3,000 ducats a year.[90] At the turn of 1600–01 the Count of Miranda began to repay his obligations to Lerma when he led the Council of Castile in handing down an even more substantive judgement in his favour, ordering that the agreement that the Catholic Kings had made with the Sandovals in 1469 should be implemented, and that the *alcabalas* and *tercias* and all other royal rights in the 'Lands of the Recompense' should be transferred to the Lerma *mayorazgo*. Forty-four *lugares* were involved, with a total of about 11,250 inhabitants (2,500 *vecinos*). All but two of the places were within a radius of 30 kilometres of Lerma and so their acquisition consolidated the Duke's landed holdings. They brought him 4,000 ducats a year of rent. However, even this success was not enough for Lerma: his lawyers now entered a plea that the award should be backdated to 1469 and that the duke should be paid the interest that would have accrued to his family over that period. They also argued that Lerma was entitled to the income from royal taxes that had been levied since 1469 and that these should also be incorporated into the award. The sums that were involved in the claim gave Philip pause and he established a commission of six councillors of Castile under Miranda to adjudicate on the claim.[91]

While Lerma tested the resolve of the judicial authorities (and indeed of the King) he let the city council of Valladolid understand that he 'would like' to be a councillor. On 8 July 1600 the council convened an extraordinary session and agreed unanimously to the proposal.[92] It then invited Philip to approve the grant when he made his solemn entrance into the city on 11 July – an occasion when, of course, a monarch would traditionally respond favourably to requests that were placed before him. Philip eagerly did so. Lerma's new councillorship gave him the first vote in the council after the *corregidor* and allowed him the honour of entering the council chamber bearing his sword and dagger.[93] However, while Lerma had no intention of carrying out the everyday duties of the office he fully appreciated that by rationing his appearances he could maximise their effect: he made his first attendance at the council on 17 August for the discussion on the ratification of the *millones* agreement, and when the councillors agreed – once again, unanimously – to ratify the grant it was he who carried the happy news to the King.[94]

The contract for the sale to Lerma of the church of *San Pablo* was agreed between himself and the Prior of the monastery at the end of September. The sale of the church and its *patronazgo* took effect on 6 December. On 29 December, Lerma bought the Camarasa palace. On 10 January 1601 it was announced that the court would move to Valladolid.[95]

The day on which Lerma and his wife bought the monastery-church of *San Pablo* was one of the proudest of his life and in 1617, after he had rebuilt the church, doubling it in height, he placed record of the purchase on both columns of the façade, in Castilian and Latin, making explicit the purposes of Catalina and himself:

Considering with dutiful thanks the great goods that have been received from
the divine hands, and bearing death in mind in life itself, they endowed this
monastery to the honour and glory of God and of the Apostle Saint Paul with
great rents and adorned it with jewels and built it up, and because it did not have
a patron, they acquired the rights of patronage in perpetuity for themselves and
their successors in the house and *mayorazgo* and chose it for their burial place and
for that of their successors.

The Sixth of December 1600

Lerma agreed to pay 4,000 ducats of *juros* to the Marquis of Camarasa for
his palace. No details have survived of the negotiations, but the hostility that
Camarasa maintained towards Lerma throughout his life suggests that the deal
was not easily struck.[96]

On 6 December, Lerma also wrote to the city council to inform it that he
had bought the church of *San Pablo* to serve as his family pantheon. He stressed
that he had done this 'because of the great love that he and his forebears have
had and have for this city' and asked permission to build a *pasadizo* from his
palace to *San Pablo* so that he could pass through it to hear the divine services.
The letter was delivered on 15 January by Francisco Calderón, himself a
town councillor. On the following day, the council unanimously agreed to
Lerma's request, recording that it did so because 'the favours which this city
has received, and hopes to receive, from His Excellency were so many and so
great'. It despatched two of its members to give Lerma the news of its decision
and to assure him that the city would always do 'everything that it could for his
service'.[97] The *corregidor* also announced that the King had ordered that entry
to the city was henceforth to be strictly restricted.[98] Lerma was the master of
Valladolid.[99]

The removal of the court to Valladolid, March 1601

Valid reasons could have been adduced for moving the court to Valladolid. The
presence of the court in the heart of Old Castile would do much to help the
region to recover after the great plague, which killed 600,000 people by the
time that it died out in 1602.[100] The King could better supervise the conduct
of the wars against the northern heretic powers and keep in touch with his
kingdom of Portugal from Valladolid. The city had twice served as the capital
of Castile and had many natural advantages. It lay at the heart of an extensive
communications network, was adjacent to the national archives at Simancas and
housed a bishopric and a regional Inquisition and the Chancellery that exercised
jurisdiction over the northern half of Castile. It was an important banking centre.
Unlike Madrid it had a cathedral, and by repute had more religious foundations

than any city in Spain, divided equally between convents and monasteries. The city also had twenty charitable hospitals. Its *plaza mayor* was one of the finest in Spain and would provide a splendid stage for courtly and religious ceremonies. Valladolid also had a university which incorporated the prestigious *colegio mayor* of Santa Cruz. The Pisuerga was – unlike the Manzanares in Madrid (which was dry in the long summer months) – a real river which, fast and wide, provided the opportunity for the court to enjoy those aquatic celebrations that were so much part of its life. On the far bank of the river lay a number of fine riverside houses which could be used for celebrations and *fiestas*.[101] Philip certainly appreciated after his visit in the summer of 1600 that he would be better able to restrict entry to Valladolid than he was in Madrid. There was, too, a feeling that Valladolid was more suited to the King's health than Madrid, with its extremes of heat in the summer and cold in the winter.[102]

There were of course disadvantages. Valladolid did not have the central position in the peninsula that Madrid enjoyed and was seriously deficient in the accommodation necessary for court and government; the monarchs had a hunting lodge at El Abrojo but otherwise did not possess property near the city. Indeed, the crown did not even own a palace in the city, although six grandee families did – Lerma, Benavente, Camarasa, Medina de Rioseco, the Duke of Híjar and the Constable of Castile.[103] But of course, the majority of nobles who lived at court in Madrid did not own properties in Valladolid, and the houses for which they now had to compete were often neither elegant nor even well-constructed.[104] The king's nobles had now to confront serious financial difficulties in moving themselves, their families and entourages to the new capital city.

In the event, the various factors which were adduced for taking the court to Valladolid were the justifications rather than the reasons for the removal. The court was taken to Valladolid because the Duke of Lerma wished to extend his control over the King and build up his patrimony in and around the city, above all in creating his family pantheon in *San Pablo*. Initially he concentrated on extending his properties in and around Valladolid and built a splendid hunting-lodge at Ventosilla. Lerma also enlarged his estates in Cea and Ampudia. Then – from 1605 – he began the long process of developing the town of Lerma into the finest aristocratic town in Spain. His ambitions formed a simple entity and they were expressed most fully in his buildings: in them he balanced with fastidious concern his determination to be the greatest nobleman in Spain and the greatest lay patron of the Church.

Changing the capital city of Spain involved moving the servants of the crown and their families, a total of perhaps 10,000–15,000 people. The problems that were involved in transporting, feeding and lodging such a large number of people meant that the turmoil lasted for several months as the carts plied back and forth between Madrid and Valladolid. Even then, there was not sufficient accommodation in the new capital for the king's servants and an unseemly rivalry arose between them for housing. The University and Inquisition of Valladolid had to give up their quarters so that members of the court and administration could take them over. The Council of Portugal had to lodge in the house of its leader while the Chancellery of Valladolid was moved to Medina del Campo and Medina's fairs had to be transplanted to Burgos.[105] At all levels of government, therefore, the removal of the court resulted in serious dislocation of the conduct of business. However, by a happy chance the arrival of a treasure fleet in December brought some eight million ducats, a quarter or so of it for the crown, and so the money was available to pay for the removal.[106]

Madrid was devastated by the departure of the court. The city had few functions beyond its status as capital, for it did not have trading or commercial functions to compensate it for the loss of the court. Its population collapsed to fewer than 40,000 people. A modern historian has remarked on 'the impression of economic disaster, psychological ruin and human loss' that Madrid suffered.[107]

The removal of the court promoted enormous resentment in Madrid and it was directed at Lerma himself: it was reported that Lerma was cursed in Madrid.[108] Churchmen were especially vocal in their criticism of Lerma for moving the court. The Cardinal-Archbishop of Toledo himself warned Lerma that criticisms were being voiced at court that 'the removal to Valladolid is for the construction of the church and house that [you] ... desire and negotiate for with such vehemence'.[109] Fray Jerónimo de Sepúlveda wrote contemptuously of Lerma's responsibility for the removal of the court. Lerma sought a reconciliation with the Cardinal; on his way to Valladolid, he travelled out of his way to meet his great-uncle and to offer him the Inquisitorship-General if he agreed to take up residence in Valladolid. The Cardinal dismissed the offer angrily and again rebuked Lerma over the removal. That the two men had argued furiously became well known.[110]

Valladolid was not ready to receive the king, and so Philip and Lerma spent a pleasant fortnight hunting at Tordesillas while preparations were hurriedly made in the new capital. When Margaret joined them from Madrid it was confirmed that she was pregnant. Naturally, it was Lerma who announced the joyous news. Happily, too, the death of the bishop of Valladolid provided Lerma with the ideal opportunity to control the religious life of the capital by having Dr Juan Bautista de Acevedo named for the bishopric.[111]

Philip formally entered his new capital city on 9 February 1601. His first major act was to issue a decree authorising the towns and cities of Castile to impose the tax on wine and olive oil within their districts to raise the first instalment of the *millones*.[112] Less than three years into his reign, Philip III had a new capital city and his subjects were subjected to a new level of taxation. For the Duke of Lerma, master of king, court and capital, there seemed little to trouble his confidence that the future belonged to him.

NOTES

1 Denia to Juan de Borja, San Lorenzo, 14 Sep. 1598, BL Add 28,422, fol. 6b; *ACC,* xv, p. 674. On the changes in government, Williams, 'Philip III and the Restoration of Spanish Government', pp. 751–8 and Martínez Hernández, *El Marqués de Velada,* pp. 361–416.

2 Cervera Vera, *La iglesia de San Pedro,* p. 33.

3 Title, 29 Sep. 1598, AGS QC 6.

4 On the ships and the Seville office, 'Imbentario', ADL 53, fols. 24v–25v and 'Petición que se dió en el consexo ...', ibid., 25, no. 32, fol. 5b; on the *escríbanía,* 'Officios de scriuanias de sacas y aduanas y regimientos', AGS CG Inv. 24, leg. 572.

5 Philip III to Francisco de Idiáquez, 20 Sep. 1598, AGS E 2636, no fol.

6 Attendance registers, councils of State and War, 1598.

7 *CSPV* ix, 27 Sep. 1598, no. 744, p. 346.

8 Gil González Dávila, *Felipe III,* pp. 44–5 and idem, *Teatro de las grandezas de la villa de Madrid, Corte de los reyes católicos de España,* Madrid, 1986 reprint of 1623 edn, pp. 51–2.

9 Philip III to Archduke Albert, San Jerónimo, 22 Sep., and Escorial, 24 Oct. 1598, in H. Lonchay and J. Cuvelier, *Correspondance de la cour d'Espagne sur les affaires des Pays-Bas au XVII siècle,* Brussels, 1923-37, 6 vols., i, pp. 8–9 and 14–15.

10 'pues en solos quarenta dias que ha seguido sus altos y heroycos pensamientos, confirmados co(n) las reglas generosas de verdadero gouierno militar, y politico, vee por experiencia q(ue) se lleua tras sí el mundo en amor y temor: y particularmente, por verse inclinado al exercicio militar, que tanto conuiene en estos tiempos', introductory note to the King, Madrid, 20 Oct. 1598, *Avisos en Materia de Estado y Guerra,* Madrid, 1599, no fol.

11 Valencia served until 1605, Acuña Vela until 1606 and Puñonrostro until 1609, while Velasco continued to attend until 1618 and Enríquez was still sitting regularly at the beginning of Philip IV's reign. See Williams, 'Restoration of Spanish Government', pp. 756–7 and 759.

12 Patrick Strange to Cecil, 3 Feb. 1599, *CSPD, 1598–1601,* p. 159.

13 Eduardo Pardo de Guevara y Valdés, *Don Pedro Fernández de Castro VII Conde de Lemos (1576– 1622),* 2 vols., Xunta de Galicia, 1977, i, 119–20; the *capitulaciones* for the marriage, dated Madrid 10 Jan. 1599, printed at ii, pp. 12–17.

14 Fernández de Béthencourt, *Historia genealógica,* iv, pp. 546–7.

15 'Fue notable este casamie(n)to, por que el Rey don Felipe nuestro señor, y su hermana la serenissima Infanta doña Ysabel, fueron los padrinos y velolos don García de Loaysa, Arçobispo de Toledo, y la nouia comio este dia con los Reyes a vna mesa; y à la tarde la lleuo el mesmo Rey en vna acanea à su lado, aco(m)pañandole por las calles de Madrid, hasta las casas de los Duques sus padres, à 16 de Nouiembre año 1598', Sandoval, *Chrónica de ... Alonso VII,* p. 240.

16 'Petición que se dió en el consexo ...', ADL 25 no. 32, fol. 8; a shorter version, 'Querella del fiscal del Consejo contra el señor Cardenal Duque de Lerma', copy, BL Eg 2081, fols. 128–30; see also *CSPV* ix, 8 Nov. 1598, no. 753, p. 349.

17 del Río Barredo, *Madrid, Urbs Regia,* p. 83; A. Cámara Muñoz, 'El poder de la imagen y la imagen del poder. La fiesta en Madrid en el Renacimiento', in *Madrid en el Renacimiento,* Madrid, 1986, pp. 73-4 and 81.

18 Danvila y Burguero, *Moura,* pp. 778–9 and C. Gaillard, *Le Portugal sous Philippe III d'Espagne. L'action de Diego de Silva y Mendoza,* Grenoble, 1983, p. 15.

19 Denia to Borja, Madrid, 12 Dec. 1598, BL. Add. 28,422, fols. 19–19b; *Relaciones,* pp. 1 and 52; J. Veríssimo Serrão, *História de Portugal,* iv, *Governo dos Reis Espanhóis (1580–1640),* pp. 50–2.

20 Denia sent his wife to the Medina Sidonia palace to order the newly-married counts of Niebla to leave for Seville. The Duke and Duchess of Medina Sidonia were so outraged by Catalina's

imperious behaviour that they vowed to leave for San Lúcar within days, *Relaciones*, p. 4.
21 Ibid., p. 10.
22 On the case of Luis de Mercado, Williams, 'A Jewish Councillor of Inquisition? Luis de Mercado, the Statutes of *limpieza de sangre* and the Politics of Vendetta', BHS, lxvii (1990), pp. 253-64.
23 Messía de Tovar, AHN OM *Prueba*, Santiago 5089; Pascual's title, 25 Dec. 1598, AGS QC 28, and AHN OM *Pruebas*, Santiago 6278; Ibáñez de Santa Cruz's title, 23 Dec., AGS QC 23; Tapia's title, 2 Nov. 1598, AGS QC. 38. On the significance of their appointments, see pp. 58–9.
24 *Relaciones*, p. 3.
25 On Albert's journey, Gilles Faing, 'Voyage de l'Archiduc Albert en Espagne', in L. P. Gachard (ed.), *Collection des voyages des souverains des Pays-Bas*, Brussels, 1974–82, iv, pp. 457–562 and Juan Roco de Campofrio, *España en Flándes. Trece años de Gobierno del Archiduque Alberto (1595–1608)*, Madrid, 1973, pp. 231–6; on Margaret's journey, González Dávila, *Felipe III*, pp. 46–63 and Bonner Mitchell, *1598 A Year of Pageantry in Late Renaissance Ferrara*, New York, 1990.
26 Anon., 'Jornada de S. M. Felipe III', printed in Simon Diaz, *Relaciones breves de ... Madrid*, p. 39; *Relaciones*, p. 5.
27 J. Torras i Ribé, *Poders i relacions clientelars a la Catalunya dels Àustria Pere Franquesa (1547–1614)*, Vic, 1998, p. 138.
28 *Relaciones*, pp. 4–5.
29 On the 'inflation of honours', Thompson, 'The Nobility in Spain', pp. 190–2.
30 Namely the cardinal of Seville, the dukes of Infantado and Terranova and the count of Alva de Liste, Anon, '*La jornada que el cardenal Arçobispo de Seuilla mi señor prosigue de Madrid a Valencia*', printed by Simon Diaz, *Relaciones breves de Madrid*, p. 40. See also Seco Serrano, 'Los comienzos de la privanza de Lerma', p. 82, n. 2.
31 Treasurers-General managed the cash that the crown kept for its immediate purposes and were also responsible for authorising payments to bankers and negotiating *asientos*, the management of alienated rents and the accounts of the armed forces and the frontier fortresses (*presidios*). On Pascual's role in military provisioning and financing, Thompson, *War and Government*, pp. 87–9, 99, 224–5 and 259.
32 See *Relaciones*, p. 48.
33 Luis Ortíz de Matienço, 'Relación de los Pliegos descargos y Dattas que ban en este libro De los cargos que an resultado contra dibersos personas por la quenta que se a tenido con pedro de Villamor, thess[orer]o gen[era]l que fue de la jornada Del casamiento de Su Mag[esta]d, por luis ortiz de matienco, su contador de Resultas y de la Razón de los gastos de la d[i]cha Jornada ...', AGS DGT Inv 24, leg. 575. See also, copy of the title of Luis Ortíz de Matienço for the journey, San Martín de la Cabeza, 22 Jan. 1599, ibid., 508.
34 *Felipe III*, p. 65.
35 Denia to Poza, Denia, 15 Feb. 1599, RB 11/2132, no. 285.
36 'El Rey mandó á Don Francisco de Roxas y Sandoval, su Sumiller de Corps y el Caballerizo Mayor, Marques de Denia, fuese á dar en su nombre la bienvenida á la Reyna, y á visitarla de su parte. Partió por la posta con sesenta caballeros y mas de ochenta criados vestidos de carmesí, con pasamanos y recamados de oro, todos en cuerpo, con sus ferreruelos de grana en sus portamanteos, y el Marques á la postre, vestido con un bohemio bordado de oro y plata, y lo mismo el chapeo ricamente aderezado', González Dávila, *Felipe III*, pp. 63-4.
37 Denia to Juan de Borja, Valencia, 5 April 1599, BL Add 28,422, fol. 53. Juan de Roco Campofrio provided a more restrained description: 'Muy blanca y corba. La boca algo hundida. De semblante muy apacible, con grandes demostraciones de humanidad y llaneça. De buena disposición y cuerpo', *España en Flándes*, pp. 231–2.
38 *Relaciones*, pp. 7–22 and González Dávila, *Felipe III*, pp. 63-70.
39 E. R. Wright, *Pilgrimage to Patronage. Lope de Vega and the Court of Philip III, 1598–1621*, Lewisburg and London, 2001, pp. 52–6.

40 N. D. Shergold, *A History of the Spanish Stage. From Medieval Times until the End of the Seventeenth Century*, Oxford, 1967, p. 245.

41 Gaspar Aguilar, *Fiestas nupciales que la ciudad y reino de Valencia han hecho al casamiento del Rey*, ed. Antonio Pérez y Gómez, Valencia, 1975 reprint, p. 9. See also *Relaciones*, pp. 18–22.

42 Anon., 'Cargos q[ue] resultan de los papeles q[ue] se an escripto contra el conde de Chinchón', no date, contained in letter of Denia to Covarrubias, el Real, 17 March 1599, RAH K-41, fols. 30–1.

43 Papal Bull, Rome, 19 April 1599, AGS BBS 5842; and *Relaciones*, p. 23.

44 García García, *La Pax Hispánica*, p. 365, n. 21.

45 Philip's letter, undated, printed by González Dávila, *Teatro de las Grandezas de ... Madrid*, p. 378. See also, Gerónimo Gascón de Torquemada, *Gaçeta y Nuevas de la Corte de España desde el año 1600 en adelante*, Madrid, 1991, pp. 19–20.

46 Denia to Juan de Borja, Vinaroz, 11 May 1599, BL Add 28,422 fols. 63b–64. On the dismissal of Vázquez de Arce, *ACC* xviii, pp. 216–35 and González Dávila, *Teatro de las Grandezas de Madrid*, p. 378.

47 Title, Barcelona, 25 May, AGS QC 30.

48 J. Yáñez, *Memorias para la historia de Don Felipe III, Rey de España*, Madrid, 1723, pp. 32–3, Ranke, *The Ottoman and Spanish Empires*, p. 52; on his services to Lerma, see pp. 48–9. 60–1, 68–9, 111, 141, 144.

49 On the removal of the court to Valladolid, below, pp. 66–93.

50 *Cntas*. Lic. Covarrubias, 20 Dec. 1598 and 27 Jan.1599, ACA CA 652, fol. 48/1 and 52; *cnta*. Covarrubias and Gaspar de Córdoba, 9 May 1599, ibid., fol. 56/3.

51 See below, pp. 228, 248–9, 252.

52 Matienço, 'Relación de los Pliegos descargos y Dattas', AGS DGT Inv 24, leg. 575.

53 Ibid., p. 31, where it is recorded that Denia was given 10,000 ducats; Covarrubias 6,000; Franqueza 3,000 and Muriel de Valdivielso 10,000. J. H. Elliott, *The Revolt of the Catalans. A Study in the Decline of Spain, 1598–1640*, Cambridge, 1963, pp. 49–51.

54 'Imbentario', ADL 53, fol. 13v.

55 *Relaciones*, pp. 33–4.

56 *Cnta*. St., 23 July 1599, AGS E 183, fol. 3.

57 Denia to Borja, 26 July 1599, BL Add Mss 28,422, fol. 80.

58 H. A. Rennert, *The Life of Lope de Vega*, New York, 1968, pp. 141–2. On the re-engagement of the court with the theatre, C. Sanz Ayán and Bernardo J. García García, *Teatros y comediantes en el Madrid de Felipe II*, Madrid, 2000, pp. 79–86.

59 P. Fernández Albadalejo, 'Lex Regia Aragonensium: Compound Monarchy and Identity during the Reign of Philip III', in E. Martínez Ruiz and M. Pazzis Pi Corrales (eds.), *Spain and Sweden in the Baroque Era (1600–1660)*, Madrid, 2000.

60 *Relaciones*, p. 43.

61 Denia to Juan de Borja, Ateca, 25 Sep. 1599, BL Add 28,422, fol. 140.

62 'Relación de la entrada de sus magestades en Madrid, el Domingo 26 de octubre de 1599 ...', printed by Simon Diaz, *Relaciones Breves*, pp. 40–2; Quintana, *Madrid*, p. 349. C. Cayetano Martín and P. Flores Guerrero, 'Nuevas aportaciones al recibimiento en Madrid de la reina doña Margarita de Austria (24 de octubre de 1599)', AIEM, xxii, 1988, pp. 387–400 and Virginia Tovar Martín, 'La entrada triunfal en Madrid de doña Margarita de Austria (24 de octubre de 1599), AEA, no. 244, 1988, pp. 385–403; E. Benito Ruano, 'Recepción madrileña de la reina Margarita de Austria', AIEM, 1, 1966, pp. 85–98.

63 J. de Santiago Fernández, *Política monetaria en Castilla durante el siglo XVII*, JCL, Valladolid, 2000, pp. 56–8.

64 del Río Barredo, *Madrid, Urbs Regia*, p. 87.

65 For instance, in *Relaciones*, p. 16 it is recorded that he received 50,000 ducats for informing the King of the arrival of the treasure fleet from the Indies in April; no record has been found of this in Lerma's private papers or in the charges brought against him at the beginning of Philip IV's reign.

66 The material in this paragraph is from 'Imbentario', ADL 53, fols. 23b–26 and 'Hacienda acrecentada por compras y mercedes de su Mag[esta]d y en otra qualquiera forma desde el año de 1599 hasta el de [1]625 en que falleció su excellenzia' (henceforth 'Hacienda acrecentada'), ADL 54, no. 9, no fol.

67 'Hacienda acrecentada', ADL 54, no. 9, no fol.; Denia to Juan de Borja, Valencia, 5 Apr. 1599, BL Add 28, 422, fol. 53.

68 *Cnta. Vicecanciller* Covarrubias, 5 May 1599, ACA CA 652, fol. 54–5.

69 This award was formally conferred on 30 November and is included here because it was negotiated during the *jornada*, 'Hacienda acrecentada', ADL 53, no. 9, no fol. and Lerma, 'Imbentario', ADL 53, fol. 23.

70 On 9 August 1599, Diego Gómez was given the *encomienda mayor* of Calatrava and Denia's *encomienda* of Hornachos, worth about half as much, was passed on to Cristóbal, 'Hacienda acrecentada', ADL 54, no. 9, no fol., 'Petición que se dió en el consexo', ibid., 25, fols. 6b–7 and 30, and Salazar y Castro, *Los Comendadores de … Santiago*, pp. 146–9 and 631.

71 Copy of *cédula* of 9 Oct. 1599, BL Add Mss 28,426, fol. 152. A fortnight later, Philip raised Borja's countship of Mayalde into a hereditary title; see Fernández de Béthencourt, *Historia genealógica*, iv, p. 199, and *Relaciones*, p. 48.

72 Lerma, 'Imbentario', ADL 53, fol. 28.

73 Ibid., fols. 26b–27; the language used here bears a remarkable similarity to the words of the king himself in a grant to Denia in 1603; see above, p. 43.

74 'TITVLO DE DVQUE DE Lerma, y mayorazgo fundado del, y de otros bienes, por el señor Rey D[on] Felipe Tercero, en 11 de Noviembre del año de 1599', appended to 'FVNDACION DEL Mayorazgo de la villa de Lerma, su jurisdicion, señorío, y vassallage, pechos, y derechos, por el señor Rey de Aragon, D. Fernando, en 18 de Iulio del año de 1412', ADL 12, no fol., a printed copy.

75 Medina Sidonia (1445), Alburquerque (1464), Alba de Tormes and Escalona (1472), Infantado (1475), Segorbe and Villahermosa (1476), Medinaceli (1479), Cardona and Nájera (1482), Híjar and Gandía (1483), Béjar (1485), Frias (1492), Arcos (1493), Luna (1495), Sessa (1507), Veragua (1537), Medina de Rioseco (1538), Alcalá de los Gazules (1558), Osuna (1562), Huesca (1563), Baena (1566), Feria (1567) and Pastrana (1572). This list is based upon my unpublished database of aristocratic titles. For some variation in dates, V. M. Márquez de la Plata and L. Valero de Bernabé, *El Libro de Oro de los Duques*, Madrid, 1994, pp. 441–2.

76 *Relaciones*, p. 55.

77 Ibid., p. 54.

78 He did not, however, feel sufficiently slighted to resign his office, Pedro de Paladiñas to Diego Sarmiento de Acuña, Valladolid, 13 Oct. 1599, RB 11/2140, doc. 111.

79 Title, AGS QC 27; *Relaciones*, p. 49.

80 On Philip II as a patron of the arts, the splendid study by F. Checa, *Felipe II Mecenas de las Artes*, Madrid, 1997. On the Escorial, A. Bustamante García, *La octava maravilla del mundo. Estudio histórico sobre el Escorial de Felipe II*, Madrid, 1994. See also F. Javier Campos y Fernández de Sevilla (ed.), *Felipe II y su época. Actas del Simposium (1) 1/5–ix-1998*, Madrid, 1998, especially F. Chueca Coitia, 'Felipe II y El Escorial', pp. 85–103.

81 Rodríguez-Salgado, 'Honour and Profit in the court of Philip II', p. 76.

82 On the history of Madrid, three outstanding works; *Madrid. Atlas histórico de la ciudad, siglos IX–XIX* (V. Pinto Crespo and S. Madrazo Madrazo, eds.), Madrid and Barcelona, 1995; Fernando Checa (ed.), *El Real Alcázar de Madrid. Dos siglos de arquitectura y coleccionismo en la corte de los Reyes de España*, Madrid, 1994 and A. Alvar Ezquerra, *El nacimiento de una capital europea. Madrid entre 1561 y 1606*, Madrid, 1989. The city remained substantially smaller than Seville, which had 125,000–130,000 people by 1600.

83 *CSPV*, ix, 31 Aug. 1598, no. 728, p. 359.

84 *Gaçeta y Nuevas*, p. 19.

85 C. Jago, 'Habsburg Absolutism and the Cortes of Castile', *AHR*, 86, 1981, pp. 307–26 and I.

A. A. Thompson, 'Crown and Cortes in Castile, 1590–1665', *Parliaments, Estates and Represen-tation*, 2, London, 1982, pp. 29–45. On the *escribanía*, see above, p. 54.

86 Williams, 'Lerma, Old Castile and the Travels of Philip III of Spain', *History*, 73, Oct. 1988, p. 384.

87 *Cnta.* St. 15 April 1603, AGS E 2024, no fol.; *Relaciones*, pp. 75 (quotation), 77–8.

88 *Relaciones*, p. 59; Hayward Keniston, *Francisco de los Cobos, Secretary of the Emperor Charles V*, Pittsburgh, 1959, pp. 159–61 and 291–8; A. Molinié-Bertrand notes that the *adelantamiento* had over 28,000 inhabitants, 'El adelantamiento de Cazorla en el siglo XVI', *CIE*, 1977, i, pp. 7–21. On the rivalry of Lerma and Camarasa, see pp. 70, 172, 178.

89 *Relaciones*, pp. 62, 79–80, 97; on the marriages, p. 177; on the tension between the Sandoval and Enríquez families, Aram, *La reina Juana*, pp. 227–33.

90 Lerma, 'Imbentario', ADL 53, fols. 7–8.

91 Ibid., fols. 3b-5; 'El Estado q[ue] tiene el pleyto que llaman de la recompenssa entre el s[eño]r fiscal del Conss[ej]o con los Duques de Lerma, es el sig[uien]te', AHN *Consejos*, 7258, fol. 1; Domínguez Ortíz, *La Sociedad Española*, p. 364; *Relaciones*, pp. 65, 86, 88–9, 96–7.

92 AMV LA 23, fols. 119r–119v, 8 and 11 July 1600, fols. 112r–112v and 119–119v.

93 Copy of cédula, Valladolid, 13 Aug. 1600, ibid., fol. 130v; copy of Philip's title to Lerma, Valladolid, 6 Aug., ibid., fols. 131r–131v.

94 'Sobre la concesion de los millones', 17 Aug. 1600, ibid., fols. 132v–135r; *Relaciones*, p. 78.

95 *Relaciones*, pp. 93–4. On the architectural history of Valladolid, Bustamante García, *La arquitectura clasicista del Foco Vallisoletano* and Martín González, *La arquitectura domestica del Renacimiento en Valladolid, passim.* On the properties belonging to *San Pablo*, Bennassar, *Valladolid*, p. 370; on the *patronazgo*, Palomares Ibañez, *El Patronato del Duque de Lerma sobre el convento de San Pablo.* I am obliged to P. Palomares Ibáñez O P for his generous advice about the history of the church and monastery of *San Pablo.*

96 See pp. 172, 178.

97 AMV LA 26, fols. 23r–24v, 16 Jan. 1601; see also, fols. 25r–25v, 19 Jan. 1601.

98 Ibid., fols. 20r–20v, 15 Jan. 1601.

99 Philip also conferred on Lerma the *alcaidía* of the royal hunting lodge and woods of the Abrojo, 10 kilometres from Valladolid (12 October). Lerma rounded out his control of Valladolid when in July 1601 he acquired the notaryship in the Chancellery of Valladolid which was responsible for recording the establishment of noble titles (*escribanía de hijosdalgo)*; this enabled him to organise searches in the archives of the Chancellery for documents about his family's past and about disputed landholdings in Castile, 'Hacienda acrecentada', ADL 54 no. 9, no fol.

100 On the plague, B. Bennassar, *Recherches sur les grandes épidémies dans le nord de l'Espagne à la fin du XVIe siècle*, Paris, 1969.

101 Bennassar, *Valladolid*, pp. 27–34, 79–114, 229–53.

102 *Relaciones*, p. 56.

103 Among lesser nobles, the counts of Salinas, Grajal, Colmenar, Vilaflor, Alba de Liste and Ribadavia and the marquises of Viana, Toral, Montealegre and Belmonte also had their own palaces. Adriano Gutiérrez Alonso et al., *Estudio sobre la decadencia de Castilla. La ciudad de Valladolid en el siglo XVII*, Valladolid, 1989, p. 110.

104 Calderón informed the Council that Philip would live in Lerma's palace, AMV LA 26, fols. 99r–99v, 15 Jun. 1601. On the quality of palaces, see, in García Mercadal, *Viajes de Extran-jeros*, ii, Pinheiro da Veiga, 'La corte de Felipe III', p. 132, and Bartolomé Joly, 'Viaje hecho por M. Bartolomé Joly', p. 90.

105 Lerma to Marquis of Poza, Villalpando, 27 January 1601, AGS CJH 293, fol. 224; the city council put guards on the gates to prevent people entering, AMV LA 26, fol. 96, 7 June 1601; Pinheiro da Vega, 'La Corte de Felipe III', in García Mercadal, *Viajes de Extranjeros*, pp. 127–56, at ii, p. 131; *Relaciones*, pp. 95, 96, 97, 103, 104.

106 *CSPV* ix, 16 Dec. 1600, no. 938, p. 437; *Relaciones*, pp. 91–2.

107 J. L. de los Reyes Leoz, 'Evolución de la población, 1561–1857', in *Madrid. Atlas histórico*, eds,

V. Pinto Crespo and S. Madrazo Madrazo, Madrid, 1995, pp. 140–5, at p. 142.
108 'y anda vna cosa en Madrid de maldiciones al duque de Lerma', Diego García de Jove to Diego Sarmiento de Acuña, Madrid, 17 Jan. 1601, RB, 11/2113, doc. 143.
109 'Papel del Cardenal de Toledo … Al Duque de Lerma', Granada, 9 May 1600, BN Mss 4013, fols. 101–104v, a copy.
110 Sepúlveda, *Sucesos del Reinado de Felipe III*, cxxiii, pp. 264–7 and *Relaciones*, p. 94.
111 Appointment, Madrid, 23 Jan. 1601, AGS PR 627, fol. 25.
112 *Relaciones*, p. 95.

4

The Court in Valladolid, 1601–06: the years of the golden keys

King, Queen and Duke

The court remained in Valladolid for five years, until the spring of 1606. These were Lerma's years, during which he exercised almost unfettered control over Philip III and bent much of court, government and Church to his will. It was as an expression of this that in the summer of 1603 the *corregidor* and city councillors of Valladolid presented Lerma with golden keys for the King and himself to a little square behind the royal palace, as if in homage to the power that he held over and within the city.[1] By the end of the residence in Valladolid he had doubled his income, from 86,227 ducats at the end of 1600 to 179,227 by the turn of 1605–06 (Appendix III). He made it his priority to lavish his new wealth on his foundations in and around Valladolid and the hunting lodge that he bought at Ventosilla, 13 kilometres north-west of Aranda de Duero. He was not concerned during these years to build up his properties in his ducal town, confining himself to a surprisingly modest expansion of his castle.

Philip resolved the immediate problems created by his lack of a palace in his new capital by taking over the palace belonging to the Count of Benavente at the western end of the *Plaza de San Pablo*. His first child, Anne, was born there on 21 September 1601, and this may well have concentrated his mind on the need to acquire a palace of his own. He and Lerma found a dramatic solution: on 11 December Lerma sold his new palace to the King. The duke made a very substantial profit; claiming that he had spent over 100,000 ducats on improving the palace during the last twelve months, he charged Philip 186,393 ducats. The King, ever grateful, accepted Lerma's valuation and reserved apartments in the palace for Lerma and his heir that were quite as splendid as his own. He also presented the duke with the governorship of the palace (*alcaidía*) in perpetuity, thereby entitling him to live in the palace whenever he wished without incurring any expense for maintaining it. More importantly, as *alcaide* Lerma could continue to organise much of the daily life of the palace and even control entry into it.[2]

Although no evidence survives to explain Lerma's remarkable volte-face in selling the palace that meant so much to him it is possible to reconstruct his motives with some degree of conviction. Most obviously, his generosity bound the King even more closely to him and afforded him an outrageous profit on his investment. Philip gave two further expressions of his appreciation. On 2 September 1601 he conferred upon Lerma the right to export 15,000 *salmas* of wheat from Sicily free of all excise duties and in November allowed him to purchase the palace on the far bank of the Pisuerga which was known as the *Casa de la Ribera*. The award in Sicily probably had a nominal annual value of about 55,000–60,000 ducats a year.[3] It is likely that Lerma negotiated both the Sicilian grant and the sales of the two palaces as the constituent parts of an agreement with Philip.[4] Moreover, it is probable that the purchase that Lerma made of a hunting-lodge at Ventosilla was also a key part of the agreement that he made with the King.[5]

The *Casa de la Ribera* occupied a commanding position on the banks of the Pisuerga and was less than 2 kilometres from the *Plaza de San Pablo*. However, both the *Casa* and the estate had fallen into disrepair and Lerma acquired them for a paltry 3,000 ducats. He then invested 80,708 ducats within the next five years on reconstructing the *casa* and organising its extensive lands so that it could serve both as a palace and an idyllic rural retreat in which he (and the King) could relax, close to the court but separate from it. The grounds were extensive enough to allow the hunting of small game. Lerma used the *plaza* in front of the *Casa* for tournaments, *juegos de caña* and bull-fights. He also introduced a variant on the bull-fight that he enjoyed in Denia and in Lerma in which the bulls were chased into the river where they were forced in their terror – and to the amusement of spectators – to learn to swim.

The gardens were divided with geometric precision into fourteen square flowerbeds in two parallel lines which were broken by six fountains and decorated by a splendid collections of statues. One of the fountains was particularly celebrated; the duke of Florence sent Lerma a sculpture by Giambologna of '*Samson and Philistine*'.[6] Lerma also planted an orchard, an orange grove and a vineyard. Philip had a wooden gallery built from his own palace down to the river so that he could cross over to it while remaining sheltered from the elements and from his own subjects.[7] For the duke, the acquisition of the *Casa de la Ribera* marked an important psychological development, for it became the first of several houses of retreat that he created for himself: after 1601 he always ensured that he had such a refuge close to the royal palace, both in Valladolid and in Madrid.

Barthélemy Joly, a French visitor, drew a particularly well-observed and rounded portrait of Philip's private and public life in his palace in 1603–04:

He is physically delicate, it is said because of a great illness that his wet-nurse had during his infancy. He rises late and hears mass at midday. He almost always eats in private. At around two or three o'clock in the afternoon he has a light snack with the Queen which is served kneeling down, as if they are divine. The two of them drink a great deal, not wine, but a light water that comes from a well at Alcalá de Henares near Madrid, and which is always brought to wherever they are. They eat around midnight, but without a regular hour. The King's exercise in the morning is to hear mass and to spend about three hours every day in his devotions ... He gives audience to those who have to deal with him. He plays at games, sings music that he composes himself and goes hunting, usually in an enclosed park. He is agreeable, pleasant and a man of great conscience ... As for his affairs, he remits them entirely to the duke of Lerma. His subjects call him '*a great Christian, a holy angel from heaven*'. But a saying goes ... '*an inclement Pope, an innocent king, a forgiving confessor and an insolent duke*'.[8]

Joly's details are confirmed by Sir Charles Cornwallis, the English ambassador, who recorded in 1607 that Philip was called 'the little saint' ('*el Santíto*') by his subjects because he was 'much inclined to devotion and observes his usuall houres with noe little strictness, than if he were ... a man in orders'. Cornwallis added that Philip's subjects were dismayed by his reliance upon Lerma but hoped that he would mature with age 'in the manner of the House of Austria'.[9] Many at court must have shared that hope, while recognising perhaps that the two men were bound together by their deep religiosity.

Philip did not travel far from his new capital city. In 1603–04 (at Lerma's insistence, as will be seen) he spent three months on a state visit to Valencia and in 1605 was away for five months, with a brief tour of Old Castile being extended when the sudden illness of his wife forced him to remain in acute discomfort in the small town of Olmedo for a month. Otherwise, he made short excursions to the Escorial, the Pardo and Aranjuez in the summers of 1602 and 1603. He also visited several of the major towns and cities of Old Castile – Zamora, Toro, Segovia, Ávila, Salamanca, Burgos, Palencia and León – but did not stay long in them, moving on promptly after performing his duties; in 1603, for instance he spent only two days on a visit to Palencia. As *caballerizo mayor*, Lerma organised these journeys, and he used them to emphasise his courtly pre-eminence by carrying the royal sword at the formal entrances into towns and cities.

Since Philip did not have access to his own complex of hunting lodges, he imposed himself on the aristocrats who had estates in the locality.[10] Typical of the hunting trips that he made from Valladolid was the first of them, which he undertook only six days after his entry into the city in 1601:

he left for the forest of San Miguel, which belongs to the Count of Villalonso and is near Toro, in order to go hunting. From there he went via Zamora to Carvajales, which belongs to the Count of Alba, and where there are mountains that are good for hunting and for recreation. He killed three wild boars and many rabbits in the three days that he spent there. The place is 20 leagues from Valladolid. From there he returned by Villalpando, which belongs to the Constable, and went on to Ampudia, which belongs to the Duke of Lerma, and on the first of this month he returned to Valladolid in order to spend Carnival there.[11]

The visit to Ampudia was unusual at this time for Philip spent only 160 days in Lerma's properties while the court was resident in Valladolid – 62 in Lerma and 98 in Ventosilla and Ampudía. The duke was not a generous host to his king. Nor did he encourage the King to return to his old capital: Philip spent less than sixty days in Madrid during these years.[12] But he spent 1061 days in Valladolid itself and its immediate district.

As was customary for a queen approaching her first delivery, in September 1601 Margaret made her Will and Testament. She named Lerma as her chief executor after the King and spoke warmly of her affection for him: 'I implore the Duke, in whose great care and good will I have always [trusted] to see to all my affairs, for I love him and owe him a great deal'.[13] However, when she gave birth in Benavente's palace rather than in Lerma's the nature of her rebuff to the duke was well understood at court.[14] Lerma put a brave face on his disappointment by having Anne baptised in *San Pablo*.[15] Margaret gave birth to a second child on 1 February 1603 but, when the news was passed round the palace that she had again produced a girl, a chilling silence engulfed the building. The child was named María, but she was weak and lived for only a month.[16]

The royal family did, however, expand with the arrival at court in August 1603 of the three eldest sons of the duke of Savoy. Charles-Emmanuel had demonstrated his determination to be independent of Spanish power in a crisis over the strategically vital marquisate of Saluzzo in 1601, and his three sons – Philip-Emmanuel (the Prince of Piedmont and heir to the duchy), Victor Amadeo, and Philibert-Emmanuel – were brought to Spain to guarantee their father's good conduct in the future. Lerma ensured that he had control over the households of the princes by ordering that they were to be established under Spanish etiquette and that all of the servants of the princes were to be Spanish rather than Savoyard.[17]

Charles-Emmanuel's frustration at having his sons live in Spain was tempered by his hope that one of them might succeed to the Spanish throne if Philip's line died out. However, when Margaret's pregnancies made it evident that this would not happen, Charles-Emmanuel began once again to assert his independence of his brother-in-law. Within months of the birth of the future Philip IV, Charles-Emmanuel deeply offended Philip by neglecting to consult him when he agreed to marry his daughter María to the heir of the Duke of

Mantua.[18] By February 1606 the Council of State was becoming anxious that – as Miranda put it – Charles-Emmanuel was showing 'little respect' towards Philip.[19]

The Duke and his city

Lerma's great building programme in and around Valladolid was financed by what was almost certainly the most generous single grant made by a Habsburg monarch to a subject. Lerma proved unable to exploit his export rights on the 15,000 *salmas de trigo* in Sicily, and on 1 September 1603 Philip took the grant back into the royal patrimony and compensated the duke with 72,000 ducats of rents and *juros* in the territories of the Crown of Aragon: 10,000 ducats of rent were on the mainland in Aragon and Catalonia, 32,000 ducats in the rents of Naples and 30,000 in those of Sicily.[20] Only sixteen aristocrats in Spain had incomes that exceeded 72,000 ducats per annum at this time and the average of the 118 incomes recorded by Núñez de Salcedo in 1595 was only 34,732 ducats, barely more than half the value of the award. The grant brought Lerma's income to about 170,227 ducats a year, ten times as much as it had been at the accession of Philip III only five years earlier. By the time that the grant was confiscated from him by Philip IV in 1621 he had earned 1,296,000 ducats from it, enough to pay for most of his building works in Lerma, Valladolid and Madrid and their environs (see Appendix III).

Secure in his wealth, Lerma now began to spend with unbridled enthusiasm, ploughing his new riches into properties and into furnishings with which to embellish them. In addition to the 80,708 ducats that he spent on the *Casa de la Ribera* in the years 1601–06 Lerma committed 138,575 ducats to rebuilding the church of *San Pablo*, 6,116 ducats to the convent of *Nuestra Señora de Belén* and 15,825 ducats to the monastery of *San Diego* (which was built within the grounds of the royal palace). In the years of the residence of the court in Valladolid, therefore, Lerma spent 241,224 ducats on his buildings in the city, at an average of 48,245 ducats annually. Two-thirds of this amount (160,516 ducats) went on his ecclesiastical foundations.

No less than 95 per cent of the 160,516 ducats were spent on reconstructing and furnishing the monastery-church of *San Pablo*. In the decade after 1607 Lerma committed a further 9,965 ducats, bringing his total expenditure on the church to 148,540 ducats. He also vested 3,000 ducats of his own rents (capital value: 60,000 ducats) to provide the maintenance of the church and its personnel. In a deeply symbolic gesture, Lerma brought the bones of Diego Gómez, the founder of the greatness of his family, from Aguilar to be re-interred in *San Pablo* at the end of 1602.[21] He then began the great rebuilding programme; he spent 73,443 ducats on doubling the height of the church by adding a baroque upper-half to the Isabelline façade, and on building the two bell towers with their inscriptions identifying his purposes in taking on the *patron-azgo* and on refurbishing the church. He committed a further 24,200 ducats to building choirstalls and presented gifts of sacred vessels valued at 32,747 ducats so that the divine services could be celebrated with appropriate splendour. He spent 2,150 ducats on creating the chapel of *San Miguel* and 16,000 ducats on funerary statues of Catalina and himself. He further identified his ownership of *San Pablo* by displaying his family crest no fewer than fifty-two times on the façade of the church, inside it and on the posts marking its limits.[22]

Lerma's commitment to supporting the Dominicans was generously acknowledged by Pope Clement VIII when he allowed the Order to name Lerma and his heirs as the patron of its Spanish Province (31 July 1603). Lerma vested 1,000 ducats of rent in *juros* to fund the provincial chapter and his *patro-nazgo* was confirmed on 5 June 1605 in the Chapter of the province held in *San Pablo* that coincided with the baptism of the future Philip IV.[23]

Lerma paid further homage to the memory of Diego Gómez by acquiring the patronage of the Bernardine convent of *Nuestra Señora de Belén* in Valladolid, which incorporated one of the houses in which Diego Gómez had lived (5 June 1601). This was a small foundation, supporting only six nuns, and Lerma paid 9,329 ducats for it.[24]

Lerma created his first major ecclesiastical foundation outside Valladolid at another ancestral property, in Ampudia, where he spent 12,000 ducats transforming his family's fine church into a teaching college. This was substantial and prestigious endowment, supporting thirty-three churchmen, but it came cheaply to the duke, for Clement VIII made 9,000 ducats available from the annual income of selected benefices to pay for the cost of maintaining the clergy.[25] Lerma committed only 1,000 ducats of rent (capital value: 20,000 ducats) to the project and so the Pope supported 90 per cent of the costs of the endowment.

At the end of April 1601 Lerma took Philip to the hamlet of Ventosilla in the wooded hills 13 kilometres north-west of Aranda de Duero. Ventosilla had formed part of the patrimony of Diego Gómez I and Lerma must have been alarmed when Philip decided to acquire it to create the hunting-lodge that he needed near his new capital. Lerma was able to persuade Philip to let him retain it and to buy up the lands around it: in all likelihood, the negotiations for the purchase of Ventosilla formed part of the deal for the sale of the Camarasa palace but no evidence directly makes the link. Certainly, Lerma made an enormous investment in the property; he spent 184,347 ducats on rebuilding and furnishing the lodge. He did so, moreover, with the same intensity that he showed in re-creating the *Casa de la Ribera;* by the time that Philip stayed there in the autumn of 1604 Ventosilla had already acquired the reputation of being one of the best country houses in Castile. The grounds were extensive enough for Lerma and the King to hunt game and also to have orchards planted in them. But as much as it was a hunting lodge, Ventosilla was also a place of spiritual retreat for Lerma, and he covered its walls with religious rather than secular paintings.[26]

Lerma rounded out the hunting and fishing facilities that Ventosilla provided by purchasing some small properties in Gumiel de Mercado and in the valley of the Esgueva. These were significant acquisitions, giving him lordship over 5,400 or so inhabitants, half of them in Gumiel. However, he erected no buildings in these properties. He now had an urban palace in the *Casa de la Ribera* and a hunting lodge and rural retreat at Ventosilla, and two major ecclesiastical foundations, the Church of *San Pablo* in Valladolid and the collegial church at Ampudia. The King of Spain did not have a complex of secular and religious possessions around his capital city, but the Duke of Lerma did.

The walled town of Lerma perched splendidly on a hill some 40 metres high overlooking the River Arlanza. Its castle, small and rustic, was quite inadequate for Lerma's new status and in March 1601 he began to enlarge it. His plans were very modest and since the new house (the 'Casa del Castillo') was very similar to the apartments he was adding to Denia it is probable that he was simply replicating in Lerma what he had done in Denia. Francisco de Mora, the King's architect, designed the new house and work began in March 1603; it was – characteristic of Lerma's building projects – to be completed 'with the greatest brevity'.[27]

Lerma spent about 20,000 ducats a year on improving his properties in Lerma. He seems to have committed most of this to creating a great park which stretched from the castle to the riverbank, filling it with fruit trees and stocking the woodlands with rabbits for the hunt. He eventually incorporated seven hermitages into the park so that he could give himself over to religious reflection while he moved around: as at the *Casa de la Ribera* and in the lodge at Ventosilla, he was carefully creating a rural and spiritual retreat for himself. He built waterworks to raise the water 42 metres from the river to the palace and created a large lake and filled it with trout and ornamental fish; he would be able to indulge his pleasure of fishing in his own lake.[28]

Not until the court was on the point of returning to its old capital did Lerma undertake to create a substantial palace in his ducal town. In October 1605 he signed a contract for 'the construction of the chief house' with Francisco de Mora.[29] It is doubtful whether he yet conceived of the transformation that he would bring about in the town into what Luis Cervera Vera has called in his magnificent study of the town, 'the greatest urban and private space created thus far in Spain'.[30] That dramatic expansion would not take place until the years 1613–17.

It was characteristic of the diffidence of Lerma's building programme in Lerma during the years of the residence of the court in Valladolid that the first two religious foundations in the town were created by female relatives.[31] Lerma's daughter-in-law Mariana, Duchess of Cea, founded the Franciscan convent of *La Ascensión de Nuestro Señor* in 1604; it became popularly known as the 'Convent of *Santa Clara*' and was completed in 1616. In truth, it was a foundation for ladies of the high aristocracy; daughters of the Count of Miranda, the Marquis of Alcañices and the Duke of Béjar all took their vows there. Lerma had quarters here and a *tribuna* so that he could assist at services. He presented the convent with a *Cristo Yacente* of Gregorio Fernández, and Queen Margaret endowed it with a relic of the Blood of Christ. Paintings by Bartolomé Carducho hung on the walls.[32] The second foundation was created by Lerma's sister Leonor, Countess of Altamira, who built the convent of *San Francisco de los Reyes* in spacious lands to the west of the town in 1606; it was finished in 1613 and had a complement of fifteen nuns.

Lerma's first religious foundation in Lerma – and the only one to which he committed himself during the years 1601–06 – was the construction of the Carmelite convent of *La Madre de Dios*. He created this in homage to the piety of his *consuegra*, Luisa de Padilla y Acuña, dowager countess of Santa Gadea. On being widowed on the death of the *Adelantado* in 1602, Luisa had retired into a Carmelite convent in Talavera de la Reina. Lerma built and endowed the convent of *La Madre de Dios* opposite the main gate of the town so that Luisa could become the first prioress. He provided lands for a substantial walled garden and proudly displayed the crests of the Sandoval and de la Cerda families on the façade. It was a substantial endowment: the duke spent 20,700 ducats on the convent and church and presented the nuns with rents worth 1,000 ducats per year for their maintenance (capital value: 20,000 ducats). He was generous with his gifts of silver, jewels, ornaments and pictures. He reserved for himself the right to name six nuns for the house. The convent was dedicated in the presence of the royal couple and the *infanta* Anne on 5 July 1608, and was formally opened in September 1616.[33] The three foundations that were begun in Lerma, therefore, during the years of the residence of the court in Valladolid were brought to fruition in the years 1613–16 – exactly at the time that Lerma was embarking on the enormous building programme that transformed his ducal town.

Lerma at fifty: the public face and the view of self

Lerma passed his fiftieth birthday in 1603. He was now at the height of his powers but descriptions of him at this time draw a contrast between his commanding authority at court and the splendid restraint that characterised the personality that he presented to the world. Nowhere is this more true than in the portrait of him written in 1603 by Jerónimo de Sepúlveda, a friar of the Escorial. Sepúlveda observed that Lerma enjoyed a *privanza* with the King such as had not been seen 'for many centuries' and noted that the duke controlled all the affairs of government 'as he wished'. Indeed, the friar suggested that 'we can say that we have two kings in Spain'. Many at court resented Lerma's power, but Sepúlveda addressed himself to the central problem created by the existence of an all-powerful favourite by observing – with the very greatest reluctance – that 'if someone has to rule the King I hold it better that it should be the Duke of Lerma than anyone else', since Lerma's personal qualities were so exceptional; he was a true gentleman, magnanimous and wise, and no one who spoke to him was ever angered by him. 'Above all', observed friar Sepúlveda, Lerma was 'a very great courtier', generous of spirit and calm.[34] The qualities of the courtier were also emphasised by Sir Charles Cornwallis, writing at the beginning of 1608: 'in all the whole course of his life, he shewes much temperance and little pompe, exceeding courteous and affable to all such as have accesse to him, and seldome gives discontenting or bitter answer to anie suitor that repayres to him, and if anie he doe, he soe sugars it over with softe words as though the denyall give a wound …'.[35]

Tomé Pinheiro da Veiga observed Lerma closely during his visit to court in 1605 and has left us a beguiling and detailed portrait of him. He characterised him as an elegant courtier, 'blessed equally with gifts of body and soul' who dressed magnificently and was surrounded by a host of servants. He was a man of presence and of good character who made a favourable impression on all who dealt with him, and Pinheiro observed – as so many observers did – that very few people left Lerma's presence discontented with him. Waspishly, however, the Portuguese added that in reality it was proverbially difficult to gain access to Lerma and that the admiration in which people held him would have been considerably enhanced if only he made himself more available for audiences; some important people had to wait two or three months to see him. Pinheiro emphasised the point by regaling his readers with the story of a soldier who was asked by the King why he had come to see him; the man replied that 'if I was able to speak to the duke I would not have come to see Your Majesty'. It was indeed Lerma's control over the King and the wealth that he accumulated as a result that remained his most enduring quality. Pinheiro wondered whether Spain had ever seen a richer man than Lerma and noted that 'every day the king makes him an award'.[36]

Lerma used his new wealth to build up his first great collection of paint-ings.[37] Sarah Schroth has calculated from the inventories of Lerma's collection that he displayed 890 pictures at the *Casa de la Ribera*.[38] Two influences lay at the core of Lerma's artistic taste. He had known Juan Pantoja de la Cruz throughout his adult life; Pantoja had been born in Valladolid in 1553, and was therefore an exact contemporary of Lerma himself. The duke commissioned Pantoja to paint the portraits of Catalina and himself that are today in the *Museo Tavera* in Toledo. More substantively, Lerma's taste had been moulded by his admiration for the great collection of Philip II in the Escorial and the Alcázar in Madrid. He shared Philip II's reverence for the work of Hieronymous Bosch and the great Titian; he owned five paintings by Bosch and at least two master-pieces from Titian, the *Ecce Homo* and the *Supper at Emmaus*. He also collected or commissioned at least nineteen copies of works by Titian, including Pantoja's admirable version of the great equestrian portrait of Charles V in 1547 that is known as the 'Mühlberg portrait' and which is now one of the glories of the Prado Museum. Pinheiro da Veiga observed that the walls of the *Casa* were hung with the works of some of the greatest masters – 'the houses ... are all full of the most beautiful pictures that there are in Spain, and many of them are origi-nals of (Raphael), Michelangelo, Titian, Leonardo, Mantegna and many other more modern artists'.

On 13 May 1603 the Flemish painter Peter Paul Rubens arrived in Vallad-olid as ambassador extraordinary of the Duke of Mantua. He announced his genius to the court with a portrait of the King, and Lerma so admired the work that he commissioned an equestrian portrait of himself from the artist. This was a daring choice of subject because the equestrian portrait was a royal genre, in which the king's mastery of the horse was a metaphor for his control of the state and his command of the arts of war. Lerma had no significant military experience but his decision to have himself portrayed on horseback could be justified not merely as an aristocratic conceit but also by reference to two great offices which he held: he had of course been the King's *caballerizo mayor* since 1598, and on 1 May 1603 Philip appointed him as *capitán general de la caballería de España* (Captain General of the Cavalry of Spain). This dignity had no real purpose other than to confer substantial military prestige upon Lerma (and to provide him with a salary of 12,000 ducats), but it neatly complemented his status as *caballerizo mayor* and Rubens emphasised the duality of Lerma's offices by having the horse ride towards the viewer rather than being portrayed sideways-on as was traditionally the case.[39] The great stallion therefore became a protagonist of the painting, almost as important as the duke himself. Lerma was depicted as a nobleman and a warrior, dressed in a breast-plate, with the Order of Santiago hanging proudly around his neck, carrying the baton that was the symbol of his office of *capitán general de la caballería* and wearing the spurs that symbolised his position as *caballerizo mayor*. Rubens added gravity to the portrait by showing that Lerma's hair was beginning to grey at the temples – a subject about which the duke himself was rather sensitive. The cavalry of Spain that Lerma commanded so elegantly charged gallantly in the lower distance, around the feet of his horse.[40] Rubens's picture was to be the finest of the portraits done of Lerma, and the most telling, for it emphasised that Lerma saw himself in these early years of the reign as a man of war as well as a Christian knight and courtier, leading the King's search for his great victory.

As part of his reconstruction of the church of *San Pablo*, Lerma commissioned a set of four alabaster funerary statues of members of the Sandoval family – of himself and his wife and of the two admired kinsmen who had risen to archbishoprics, Cristóbal de Rojas of Seville and Bernardo de Sandoval y Rojas of Toledo. The reference to the two groups of statues of the families of Charles V and of Philip II that Pompeo Leoni had created in the Escorial was explicit and unmistakeable. Indeed, Lerma originally tried to persuade Leoni to produce the statues. However, perhaps because the sculptor was now too old to carry out the work, Lerma commissioned the distinguished silversmith Juan de Arfe Villafañe to carry out the commission. Arfe in turn brought in Lesmes Fernández del Moral to help him and Leoni agreed to provide some technical guidance.

The statues of Lerma and Catalina were finished in 1606. Both were kneeling in prayer. Lerma was once again dressed in armour, with his vizier by his side, resplendent in the cape of Santiago; the sword that undoubtedly formed part of the statue has been lost. A loving husband, a devout Catholic, a soldier of valour and a gentleman of the leading Spanish military order: Lerma's statue remains the defining image of his perception of self, emphasising his pre-eminence among the aristocratic and courtly elite of Spain.[41] Catalina was portrayed as an elegant and devout lady, a woman of great rank and deep piety. In the inscription that he placed by the statues Lerma expressed the range of motives that inspired his life (and, indeed, his exercise of the *valimiento):*

> To God, our greatest hope. Francisco, Duke of Lerma, head of the illustrious family of Sandoval, and dedicated entirely to the service of the very great monarch, Philip III, and exceedingly decorated by [him] through his royal magnificence; serving [him] with the greatest fidelity and gratitude to God, the king and author of all favours and prostrated before [Him] ... Bearing death in mind and while in good and robust health, [he] ordered that this monument be created for himself and for his wife the Duchess Catalina de la Cerda, *camarera mayor* of the most holy Queen Margaret, and also for his children and heirs. Year of 1604.[42]

The first challenge: the Marchioness del Valle, 1603–04

Catalina did not live to see the statues. By the end of 1602 it was evident that she was terminally ill with what seems to have been cancer of the bowels. She and Lerma drew up and signed their joint will and testament on 4 April 1603. On 2 June, Catalina died in Buitrago. In distressing circumstances, her body was brought to *San Pablo*, where a splendid burial service took place; it was organised by Lerma's treasurer, Tomás de Ángulo.[43] Lerma was so deeply shocked at the loss of his beloved wife that he obtained permission from the Pope to enter the Jeronimite order at a time of his own choosing and with dispensation from the requirements of the novitiate. It was the first indication during the years of his *valimiento* that he was still thinking of retiring into religious life. However, he was not yet ready to leave court and did not push the issue with Philip, who in any event refused to let him retire.[44]

The will and testament of Lerma and Catalina provided for the establishment of *mayorazgos* for their sons. Diego Gómez's *mayorazgo* was to be worth 20,000 ducats annually, and although he was only to inherit it after Lerma's death his prospects were sufficiently well established now for his father to negotiate a marriage for him with Luisa de Mendoza, the heiress of Ana de Mendoza, IV duchess of Infantado. Luisa's father, Rodrigo de Mendoza, had died before her mother had inherited the title, and when Ana remarried, to Juan Hurtado de Mendoza, it was he who assumed the title of VI duke. Until Luisa inherited the Infantado title, she and Diego Gómez were to be known as the counts of Saldaña; one of the titles that had been confiscated from Diego Gómez I in the fifteenth century was to be enjoyed by Lerma's son. Once again, Lerma made explicit to everyone at court the advantages that accrued at the highest levels of the court to those who allied themselves to him: the VI duke of Infantado was appointed as a *gentilhombre de la cámara* and a councillor of State. As a further reward, Infantado's fractious brother Francisco, Admiral of Aragon, was released from imprisonment.[45]

When Catalina's health finally collapsed in the spring of 1603 Lerma had her replaced as the Queen's *camarera mayor* by his sister Catalina, the dowager countess of Lemos.[46] The cavalier fashion in which the duke effectively converted the queen's *camarería mayor* into a Sandoval fief was deeply resented by Margaret. Moreover, the appointment was part of a programme through which Lerma reasserted his control over the major organs of Church and State. In February 1603 he had secured the appointment of Dr Juan Bautista de Acevedo as Inquisitor General and in April had the Count of Lemos appointed as President of the Council of Indies (at the age of twenty-seven).[47] In May Lerma himself was raised to the dignity of *capitán general de la caballería de España*, which further enhanced his standing at court and conferred significant – if, frankly, spurious –

military prestige upon him. His position at court now appeared unassailable.

Lerma was deeply attached to his sister, but he knew well enough, as did everyone at court, that she was a domineering and abrasive character. Certainly, Catalina announced her return with a stunningly grand entrance at the Escorial, which friar Sepúlveda considered to have been without precedent.[48] Lerma must surely have calculated – planned, even – that Catalina would come into conflict with doña Magdalena de Guzmán, Marchioness del Valle, *aya* of the *infanta* Anne, who was perhaps the most tempestuous of the ladies of the court.[49] In September, Catalina withdrew from del Valle her right to sleep in Anne's bedchamber. Furious, del Valle demanded to be allowed to retire from court. Her wish was granted with brutal alacrity: Pedro de Franqueza, Count of Villalonga, and Lerma's most trusted man of business, ordered her to leave the palace within three hours.

Worse soon followed for the Marchioness; on 11 December she was arrested by *alcalde de casa y corte* Silva de Torres. There could now be no misunderstanding the nature of the conflict in which del Valle was involved, for Silva de Torres was a trusted *hechura* of Lerma's, and had indeed been introduced into his service through his close friendship with Villalonga. Moreover, the very day on which del Valle was arrested was chosen with fastidious care, for Philip had left Madrid on 10 December for his state visit to Valencia: once again – as he had done, for instance in 1599 in his attacks upon Rodrigo Vázquez de Arce and the Count of Benavente – Lerma moved against an opponent when he was on the road with the King.[50]

No explanation for del Valle's disgrace was made public and the affair remained shrouded in mystery. However, in a series of twenty-six letters written early in 1604 a Flemish merchant named James van Castre gave informed and detailed accounts of the affair.[51] Van Castre reported that the dowager Countess of Lemos had challenged del Valle's influence with the royal couple as soon as she had become *camarera mayor*, and that del Valle had complained to Margaret that Lerma's dominance over Philip meant that he was not a real king but merely the image of one. Margaret dutifully reported this to Philip who, furious, passed it on to Lerma. The duke then confronted del Valle, who claimed that the words were Margaret's and not her own. Lerma rebuked the Queen and had del Valle expelled from court.

A few days after Silva de Torres arrested del Valle he imprisoned her niece, Ana de Mendoza, who was a lady-in-waiting to the Queen. It was now evident that the leading members of the Queen's circle were being picked off one by one. Van Castre wrote of the hatred that Margaret had for Lerma and described her as 'the centre' of the 'mass of turmoil'.[52] What was at issue now was not merely the fate of the Marchioness del Valle but the welling hostility between the Queen of Spain and her husband's *valido*.

Margaret's resentment of Lerma's dominance of her husband was compounded by her anger at the methodical manner in which he had seized control of her own household. In 1599, of course, he had the Duchess of Gandía replaced as Margaret's *camarera mayor* by his wife and in 1603 he imposed his sister in her place. He had also had Pedro Franqueza named as Margaret's private secretary in August 1602. The dismissal of del Valle was a final humiliating rebuff to Margaret and it came, moreover, at the end of a traumatic year for the Queen; her second child, María, had died on 1 February and the Empress María, her compatriot and chief supporter, on 26 February. On 10 September she had begun a miscarriage in public at a court *fiesta*. Most distressing of all: when Philip was preparing to leave for Valencia, Margaret begged Lerma to allow her to travel with her husband and had been rebuffed.[53] She never forgave the duke for the distress and humiliations that he had imposed on her. By the turn of 1603–04, Margaret had become an implacable opponent to Lerma, determined to break his hold over her husband and his control of her own household.

The most important information provided by van Castre makes it evident that the dismissal of del Valle had come about when Lerma discovered that she was involved in a wide-ranging conspiracy against him which involved some of the greatest figures in the land. Van Castre recorded that del Valle had formed an alliance – 'a most straight league of friendship'[54] – with, among others, the Count of Miranda and the Constable of Castile. It is on Miranda's role that van Castre's evidence is most interesting, and indeed most tantalising, for no other source associated him with the attempt to overthrow Lerma. Van Castre recorded that Miranda was offered generous terms to resign the presidency of the Council of Castile and that when he refused to do so it was decided to leave him in office until another opportunity presented itself to remove him: Miranda was, as van Castre put it, 'too great a fly to be taken in a cobweb'.[55] Moreover, having dismissed one president of the Council of Castile in 1599, Lerma – and perhaps even Philip himself – dared not risk the scandal of removing another one only four years later.

The Constable of Castile was not allowed to remain at court. In November, he was despatched to Brussels to reform the Army of Flanders, with instructions to then proceed to England to make peace with James I. He did not return to court until the end of 1605. He was rewarded with grants of money and a councillorship of State and – exceptionally – was allowed to retain the presidency of the Council of Italy during his absence. Indeed, Lerma ordered that the dispositions that the Constable had made for the government of the Council of Italy were to be observed 'to the letter'. The generosity of the settlement and the warmth of Lerma's support attracted no immediate comment at court. They should have done, for the Constable was the brother of the Duchess of Gandía, who had been so cruelly dismissed as Margaret's *camarera mayor* in 1599.

The Constable and Lerma were divided over two other issues. The Constable made no secret of his resentment that Lerma had taken over many of the ceremonial duties that pertained to him with his ancestral office of *copero mayor*.[56] Moreover, he stood in the forefront of those who wanted to carry on the wars in northern Europe and, bluff and tactless – as van Castre put it, 'a stout and free spirit'[57] – he regularly gave vent to his views. To be called upon to negotiate a peace with England was therefore humiliating for him. However, he was acutely aware that he needed to retain the royal grace in the hope of rebuilding his family's wealth, which had suffered a dramatic decline during the sixteenth century (Appendix I). Having failed to overthrow Lerma, the Constable was therefore painfully conscious of the need to reach an accommodation with him: Lerma had his hold over him.[58]

Van Castre also recorded that don Juan Hurtado de Mendoza, Marquis of San Germán, was involved in the conspiracy. This must have been wounding to Lerma, for not only was the Marquis his kinsman but he had advanced him to be a Gentleman of the King's Chamber (1599) and his own lieutenant in the cavalry of Spain (1603). Quite what San Germán hoped to gain from conspiring against his master is not clear; perhaps he simply fell under the spell of the Marchioness. On the discovery of the conspiracy, he too was sent away from court, appointed as *capitán general de la caballería de Portugal*.[59] It was not the last time that San Germán would embarrass his patron; as Marquis of la Hinojosa – a title to which he was raised in 1612 – he played a key role in discrediting Lerma by the incompetence with which he served as Governor of Milan.[60] His career was marked by an egregious impetuousness: in 1603 he demonstrated this for the first time. He also became one of the first of Lerma's kinsmen or *hechuras* to demonstrate how the great patron could be damaged by men to whom he had given his trust and confidence.

The journey to Valencia and the dukedom of Cea

When Lerma uncovered the conspiracy of the Marchioness del Valle he seems to have intended to have the King undertake a state visit to Portugal. In September 1602 Lerma led a *junta* which urged Philip to travel to Portugal to deal with the growing crisis in the kingdom (which had not seen its king since Philip II departed in 1583). The King approved the journey for November but did not go, and in December the Council of War advised him that the situation in Portugal was so grave that it could only be worsened 'by a rebellion' and that it was imperative that he visit the kingdom. Philip was eager to go; in February 1603 he asserted that 'the more I think about it, the more necessary I believe my journey to Portugal to be'.[61] Within a few days Lerma announced that the

King would be 'going to Portugal for the whole of April'.[62] In November 1603 the Council of State unanimously urged Philip to visit Portugal; once again, the King agreed. However, within weeks Lerma announced that Philip would be making a state visit not to Portugal but to Valencia.[63]

The reasons for the decision to visit Valencia were Lerma's. In the spring of 1603 Philip had extended Lerma's concession on the tunny-fishing rights of Valencia to the whole of the eastern coast, and Lerma was determined to have the cortes of Valencia validate the grant so that it could never be taken from his family. Even more substantively, Lerma was determined that the cortes should ratify all grants that had been made to his family in the kingdom of Valencia since the establishment of its *mayorazgo* in 1431; Philip III's state visit to Valencia was designed so that the Duke of Lerma could organise his family's affairs in the east – to mark, in other words, Lerma's determination to wind down his commitments in the east so that he could concentrate on his interests in Old Castile. Indeed, it was announced that the cortes would meet in Denia rather than in the capital city, as if the primary purpose of the royal visit was to conduct Lerma's family business rather than to deal with affairs of state.[64]

The King arrived in the city of Valencia on Christmas Eve. Lerma retreated from his intention to hold the cortes in Denia – probably to save himself expense – and the cortes opened in the city of Valencia on 9 January. The members voted a record *servicio* of 400,000 *lliures* and donated 50,000 *lliures* to the ministers who had assisted in its deliberations; 15,000 – the largest amount, naturally – went to Lerma.

The real justification for holding the cortes of Valencia now became evident. Philip agreed to the request of the cortes that all grants that the crown had made to the Sandoval family since 1431 should be confirmed in perpetuity. Moreover, to ensure that the arrangement was smoothly supervised, he appointed Lerma's brother Juan, Marquis of Villamizar, to the viceroyalty of the kingdom; there could be no doubt now that the duke's affairs in Valencia would be properly managed.

Even the advancement of Lerma's brother to the viceroyalty of Valencia was dwarfed by the elevation of his son to a dukedom when Cristóbal became Duke of Cea – and when, therefore, the Sandovals became the only family in Spain in which father and son both held dukedoms. The documentation for the creation of the dukedom has not survived and so the date during the *jornada de Valencia* when Cristóbal was raised to the title cannot be precisely established. The new dukedom had as its core the town of Cea in León and twenty-six *lugares* which had formed part of the original Lerma *mayorazgo* and which were now given by Lerma to his son. Philip departed from the city of Valencia on 21 February but for the first time on a journey of state, Lerma travelled separately from him, ostensibly because of his ill-health but probably as a stratagem to begin the process of grooming his son to begin taking a substantial role in the King's household.[65]

Lerma's income from his eastern properties was now 21,500 ducats, nearly three times greater than it had been in 1598, but he had no ambitions to further extend it. On leaving the city, he presented his town house in Denia to the Carmelite nuns. He never returned to the east. His destiny – and that of his family – lay in Castile.

By the time that the King returned to Madrid (10 March 1604), the judges in the case of the Marchioness del Valle had ordered that she be imprisoned in the fortress-archive of Simancas. This verdict carried terrifying implications for the Marchioness, for incarceration in Simancas was traditionally inflicted upon people who had offended seriously against the majesty of the crown. However, when the sentence was handed down in February 1605 it proved to be fairly innocuous: del Valle and Ana de Mendoza were exiled to Logroño during the King's pleasure. Once again, Lerma was careful not to push an opponent – and her powerful family and supporters – too far.

The case of the Marchioness did, however, create serious tension within Lerma's *clientela*, for Gaspar de Córdoba rebuked Lerma for his conduct towards del Valle. Fray Gaspar died (2 June) before he could pursue his objections and Lerma, confident of the completeness of his power, had his own confessor, fray Diego de Mardones, appointed to succeed him as Philip's confessor.[66] But as Lerma demonstrated yet again his apparently effortless command of the royal grace, he failed to realise that he had provided the King with a confessor who had the deepest hostility towards his two most trusted confidants, Rodrigo Calderón and the Count of Villalonga, and who was, moreover, an accomplished and sophisticated politician. Lerma had withstood – swept aside, even – the attack on him by the Queen and the impetuous Marchioness del Valle and her allies: he would find it much harder to deal with the sustained challenge posed by a confessor to the King, especially when Mardones, too, made an alliance with the Queen. Once again, an assault on Lerma would be mounted by a man who had made his career within his *clientela*.

Return of the court to Madrid

Almost from the beginning of the residence in Valladolid, Lerma indicated that the court would not be away from Madrid indefinitely. Indeed, he replicated exactly with the old capital the manoeuvres that he had taken with Valladolid in 1600. On 2 June 1602, at the request of the city council of Madrid, Philip endowed Lerma with a councillorship which carried the first vote in the council after the *corregidor*. He also vested the privilege in perpetuity in Lerma's *mayorazgo* so that it would pass in time to his descendants.[67] Lerma had three properties in Madrid – a town house near the church of San Ginés, three rather ramshackle houses in the *Plaza de las Descalzas Reales* and a small palace with gardens off the Prado San Jerónimo that he knew as the '*huerta*' ('gardens').[68] It is evident from the testamentary provisions that Lerma made with his dying wife in 1603 that he intended at this time to subsume the *huerta* into the *mayorazgo* of Diego Gómez. However, by the spring of 1604 he had decided to build a palace not for his son but for himself; on 20 April 1604 he began the process of buying up properties around it when he paid Pedro Álvarez Pereira 12,000 ducats for his palace adjacent to the *huerta*.[69] The city council generously presented him with parcels of land that would enable him to build a *plaza* in front of the new palace.[70]

When the court returned to Madrid, Lerma would need a network of lodges and houses around the capital, and in 1602 he began the process of acquiring these by paying the Marquis of Auñón 45,290 ducats for the small town of Valdemoro, which had 600 inhabitants, 22 kilometres south of the capital and half-way between Madrid and Aranjuez. He then began one of his most ambitious and expensive building projects, spending 128,280 ducats on a complex that incorporated a small palace, a *plaza* and the church. Revealingly, in describing his purposes in buying and developing Valdemoro, Lerma reproduced the phrase that he had used about Ventosilla in 1601 – that he had bought it so that it could be used as 'a place of recreation' for Philip.[71] Valdemoro would provide the ideal stopping-off place for the King as he moved into and out of Madrid on the southern road. As he had done in Valladolid, so now in the environs of Madrid Lerma was creating a complex of properties adjacent to the capital city. Once again, he was preparing with cool calculation to move the court of Spain.

On Good Friday (9 April) 1605 Margaret was delivered of her third child, and to the unrestrained delight of King and court it was a boy. Despite the solemnity of the day the bells sounded joyously to mark the birth of the first male child to a sovereign since Philip III himself had been born in 1578. The celebrations, as we have seen, marked an apogee in the expression of Lerma's power in Court, State and Church.[72] After the official festivities were concluded, the duke took Philip and Margaret to Lerma to relax: bulls were run, jousting tournaments were held and a number of religious celebrations took place [27 June–31 July]. Lerma did not, however, pay for the celebrations; the royal exchequer spent 76,000 ducats on the expenses of the progress, and once again it was Muriel de Valdivielso who controlled the accounts.[73]

Philip returned to Valladolid on 7 September and spent only nine days there before leaving on 16 September for a brief progress to the monastery of the Escorial. However, he was detained for nearly four weeks in Olmedo when Margaret fell seriously ill. Not until the end of November did the King take up residence again in Valladolid: he had been away for nearly five months.[74] The most serious problem awaiting him was the need to respond to the news of the attempt by English Catholics to blow up Parliament with James I inside. Philip was genuinely horrified by the attempt on the life of a fellow monarch and especially so a few months after he had personally ratified a treaty of peace with James. After long meetings of the Council of State it was decided that Lerma himself would visit the English ambassador to offer congratulations on James's escape and that he would be followed by all the members of the Council. There was intense relief when James absolved foreign powers from complicity in the plot. The new amity between Spain and England had survived, although the English Catholics suffered renewed and systematic persecution.[75]

The capital city to which Philip returned was unpleasant and overcrowded. Valladolid now housed twice as many people ($c.60,000$) as it had done in 1601.[76] Pinheiro da Veiga described it as an intolerable place in which to live, the overcrowding aggravated by the stench caused by the rivers which coursed through the city.[77] As early as the spring of 1604 the Council of State had to address the problems created by the influx of people into the city.[78] Several members of Lerma's *clientela* had the shortcomings of the capital city impressed upon them. Pedro Franqueza (who had been raised to the countship of Villalonga in 1603) was ordered to investigate the causes of the spread of disease in the city.[79] Sarmiento de Acuña, as *corregidor*, received many complaints about the dirtiness of the city.[80] Juan de Borja echoed the thoughts of many courtiers when he cursed Valladolid as 'this Babylon', and the reputation that Valladolid had acquired as an unhealthy city during the hunger and plague of 1598–99 was confirmed; Miguel de Cervantes's 'Glass Graduate' 'heard one man telling another that as soon as he got to Valladolid, his wife had fallen very ill'.[81]

By the autumn of 1605 Lerma had decided that the court would shortly return to Madrid. In November, he opened negotiations for new water supplies for his *huerta* in Madrid.[82] On 21 January 1606 he took the royal couple to Ampudia to celebrate the elevation of his church there to collegial status, and he arranged for a delegation of *regidores* of Madrid led by Silva de Torres to travel to the town to negotiate for the return of the court. Lerma instructed the *regidores* to travel around Valladolid so that their presence in Ampudia should not be known in the city.[83] On arriving in Ampudia, the *regidores* humbly asked Lerma to urge the King to return the court to the old capital. Lerma was of course now a *regidor* of Madrid and Silva de Torres flatteringly addressed him as 'the Protector of Madrid'.[84] Villalonga assured Lerma that the city of Valladolid would accept a decision to return to Madrid with good grace since 'no republic owes more to any individual' than Valladolid did to him.[85] Silva de Torres and

Villalonga then engaged in a *comedia* in which they negotiated the terms of the return, representing respectively the interests of Madrid and of Valladolid. The deal was soon struck: the two men agreed that Madrid would pay the King 250,000 ducats as a lump sum together with the income from one-sixth of the rents in the city for a decade in return for taking the court back to Madrid.[86]

When Villalonga informed the councils that the decision had been taken to return to Madrid, he emphasised that it had been Lerma who, as the 'author and promotor' of the decision, had asked the King to take the court back to its old centre.[87] Lerma himself wrote to the city council of Madrid informing them of the King's decision and he left no room for doubt that he had been instrumental in persuading Philip to return.[88]

Lerma ensured that he and his *hechuras* controlled the return of the court to Madrid and the management of affairs in the restored capital. Silva de Torres was given the responsibility of organising the journey of court and government back to Madrid. He was also appointed as *corregidor* of Madrid with retention of his seniority in the *Sala de alcaldes de Casa y Corte*; he would manage the affairs of Madrid as Sarmiento de Acuña had done those of Valladolid.[89] The duke also ensured that he was represented in the councils of Valladolid and Madrid: Rodrigo Calderón was appointed as a city councillor in Valladolid so that he could keep his eye on Lerma's interests there while Villalonga was named to a similar position in Madrid.[90]

Philip was joyously received in Madrid on 4 March 1606, and he shared the pleasure of the citizens of the restored capital, for he once again had available to him the facilities not only of Madrid itself but of the palaces and hunting lodges that were adjacent to it.[91] For Valladolid, the loss of the court was devastating: not until the nineteenth century did it regain the population level that it had enjoyed in 1605.[92] For Lerma, too, the implications of the return to Madrid were very serious, for he only owned three comparatively small properties in the restored capital, none of which compared in size or in grandeur with the properties that he had available to him in Valladolid; quite simply, he did not have a palace in Madrid that was worthy of his social and political status.[93] Nevertheless, he fully recognised that the court would not return to Valladolid; on 11 June 1606 he sold the *Casa de la Ribera* to the King. Moreover, he systematically broke up his great collection of paintings, acknowledging that he no longer had the space in which to house it. He retained most of the more important pictures, particularly those of a religious or contemplative nature, which he hung in *San Pablo* and in the hunting lodge of Ventosilla. Otherwise, in the year or so after the court returned to Madrid he disposed of probably two-thirds of his pictures, including even the great equestrian portrait of him by Rubens. His days as a soldier were over, but so too, at least for the moment, was his mania for collecting pictures on the grandest of scales. He would now become a gentleman of a court that was resident once again in its natural capital. Lerma took over one-third or so of the rooms in the Alcázar while he pondered on the problem of acquiring or creating a palace that was suitable for him.[94]

NOTES

1 'Y el corregidor y regidores de esta ciudad llevaron al dicho Duque un dia de esta semana las llaves doradas de las puertas de la plazuela que se ha hecho detrás de Palacio, á costa de la ciudad, y se las entregaron con una salvilla de oro en que iban, que pesaba mas de 600 escudos; las cuales eran dos, una para el Rey y otra para el Duque, porque con cada una se abren las cuatro puertas que tiene la plazuela', *Relaciones*, 9 Aug. 1603, p. 186.

2 'Estado de Lerma: Bienes en Valladolid. Alcaydía del Palacio real de Valladolid', Valladolid 11 and 29 Dec. 1601, ADL 8, no fols. On the palace, J. Martí y Monsó, 'Felipe III y el Duque de Lerma en Valladolid. Los palacios reales', in his *Estudios histórico-artisticos relativos principalmente a Valladolid*, Valladolid-Madrid, 1898–1901, pp. 599–626.

3 On the sale of the *Casa de la Ribera*, 'Relación de las cédulas escrituras ynbentarios y otros recados q[ue] el Duq[ue] de lerma presenta en el Conse[ejo] de haz[ien]da de su Mag[esta]d para q[ue] los vea y reconozca el s[eño]r fiscal', Madrid, 4 Sep. 1607, AGS DGT Inv. 24, leg. 1288, no fol.

4 See p. 83.

5 See pp. 84–5.

6 On the palace, J. Pérez Gil, *El Palacio de la Ribera. Recreo y boato en el Valladolid cortesano*, Valladolid, 2002.

7 'Ribera casa y Jardin de Vall[adol]id don fran[cis]co Gómez de Rojas y Sandoual Duque de Lerma. Quenta de 30,265,466 que a de auer por la Riuera cassa y Jardines que tenia en la ciudad de Vall[adol]id de la otra parte del Rio y Su Mag[esta]d para su seruicio, y de como se le pagan. Año de 1607', AGS DGT Inv. 24, leg. 1288, no fol.

8 Joly, 'Viaje por España', in García Mercadal (ed.), *Viajes de extranjeros en España*, ii, pp. 94–5; 'inclement' was of course a pun on the name of Pope Clement VIII. Italics in original.

9 'A discourse of the State of Spayne', BL Add 39,853, fols. 150–61.

10 Williams, 'Lerma, Old Castile and the Travels of Philip III of Spain'.

11 *Relaciones*, pp. 95–6.

12 Itinerary, Philip III.

13 'TESTAMENTO Y CODICILIO DE LA REYNA D[OÑA] MARGARITA DE AUSTRIA ...' Valladolid, 20 Sep. 1601, AGS PR 31 D20, at fols. 18r–18v.

14 AHV LA 26, fols. 155r–155v, 21 Sep. 1601 and *Relaciones*, p. 113.

15 'Relación del cristianisimo de la Srma. Infanta'; *Relaciones*, pp. 119–22.

16 Ibid., pp. 166–7, 169–71.

17 *Cntas*. St. 11 July 1600 and 22 Nov. 1603, AGS E 1937, fols. 12 and 17; 'Instrucción dada sobre la manera en que ha de ser servido los principes de Saboya ...', San Martín de la Vega, 2 Dec. 1603; see also the orders issued by Pedro Franqueza, 'La forma que han de guardar los oficiles de bocco de sus altezas', Valladolid, 12 April 1605 and 'Relación de lo que mande S[u] M[ajestad] se observe y dé a los criados de S[us] A[ltezas] [Felipe-Manuel de Saboya y Manuel-Filiberto de Saboya] de gajes, raciones à cada uno que le toca ...', Valladolid, 19 April 1605, RAH F-18, fols. 116–145v. On the Saluzzo crisis, Parker, *Army of Flanders*, p. 58. On Savoy, Toby Osborne, *Dynasty and Diplomacy in the Court of Savoy. Political Culture and the Thirty Years' War*, Cambridge, 2002.

18 *Cntas. Junta de Tres*, 28 Aug. and 12 Dec. 1602 and 25 May 1605, AGS E 1937, fols. 20, 22, 62.

19 *Cnta*. State, 28 Feb. 1606, ibid., fol. 85.

20 Lerma, 'Testamento ... (1617)', ADL 12, pp. 28–9 and 'Hacienda acrecentada', ADL 54, no 9, no fol.

21 Anon., 'Relación General de los Patronazgos que tiene el Duque de Lerma mi señor adelantado mayor de castilla perpetuos en los Reynos de Castilla, Aragón y Valencia y la Renta que por Raçon dellas les dejo situada El Cardenal Duque mi s[eñor] que aya gloria', 22 Feb. 1623, ADL 54 no. 9 and Lerma, 'Imbentario', ADL 53, fols. 28b–30. On the architecture,

Bustamante García, *La arquitectura clasicista*, pp. 410–17 and Martín González, *La arquitectura doméstica del renacimiento en Valladolid*, pp. 178–9.

22 I am obliged to Katharine Williams for counting these crests.
23 L. Cervera Vera, *El convento de Santo Domingo en la villa de Lerma*, Madrid, 1969, pp. 16–23.
24 'Relación general de los patronazgos que tiene el Duque de Lerma, mi señor', ADL 54, no 9, no fol.
25 Lerma also paid 500 ducats for a house in Ampudia for a small community of Franciscans.
26 Pedro de Herrera, *Translación del Santíssimo Sacramento a la iglesia de San Pedro de la villa de Lerma*, BN Mss 15880, pp. 35–70 and *Relaciones*, p. 228. A plan of the lands around Ventosilla in 1610 is printed in Palacio Real, Biblioteca, *Las Trazas de Juan de Herrera y sus seguidores*, Patrimonio Nacional, Santander 2001, p. 250.
27 L. Cervera Miralles, 'El palacio del Duque de Lerma', in E. González Pablos (ed.), *El palacio ducal de Lerma de ayer a hoy*, JLC 2003, pp. 35–50.
28 Cervera Vera, *El conjunto palacial*, i, p. 282; see his sketch of the grounds on p. 288.
29 'Cuentas del Duque de Lerma de 1602 y 1603', AHPM Protocol 1849, fol. 1210; Cervera Vera, *El conjunto palacial*, i, pp. 41, 249–50, 263–9, 319–21. On Lerma's building programme after 1613, see below, pp. 186–9.
30 Cervera Vera, *El conjunto palacial*, i, pp. 21–53. For a plan of the project, Palacio Real, Biblioteca, *Las trazas de Juan de Herrera y sus seguidores*, pp. 252–3.
31 The following is based upon 'Relación general de los patronazgos que tiene el Duque de Lerma mi señor', ADL 54, no. 9, no fol and 'Hacienda acrecentada', ibid.
32 R. J. Payo Hernanz, *Lerma*, Centro de Iniciativas Turísticas de Lerma, 2004, pp. 60–9.
33 'Relacion general de los patronazgos que tiene el Duque de Lerma mi señor', ADL 54, no. 9, no fol.; Lerma, 'Testamento … (1617)', ibid. 12, p. 18b; Lerma, 'Imbentario', ibid. 53, p. 34b. The convent was designed by Francisco de Mora and completed after his death by fray Alberto de la Madre de Dios.
34 *Sucesos del Reinado de Felipe III*, cxxix, pp. 416–17.
35 'Discourse of the State of Spayne', BL Add 39,853, fol. 160.
36 *Fastigiana*, pp. 77–8.
37 I am obliged to Xanthe Brooke and David Davies for their advice on Lerma's collection of paintings and to Nigel Glendinning who guided me in the analysis of the important series of inventories in the Lerma archive in Toledo. Two important theses deal with the subject: X. Brooke, 'The Patronage and Art Collection of the Duke of Lerma', MPhil. thesis, Courtauld Institute, London University, 1983 and Sara Schroth, 'The Private Picture Collection of the Duke of Lerma', PhD diss., New York University, 1990, which expertly analyses the inventories in Toledo.
38 Brooke, 'The Patronage and Art Collection of the Duke of Lerma', pp. 32–6.
39 Lerma, 'Imbentario', ADL 53, pp. 24v–25 and 'Cédula del rey (Felipe III), por la que hace merced del oficio de capitán general de la caballería de España al duque de Lerma', Aranjuez, 1 May 1603, RAH M-73, fols. 144–6. When Lerma renounced the office (1 October 1609) he had taken 76,000 ducats from it. See also, García García, *La Pax Hispánica*, pp. 109–10.
40 There is an extensive literature on this painting; see especially, Frances Huemer, *Corpus Rubenianum*, London, 1977, pp. 21–5, C. White, *Peter Paul Rubens. Man and Artist*, New Haven, 1987, pp. 29–30. On the portraiture of favourites, J. Brown, ' "Peut-on assez louer cet excellent ministre?" Imagery of the Favourite in England, France and Spain', in Elliott and Brockliss, *The World of the Favourite*, pp. 223–35. On the iconography of the equestrian portrait, D. Howarth, *Images of Rule. Art and Politics in the English Renaissance, 1485–1649*, Basingstoke, 1997, pp. 132–44.
41 The statue of Cristóbal de Rojas was placed in the church of *San Pedro* in Lerma in August 1609 but for reasons that are not clear work did not proceed on the statue of Cardinal Sandoval y Rojas. Martí y Monsó, 'Estatuas orantes de los Duques de Lerma', in *Estudios histórico-artisticos relativos principalmente a Valladolid*, Valladolid, 1901, pp. 247–300; Cervera Vera, *La iglesia de San Pedro*, pp. 52–8 and B. Gilman Proske, *Pompeo Leoni. Work in Marble and Alabaster in Relation to Spanish Sculpture*, New York, 1956, pp. 38–9.

42   Matías Sangrador, *Historia de la muy noble y leal ciudad de Valladolid*, 2 vols., Valladolid, 1854, ii, p. 243.

43   'Traslado del cuerpo de la Duquesa de Lerma', 1603, AHPM, 1847, fol. 699 and Fr Juan de la Puente O. P. to ?, Valladolid, ? June 1603, PB 11/2116 doc. 228. See also Sepúlveda, *Sucesos del Reinado de Felipe III*, vol. 130, pp. 347–50; *Gaçeta y Nuevas*, pp. 22–3; and Palomares Ibáñez, *El convento de San Pablo*, p. 364.

44   Lerma's fullest expression of his desolation, in October 1604: 'estoy cansadísimo y que de boníssima gana me rretiraría a donde nadie se acordase de mí' – see García García, *La Pax Hispánica*, p. 372, n. 56.

45   'Testamento ... (1617)', pp. 26v–28 and *Relaciones*, pp. 184–5. The Admiral had served as commander of the Army of Flanders (1597–1600) but was so incompetent that he contrived to be captured by the enemy and had to be ransomed. After resuming his command, he then fought such a feeble campaign in 1602 that he was summoned to Spain and arrested on his arrival, A. Rodríguez Villa, 'D. Francisco de Mendoza, Almirante de Aragón', in *Homenaje a Menéndez y Pelayo*, ii, 1899, pp. 487–610. On the Admiral's feud with Lerma, see below, pp. 136–8, 150–1, 156–7, 167, 178.

46   *Relaciones*, pp. 165, 171.

47   Bautista de Acevedo's appointment, H. C. Lea, *A History of the Inquisition of Spain*, 4 vols., New York, 1906/07, i, p. 557; Lemos's title, 6 April 1603, AGS QC 36.

48   'La condesa de Lemos entró hoy sábado, en la noche, seis de julio, y bien noche, con grandísimo acompañamiento. Vienen con ella acompañandola tres potentados de Italia con otros muchos caballeros. Ella sola trae tan solamente ochocientos criados y ansi no caben, de pies en El Escorial, ni en el Sitio no se ha visto tanta gente para siempre jamás', *Sucesos del Reinado de Felipe III*, vol. 129, p. 178.

49   On del Valle, L. Fernández Martín, 'La Marquesa del Valle: Una vida dramática en la corte de los Austrias', *Hispania*, 143, 1979, pp. 559–638.

50   *Relaciones*, pp. 191–2, 194–5, 201–2; Fernández Martín, 'La Marquesa del Valle', pp. 596–624; M. J. Pérez Martín, *Margarita de Austria, reina de España*, Madrid, 1961, pp. 121–7, and Sánchez, *The Empress, the Queen, and the Nun*, pp. 20, 42–4, 51–2, 93–4 and 100–1.

51   Van Castre's letters to the Marquis of Veras between 9 Dec. 1603 and 2 June 1604 give a detailed and remarkably accurate account of court politics during these months, NA SP 94/9 and 10. The following paragraphs are based upon the letters to Veras, Madrid, 4/14 and 12/22 Jan. and two letters of 9/19 March 1604, NA SP 94/9, fols. 94–94b, 129–30, 131–2 and 157–9. The fullest Spanish account, Sepúlveda, *Sucesos del Reinado de Felipe III*, vol. 130, pp. 16–20 and 352–4.

52   Van Castre to Veras, Madrid, 12/22 Jan. 1603, at fol. 131.

53   *Relaciones*, pp. 189–90.

54   Van Castre to Veras, Madrid, 4/14 Jan. 1604, at fol. 129b.

55   Ibid., at fol. 130.

56   On the resentment of the Constable at having to cede some ceremonial precedence to Lerma, del Río Barredo, *Madrid, Urbs Regia*, pp. 130–1.

57   Van Castre to Veras, Madrid, 14 Jan. 1604, at fol. 129b.

58   Constable to Lerma, Valladolid 11 Oct. 1603 and reply, San Lorenzo, 9 Nov. 1603, BL Add 28,465, fols. 13b–14b; *Relaciones*, pp. 174, 190–1, 195, 203.

59   *Relaciones*, pp. 171, 182.

60   See below, pp. 194–5.

61   *Cntas. Junta de Tres* (Lerma, Idiáquez and Gaspar de Córdoba), 9 Sep. 1602 and 12 Feb. 1603, AGS E 2023, fols. 82 and 84 and *cnta*. War 9 Dec. 1602, AGS GA 589, no fol.

62   To Juan de Borja, Valladolid, 24 Feb. 1603, BL Add 28,425, fol. 25.

63   *Cnta*. St., 2 Nov. 1603, AGS E 2636, fol. 125; Lerma to Juan de Borja, El Pardo, 24 Nov. 1603, BL Add 28,425, fol. 144.

64   *Relaciones*, pp. 176, 196–7, 203; James Casey, *The Kingdom of Valencia in the Seventeenth Century*, Cambridge, UK, 1979, pp. 234–6.

65 I have not located the documentation founding the dukedom, but they are summarised in the agreements between Lerma and his son in 1607; see below, pp. 141–4; also *Relaciones*, p. 208 and *Gaçeta y Nuevas*, p. 24. The first evidence of Cristóbal's involvement in government, *cnta.* War, 17 Aug. 1601, AGS GA 580, fol. 147, referring to a note that he had sent the Council. See also, *Relaciones*, pp. 138, 198, 203–4; on the Cortes, Eugenio Ciscar Pallares, *Las corts valencianas de Felipe III*, Valencia, 1973, pp. 84–5. Philip returned from Valencia to the Pardo, and when he moved on some of the Queen's ladies left a fire burning which spread throughout the palace, destroying most of it. Since the larger pictures could not be taken out through the narrow doors, only the smaller pictures were saved. A graphic account of the circumstances of the fire, van Castre to Veras, n. p., 9/19 March 1604, NA SP 94/9, fol. 159.

66 *Relaciones*, pp. 211–13, 218, 236; Edouard Rott, *Philippe III et le Duc de Lerme (1598–1621). Étude historique d'après des documents inédits*, Paris, 1887, pp. 367–8.

67 Lerma, 'Inbentario ...', ADL 53, fol. 21v.

68 'Casa del prado en la V[ill]a de M[adri]d', 'Estado de Lerma', ADL 8, no fol.; *Relaciones*, p. 145.

69 'Copia simple de la escritura de Venta que otorgó Pedro Álbarez de Pereyra, de las Casas, Huertas, Jardines, y Solares, que llamavan la Quinta del Prior, en el Prado de s[a]n Gerónimo de Madrid, a fauor del s[eño]r Duque de Lerma, en precio de 12,000 duc[ado]s', Valladolid, 20 April 1604, ADL 8, no fol.

70 'Hacienda acrecentada', ADL 54, no. 9, no fol.

71 Ibid., *Relaciones*, pp. 134, 139, 144, 303.

72 See above, pp. 1–8.

73 Pedro Ramírez, 'Cargo de los m[a]r[avedi]s que r[eccivi]o ... los gastos de la xornada que su m[agest]ad hizo a Burgos y lerma el año de 605, AGS CMC 3a Epoca, leg. 3532, no. 5; Cornwallis to Lords of the Council, Valladolid, 9 July 1605; Winwood, *Memorials*, ii, 85–6; *Relaciones*, pp. 255–6.

74 *Relaciones*, pp. 260–1, 264.

75 *CSPV*, x, 8 and 24 Dec. 1605, nos. 452, 460, pp. 299, 307.

76 Gutiérrez Alonso, *Valladolid*, pp. 30, 42, 53, 90, 101.

77 *Fastigiana*, p. 130.

78 *Cnta.* St. 3 April 1604, AGS E. 198, no fol., draft.

79 'Mucha diligencia he hecho para saber el verdadero stado de las enfermedades de aqui', Villalonga to Lerma, Valladolid, 27 April 1605, AGS. E. 201; *Relaciones*, pp. 259, 261.

80 José García Oro, *Don Diego Sarmiento de Acuña, conde de Gondomar y embajador de España (1567–1626)*, La Coruña, 1997, p. 124.

81 Borja to Lerma, Valladolid, 12 March 1604, BL Add 28,425, fol. 209b; Miguel de Cervantes, *Exemplary Stories*, ed. C. A. Jones, Harmondsworth, 1972, p. 143.

82 'Casa del prado en la V[ill]a de M[adri]d, 'Estado de Lerma', ADL 8, no fol.

83 Lerma to Franqueza, Ampudia, 20 Jan. 1606, in reply letter from Valladolid, of same date, AGS E 205, no fol.; José Miguel López García, *El impacto de la corte en Castilla. Madrid y su territorio en la época moderna*, Madrid, 1998, p. 148.

84 Silva de Torres to Lerma, Madrid, 20 Jan. 1606, AGS CJH 487–27–1, 2.

85 Franqueza to Lerma, Valladolid, 29. Jan. 1606, AGS E 205, no fol.

86 Torras i Ribé, *Franquesa*, p. 166.

87 *Cnta. Junta de Tres*, 24 Jan. 1606, AGS E 205, no fol.

88 'Por las cartas que el alcalde Silva de Torres me ha ido escribiendo, he entendido las necesidades y trabajos que esa Villa tenía, y doliéndome, como es razón, en general y particular por lo que toca a cada uno de Vuestra Senoría, lo represente al Rey nuestro Senor y le supliqué que fuese servido de mandarse informar lo que en esto pasaría y de otros inconvenientes que la experiencia ha ido mostrando de que la corte no volviese a Madrid; y su Majestad, Dios le guarde, hallándose con el mismo celo del bien universal de sus Reinos que tuvo en la venida de Valladolid, ha resuelto la vuelta a Madrid, y con lo que ha oido a los embajadores

de la Villa, espero en Dios que le mandará abreviar todo lo que fuere possible, de que yo quedo contentísimo, y lo que deseo servir a Vuestra Senoría y todo le vaya bien de esa Villa, y a darles esto quisiera ir en persona luego; pero remítome a la licencia de Silva de Torres y a los Regidores que han venido con él, que dirán lo demás. Dios guarde a Vuestra Senoría. De Ampudia, 23 de enero de 1606. – El duque de Lerma, marqués de Denia', Antonio León Pinelo, *Anales de Madrid. Reinado de Felipe III. Años 1598 a 1621*, ed. R. Martorell Téllez-Girón (Madrid: 1931), p. 237, n. 98.

89 Ana Guerrero Mayllo, *Familia y vida cotidiana de una elite de poder. Los regidores madrileños en tiempos de Felipe II*, Madrid, 1993, pp. 184–5, 193, 202.

90 Gutiérrez Alonso, *Valladolid*, pp. 297–330 and Torras i Ribé, *Franquesa*, p. 90.

91 *Gaçetas y Nuevas*, p. 26; on the return, Alvar Ezquerra, *El nacimiento de una capital europea*, pp. 292–7. On Philip's pleasure in the return, see below, p. 134.

92 *Cntas.* Fin. 15 Jul. 1608, 4 Dec. 1616 and 10 Jan. 1621, AGS CJH 352, fol. 32, 395, fol. 43 and 414, no fol. On Valladolid, Gutiérrez Alonso, *Valladolid*, pp. 90–5.

93 See below, pp. 95–6, 188–9.

94 Cornwallis recorded that 'contrary to the custome of all other officers, he not onlie lodgeth in the Pallace, but hath almost a whole third part of it to his owne use', 'Discourse of the State of Spayne', BL Add 29,853, fol. 159b. See also, 'Ribera casa y Jardin de Vall[adol[id … Año de 1607', AGS DGT Inv. 24, leg. 1288, no fol.

5

Government and policymaking: the apogee of power, 1598–1606

Men and offices

King and valido

The weight of decision-making in the Spanish Monarchy fell squarely upon the king: councils, ministers and servants made recommendations to him but only the monarch could take decisions.[1] Insecure and lacking in confidence as he was in his early years, Philip III yet applied himself with commendable if mechanical seriousness to the business of government. It is extraordinarily rare, for instance, to find a *consulta* of a council to which he had not appended a comment in his own hand. Nevertheless, on three occasions he formally conferred authority on Lerma to manage affairs – in the first days of the reign when he ordered the councils to obey his orders; in 1605 when he gave Lerma the right to manage the distribution of papers from petitioners for favours and office; and in 1612 when he issued the decree instructing the councils to do whatever Lerma ordered them to do.[2] Each of these orders gave Lerma exceptional powers, and taken together they conferred on him a range of authority that was unique for even the most senior of crown ministers in Habsburg Spain.

Lerma's strategy for exercising his extraordinary authority was very carefully considered. He was especially punctilious in always making it clear that he was giving orders in the King's name and not in his own – 'His Majesty has instructed me' was the stock phrase through which he issued instructions. Moreover, he presented himself to the world as the diligent servant of the King, working incessantly to carry out his duties; in September 1603, for instance, he wrote to Juan de Borja that 'no man has worked at such great tasks, and so many of them, as I have had to'.[3] He displayed his concern to be involved in government as well as being at the centre of courtly occasions, interviewing ambassadors and supplicants, receiving and distributing papers from administrators, giving orders to councils and defining which business they should deal with and which should be delegated to *juntas*.

Lerma's presentation of himself as a hard-working and dedicated servant of the King was clearly at variance with the impressions of many observers; we have seen, for instance, how Tomé Pinheiro da Veiga commented on the proverbial difficulty of having an audience with the duke.[4] He was highly selective in choosing the subjects on which he would involve himself and how much attention he would pay to them. He had neither the temperament nor the energy to impose himself on the machinery of government. He tended to work when it suited him – and sometimes when he could no longer avoid doing so. Indeed, he often complained about the restrictions placed on his ability to work by his ill-health; in 1605, for instance, he observed that 'after having been in bed for three days, I got up to see some bulls that were being run ... but the wind was so fierce that day that it did me damage and thus I am once again in bed, although I am not as ill as I was before'.[5] Complaints about his ill-health litter his correspondence. There was mannered study here: Lerma's apparent devotion to duty even when he was ill helped to convince Philip of the sincerity of his commitment to his service while at the same time his illnesses conveniently created another avenue through which he could distance himself from decision-making.[6] So too there was careful study in Lerma's practice of writing only very rarely in his own hand; the overwhelming majority of his letters were written by secretaries – most notably, Calderón, Villalonga and Juan de Ciriza – and initialled by him, 'the Duke'. The rarity value of Lerma's holograph letters may perhaps have contributed, paradoxically, to the impression of a minister who was working so hard that he did not have the time to write his own notes. Most certainly, administrators who received a note in Lerma's hand understood that it carried special significance.

Lerma naturally took a particular interest in the papers of the Council of State. He was able to influence the setting of the agenda of its meetings: for instance, in 1604 he ordered Andrés de Prada that 'for the moment' the Council was not to consider papers that had arrived about England.[7] Similarly, in 1607 he instructed Prada to retain some papers from Ambrosio Spínola and others about the Low Countries until the King had made a decision on them; clearly they were not to be shown to the Council.[8] Conversely, when some papers arrived from Baltasar de Zúñiga in Brussels in 1605 Lerma ordered that they should be considered by the Council without the identity of their author being revealed.[9] He could also influence the make-up of the Council for particular debates; in 1604 he ordered that the papers from Milan were only to be considered by the Council when the Constable of Castile (who had been Governor of Milan) was present.[10]

Lerma paid particular attention to the finances of the royal households and could be forceful in ordering that monies be found for them. In 1601, for instance, he instructed the Marquis of Poza, President of the Council of

Finance, to promptly pay the ordinary expenses of the royal households since these 'cannot suffer any delay'[11] and in 1603 he ordered Poza's successor to take 190,733 ducats from any source that he could find to pay the servants of both royal households and of the chapel 'because they are the neediest of people'.[12]

The duke often paid detailed attention to the negotiations for *asientos*. At the turn of 1602–03 he and Franqueza negotiated an agreement with the Genoese banker Ottavio Centurione for the provision of over three million ducats annually for three years. Lerma gloried in the agreement, christening it the '*asiento grande*': for a loan of such magnitude he would take the plaudits.[13] He kept an eye on more routine agreements; in July 1603 he ordered the Council of Finance to renegotiate an *asiento* that it had arranged because the conditions it contained were not strict enough.[14] When the Council of Finance suggested in 1604 that the terms that he himself had agreed for an *asiento* for 200,000 ducats were too generous, he allowed it to reconsider them and make recommendations to the King.[15] Lerma had to balance his wish to take the credit for successful or important decisions with his need to distance himself from responsibility for the decisions that might prove to be contentious.

The clients

Lerma maintained an overview of affairs in court and government through a network of placemen (and women) whom he advanced with precise care. Normally, he dealt directly with the King to have his clients and relatives appointed to office on a case-by-case basis; only on one occasion, in 1602 when he attempted to 'pack' the reformed Council of Finance with his *hechuras*, did he try to have several of them appointed at once. However, it is remarkable that virtually all of the leading figures in his *clientela* were placed in office by 1604 and it is remarkable, too, how many of them were appointed while the King was on the road, away from his capital.

The men and women used by Lerma to assist him in the management of court and government may usefully be divided into four groupings – his relatives; the members of his household and the staff of his private offices; his friends and associates; and opportunists who attached themselves to him to advance their own careers.

When the court moved to Valladolid, Lerma had already won major appointments for relatives across the face of court, Church and government – most notably, the archbishopric of Toledo, the presidency of the Council of Castile, the *mayordomía mayor* and *camarería mayor* of the Queen and the viceroyalty of Naples.[16] He then secured the succession of his sister to the *camarería mayor* of the Queen but otherwise the only major court office that he acquired for a relative during the residence in Valladolid came about when in 1603 he had one brother-in-law, the Count of Altamira, moved from the position of

Margaret's *mayordomo mayor* to that of her *caballerizo mayor* and replaced as *mayordomo mayor* by another brother-in-law, the Marquis of la Laguna.[17] The Marquis of Velada retained his position as Philip's *mayordomo mayor* but was under increasing pressure from Lerma; in 1602, the duke hinted that Velada might earn *grandeza* if he made his position available to him but the Marquis hung on to his office, resentful of Lerma's arrogance but not yet confident enough of his own strength to move into open opposition to him.[18]

Lerma advanced members of his household and private staff to offices across court and government. Four of his own confessors were promoted to positions with the king and his heir – Diego de Mardones, Jerónimo de Xavierre and Luis de Aliaga to the confessorships of Philip himself and Jusepe de González to that of the heir.[19] He raised another four men who had worked for him as household servants to courtly and political eminence: Rodrigo Calderón had been his page; Dr Juan Bautista de Acevedo, tutor to his children; Juan de la Serna, his *camarero mayor*; and Duarte Coronel, his Master of the Wardrobe. A group of men who had served in Lerma's private offices were raised to important positions in government and administration, for the most part in the early years of the reign: his secretaries, Alonso Muriel de Valdivielso, Iñigo Ibáñez de Santa Cruz, Bernabé de Bibanco, Tristán de Ciriza, Dr Juan González Centeño and Pedro de Solórzano; his accountants and treasurers, Tomás de Ángulo, Juan de Ciriza (brother of Tristán), García Mazo de la Vega, Jorge de Tovar y Valderrama and Juan Ladrón de Guevara; and his paymaster of building works, Diego López de Gojenaga. Philip was prepared to formally acknowledge that service to Lerma was itself a qualification for governmental office: for instance, Tristán de Ciriza's title of appointment in 1604 to the strategically important patronage office of *contador de mercedes* specifically recognised his achievements in Lerma's papers.[20]

The friends of Lerma who were advanced to office included Diego Sarmiento de Acuña, Pedro Messía de Tovar, Juan Bautista de Tassis, Diego de Covarrubias, Agustín Álvarez de Toledo, Francisco de Contreras, Diego de Colmenares and Diego de Silva y Mendoza, Count of Salinas. A sub-grouping here was made up of Lerma's business associates – the members of the Spínola family who had helped him in the 1580s and Juan Pascual, son of the banker who had salvaged his financial position in the 1590s. Villalonga and Gaspar de Córdoba should also be included in this group since they had formed strong contacts with Lerma in the 1590s.[21] So too should a number of men from the city of Valladolid whom Lerma had come to know and trust – Juan and Diego de Alderete, Pedro Manso and Dr Fernando de Villagómez, who had acted in legal capacities for him; Cristóbal and Miguel de Ipeñarrieta and Baltasar Gilimón de la Mota, who were prominent citizens of Valladolid; and Dr Antonio Bonal and Lic. Pedro de Tapia, *oidores* of the Chancellery of Valladolid.

The grouping of opportunists who attached themselves to Lerma at the beginning of the reign were led by Lic. Alonso Ramírez de Prado and Pedro Álvarez de Pereira, both of whom drew themselves to Lerma's notice during the journey of 1599. We could also include here men such as Juan de Idiáquez and Francisco González de Heredia, senior servants in Philip II's government who made the transition to even greater importance under Philip III.

A number of these men – most notably Calderón, Villalonga, Ramírez de Prado and Álvarez Pereira – became notoriously corrupt, but it should not be assumed that the *hechuras* of Lerma were by definition corrupted or corrupting of others. While Lerma tolerated – and probably encouraged – the behaviour of Calderón and Villalonga he appreciated that he would not last long in power if membership of his *clientela* became synonymous with corrupt or dishonest activities.[22] It is also salutary to remember that many of his *hechuras* had distinguished careers after Lerma had left court, most surprisingly perhaps Juan de Ciriza and Pedro Messía de Tovar, both of whom were raised to noble titles by Philip IV. Political and personal affiliations at court were complex and ever-changing matters. What Lerma required of the men and women whom he placed in office was that they should be efficient and discreet in their work and that they should keep a watching brief for him, finding out what was happening – or what was likely to happen – and who was manoeuvring for advantage or seeking opportunity. Above all, like any patron, Lerma required loyalty: that the men and women who owed their positions to him were committed to him and to his service and would perform whatever duties he required of them.

This naturally created tensions, both because everyone in the King's service owed their primary loyalty to him and because personal rivalries were endemic within court, Church and government. It was ironic that the men who inflicted most damage upon Lerma came from within his own *parentela* and *clientela*. Even his own son Cristóbal eventually broke with him – albeit somewhat half-heartedly – while his great-uncle, the Cardinal-archbishop of Toledo, led the opposition to the removal of the court to Valladolid in 1601. Similarly, Miranda and San Germán involved themselves in the del Valle conspiracy in 1603 while the Duke of Infantado broke with Lerma over his treatment of the Admiral of Aragon.[23] But most devastating of all was the treachery – as Lerma regarded it – of the men whom he had raised to the king's confessorship, Mardones, Xavierre and Aliaga, all of whom broke with him and involved themselves in intrigues against him: Lerma may well have reflected ruefully on the difficulties that were created for him by the consciences of the Dominicans whom he had advanced. So, too, some lawyers turned against him, most notably Fernando Carrillo, who worked briefly for him in 1603 but who became a powerful and strident opponent in the second half of the reign. Raising men to important or strategic offices carried its own danger for the great patron: Lerma learned the lesson most painfully in the cases of Luis de Aliaga and Fernando Carrillo.

Control of the city of Valladolid: Rodrigo Calderón and Diego Sarmiento de Acuña

The President and Council of Castile were responsible for maintaining order throughout the kingdom but they had of course a very particular obligation to control law and order in and around the court, and this they carried out through the *alcaldes de casa y corte*, who served as the court's police force. Lerma worked closely with Miranda and his council to ensure that the court and the capital city were tightly under his control during the years of the residence of the court in Valladolid and he was careful to promote members of his *clientela* to the *alcaldía de casa y corte*.[24] He further extended his control of the institutions of the city itself by making use of two of his most trusted confidants, both of whom were citizens of Valladolid, Rodrigo Calderón and Diego Sarmiento de Acuña.

Rodrigo Calderón was born (*c.*1576–68) in Antwerp while his father Francisco was serving in the Army of Flanders. The Calderón family were leading citizens of Valladolid and when Francisco returned home he was taken on by Lerma as his man of business in the city.[25] In 1589 Francisco secured a place for Rodrigo as a page in Lerma's household. Sharp-witted and diligent, the young boy rose quickly in his master's service and by 1598 had become his chief private secretary.[26] Lerma developed a deep affection for Rodrigo and seems almost to have regarded him as a favoured son – a characteristic that was to create grave tensions between Lerma and his own sons. When the court moved to Valladolid, Rodrigo entered into his own and became much more important in Lerma's service than his own father; he was appointed as Chief of Public Works, Chief of Police, Archivist, Registrar of the Chancellery and Governor of the Royal Prison. He therefore played a central role in managing the affairs of the city for Lerma.

The duke's confidence in Calderón – indeed, his reliance upon him – also led him to place him in palatine offices that put him in daily proximity to the King. As Secretary of the King's Chamber (1600), Calderón even dealt with some of Philip's correspondence, while as Captain of the German Guards (1601) he assumed a leading responsibility for guarding the King. Four companies of guards served the King as his bodyguards – the *Monteros de Espinosa* from the *Casa de Castilla* and the 'Guards of the three Nations' (Flemish, Spanish and German) from the *Casa de Borgoña*. One of these companies was always on duty within the palace when the King was resident while two other troops patrolled the palace and its grounds at night. When the King walked through his palace the Spanish and German guards had the privilege of preceding him while the Archers followed behind.[27] Don Rodrigo, therefore, was often in close proximity to the King, and Philip came to know him well.

While carrying out these roles, Calderón continued to act as Lerma's secretary and managed his appointments diary; people wishing to see Lerma had to seek permission to do so through Calderón. In practice, Calderón tended to see the supplicants whose cases had been unsuccessful, since when there was good news to tell Lerma generally imparted it. The duke also gave Calderón special responsibility for gathering information. As early as 1603, Cabrera de Córdoba observed that Calderón 'is empowered of all businesses' and that he carried enormous personal influence with Lerma.[28]

Unfortunately, don Rodrigo's power went to his head and he became proverbially arrogant. He treated the greatest men in the land with measured contempt, among them the Duke of Infantado and the marquises of Velada and Camarasa. Even Lerma's younger son felt the weight of his hostility; the Count of Saldaña came to see Calderón as a rival for his father's affections. More important still was the hostility felt towards Calderón by the royal couple and their confessors. Margaret soon appreciated that she could damage Lerma by moving against Calderón, and she secured the support of Philip's confessors Diego de Mardones and Luis de Aliaga in what became a sustained and highly personalised campaign against don Rodrigo. In 1607, Margaret almost destroyed Calderón's position at court, and when she died after childbirth in 1611, Philip came to believe that Calderón had been involved in her death; then, not even Lerma could save him. Indeed, Lerma's sustained defence of Calderón began after 1611 to drive a wedge between the King and himself.[29] All that lay in the future while the court resided in Valladolid, but in September 1604 one of Calderón's enemies tried to kill him as he left Lerma's palace. Don Rodrigo's luck held; the musket that was aimed at him jammed and the gunman escaped. The incident marked the beginning of Calderón's familiarity with violence. In time, he commissioned murders on his own account and in doing so – like Antonio Pérez before him – provided his enemies with the means to destroy him (and to gravely undermine Lerma himself).[30]

Diego Sarmiento de Acuña could not have been more different to Calderón. A Galician nobleman, Sarmiento was discreet and self-effacing and became in time the greatest Spanish diplomat of his generation, known from 1617 as the Count of Gondomar. He took possession of the office of *corregidor* of Valladolid in September 1602. A practical and efficient man, he supervised improvements to the amenities of the city, paving streets and squares, building a bridge over the Pisuerga, planting trees and extending parks and gardens to accommodate the needs of the court. His most valuable service to Lerma was to restrict entry into the city. His term of office came to an end a few weeks before the baptism of Prince Philip in 1605, and he was replaced by the Count of Saldaña. He then earned further gratitude from Lerma by agreeing to stay on to guide the young man in his duties; Sarmiento did the work of organising the city of Valladolid, particularly in the weeks leading up to the royal baptism of 1605, but Lerma's son gallantly took the credit for the brilliant success of the *fiestas*. In return for his discretion as much as for his loyal service to King and *valido*, Sarmiento was appointed first as *alférez mayor* of the city of Valladolid and then as a councillor of Finance in 1604.[31]

The offices

Lerma had the keenest appreciation of the value of information; he needed to know what was happening (or likely to happen) at court and to be able to act promptly, preferably in a pre-emptive capacity. Nowhere was his determination to manage the flow of information more evident than in the steps he took to manage the correspondence of the royal couple: several of Philip's personal secretaries in the years to 1618 were Lerma's men – Iñigo Ibañez de Santa Cruz, Rodrigo Calderón, Tristán de Ciriza, Bernabé de Bibanco and Juan González Centeno. Similarly, the Queen had to tolerate Villalonga and García Mazo de la Vega in her private office.[32] Although no evidence exists on the matter, it may reasonably be presumed, therefore, that Lerma therefore knew on a daily basis what information was coming to the royal couple and what letters they were writing.

Control of government started with the conciliar presidencies. By the end of 1603 Lerma had secured the presidencies of the councils of Castile and the Indies and the leadership of the Council of Portugal for relatives (Miranda, Lemos and Borja) and those of Inquisition and Aragon for *hechuras* (Bautista de Acevedo and Covarrubias). In addition, the presidencies of Finance and Military Orders were held by men who had discreetly accommodated themselves to him (Juan de Acuña and Juan de Idiáquez). Only Italy remained in the hands of an outright opponent, the Constable of Castile, and he was banished abroad in 1604–05.

The most important and prestigious of the presidencies were those of the councils of Castile and Inquisition (i.e. Inquisitor-General); both were dominated throughout the reign by Lerma's men. Miranda was the first of five presidents of the Council of Castile who were *hechuras* of Lerma's; he was followed by Juan Bautista de Acevedo (1608), Pedro Manso (1608–10), Juan de Acuña (1610–15) and Fernando de Acevedo (1616–21). For the whole of Philip III's reign after the dismissal of Rodrigo Vázquez de Arce in 1599, therefore, the Council of Castile was led by men who were committed to Lerma's service. However, control of the presidency was not in itself sufficient: for example, Miranda could not have handed down so many verdicts that were favourable to Lerma's seigneurial ambitions without the support of a number of his councillors.[33] Eight of the fifteen men who were appointed to councillorships of Castile between the beginning of the reign and the return of the court to Madrid may with confidence be described as *lermistas*. Pedro de Tapia, Juan de Ocontrillo, Francisco de Contreras, Antonio Bonal and García de Medrano had come to know Lerma in the 1590s; indeed, Ocontrillo and Contreras (who were the first *lermistas* appointed to the Council) were both named on the same day, in Anguita on 5 October 1599.[34] Álvaro de Benavides was married to a Sandoval.[35] Lic. Juan de Alderete was described by Juan de Borja as 'a senior servant' of Lerma and the duke himself freely acknowledged that he had 'always desired the good of Juan Alderete because I have many reasons to do so'.[36] Remarkably, Juan and his brother Diego were appointed to councillorships of Castile on the same day in February 1604 while the King was in Valencia.[37] These men served Lerma well; indeed, in 1607 the President and councillors of Castile declared themselves 'the faithful servants' of the duke.[38]

In one case there was serious tension within Lerma's *parentela*, and he had to arbitrate in a conflict which arose between Miranda and Juan de Borja, over the advancement of García de Medrano. For reasons that are not known, Miranda insistently refused Borja's demands that García de Medrano be promoted to a councillorship of Castile.[39] Certainly, Borja became very angry at the President's obduracy.[40] Lerma negotiated a compromise whereby Medrano was appointed to a councillorship of the Military Orders in 1600.[41] Not until June 1604 did Miranda agree that Medrano should be named for Castile itself.[42]

It has been observed that the Council of Castile maintained law and order in and around the court and the crown's palaces and hunting lodges through its *alcaldes de casa y corte*. Nine men were appointed to the *alcaldía* while the court was resident in Valladolid and three of them were prominent *hechuras* of Lerma's – Diego de Alderete (1601), Silva de Torres (1603) and Pedro Manso (1604).[43] Each in turn followed the normal *cursus honorum* for successful *alcaldes* and passed on to councillorships.

When Lerma engineered the appointment of Dr Juan Bautista de Acevedo as Inquisitor General in 1603 Cabrera de Córdoba permitted himself to observe that 'many wondered at this, because this position had always been given to men who were well qualified and who had great experience of Inquisition affairs and of other matters, but as he is a creature of the Duke of Lerma everything will be made easy'.[44] The appointment proved to be only the beginning of Lerma's systematic subornation of the Council of Inquisition. Bautista de Acevedo was followed as Inquisitor-General by Cardinal Bernardo de Sandoval y Rojas of Toledo (1608–18) and then by Luis de Aliaga (1619–21).[45] The Inquisitorship-general, therefore, like the presidency of the Council of Castile, was in the hands of Lerma's men for virtually the whole of the reign.

It was appropriate, therefore, that the first councillorship of Inquisition of the reign should have gone to a kinsman when Tomás de Borja was appointed in

November 1598.[46] Borja was followed in 1600 by Felipe de Tassis, the brother of Juan Bautista de Tassis,[47] and in 1603 by Pedro de Tapia.[48] Bautista de Acevedo also took advantange of his position as Inquisitor-General to advance two of his brothers within the Council: Francisco to the *fiscalía* (1605–08) and Fernando to a councillorship (1608–15).[49] Moreover, three of Lerma's leading *hechuras* became secretaries of the Council – Franqueza (1601), Tristán de Ciriza (1613) and Bernabé de Bibanco (1614).[50] Lerma therefore knew of everything that was happening within the Council's offices. Indeed, *la Suprema* was for all practical purposes controlled at every significant level by *lermistas* for virtually the whole of the reign.

The Council of the Indies managed the enormous territories of the crown in the Americas and had special responsibility for the treasure fleets that brought the silver to Seville each autumn. It will be recalled that in 1603 Lerma secured the presidency of the Council for his nephew and son-in-law, the Count of Lemos.[51] The new president was a man of wide abilities; he had served with distinction as a soldier at the siege of Ostend and was a celebrated intellectual who employed Lope de Vega as his secretary and whose support for Miguel de Cervantes was so appreciated by the author that he conferred immortality upon the Count by dedicating the 'Second Part' of *Don Quixote* to him in 1615.[52] Lemos struggled to earn a reputation at court for his abilities rather than for his connections with Lerma.[53] He inherited one councillor who was a *lermista* (Juan de Ocontrillo) but, determined to demonstrate his independence of his uncle, he added only two more – Luis Gudiel, whom Lerma went out of his way to help in 1604, and Juan de Ibarra, who was promoted from the secretaryship to a councillorship *de capa y espada* in November 1604.[54]

The Council of Portugal had a turbulent history under Philip III. Juan de Borja replaced Moura in 1600 as leader of the Council but he left Valladolid in 1601 to serve as *mayordomo mayor* to the Empress María. Lerma attempted to have him replaced by Diego de Silva y Mendoza but was unable to push the appointment through, probably because of opposition within Portugal to the appointment of non-Portuguese.[55] Borja returned to court on the Empress's death in 1603 and resumed the leadership of the council, serving until he died in 1606. He was then succeeded by his son, Carlos de Aragón Borja y Gurrea (who was only 26 years old) and who served until 1614.[56] Lerma also had Pedro Álvarez Pereira appointed as a councillor of State of Portugal in 1599 and raised to a councillorship of Portugal in 1602.[57] He therefore had his supporters placed in the key positions in the Council.[58]

The expansion of government under Philip III resulted in a substantial growth in the size and importance of the conciliar secretariat. Lerma was aware of the implications of this expansion and placed *hechuras* within the secretariats of

Table 4 Secretarial offices held by *hechuras* and associates of the Duke of Lerma

The major councils	
State	Pedro Franqueza, Count of Villalonga, (Italy, 1600–07)
	Juan de Ciriza (Flanders, 1612–14)
War	Juan de Ciriza (Sea, 1610–12)
Castile	Francisco González de Heredia
	(Patronato Real, 1588–1614)
	Juan de Amezqueta
	(Justicia, 1602–05)
	(Cámara y Estado, 1605–08)
	Tomás de Ángulo
	(Justicia, 1605–08)
	(Cámara y Estado, 1608–21)
	(interim holder, *Patronato Real de la Iglesia*, 1614)
	Jorge de Tovar y Valderrama
	(Justicia, 1609–14)
	(Patronato Real de la Iglesia, 1614–24)
Finance	Cristóbal de Ipeñarrieta (1596–1601)
	Miguel de Ipeñarrieta (1614–18)
Indies	Juan de Ciriza (New Spain, 1605–10)
Inquisition	Pedro Franqueza (1601–07)
	Tristán de Ciriza (1612–24)
	Bernabé de Bibanco (1614–16)
Military Orders	Francisco González de Heredía
	(Santiago, Calatrava and Alcántara, 1588–1614)
Portugal	Pedro Álvarez Pereira (1600–1607)
Crusade	Tomás de Ángulo (1604–05)
Junta de Obras y Bosques	Juan de Ibarra (1586–1604)
	Pedro Franqueza (1604–06)
	Tomas de Ángulo (1612–21)

nine councils, chief among them those of State, Castile and Inquisition. Two major *hechuras* were placed in office in the Council of State; Pedro Franqueza served 1600–06 and Juan de Ciriza from 1612 until the accession of Philip IV in 1621.[59] The three offices of the Council of Castile were filled by trusted *hechuras* of Lerma for virtually the whole of the reign: *Justicia* (1602–14), *Patronato Real de la Iglesia* until 1624; and *Cámara y Estado de Castilla* (1605–21). These offices managed patronage affairs in Church and State, and Lerma therefore had access to influence and information across the whole range of these areas of government throughout the kingdom of Castile.

Francisco González de Heredia had been so greatly trusted by Philip II that in 1588 he had been appointed to the secretaryship of the *Patronato Real* and to that of the Council of Military Orders. In the first capacity he had responsibility for the administrative arrangements for all senior ecclesiastical appointments in Castile, while in the second he managed the documentation for appointments to the lucrative range of *encomiendas* in the Orders of Santiago, Calatrava and Alcántara.[60] González de Heredia then travelled the well-worn path to Lerma's favour through the good offices of Juan de Borja and was allowed to retain his lucrative array of offices until he died in 1614. He therefore exercised uniquely wide influence over many key areas of patronage and when he died he left a substantial fortune. However, he was wise enough not to endanger his great power and wealth, and no suspicion of corruption attached to his name. His son, Jerónimo, was advanced to a royal secretaryship in 1606.[61]

Juan de Amezqueta, secretary of the Count of Miranda, was appointed to the secretaryship of *Justicia* in 1602 and so undertook responsibility for managing the documents of all judicial cases dealt with by the Council. In 1605 he was promoted to the secretaryship of the *Cámara y Estado de Castilla*, which dealt with the crown's secular patrimony in Castile. He served until his death in 1608.[62] He was replaced on *Justicia* by Tomás de Ángulo.[63] In turn, Jorge de Tovar succeeded Ángulo in 1609 and followed González de Heredia in that of the *Patronato Real de la Iglesia* in 1604, serving until his death in 1624.[64]

Cristóbal de Ipeñarrieta, Secretary of the Council of Finance since 1596, came from a leading family of Valladolid and was well known to both Lerma and Juan de Borja. In January 1603 he was promoted to a councillorship of Finance, which he served until 1612.[65] His brother Miguel also made a career in the offices of the Council of Finance, becoming secretary in 1614 and councillor in 1618.[66] Like González de Heredia and Amezqueta, the brothers mastered the complex art of serving Lerma while remaining at some distance from him.

This was certainly not true of Pedro Álvarez Pereira, who played a key role for Lerma on the Council of Portugal and on *juntas* managing financial affairs. In 1599 Lerma had Álvarez appointed to a councillorship of Portugal and, reassured by his assiduity, began then to promote him to important *juntas* at the centre of Castilian government as well as in Portuguese affairs. Álvarez Pereira specialised in financial work and he became corrupted by his contacts with bankers and businessmen – and above all, by his work with the Count of Villalonga.[67]

Corruption personified: Pedro Franqueza, Count of Villalonga

Few men were more appropriately named than was Pedro Franqueza, for in Spanish the word '*franqueza*' means 'bribe'. Franqueza was a Catalan who was a contemporary of Lerma's, born in 1550. His relationship with Lerma was founded in his ability to work enormously hard at a number of tasks, and had none of the intimacy that characterised Lerma's bond with Rodrigo Calderón. He was consumed by his commitment to his work – and, after the court moved to Valladolid, by an unbridled determination to become wealthy.

Already by 1598 Franqueza had thirty-five years' service in the secretariat of the Council of Aragon behind him. He had come to know Lerma during the 1590s and, as we have seen, committed himself to his service during the *jornada* of 1599.[68] He rose dramatically, being appointed to three major secretaryships, which he exercised simultaneously – to the senior secretaryship of the Council of State, responsible for Italian affairs (1600); to one of the two secretaryships of the Council of Inquisition (1601) and then to the private secretaryship of the Queen (1602). He became so important to Lerma that in 1600 he was given lodgings in the royal palace to be close at hand for the duke. Cabrera de Córdoba, who watched Franqueza's career with fascinated horror, observed in 1602 that he 'is empowered with the (control) of the machine of all the important business through the favour that the Duke of Lerma gives him'.[69] However, Franqueza's seizure of the levers of power had only just begun. In 1602 he was given control of the correspondence with Baltasar de Zúñiga, ambassador in Brussels, and he began to gain influence over the Council of State's papers dealing with the Low Countries that belonged by right to his colleague Andrés de Prada.[70] In the following year he tried to take over complete control of Prada's office but Prada, who was an experienced administrator, managed to fight off his challenge.[71]

Franqueza now began to accumulate the secretaryships of key *juntas* with financial responsibilities.[72] At the height of his power, in 1605–06, he held five of these – of *Hacienda* and of *Desempeño Real*, both of which challenged the reformed Council of Finance for control of the crown's finances; *Obras y Bosques*, in charge of the royal palaces and estates; *Armadas*, which supervised the financing, building and provisioning of the royal fleets; and *Hacienda de Portugal*, which managed the financial affairs of the kingdom of Portugal.[73] In co-ordinating the work of these *juntas*, Franqueza was able to divert work away from the councils and to abrogate to himself much of the most important financial affairs of government; more than anyone else – more even than the President of the Council of Finance – he was the man who managed the resources of the royal exchequer in these years.[74]

Franqueza lived in dazzling luxury and invested large amounts of money in landed estates, and like Calderón he chose to do so in lands that were adjacent to the marquisate of Denia – in 1603 the town of Villamarchant and the *lugares* belonging to the town of Villalonga; in 1604 the town of Navajas. He also acquired a range of municipal and trading offices in Valencia and the south-east – an *escribanía* in Verguer; an *alcaidía* in Cartagena; rents drawn on the *bailía* of Valencia and the *procuración real* of Mallorca.

Franqueza's career reached a double pinnacle in the autumn of 1603 when he and his eldest son, Martín Valerio, both gained noble status. In August, Martín Valerio married Catalina de la Cerda y Mendoza, daughter of Bernardino de Mendoza, Count of Coruña. Such was Franqueza's stature at court that the marriage ceremony was held in the house of the President of the Council of Castile (who now addressed Franqueza as 'cousin') and was conducted by the Inquisitor-General with the Duke of Infantado and the Countess of Miranda serving as *padrinos*. In September, Franqueza was raised to the countship of Villalonga, a small town 40 kilometres to the west of Denia with rents worth about 20,000 ducats annually.[75]

The King continued to lavish his favour on his new count. On 24 November 1604 he presented Villalonga with a *juro* worth 5,500 ducats annually. More substantially, on 4 May 1605 Philip issued a decree which absolved Villalonga and his successors from the sanctions of the law if any of them were found guilty of crimes 'so that the goods of the said *mayorazgo* can at no time or for any reason be confiscated because of the actions of an individual or successor who is badly led or ill-advised...' Villalonga took advantage of the royal generosity to establish his *mayorazgo* (18 July). He then made his will and testament, and in acknowledging his obligations to Lerma set out a classic statement of the relationship between a *hechura* and his patron:

> For many years I have had occasion through working in the royal service and living at the court to have especial closeness and contact with Don Francisco Gómez de Sandoval y Rojas, Duke of Lerma, a man who is known throughout these kingdoms for his high nobility and the greatness of his blood and the seniority of his family and also for his rare and excellent virtues [which have been employed with so much benefit to the royal service and the public cause of these kingdoms] ... The benefits, grants, friendship and great love with which he has bound me to his person and house [causes my family] to recognise that all the goods, honours, graces, favours and royal grants, offices and our position in great affairs have come to us through the confidence that he has placed in us. Accordingly, as is well known, I despatch all of these businesses in the royal name ... Through his great generosity and nobility [the Duke of Lerma] has wished to honour and favour us; his favour is the first and only reason for His Majesty giving us the place in his royal service together with the grants, honours, favours and confidences that we have received [and which we hope that we will continue to receive throughout the life of His Majesty] ... It is right that we should demonstrate our obligation to His Excellency in testament to the love and gratitude that we owe to him and to his house, in part payment and remuneration for all that he has given to us [by making] the most substantial offering that ... we can make, by subrogating our house and *mayorazgo* into that of His Excellency in recognition of our debt and obligation ... In the event that our family line dies out and is extinguished it is our will that this *mayorazgo*, together with the house and goods that are incorporated to it, should be joined with and incorporated

into the house and *mayorazgo* of the said lord duke of Lerma and that it should
stay within it for ever [to be enjoyed] by his descendants.

Villalonga charged Martín Valerio and his heirs to remain 'creatures, sons and
dependents' of Lerma and his heirs.[76]

Such was Villalonga's admiration for his master that he forced Pedro de
Medicis to sell him his palace on the *Prado de San Jerónimo* near to Lerma's
town house – at a knock-down price – so that he could be near to Lerma and
always available to him.[77] He paid a deeply personal tribute to him when on 10
December 1606 he commissioned Pompeo Leoni to make a marble tomb with
funerary figures of his wife and himself in emulation of the statues of Lerma and
his wife in *San Pablo*.[78] But the statues were never made: on 18 January Lerma
advised the King to arrest Villalonga for mismanaging the financial affairs of the
crown.[79] To save himself, Lerma abandoned the Count.

The Councils of Finance and State

The struggle for control of the crown's finances: Juan de Acuña, the Council of Finance and the Count of Villalonga

The insistent peripateticism of Philip III during the first two years of his reign
accentuated the difficulties of financial management that he had inherited and
stimulated the use of short-term expedients to raise revenues.[80] Not until the
autumn of 1600 did Philip seriously turn his attention to reconstructing the
Council of Finance: he then appointed Juan de Acuña, a senior councillor of
Castile, as examining judge of the Council with a mandate to draw up a detailed
report into its activities. Acuña, an illegitimate son of the Count of Buendía,
was an experienced administrator who had a reputation as a stern and impartial
judge.[81] He promptly established that the Marquis of Poza had mismanaged his
responsibilities and recommended that he be dismissed.[82] Once again, it fell to
the unfortunate royal confessor, fray Gaspar de Córdoba, to inform a man of
his disgrace, and it was no comfort to Poza that his humiliation was disguised
with a councillorship of State. Poza sought an audience with Lerma to protest
against the decision but the duke refused to see him and Poza was forced to
vent his fury on the Count of Miranda. He wrote curtly to Lerma, who replied
by assuring him that he had done his best for him 'as a friend' and insisted that
he could not intercede for him.[83] It was with the most exquisite courtesy that
Lerma abandoned Poza.

While Philip supported Acuña over the dismissal of Poza he continued to
allow *juntas* to take over many of the responsibilities of the Council of Finance.[84]
In November 1600 a *junta* was established to negotiate *asientos* with bankers,

and it was dominated by Lerma's men – Juan de Borja, Gaspar de Córdoba and Franqueza among them.[85] Philip emphasised the importance of the new body by ordering that it should deal with a scheme to raise one million ducats 'because it is my wish that this be done without the Council of Finance having a hand in it'.[86] When the *contadores* of the Council of Finance objected in January 1601 about the decisions being made by the *Junta de Hacienda*, Philip bluntly ordered them to carry out his orders – 'when I order a despatch to be made the Council is not required to know how or with what advice I have decided upon it, for this is not its concern, [which is] only to carry out the orders sent to it in my name'.[87]

Acuña presented his report to the King on 6 February 1602.[88] He recommended that the Council of Finance should be enlarged and united with the *Contaduría Mayor de Cuentas*. Most importantly, Acuña insisted that the duties of the Council should be clearly defined so that it was responsible for 'the administration, government and collection of the resources of the royal exchequer'.[89] Philip demonstrated his satisfaction with Acuña's report in the most vivid manner: in April he appointed him as President of the Council of Finance.[90]

The *Junta de Reformación de los Tribunales de Hacienda* was then established to recommend men for councillorships and other offices in the new body. Acuña was joined by the presidents of Castile and Indies (Miranda and Laguna) and by Alonso Ramírez de Prado and Cristóbal de Ipeñarrieta.[91] Of these men, Miranda, Ramírez de Prado and Ipeñarrieta kept a watching brief for Lerma, and tension developed within the *Junta* as they fought to have their colleagues appointed.

The key figure among the *lermistas* was Ramírez de Prado. A councillor (*oidor*) of the Council of Navarre, he was a cultivated networker who had, like so many others, found his way into Lerma's service in 1599 through Juan de Borja.[92] He rose rapidly; in October 1600 Philip appointed him to a councillorship of Castile but ordered that he was not to sit on the Council because he could not be spared from the Council of Finance; Ramírez was clearly destined to play a key role in the appointments of the members of the Council and in the management of financial affairs after the reforms had been implemented.[93]

The *Junta de Reformación* made its recommendations in September 1602.[94] It suggested that two experienced *contadores mayores*, Luis Gaitán and Francisco de Salablanca, should be retained and that secretary Esteban de Ibarra should be appointed because of his great knowledge of financial affairs. Otherwise, it proposed a number of *lermistas*. Ramírez de Prado received the strongest commendation – 'a minister who is so capable and useful and who has such experience and intelligence' – while Pascual was described as an 'intelligent person'. The *Junta* also supported the nominations of Cristóbal de Ipeñarrieta, Diego Sarmiento de Acuña, Domingo de Cabala, Alonso Fernández de Espinosa and Gaspar de Pons, all of whom were closely associated with Lerma. Ramírez de Prado then proposed that the royal confessor should be appointed 'because of the great understanding that he has of affairs of the exchequer'. In reality, fray Gaspar had no financial expertise and his nomination was tactfully opposed by the three presidents on the grounds that he was fully occupied with the King's confessorship and a councillorship of State.

Philip was in Lerma when he despatched the titles for the new council-lors on 26 October 1602 – the only occasion when he appointed a tranche of *lermistas* to governmental office while he was living in one of Lerma's proper-ties. He named Salablanca and Gaitán de Ayala from the old *contadores*, and Ramírez de Prado, Ipeñarrieta, Cabala, Fernández de Espinosa, Pascual and Pons from the *lermistas*. He rejected the claims of Gaspar de Córdoba, Messía de Tovar and Sarmiento de Acuña.[95] The new president and the new *ordenanzas* transformed the Council, which now sat 50 per cent more frequently than it had done and with an average attendance that was doubled.[96] However, when vacancies arose on the Council, Lerma had Messía de Tovar (July 1603) and Sarmiento de Acuña (September 1604) appointed; having failed to secure their nomination as part of his grouping of councillors, he was successful in having them named on an individual basis.[97]

Lerma also extended his control over the Council's patronage offices. In 1603 Diego López de Gojenaga, who had been Lerma's private accountant, was named as *contador del sueldo*, charged with responsibility for despatching the decrees for conciliar salaries.[98] In 1604 Tristán de Ciriza was appointed as *contador de mercedes* and assumed responsibility for supervising the despatch of royal decrees involving grants or *mercedes*.[99]

Lerma continued to undermine the new Council of Finance by having *juntas* created to take over many of its responsibilities. On 5 May 1603 – almost unnoticed in the great reforms of the financial institutions – the *Junta del Desem-peño* was established.[100] It came into being as a direct result of an initiative by Franqueza and Ramírez de Prado, who in a working document proposed that the crown needed to correlate its expenditure against its income, establishing what monies were available to it, where they were and what was committed against them. In this, the two men were quite correct: this role should have gone under the *ordenanzas* of 1602 to the renewed Council of Finance. The solution proposed by the two men threatened to fracture the management of financial affairs. Franqueza and Ramírez de Prado went on to suggest that the crown could achieve solvency by buying its alienated rents out of pawn (*desem-peñar*). In practice, this involved nothing more sophisticated than recycling the crown's debts by massively alienating its resources in Castile; loans would be piled upon loans to create the impression that the crown was overcoming its debts when in reality it was extending them. The *Junta del Desempeño* was given the right to intervene in any of the crown's financial matters. It had access to the financial dealings of all the councils but was answerable to none of them. It had, too, direct access to the King so that he could sign decrees authorising disbursements of money. Central to the justification for the *Junta*'s existence was that it should ensure that the royal households had first call on resources.

The contest between the Council of Finance and the *Junta del Desempeño* allowed Lerma to play the two bodies off against each other. Certainly, the ground over which they fought for control was extraordinarily lucrative: the grant of the eighteen *millones* by the Cortes of Castile in 1601 had given the crown the assurance of receiving 3,000,000 ducats a year in cash for six years while the boom in the Indies trade in the period 1601–05 brought it an average of 2,156,250 ducats per annum.[101] The crown therefore regularly had vast injections of cash, and much of it found its way, directly or indirectly, into Villalonga's own coffers.

As Jean-Marc Pelorson demonstrated in a seminal article, Villalonga and Ramírez de Prado took advantage of their membership of the *Junta del Desempeño* to profit enormously from their control over negotiations with bankers and financiers.[102] Certainly, Villalonga had the complete trust of the King. He travelled with Philip and had the freest access to him. Indeed, he was even allowed to speak directly for the King on the most important of matters: in May 1605, for instance, Philip trusted him to 'explain' his policy toward his fractious brother-in-law the Duke of Savoy to a *junta* comprised of councillors of State.[103] Villalonga was able to turn the King against his reformed Council of Finance to the point where Philip rebuked it in writing for failing in its duty to him.[104] He was able, too, to demonstrate apparently brilliant success in managing the crown's finances: on 16 August 1605 he and Ramírez de Prado sent a *consulta* to Philip claiming that the crown had benefited by 14,728,890 ducats from the *desempeño*. Philip failed to attach any importance to the fact that only two members of the *Junta* had signed the *consulta*, and retained his confidence in Villalonga.[105]

Within a year of the establishment of the *Junta*, Villalonga was personally agreeing the terms of major *asientos*, controlling the farming-out of taxes, manipulating the return on *juros*, trading in crown rents, and organising major shipbuilding contracts. From every operation he took his cut and everyone dealing with him understood how his favour could be won by the gift of valuables and presents. Soon he was managing frauds that were often worth hundreds of thousands of ducats and which in total cost the royal exchequer millions of ducats. As a master of administrative procedures he ensured that his misdeeds left little evidence behind him.[106]

Villalonga was able to disguise the shortage of silver, if only temporarily, by yet another debasement of the coinage in September 1603 – the very month, as it happened, in which he was raised to the countship, as if in tribute to his work in devastating the country's coinage.[107] Another device which Villalonga pushed through was the grant of a papal pardon for the Jews of Portugal in return for their gift to the crown of 1,860,000 ducats. While Villalonga may have received as much as 70,000 ducats for arranging the deal, Philip's reputation fared less well: he was mocked in Portugal as 'The King of the Jews'.[108]

Responsibility for maintaining the navy was handed in 1603 to the *Junta de Fábricas y Armadas*, and it too was controlled by Villalonga. The *Junta* negotiated government contracts for shipbuilding and for repair work and effectively privatised the crown's interest in the industry. The contracts were neither public nor competitive: they went, as did so much else in these years, to those who came to agreements with Villalonga. But the ships that the Count sent to sea were often inadequate and frequently unsafe. In 1603 the home fleet was reorganised into three squadrons. With fine symbolism, the money for the operation was kept in the monastery of *San Pablo* itself and managed by Villalonga and the two treasurers-general, as if it was for the personal use of Lerma and his *hechuras*.[109]

Villalonga was able to involve himself in some appointments to major offices even though he did not hold a secretaryship responsible for patronage. He sold titles, manipulated the grant of royal *mercedes* and sealed despatches. He negotiated with the greatest men at court; for instance, the Count of Benavente paid him 6,000 ducats for despatching his title as Viceroy of Naples. However, Villalonga was not always discreet. It was foolish of him to flaunt his role in facilitating the appointment of Bautista de Acevedo as Inquisitor General in 1603 – 'the Inquisitor General is all mine, and I alone [knew about the appointment] other than his Majesty and the Duke of Lerma.'[110]

The first doubts about Villalonga's methods were raised at the turn of 1604–05 when Diego de Mardones warned Lerma of the increasing tension between Juan de Acuña as President of the Council of Finance and the members of the *Junta del Desempeño*. When Villalonga and Ramírez de Prado repeatedly assured Philip over the winter of 1605–06 that the *desempeño* had dramatically improved the crown's financial position, they were responding to the observable truth that the royal finances were at the point of collapse. They were also defending themselves against the corrosive criticism being levelled against them by Mardones. Acuña decided to distance himself and his council from responsibility for the financial disaster that was manifestly imminent, and on 13 February 1606 he joined Mardones in sending a *consulta* to Philip giving the real figures for the *desempeño*. The Queen supported them by making public her criticisms of Villalonga.[111] Villalonga's house of cards now collapsed with alarming rapidity, and as it did so the authority of Lerma in court and government was placed gravely at risk.

*The Council of State, Ambrosio Spínola and the privatisation of the war
in the Low Countries*

While the Count of Villalonga suborned the crown's management of financial
affairs, the Council of State reasserted its importance in government and in
doing so assumed a role at the centre of policymaking that it would maintain
throughout the seventeenth century. During the years of the residence of the
court in Valladolid, the Council of State met on average twice a week and was
attended by sixteen men who maintained a healthy enough average of five
councillors per meeting. At the core of the Council in these years were six men
of substantial and variegated experience: Idiáquez, Chinchón, Miranda, Velada,
the Constable of Castile and the Count of Olivares. Lerma attended only thirty-
eight of 1,704 meetings for which membership has been tabulated in the years
of his *valimiento*. Clearly, he was not concerned to dominate the policymaking
process from the council table. Nor did Lerma attempt to dominate the Council
through his relatives. The members of his *parentela* who attended the Council
during these years – Miranda, the Cardinal of Toledo, Juan de Borja and the
Duke of Infantado – formed only 22 per cent of attendances at the Council.
Miranda was the only one of these men who became an important councillor,
attending 220 times in Valladolid. Juan de Borja, obsessed by his own ill health
(and obliged to live in Madrid until the death of the Empress María in 1603),
spent such energies as he had in trying to evade work and made little impression at the council table (113 attendances). The Cardinal-archbishop of Toledo
sat thirty-seven times in 1603 but thereafter his refusal to live in Valladolid
meant that he attended only a handful of meetings before the court returned
to Madrid. Nor did the men whom Lerma had placed in the king's confessorship make a significant contribution at the Council. Gaspar de Córdoba was
the only one who made any impression on the Council in these years; he sat
regularly in 1600–03 (170 attendances) but only eight times in 1604 as illness
restricted him. When Diego de Mardones was appointed to succeed Córdoba
in January 1606 it was expressly recorded that he would confine himself to
fulfilling his duties as confessor to the King and that he would not play a part in
governmental affairs as his predecessor had done.[112] Five laymen made limited
impact on the Council.[113]

   Philip and Lerma set themselves to reshape the Council of State in the
spring of 1600. They had first to address themselves to the question of which
of the senior servants of Philip II they should retain. There was certainly to be
no place on the Council for the Marquis of Castel Rodrigo.[114] When his tenure
of office as Viceroy of Portugal came to an end in 1603 he wrote to the King
asking for permission to come to court, as was traditional, to present his report
in person to the King. Philip did not even deign to reply and in 1604 Castel
Rodrigo bitterly reproached him that 'men of my quality and services should

be treated in this manner'. Still, Philip still did not reply, but he instructed Villalonga to inform the Marquis that Lerma would write to him ordering him to remain in Portugal.[115]

By contrast to his old colleague, Juan de Idiáquez survived in office to exercise much greater influence on policymaking under Philip III than he had under Philip II. He attended 70 per cent of the meetings of the Council of State between the beginning of 1599 and his death in August 1614 (with 983 attendances out of 1403 meetings). Idiáquez also managed a very substantial burden of work as President of the Council of Military Orders and as a member of several major *juntas*. His knowledge of European politics and the understated but authoritative manner in which he delivered his *pareceres* at the Council were admired equally by his king and his colleagues and he became the recognised leader of the Council, the councillor who set the tone and the framework for discussions.

The Count of Chinchón almost shared Moura's fate. The severity of his personality did not make him an agreeable colleague and he probably survived in office because he was not a threat to Lerma and because it was useful to have a representative of the eastern nobility at the centre of government.[116] Chinchón sat on the councils of Aragon and Italy as Treasurer-General until his death in 1608. He came to exercise significant, if subordinate, influence at the Council of State in the shadow of Idiáquez; his attendance has been recorded at 591 meetings in the years to his death in 1608.

The Marquis of Velada was well regarded by the King and since he was a prominent member of the powerful Toledo clan he could not easily be swept aside. Velada was quiescent in Lerma's seizure of power but as Santiago Martínez Hernández has demonstrated in a brilliant biography, he challenged Lerma in the middle years of the reign and emerged with his position at court substantially enhanced. Perhaps even Lerma was beguiled by the circumspection with which Velada conducted himself into failing to realise that the languid marquis was a politician of substance and determination.[117] He attended 377 meetings in the years to 1616 (25 per cent).

It was significant of the reinvigoration of the Council of State that two men who had good cause to resent Lerma became major councillors. The Constable of Castile sat regularly in Valladolid before leaving for northern Europe, and when he returned to court at the end of 1605 he became a councillor of real substance, sitting consistently until he was sent to Milan in 1610 (660 attendances, 1601–10).[118] Enrique de Guzmán de Guzmán, second count of Olivares, was the brother of Ana Felix, Marchioness of Camarasa, and doubtless shared her resentment at the treatment of her husband by the *valido*. Lerma was careful to reach an accommodation with him and praised his appointment to the Council in 1602: 'there has been great pleasure here with this appointment, which I consider to be very appropriate because of the many and great qualities that the Count has through his wide experience'.[119] Olivares became a major councillor, imaginative and broad in the perspectives he brought to the Council. He was encouraged to reconcile himself to Lerma because the duke toyed with the thought of having him sent as ambassador to the imperial court in 1602. This was a potent threat in view of Olivares's acute financial difficulties, and it was doubtless Lerma who was behind the King's refusal in 1603 to grant Olivares the grandeeship that was the chief ambition of his family and himself. For good measure, Poza and Chinchón were also refused at the same time. Lerma would keep the three men under his control as they strove to win *grandeza*: none of them ever conspired against him – but none of them was raised to the grandeeship.[120]

Lerma took a close interest in the first two major projects to which the renewed Council committed itself to enhance the status of Spanish arms, but both brought humiliation rather than the great victory for which the King had yearned: a naval expedition against Algiers failed even to land men, while the men who made it to shore in Ireland in 1601 were easily crushed by the English. Philip reluctantly accepted that he could no longer intervene in England and determined to concentrate his resources on the war in the Low Countries, proclaiming that he would make a war of 'blood and iron' on the Dutch.[121] Few of his senior policymakers doubted that the best that could be hoped for would be to win an acceptable peace settlement.[122]

Appreciating full well how deeply Philip yearned to win a great victory to mark the beginning of his reign, Lerma led the search for a triumph in what Bernardo García has termed a 'foreign policy of reputation'. He knew, as did all senior policymakers, that success would have to be found on the cheap, for the resources no longer existed to fund major expeditions on land or sea. He was a member of a *junta* in February 1602 which accepted Federico Spínola's offer to operate eight galleys out of Sluys to harass Dutch shipping. This imaginative enterprise proved to be a sad, if heroic, failure.[123] In 1602 the Englishman Thomas Wintour arrived in Valladolid to ask for support for a conspiracy of Catholic gentlemen to baulk the succession of King James VI of Scotland to the English throne. Lerma was beguiled by the prospect of winning a great victory for his king in England and he and Franqueza interviewed Wintour and then passed him on to Miranda and the King. It was a crass response by Lerma, for it encouraged Wintour and his associates to carry on plotting, and in 1603 Guy Fawkes travelled to Spain to win support for the enterprise. Fawkes trekked around Old Castile in pursuit of the duke but never secured an audience with him. Nevertheless, it was foolish of Lerma to leave himself open to the charge of conspiring with the English Catholic plotters.[124]

Queen Elizabeth died on 24 March 1603, and James VI succeeded without challenge, becoming James I of England. He promptly brought the war with Spain to an end by proclaiming that he himself had never been at war with Spain, and Juan Bautista de Tassis, a close friend of Lerma's, was sent to England as extraordinary ambassador to re-establish relations. He was rewarded with the title of Count of Villamediana (12 October 1603). Once Tassis had established that James was serious about making peace, the Constable of Castile was appointed as the peacemaker.[125]

When Federico Spínola died in an engagement off Sluys (26 May), his brother Ambrosio redoubled his commitment to Spain's cause in the Low Countries in homage to him. The Army of Flanders was tied down in an interminable siege of the town of Ostend, and on 7 October Ambrosio wrote to Philip offering to conquer Ostend within one calendar year and to provide half of the 120,000 ducats a month that would be required to do so.[126] With his astonishing offer Spínola began one of the most important – indeed extraordinary – careers in Habsburg Spain; he became a major figure in the government of Philip III and assumed even greater importance under Philip IV. Spínola's career was marked not only by its military and political brilliance but also by the unusual determination to become a great lord in Spain; indeed, he became in this regard almost more Spanish than the Spaniards. Sublimely self-confident, he measured himself in battle against Maurice of Nassau and at court against the Duke of Lerma (and indeed against the whole body of the Castilian military élite). He had an intriguing relationship with Lerma, whom he much admired. Lerma was vexed by Spínola's ability to make himself indispensable to him and, try as he might, he could neither cope with Spínola nor do without him – a characteristic that he shared with the Count-Duke of Olivares in the 1620s.

For its part, the Council of State had no alternative but to accept Spínola's offer to conquer Ostend. The general kept his promise, concluding the siege – if at a dreadful human cost; 50,000 men died in the campaign – on 22 September 1604.[127] At last Philip had his great victory. The capture of Ostend came one month after the conclusion of peace with England (Treaty of Hampton Court, 28 August 1604).[128] The conjuncture of the two events raised hopes that Spain's war effort could now be concentrated on the Low Countries. This was the more true because it was evident to the King and his leading advisers that for the first time since Parma's death in 1591 Spain once again had a general of the first rank to lead the war effort.

Unfortunately, Spínola then demanded that in reward for his triumph he should be appointed *maestre de campo general*, or field marshal, of the Army of Flanders.[129] Members of the councils of State and War found this an intolerable presumption, not least because it focused all of their resentment at the alienation of control over the war in the Low Countries that had come about with

Philip II's devolution of authority in 1598. Lerma was among the policymakers in Madrid who resented Spínola's overweening ambition and in September 1604 sneered that his status as a soldier derived solely from his wealth – 'he would not be a soldier if it was not for his money'.[130] Spínola set such store on winning the *maestrazgo* that he came to Spain and spent the winter of 1604–05 waging a campaign for the office that was quite as methodical as the one that he had fought at Ostend. It was a pivotal moment, in which Spínola once again confronted the Castilian nationalists who so resented him and indeed measured himself against Lerma and his *clientela*. As Philip II's wars were finally run down, it was the Genoese banker-general who forced the Spanish government to confront the realities of its position in the Low Countries and even to address some fundamental questions about the nature of the Spanish monarchy itself.

Spínola startled the councillors of State by informing them that in 1605 he would cross the Rhine and invade Frisia, dividing the United Provinces into two and hindering communications with their allies in the Empire. He also promised, as a point of family honour, to recover Sluys, which Maurice of Nassau had captured while he was concentrating on Ostend. The Council baulked at giving control of the Army of Flanders to a foreigner: in January, Agustín Mejía was appointed *maestre de campo general* in Flanders.[131]

Spínola was then referred to Villalonga. The Count informed Spínola that Philip was honouring him with the dukedom of Santa Severina in Naples and – a most singular honour, this, coming as it did from Villalonga's lips – that he would not have to pay anything for it. Spínola would be given a small army with which to attack Sluys. Spínola dismissed the offer and may well have confused Villalonga by stating the principle that guided his determination: 'his purpose was to win honour and reputation, making his name in great affairs'. Villalonga argued with him, but to no avail.

As Spínola had doubtless anticipated, he was now granted an interview with Lerma. He threatened to retire from the service of the King if the *maestrazgo* was not conferred upon him. The financial and military implications of that threat were irresistible and Spínola was appointed as *maestre de campo general* and also given control over the financial management of the war as *superintendente de hacienda de Flandes*. Mejía was appointed as Inspector of the Frontiers and Coasts of Spain and given a councillorship of War as compensation.[132]

Once again Spínola was as good as his word. In a campaign that rocked Europe and came close to demoralising the Dutch, he led his army into the north-eastern territories of the United Provinces. Fearful that he might thrust deeper into their territory in 1606 and split it into two, the Dutch began constructing a fortified rampart for some 240 kilometres along the Yssel and Waal rivers.[133]

The most extraordinary aspect of the campaign of 1605 was that it was fought without benefit of any Indies silver: no American treasure arrived in Spain throughout 1605.[134] Even Spínola could not fund the war by himself, and at the end of the campaigning season he returned to Spain to win the resources for the 1606 campaign. Lerma vigorously opposed his return, fearful that Spínola would once again prove irresistible at court. However, in October 1605 the *flota* from New Spain arrived in Seville without any treasure, having had to deposit its precious cargo in Havana to await the galleons of 1606.[135] As Spínola travelled to Spain he could not have known that the crown had more desperate need of his financial credit than ever before.

NOTES

1 M. Artola, *La monarquía de España*, Madrid, 1999; see esp. pp. 41–66, 253–79.
2 See pp. 54, 174–7.
3 Palace, 11 Sep. 1603, BL Add 28,425, fol. 109.
4 See above, p. 87.
5 Lerma to Juan de Borja, Lerma, ? Jul. 1605, BL Add 28,425 fols. 296–296b.
6 See the important examples cited by García García, *La Pax Hispánica*, pp. 270–1, nn. 70–5.
7 Prada to Lerma, Valladolid, 16 Oct. 1604 and reply, Ventosilla, 26 Oct., AGS E 841, fol. 180.
8 Prada to Lerma, Madrid, 16 Jul. 1607 and reply, San Lorenzo, 22 Jul., copies, BN Mss 1492, fol. 269v.
9 Lerma to Prada, Tordesillas, 26 Feb. 1605, ibid., fol. 268v, copy.
10 Prada to Lerma, Valladolid, 16 Oct. 1604 and reply, Palace, 28 Oct., AGS E 841, fol. 180.
11 Lerma to Poza Valladolid, 11 Mar. 1601, AGS CJH 293, no fol.
12 Same to Acuña, de casa, 30 Oct. 1603, AGS CJH 432, fol. 342.
13 Same to Juan de Borja, Valladolid, 25 Dec. 1602, BL Add 28,424, fol. 437. See also, Lerma to Juan de Acuña, Campillo, 30 Oct. 1603, AGS CJH 432, fol. 350.
14 Lerma to Juan de Acuña, President of Council of Finance, Valladolid, 12 Jul. 1603, AGS CJH 432, no fol.
15 Same to same, Ventosilla, 17 Oct. 1604, CJH 321 (MOD), no fol.
16 See above, pp. 56, 60–1.
17 Juan de Borja was also *mayordomo mayor* to the Empress María until her death in 1603. A *cédula* of 29 October 1601 raised all of Borja's sons to the rank of *mozos fidalgos* of the *Casa de Portugal*, Fernández de Béthencourt, *Historia genealógica*, iv, 189–204. For a discussion of Lerma's use of his authority, Feros, *Kingship and Favoritism*, ch. 5 'In his image and likeness', pp. 91–109.
18 See a brilliant analysis of the tensions between Lerma and Velada in Martínez Hernández, *El Marqués de Velada*, pp. 431–559.
19 On Mardones's role in government, *Relaciones*, pp. 282 and 283; González was Prior of *San Pablo* when he was appointed as Lerma's confessor, ibid., p. 387.
20 On Calderón, above pp. 109–10; Bautista de Acevedo, above, pp. 3–4; de la Serna, Lerma to Juan de Borja, Valladolid, 4 Mar. 1603, BL Add 28,425, fol. 39; on Juan de Ciriza, same to same, Valencia, 31 Jan. 1604, BL Add 28, 425, fol. 192; see also *Relaciones*, p. 463; Tristán de Ciriza's title, Valladolid, 14 Dec. 1604, AGS QC 40.
21 Juan López, *Tercera parte de la historia general de Sancto Domingo y de su orden de predicadores*, Valladolid, 1613, pp. 221–7.
22 The career of a minor *hechura* demonstrated how Lerma could be damaged by overethenthusiastic efforts from a follower. Iñigo Ibáñez de Santa Cruz's career was distinguished by self-damage. He had served in Lerma's household in the 1590s and severely embarrassed his master at the beginning of the reign by circulating a tract attacking the 'confused and ignorant government' of Philip II and his ministers in contrast to that of Philip III. Lerma saw to it that

GOVERNMENT AND POLICYMAKING: 1598–1606 129

Ibáñez's punishment was a lenient one and allowed him to return to work. Unfortunately, Ibáñez was not a man to learn a lesson; in 1603 gave a paper to Gaspar de Córdoba urging him to have Villalonga and Calderón dismissed. He was condemned to death and to the sequestration of his property. Once again, Lerma inteceded for him and against all expectation Ibáñez found himself again employed in the royal service as a secretary. Lerma clearly had real affection for Ibáñez but did not thereafter advance him to significant office in government or court. On his services, *cnta.* Indies, 16 Feb. 1612, AGI IG 751, no fol., and *Relaciones*, pp. 56, 243, 413.

23 See below, pp. 156–7, 167, 178.

24 See above, p. 112.

25 For convenience's sake, I use the title of Lerma rather than that of Denia in this paragraph and refer to Valladolid as a 'city', a rank that it only received in 1595.

26 Salazar y Castro, *Comendadores de … Santiago*, pp. 224–5; J. Juderias, 'Un proceso político en tiempo de Felipe III. Don Rodrigo Calderón, Marqués de Siete Iglesias. Su vida, su proceso y su muerte', *RABM*, 3a época, v, May 1905, pp. 334–65; ix, Dec. 1905, pp. 349–63; x, Jan. 1906, pp. 1–31 and 406–13.

27 Trewinnard, 'The Household of the Spanish Monarch', pp. 113–14.

28 *Relaciones*, p. 351.

29 See below, pp. 168–9, 170–2.

30 *Relaciones*, p. 227 and T. W(ilson) to Sir Robert Cecil, Valladolid, 30 Sep./10 Oct. 1604, NA SP 94/10, fol. 112. Also, below, pp. 250–1.

31 García Oro, *Conde de Gondomar*, pp. 123–4, and L. Tobío, *Gondomar y su triunfo sobre Raleigh*, Santiago de Compostela, 1974, pp. 187–97; Gutiérrez Alonso, *Valladolid*, pp. 297–301.

32 On Villalonga, *Relaciones*, pp. 150; Mazo de la Vega's title as councillor of Finance, Madrid, 14 Feb. 1614 refers to his having been Secretary of the Queen, AGS QC 20.

33 The records of the *Cámara de Castilla* have scores of requests from Lerma for favours and privileges; for example, in July–August 1607, the Council of Castile gave favourable verdicts to him over a grant to a convent in Valladolid; exemption from the provisions of law so that the Duchess of Santa Gadea could be given some money to live on, privileges on the sale of the *Casa de la Ribera*, and the conditions of the market held in Valladolid. AGS CC Leg. 918, fols. 73, 74, 99, 8, and 149. On the councillors of Castile, Jean-Marc Pelorson, *Les Letrados juristes castillans sous Philippe III. Recherches sur leur place dans la société, la culture et l'état*, Poitiers, 1980, and Janine Fayard, *Les Membres du Conseil de Castille à l'époque moderne (1621–1746)*, Geneva-Paris, 1979.

34 Tapia's title, Madrid, 7 Feb. 1600, AGS QC 38; Ocontrillo's and Contreras's, 5 Oct. 1599, AGS QC 28 and 16; Bonal's, San Lorenzo, 14 Mar. 1604, ibid.

35 He was the first man appointed in the reign to councillorship of the Military Orders (Jan. 1599) and was promoted to Castile on 7 Feb. 1600, AGS QC 6.

36 'es tan benemerito y es tan antiguo servidor de la casa de V. Ex[celenci]a', Juan de Borja to Lerma, Madrid, 27 Mar. 1602, and reply ('Yo he deseado siempre el bien de Joan Alderete'), Valladolid, 6 Apr. 1602, BL Add 28,424, fol. 303b. See also, Borja to Lerma, Madrid 21 Sep. 1600 and reply, San Lorenzo, 23 Sep. in which Lerma acknowledged that 'alderete merece toda la merced que Su Mag[esta]d le iciere …', BL Add 28,423, fol. 217.

37 Titles, Valencia, 18 Feb. 1604, AGS QC 24 (Juan) and 11 (Diego).

38 'Todos somos hechuras y criados de V[uestro] Ex[celenci]a', Council of Castile to Lerma, Madrid, 7 Jul. 1608, BN Mss 12179, fol. 109, copy.

39 Borja to Denia, Madrid, 29 Jul., 7 Aug., 4 and 25 Sep. 1599, BL Add 28,422, fols. 89, 112, 132–3, 146b.

40 'Malissima obra recebimos en no querer el conde publicar la placa de don Garcia de Medrano perdonesselo dios', same to same, Madrid, 23 Jan. 1600, ibid., fol. 261b. Lerma replied, 'Yo juro a VS. que no me queda nada por hazer' and promised that he would speak to Miranda that day, reply, 24 Jan. 1600, ibid.

41 'Beso las manos a V[uestra] Ex[celenci]a por la provision de Don García de Medrano, Borja

to Lerma, Madrid, 17 Feb. 1600, ibid., fol. 305; Medrano was sworn in on Orders on 3 Mar. 1601, AGS QC 20.

42 Title, Buñol, 21 Feb. 1604, ibid.

43 Diego de Alderete, Valladolid, 13 Sep. 1601, QC 11; Silva de Torres, Aranjuez, 6 May 1602, QC 31; Manso, San Lorenzo, 7 Oct. 1604, QC 37.

44 *Relaciones*, p. 168.

45 Cardinal Sandoval took possession 8 Oct. 1608, AHN Inq. Lib. 361, fol. 58; Aliaga on 28 Jan. 1619, ibid., lib. 362, fol. 362. On the Council in the early years, Williams, 'A Jewish Councillor of Inquisition?' Luis de Mercado, the Statutes of *limipieza de sangre* and the Politics of Vendetta (1598–1601), *BHS*, lxvii, 1990, pp. 253–64.

46 Oath, 23 Nov. 1598, AHN Inq. lib. 1338, fol. 24; Lerma wrote to Juan de Borja on 31 May 1599 that 'Las cossas del s(eñor) Don Thomas de borja Tengo por tan propias como es Razon, y a nadie le esta mejor que A mi el verle en el lugar q(ue) meresce hago y Hare quanto es en mi por cumplir a oblig(acio)n', Barcelona, BL Add 28,422, fol. 68.

47 Oath, 31 Jul. 1600, AHN Inq. lib. 1338, fol. 26.

48 Oath, 26 June 1603, ibid., lib. 367, fol. 10.

49 Francisco, title, 5 Jul. 1605, AHN Inq. lib. 1338, fol. 38b; Fernando's oath, 24 Jan. 1608, ibid., fol. 223.

50 Franqueza, oath, 26 May 1601, AHN Inq. lib. 1338, fol. 29; Ciriza, 11 Jan. 1613, ibid., fol. 50; Bibanco, 3 Mar. 1614, ibid., fol. 55b. Curiously, Ciriza's title was given to him in 1613 to replace Franqueza, who had of course lost his office early in 1607, Madrid, 10 Jan. 1613, AHN Inq. lib. 366, fol. 113. Bibanco then replaced Ciriza, title, 2 Mar. 1614, ibid., fol. 161.

51 Lemos's title, Olmedo, 6 Apr. 1603, AGS QC 36; Borja's appreciation ('a sido muy acertada esta eleçion'), to Lerma, Madrid, 12 Apr. 1603, BL Add 28,425, fol. 76b.

52 Fernández de Béthencourt, *Historia genealógica*, iv, pp. 550–8.

53 Cornwallis wrote of him that he was 'much riper in Understanding' than many others, to Salisbury, Valladolid, n. d. (1605), in Sir Ralph Winwood, *Memorials of Affairs of State in the Reigns of Queen Elizabeth and King James I*, 3 vols., London, 1725, ii, p. 150.

54 Ocontrillo's title, 14 Jan. 1599, AGS QC 28; Gudiel's title, Denia, 24 Jan. 1604, ibid. 17. Juan de Ibarra was secretary of the Council and of the *Junta de Obras y Bosques* when he was appointed, title, 20 Nov. 1604, AGS QC 27.

55 Gaillard, *Le Portugal sous Philippe III*, pp. 15, 59, 71, 81–91; T. J. Dadson, 'The Duke of Lerma and the Count of Salinas. Politics and Friendship in Early Seventeenth-Century Spain', *EHQ*, vol. 25, 1995, pp. 5–38, p. 9.

56 *Relaciones*, pp. 52, 184, 288–9.

57 Álvarez Pereira to Lerma, Madrid, 1 Dec. 1599, BL Add 28,426, fol. 193, *Relaciones*, pp. 145–6, 199.

58 Felipe de Tassis was appointed as *Comisario General de la Cruzada* in 1599 and served until 1607. The Council of the Crusade was a minor body whose only real function was to deal with the administration of the *cruzada* tax. Nothing is known of Tassis's conduct of his office.

59 Martín died in October 1599 and Francisco accepted generous terms to retire in February 1600, *Relaciones*, p. 62. No title survives for Prada's appointment to State; Franqueza's title, Toledo, 5 Apr. 1600, AGS QC 36.

60 Title of *Patronato Real de la Iglesia*, Madrid, 6 Jan. 1588, AGS QC 17; copy of *cédula* of 6 Jan. 1588 appointing him Secretary of the Council of Military Orders, BL Add 28,701, fol. 189–99b.

61 'toda la merced que hiziere V[uestra] Exc[elenci]a al S[ecretari]o Francisco gonzález de Heredia terné yo por propria por que se lo devo', Borja to Lerma, Madrid, 29 Jan. 1605, BL Add 28,425, fol. 14. *Relaciones*, p. 551; Jerónimo's title, Madrid, 4 Mar. 1606, AGS QC 21.

62 Titles, *Justicia*, Valladolid, 25 Aug. 1602 and *Cámara y Estado de Castilla*, Lerma, 2 Sep. 1605, AGS QC 24.

63 Ángulo, titles, *Justicia*, Olmedo, 19 Sep. 1605, and *Cámara y Estado de Castilla*, El Pardo, 19

Nov. 1608 AGS QC 40. At the same time Lerma had Juan de Ciriza raised to the Indies office dealing with New Spain. These key strategic appointments were made while the King and his household were stranded in Olmedo by the Queen's illness; Ciriza's title, Olmedo, 24 Sep. 1605, AGI IG 965, no fol. Ángulo was also raised briefly to the secretaryship of the Council of Crusade in 1604 and so had knowledge of the collection of the *Cruzada* tax.

64 Titles, Madrid, 9 Jan. 1609 and Madrid, 31 Dec. 1614, AGS QC 23.

65 Borja suggested Ipeñarrieta for a place on a junta, 'por ser muy suficiente para el servicio de Su M[agestad]', and Lerma noted that he held him in high regard and that he was 'un gran ministro', Borja to Lerma, Madrid, 21 Jan. 1601 and reply, Tordesillas, 26 Jan., BL Add 28,423, fol. 387b. No title has survived for his appointment as councillor of Finance, but he began attending from 8 Jan. 1603, Attendance Register, Council of Finance. See García García, *La Pax Hispánica*, pp. 348–9.

66 Title as secretary, Madrid, 31 Dec. 1614 and oath as supernumerary councillor of Finance, 19 Mar. 1618, both AGS QC 35.

67 *Relaciones*, pp. 145–6

68 See above, pp. 59.

69 Title to secretaryship of Inquisition, 26 May 1601, AHN Inq lib., 1338, fol. 29; *Relaciones*, pp. 92, 150 (quotation), 185, 192, 193, 212–13.

70 *Cnta. Junta de Dos*, 26 Feb. 1602, AGS E 2023, fol. 83.

71 It was reported that Prada would be appointed to a secretaryship of the Council of War and that Franqueza would take over his office 'para que lo sea enteramente de todo el de Estado', *Relaciones*, p. 174.

72 Williams, *Philip II*, pp. 141–9.

73 The following is based upon 'ESCRITVRA de Mayorazgo [que ottorgaron los Señores Don Pedro] Franqueça [y Doña ana grabiel Franqueça Su muxer Conde y Condesa de Villalonga]', in 'Tanto autentico sacado con autoridad Judicial de la esc[ritu]ra de mayorazgo fundado p[or] d[on] Pedro Franqueza, conde de Villalonga, a favor de su hijo mayor y sus descendientes; llamando en falta de sucesores a los de la Casa de Lerma', Valladolid, 18 Jul. 1605, ADL 12, no. 2; 'VISITA Y CARGOS DE DON PEDRO FRANQUEZA [CONDE DE VILLALONGA, SECRETARIO DE ESTADO DEL SEÑOR REY DON FELIPE III DE ESTE NOMBRE. EN MADRID A 22 DE DICIEMBRE DE 1609]', printed by José Antonio Escudero, *Los Secretarios de Estado y del Despacho*, 4 vols., Madrid: 1976, at iii, pp. 792–818; parts of this document not printed by Escudero are also used, BL Mss Eg 2060, fols. 5–35; Thompson, *War and Government*, pp. 80, 195–6, 267 and Torras i Ribé, *Franquesa*, pp. 173–89.

74 See above, pp. 120–2.

75 'ESCRITVRA de Mayorazgo ... Franqueça', ADL 12, no. 2, fol. 2b; *Relaciones*, p. 188; Torras i Ribé, pp. 109–20 and Guerrero Mayllo, *Franquesa*, pp. 213, 279.

76 'ESCRITVRA de Mayorazgo ... Franqueça', ADL 12, no. 2, fols. 26b–28.

77 See above, p. 190.

78 Gilman Proske, *Pompeo Leoni*, pp. 25–6.

79 Torras i Ribé, *Franquesa*, p. 193; García García, *La Pax Hispánica*, p. 292, n. 131.

80 Carlos Morales, *El Consejo de Hacienda de Castilla*, pp. 167–78; on financial structures, Thompson, *War and Government*, especially pp. 67–100.

81 Acuña had been appointed councillor of Castile 1 Sep. 1587 and councillor of the *Cámara*, 15 Nov. 1595, AGS QC 24.

82 Poza's defence, to Philip III, Valladolid, 26 Nov. 1601, a draft, BL Add 28,378, fols. 247–56b; *Relaciones*, pp. 132, 136.

83 Poza to Lerma, Valladolid, 18 Jan. 1602, and reply, Valladolid, same date, RB 11/2132, doc. 141.

84 P. Medina Encina, 'El Consejo de Indias', in P. González García et al. (eds.), *Archivo General de Indias*, Barcelona and Madrid, 1995, pp. 196–248.

85 Carlos Morales, *El Consejo de Hacienda*, p. 176.

86 *Cnta. Junta de Hacienda*, 22 Nov. 1600, AGS CJH 284, fol. 13.

87 *Cnta.* Fin., 15 Jan. 1601, AGS CJH 293, fol. 223.

88 *Cnta. Junta de la reformación de los tribunales de hazienda sobre la Cont[aduria] May[or] de Quentas y su reformación*, copy, Valladolid, 6 Feb. 1602, BL Eg 2055, fols. 3–9.

89 Taken from title of Francisco de Salablanca, Lerma, 26 Oct. 1602, AGS QC 24.

90 Title, Valladolid, 20 Apr. 1602, AGS QC 24 and *Relaciones*, p. 140.

91 *Cnta. Junta de reformación de los tribunales de hacienda*, Valladolid, 3 Apr. 1602, copy, BL Eg 2055, fol. 9b–12b.

92 In July 1599 Borja thanked Lerma for promoting Ramírez to the position of *contador* in the *Contaduría Mayor de Hacienda* and was told that Ramírez was a very good minister who deserved to be rewarded, Borja to Denia, Madrid, 29 July (and reply, from Denia, 1 Aug.) 1599, BL Add 28,422, fols. 89 and 151. See J. de Entrambasaguas, *Una familia de ingenios. Los Ramírez de Prado*, Madrid, 1943.

93 Title, San Lorenzo del Escorial, 17 Oct. 1600, AGS QC 6.

94 *Cnta. Junta de Reformación*, Valladolid, 10 Sep. 1602, BL Eg 2055, fols. 13–14b.

95 Gaitán de Ayala, AGS QC 32; Salablanca, ibid., 19; on Ramírez de Prado, see n. 92; no title exists for Ipeñarrieta, but see this ch. n. 65; titles for Cabala, AGS QC 13; Fernández de Espinosa, 5; Pascual, 28; Pons, 20; and Pedroso, 9.

96 Attendance Register, Council of Finance.

97 Messía de Tovar, 2 Jul. 1603, AGS QC 37 and Sarmiento de Acuña, 13 Sep. 1604, ibid., 12.

98 López de Gojenaga's title has not survived but the title of his son, Diego, to succeed him refers to it, Madrid, 21 Dec. 1610, AGS QC 12.

99 Title, Valladolid, 14 Dec. 1604, ibid., 40.

100 The following is based upon the history of the *Junta del Desempeño* in cnta. Fernando de Carrillo, 4 Aug. 1616, AGS CJH 547, no fol., copy, and 'Visita y cargos de don Pedro Franqueza', Escudero, *Los Secretarios*, iii, pp. 792–818; Thompson, *War and Government*, pp. 61–2, 80–1, 195–6, 229, 267–8, 274–5.

101 A total of 34,500,000 ducats were registered at Seville, of which about one quarter (8,625,000 ducats) belonged to the crown: M. Morineau, *Incroyables gazettes et fabuleux métaux*, Cambridge, UK, 1985, p. 168.

102 J.-M. Pelorson, 'Para una reinterpretación de la Junta del Desempeño General (1603–1606) a la luz de la "visita" de Alonso Ramírez de Prado y de don Pedro Franqueza, Conde de Villalonga', *Actas del IV Symposium de Historia de la Administración*, Alcalá de Henares, 1983, pp. 613–17; Torras i Ribé, *Franquesa*, pp. 173–89.

103 *Cnta. Junta de Tres*, 25 May 1605, AGS E 1937, fol. 62.

104 'Visita y cargos de don Pedro Franqueza', BL Eg 2060, fol. 168.

105 Escudero, *Los Secretarios*, iii, pp. 798–9.

106 Francisco de Monçon, 'Visita y cargos de don Pedro Franqueza', Madrid, 20 Oct. 1611, BL Eg 2060, fol. 916.

107 Santiago Fernández, *Política monetaria en Castilla*, pp. 58–62.

108 *CSPV* ix, 21 Mar. 1602, no. 1065, pp. 498–9.

109 *Relaciones*, pp. 167–8.

110 Torras i Ribé, *Franquesa*, pp. 168–9.

111 García García, *La Pax Hispánica*, pp. 370–2; see esp. p. 370, n. 45.

112 *Relaciones*, pp. 234–5.

113 These were: the Marquis of Poza (159 attendances, 1602–04); Enríque de Henríquez de Guzmán, V Count of Alva de Liste (235; 1599–1604); Antonio Fernández de Córdoba, VI duke of Sessa (91; 1604–05); Cardinal Fernando Niño de Guevara (133; 1600–01) and the Count of Fuentes (47; 1599–1600); Attendance Register, Council of State. Neither Diego de Mardones nor Jerónimo de Xavierre made any appreciable impact.

114 Gaillard, *Le Portugal sous Philippe III*, pp. 15–16.

115 Moura to Philip III, Castel Rodrigo, 21 May 1604, AGS E 198, no fol.

116 Williams, *Philip II*, pp. 145, 214–15.

117 Martínez Hernández, *Velada*, pp. 476–92.

118 Lerma to Carrillo, Lerma, 13 Sep. 1610, AGS CJH 495, no fol.; *Relaciones*, pp. 414–15, 417, 479, 488, 496.
119 He had served as ambassador to the papacy (1582–93) and Viceroy of Naples (1595–99); see Elliott, *Olivares*, pp. 7–16; he was sworn in on 24 September 1602, Lerma to Juan de Borja, Valladolid, 25 Sep. 1602, BL Add 28,424, fol. 413b (quotation).
120 *Relaciones*, p. 191.
121 Cnta St. 26 Nov. 1602, printed by M. Alcocer y Martínez, *Consultas del Consejo de Estado*, 2 vols., Valladolid, 1930–32, i, pp. 252–81; see García García, *La Pax Hispánica*, pp. 38–9, 42 and P. C. Allen, *Philip III and the Pax Hispánica, 1598–1621 The Failure of Grand Strategy*, New Haven, 2000, pp. 141–55.
122 In 1600 discussions took place with the Dutch in a peace conference at Boulogne in which Baltasar de Zúñiga and Fernando Carrillo attempted to win a settlement. Albert did his part, too: at the 'Battle of the Dunes' (2 July 1600) he led his cavalry with great gallantry, conspicuous to friend and foe alike on his splendid white horse. See García García, *La Pax Hispánica*, p. 52.
123 A. Rodríguez Villa, *Ambrosio Spínola, primer marqués de los Balbases*, Madrid, 1905, 19–37. On Isabella's appraisal of the situation in the Low Countries, García García, *La Pax Hispánica*, pp. 283–4.
124 Anthony Dutton took Fawkes with him and noted that 'I have been entertayned from Veosilio to Escuriall, and thence to Lerma, from Lerma to Burgos … and thence to Palencia, and thence to Ampudia and so hither', A. J. Loomie, 'Guy Fawkes in Spain. The "Spanish treason" in Spanish documents', *BIHR*, 9, London, 1971, p. 21.
125 *Relación de la iornada del … Condestable*, Valladolid, 1604.
126 Allen, *Philip III*, pp. 65–70, 125–6, 131, 139; García García, *La Pax Hispánica*, pp. 54–5.
127 Roco de Campofrio, *España en Flándes*, p. 290; Jan den Tex, *Oldenbarnevelt*, Cambridge, UK, 2 vols., 1973, i, 338–40.
128 García García, *La Pax Hispánica*, pp. 45–8.
129 The following is based upon Rodríguez Villa, *Spínola*, pp. 91–104, and *Relaciones*, pp. 234, 237–8. On the structure of the Spanish Army, Parker, *Army of Flanders*, 'The Chain of Command', p. 277.
130 To Andrés de Prada, Valladolid, 9 Sep. 1604, BN Mss 1492, fol. 134, copy.
131 *Relaciones*, pp. 234. On his career, González Dávila (1623), pp. 92–6, Diego de la Mota, *Libro del principio de la orden de la Cavalleria de S. Tiago del Espada*, Valencia, 1599, pp. 302–3; Allen, *Philip III*, p. 145.
132 *Relaciones*, pp. 237–8 and González Dávila, *Teatro de las Grandezas de … Madrid*, p. 93.
133 Parker, *Dutch Revolt*, pp. 236–7.
134 Morineau recorded that a fleet arrived in January 1605 but it docked at Seville in the last days of 1604, *Incroyables gazettes*, p. 74; *Relaciones*, pp. 233–4.
135 Cntas. Indies 23 May and 24 Oct. 1605, AGI IG 748, fol. 69 and no fol.; *Relaciones*, pp. 261–2, 263.

6

Humiliation,
1606–07

Disaster: the treasure fleets of 1605–06 and the arrest of Villalonga

In the seven months after the court returned to Madrid in March 1606, Philip
spent only three in the city. The suddenness with which the decision to return
the court to Madrid had been taken had not allowed time to prepare the Alcázar
to receive the King and his court and refurbishment hurriedly took place.
However, Philip, Margaret and Lerma each had reasons of their own for spending
the summer of 1606 away from Madrid. The unbridled enthusiasm with which
Philip threw himself into the pleasures that were now available to him in his
palaces and hunting lodges in and around Madrid suggested that he was delighted
to be back in a real capital. He made short trips to Aranjuez and Toledo before
spending nearly three months in the Escorial (18 July–8 October). He rose early
each morning to hunt and made it clear that he was determined to relax from
the cares of the world – 'it is said that their Majesties have gone (to the monastery) to enjoy themselves and not to treat of business', reported Cabrera de
Córdoba.[1] Margaret was also eager to prepare for childbirth in the cool of the
Escorial.[2] She gave birth to a third daughter on 18 August, and the child was
named María in tribute to the child who had died in 1603.

For his part, Lerma was grateful to spend the summer in the Escorial
so that he could isolate Philip from his own opponents, and he ordered that
anyone wishing to bring government business to the King's attention had to do
so through Villalonga.[3] It was not immediately evident that a new pattern was
being created in which the King spent months away from his capital; in each
of the years 1607–11, Philip and Lerma travelled into Old Castile and stayed
there for weeks or months at a time. Moreover, they spent a total of 347 days,
nearly one-fifth of the period, in the Escorial.

Lerma was at a low point in the late summer of 1606. He was forced to
endure the prolonged crisis which followed on the disaster to the treasure ships
without the active support of his senior allies in government; Juan de Borja

died in September 1606 while Miranda's ill-health forced him to withdraw from governmental activity after the return to Madrid.[4] Since Cristóbal, Duke of Cea, showed no sign of developing into an able and conscientious politician, Lerma was forced to rely for support on Rodrigo Calderón. Unfortunately, don Rodrigo was manifestly unequal to the burden that now fell upon him and compensated for his shortcomings by displaying an increased arrogance in his conduct of business. Calderón's enhanced profile at court therefore served only to increase the hostility to both him and his master. As Lerma crumbled, so too did the quality of advice available to him.

Even before the court returned to Madrid it had become evident that the crown would not be able to finance a major campaign in the Low Countries to drive home Spínola's successes of 1605; as early as February 1606, Lerma told an envoy from the Archdukes that he 'could not see how more money could be spared'.[5] Exactly as he did so, the first news of the missing fleet began to arrive at court, and the full details of the disaster that had befallen it were confirmed in May 1606. On or about 6 November 1605 a hurricane scattered the eight galleons carrying the Peruvian silver from Cartagena to Havana. Four ships sank, with the loss of 1,300 men, including General Fernández de Córdoba. Three ships reached safety in Jamaica and a fourth made it back to Cartagena only hours before it would otherwise have sunk. About one-half of the Peruvian silver shipment for 1605 was lost. Moreover, since there was no specie with which to pay for the merchandise that was to be carried on the outward-bound fleet of 1606, that fleet remained at anchor in Seville.[6] The Indies silver trade was dislocated, and at a time of heightened crisis both at home and abroad the King was forced to manage his finances without access to American silver.

The continuance of the war effort in the Low Countries was placed further at risk by the crown's need to deploy a large army in northern Italy to resolve a dispute between the papacy and the Republic of Venice.[7] As it happened, the crisis was resolved without resort to arms, but it proved to be an expensive alarm. Once again salvation for the war in the Low Countries came from Ambrosio Spínola. His fellow Genoese bankers refused to advance credit on the sureties of the King of Spain but when Spínola pledged his own estates as security they agreed to provide credit for a new campaign: in 1606 therefore, 3,955,677 ducats were sent to the Low Countries by the Spanish government and it was Spínola who facilitated the provision of virtually all of it.[8] For the second year in succession he was funding his own campaign.

Unfortunately, Spínola was not able to begin his campaign until late in the season. He fell ill in Genoa and only arrived in Brussels at the end of June. He then found that much of the credit that he had secured had been frittered away. He captured Groenlo (12 August) but was then forced to recognise that he could not carry on with an effective campaign. On 24 August he wrote to Philip that 'God, Your Majesty and the whole world will bear me witness that I have done all that I can, but I am only an individual and cannot have the resources to maintain an army'. He held his army together long enough to take Rheinberg (2 October), but 600 veterans then marched to Breda to offer their services to the enemy in the first mutiny in an army under Spínola's command.[9]

During 13 to 15 October, seventy-three ships docked at Seville, carrying more than six million ducats'-worth of silver and merchandise. The fleet also brought the assurance that the *Tierra Firme* fleet would arrive six weeks later with the bullion shipment for 1606 together with the treasure salvaged from the galleon at Cartagena. It was one of the high points of Spain's silver trade but it came too late to save the campaign in Flanders; the Council of Finance calculated that even the arrival of the second fleet would not provide enough silver to satisfy the crown's debts.[10]

Philip and Lerma were in Ventosilla when they were informed of this dismal financial projection. As Bernardo García has demonstrated, Lerma turned on Villalonga, making it brutally clear to him that he and the *juntas* through which he had worked would be held responsible for the crown's financial predicament, and that he was abandoning him to his fate:

> And so His Majesty has resolved to leave his recreations and return to Madrid to see everything for himself and to help to find the remedy … Please God that the successes will be those that are hoped for and that with them I will be disabused of the lack of confidence in which I live because experience has shown that we always find ourselves with less money and less time and less care than we have been promised by our *juntas*.[11]

Lerma's enemies gathered, chief among them the Queen. In October the papal nuncio reported that Margaret 'thinks of nothing else but how to defeat the Duke of Lerma' and was only 'awaiting the right opportunity' to move against him. Indeed, the nuncio went so far as to refer to 'a civil war' between Margaret and Lerma.[12]

Margaret found a resourceful and determined ally in her husband's confessor. It is probable that Diego de Mardones's primary objection to Lerma's control of the King lay in confessional matters, but he chose to undermine the duke indirectly by attacking his closest *hechuras*; he joined with Margaret to undermine Calderón and consolidated his alliance with Juan de Acuña against Villalonga.

Mardones was presented with the exactly the weapon that he needed to use against Calderón when he was approached by Pedro de Gamboa, a secretary of Calderón's, with allegations about his master's behaviour. The confessor eagerly passed these on to his friend, the Admiral of Aragon. The Admiral detested Lerma but he did not have the sophistication to manage an intrigue against a politician who was as calculating as was the duke. Short-tempered and utterly lacking in judgement as he was, however, the Admiral did possess two qualities which made him an ideal tool for others in pushing a conspiracy forward: he was fearless and he had access to the King.

When Calderón heard about Gamboa's treachery he terrified him into claiming that the Admiral had urged the Archduke Albert to return the sovereignty of the Low Countries to Philip III and to oppose the policies, both domestic and foreign, of Lerma. The Admiral denied that he had encouraged Albert to turn against Lerma but his denials were unsustainable, given the evidence in his own hand.[13] When in November 1606 one of the gentlemen of his suite struck a porter of Villalonga's, the Admiral himself was held responsible and placed under arrest. It took some time for courtiers to understand that Lerma and the Admiral were locked in a bitter feud and that it was being fought over the the question of making war or peace in the Low Countries.

On 14 December 1606 the Council of State advised Philip that the war in the Low Countries could not be sustained and that expenditure on the Army of Flanders would have to be be halved. However, almost simultaneously the Council received news that the United Provinces were prepared to discuss a cessation of hostilities for they could not support the growing cost of its own army, which had doubled in size since 1597.[14] Exactly as the governments of Spain and the United Provinces edged towards a cessation of hostilities, 4,052 veterans of the Army of Flanders began the largest mutiny that the Army had seen for thirty years (11 December).[15] Were the very different decisions of the United Provinces and Philip's mutineers each inspired by the realisation that the King of Spain now had fabulous amounts of silver available to him – the United Provinces fearful that Spain would now be able to continue the war: the mutineers, determined to win their share of the silver? Philip soon had more wealth, for the *Tierra Firme* fleet reached Seville in that same week with a further 4,500,000 ducats of bullion and perhaps half as much again in valuables and merchandise.

Once again, it was too late: at the end of a year during which 16,000,000 ducats'-worth of bullion had reached Seville, there was a shortage of silver in the city.[16] Lerma established a new *junta* to deal with the *desempeño* of the royal exchequer, but it was no longer possible to disguise the realities of the crown's financial situation: on 26 December, Alonso Ramírez de Prado was arrested. On 2 January 1607 Lic. Fernando Carrillo, a councillor of Castile, was commissioned by the King to investigate the conduct of Ramírez de Prado.[17]

A Jesuit-educated laywer from Córdoba, Carrillo was highly respected at court (and beyond) as a man of unbending probity. He had earned the good opinion of the Archdukes Albert and Isabella and of Baltasar de Zúñiga by the singlemindedness with which he had negotiated with the English for peace in 1600 and had managed the finances of the Army of Flanders in the years 1600–03. Indeed, Zúñiga found only one fault in him, in that his bluntness with his

juniors and equals extended into his dealings with his superiors.[18] Ruthlessness
in the pursuit of his duty was, however, precisely the quality that distinguished
Carrillo.[19] When he returned to Spain at the turn of 1602–03 Lerma and
Villalonga tried to win his support, persuading him to act as a witness to some
of the legal deeds founding the *mayorazgo* of Villalonga.[20] However, Carrillo was
too honest to be swayed by favour, too ambitious to be intimidated by Lerma,
and his appointment to lead the *visita* proved to be the making of a remarkable
career. The first display of his independence was to the point: at midnight on
19 January he personally arrested Villalonga. He also had Pedro Álvarez Pereira
taken into custody. No one at court could fail to understand the significance of
the arrest of three leading members of Lerma's *clientela:* the authority of the
duke himself was now under direct challenge. On 29 January the Admiral of
Aragon was released from prison.[21]

On 27 January, Cristóbal and Miguel de Ipeñarrieta entered Villalonga's
palace to compile an inventory of his possessions.[22] They found a veritable
Aladdin's cave, packed with jewels, objets d'art, exquisite furniture and precious
stones. Only the very best had been good enough for the Count; for instance,
his bedsheets were Dutch and his carpets were Turkish while his stables housed
thirty thoroughbreds, twelve coach horses and six coaches for himself and his
wife. Villalonga had evidently known that he was to be investigated – perhaps
this was the purpose of Lerma's letter of October 1606? – for he had moved
his money away: the Ipeñarrietas found only 3,200 ducats in cash but invoices
revealed that bankers were holding another 83,244 ducats on Villalonga's
behalf. The brothers were readily able to demonstrate, too, that Villalonga had
received presents from virtually everyone with whom he had done business,
including Rudolf II, Henry IV and the Senate of Venice. Carrillo would have to
tread carefully not to embarrass some of the crowned heads of Europe.

The Ipeñarrietas calculated that Villalonga's annual income from salaries
amounted to 22,446 ducats – 16,000 from his governmental offices and 6,446
from his municipal offices and his *encomienda*. His rents and government bonds
produced 32,470 ducats, bringing his legitimate annual income to 54,916
ducats. However, their preliminary inventory (which accounted for 3,044
valuable items) put a capital value on Villalonga's possessions of 917,034 ducats,
including jewellery worth 160,000 ducats. They made no attempt to correlate
Villalonga's income with his expenditure, much less to reach a realistic figure
of how much money he received in any one year: probably the task would have
been impossible. The brothers noted – but did not emphasise – that Villalonga
owned three books of copies of letters written by Lerma to the presidents of
Finance, demonstrating that he had kept closely in touch with Lerma over the
management of financial affairs. Here, too, Carrillo would have to be discreet.

In January 1607, three of the King's senior ministers met as the '*Junta* of Three' to consider the Dutch offer of an armistice – Juan de Idiáquez, President of the Council of Military Orders and Philip's pre-eminent adviser on foreign affairs; the Count of Miranda, President of the Council of Castile, and Jerónimo de Xavierre, confessor of the King. Lerma had often attended this *junta* but he chose not to be present for this meeting and it was left to members of the *junta* to recommend that Philip should agree to end hostilities.[23] By the end of March, Albert had negotiated a ceasefire that would operate on land for eight months, to come into effect one month later.[24] Emphasis was added to Albert's insistence on making peace when on 24/25 April a Dutch fleet sank three galleons of the Straits Squadron off Gibraltar, with the loss of 1,200 men. When the Dutch anchored off the Straits and Spain was unable to muster fighting ships to protect the incoming silver fleets, Philip noted despondently that 'the enemy possess the sea'.[25]

In August, Albert informed Lerma that it would be 'impossible' to pursue the war unless the King provided at least 300,000 ducats a month for a year. More bluntly still, he expressed the view that the war had been a shattering waste of men and money.[26] Spínola carried on the negotiations and sufficient progress was made that on 1 February 1608 he and Maurice of Nassau led dazzling entourages to begin what has been called 'the first European peace congress'.[27]

Retirement – or survival?

Lerma sank into depression at the attack on his *hechuras* and at the implications for his own continuance in office of the disintegration of the crown's financial and foreign policies. In November he and Philip went (as was normal at this time of year) to the Pardo to hunt small game. Isolated with Philip in the hunting lodge, Lerma insisted, as he had done in 1603 after the death of his wife, that he wished to renounce the world and enter the Jeronimite order.[28] Lerma's despair lasted for several months. In January 1607 it became known that he was suffering from loss of sleep and was in pain from gout. In February the papal nuncio confirmed that Lerma intended to retire from affairs and hand over his responsibilities to his son.[29]

The duke rallied sufficiently to demonstrate to the King his concern for good government by instigating a wide-ranging reform of all military and naval expenses at home and abroad. Some of these reforms proved to be of enduring value.[30] However, it was a sign of his vulnerability that attacks continued to be mounted on members of his *clientela*.[31]

Sensational confirmation of Lerma's decline came in May 1607 when Calderón was arrested and charged with having systematically abused his position

– by receiving presents; trading in secular and ecclesiastical offices; revealing state secrets for money; passing confidential information to litigants; accepting money, jewels and presents for facilitating the conduct of cases; committing frauds in association with bankers, and so on. The King ordered an investigation by 'persons of complete confidence, honesty, truthfulness and intelligence'.[32] Calderón was even more closely associated with Lerma – and more important to him – than Villalonga, Ramírez de Prado and Álvarez de Pereira: if Lerma could not save him it was unlikely that he himself could survive.

Lerma adopted his customary strategy in crisis, taking Philip away from his capital: they left Madrid at the beginning of May 1607 and did not return until 1 August, spending time in Aranjuez and the Escorial and travelling to Lerma, Valladolid and Burgos. Once again, Lerma used a *jornada* to extract great favours from the King; once again, Philip caved in to Lerma's demands. The first of them was familial and seigneurial; on 25 May, in Aranjuez, Philip presented Lerma with perhaps the most significant grant of his *valimiento* when he confirmed the settlement of the century-long case over the lands confiscated from Diego Gómez in 1436.[33] The second of Lerma's demands was more personal; on 7 June, in Buitrago, Philip despatched a decree to his councils declaring that Rodrigo Calderón was innocent of all charges against him: 'we ought to declare, as we now do declare, that the said Rodrigo Calderón, is free'. The King ordered that 'perpetual silence' should henceforth be observed on the allegations against Calderón and that they were never to be investigated again under any circumstances.[34]

It was not enough for Lerma. On or about 18 October 1607, he let it be known publicly for the third time that he wished to retire from court:

> It has been announced that he wants to go to Lerma (to where he has ordered that all his property be taken) to recuperate. He instructs his servants that those who wish to follow him may do so and the others are to be dismissed. This news has come as a very great surprise for the whole of this court, and no one believes that it will take place, but rather that there has to be some purpose behind it which will be discovered in time. What is being said publicly is that he has debts and wishes to find time to himself so as to pay them and organise his life.[35]

Philip refused to allow Lerma to retire; in November Cabrera de Córdoba recorded that 'the retirement that has been announced that the Duke of Lerma wished to make has been hushed up around here, because it is being said that his Majesty did not wish to give him licence for it'. However, Lerma continued to insist that he was leaving; in January 1608 he sent many of his possessions to Lerma and let it be known that he would shortly depart there himself.[36]

Philip showered gifts on Lerma to reassure him (and the court) of his enduring affection. He presented him with jewellery that was reputedly worth 40,000 ducats and appointed him to three governorships in royal houses. The governorships of the *Casa de Campo* (6 July) and the *cavallerizas* of Madrid (6 September) were unsalaried but Lerma's acceptance of them clearly implied that he was prepared to remain at court.[37] By contrast, on 15 November Philip conferred upon Lerma the governorship of the *Casa de la Ribera*: Lerma would surely only have needed this if he was thinking of retiring to Valladolid.[38] The duke was pushing the King very hard, trying to convince him that he was intent on leaving court. Would he go or would he stay? Was he crumbling – or was he negotiating with the King?

The second settlement of the Lerma estates: the agreements of 1607 with the Duke of Cea

Lerma accompanied his threats to abandon court by securing in law the financial, seigneurial and territorial advances that he had made in Castile since his elevation to the dukedom of Lerma. On 31 January 1607, Philip issued a decree which defined the Lerma *mayorazgo* as it had developed since 1599 and exempted the duke from the provision of Castilian law which allowed the holder of a *mayorazgo* to dispose of only one-fifth of his *bienes libres*. In doing so he made it difficult for any future monarch – even indeed for himself – to confiscate from Lerma or his successors any of the gains that he had made since 1599. Philip also gave Lerma permission to found one or two or more *mayorazgos* for Cristóbal from the *bienes* that he had at present or at the time of his death, 'the more to enlarge and elevate the memory of your person and house'.[39]

In the spring of 1607 Miranda and his commission of councillors of Castile awarded judgement in Lerma's favour over his claim that he was entitled to enjoy the royal taxes – the *servicios ordinarios y extraordinarios*, the *millones*, *moneda forera* and *galeotes* – in each of forty-four places of the 'Lands of the Recompense'. The Council of Finance then calculated that these were worth 7,694 ducats annually (capital value: 209,393 ducats) and added 53,857 ducats to compensate Lerma for the income that he would have had from the rents in the years since the verdict in 1600. The award therefore totalled 263,250 ducats – a sum equivalent to about 4 per cent of the crown's free income.[40] On 25 May, as we have seen, secluded with Lerma in his palace at Aranjuez, Philip ratified the agreement and, in an order which he formally stated to be 'an irrevocable contract', ordered the payment of the monies.[41] Diego Gómez I had been avenged.

Both king and duke knew full well that the crown could not pay the award, for it was only months away from suspending payments to its bankers.[42] Lerma therefore agreed to accept eleven *villas de behetría* from the royal patrimony. Such towns were immune from many fiscal dues and in theory had the right to choose their own lord. In agreeing to hand the towns over to Lerma Philip simply disregarded this latter privilege. The duke ensured that two of his most trusted *hechuras* managed the transactions on behalf of the crown; as Treasurer General, Garci Mazo de la Vega calculated the value of the towns while Jorge de Tovar, Secretary of *Justicia* of the Council of Castile, took possession of them for Lerma. The duke had chosen the towns very carefully. The *villas* were very substantial places – two of them had more than two thousand inhabitants – but their situation was as important as their size; three lay to the south-west of Burgos and the remainder were clustered around Palencia, seven of them being within 15 kilometres or so of Ampudia. Their acquisition therefore represented a significant concentration of the lands of Lerma's estate. They were, too, much more manageable, for Lerma was better able to exploit the resources of eleven sizeable towns than he was the forty-four scattered villages of the 'Lands of the Recompense'. The jurisdictional and seigneurial rights that Lerma enjoyed over the *villas* were worth 8,265 ducats annually (capital value: 165,312 ducats). In addition, Philip gave Lerma improved rates of interest on the *alcabalas* in Valdemoro that were earmarked for the *mayorazgo* of Diego Gómez. It was estimated that this was worth a further 44,009, bringing the capital value of the two transactions to 209,321 ducats.[43]

Lerma subsequently bought the right to levy *alcabalas* and *tercias* in the *villas;* this produced 13,100 ducats in annual rent (capital value: 432,300 ducats). He acquired the *mojonerías* and other minor rents as a grant from the King and bought a variety of municipal offices in the *villas*. By 1612, the *villas* brought Lerma 21,961 ducats of rent (capital value: 609,547 ducats) – as much income as senior noblemen such as the counts of Chinchón and Barajas (who jointly occupied fifty-third place on the list of aristocratic incomes in 1612) had from all their landed rents (Appendix I).

While Lerma was initiating these transactions, the city council of Valladolid asked Philip for permission to present the duke with the town of Tudela de Duero, 18 kilometres east of Valladolid. Tudela had a population of just over 2,000 and brought Lerma another 3,595 ducats of annual rent. The city of Valladolid was clearly anxious to retain Lerma's favour – perhaps even in the hope that he might bring the court back? – and it was amply rewarded for its generosity to the duke by having its *alcalaba* payments reduced by two-thirds.[44] Lerma was in deep political crisis but he could still dispose of the royal grace to those who supported him.

The purchase of the *villas de behetría* and the acquisition of Tudela de Duero therefore increased Lerma's annual income by 25,556 ducats. Yet more wealth cascaded on to the duke when in September Philip and Lerma agreed that the crown would pay Lerma 80,709 ducats in the final settlement for the sale of the *Casa de la Ribera*.[45] The transactions that Lerma initiated during his

**Table 5 The increases in the value of the Lerma estate initiated in
1607. Capital value of the transactions (in ducats)**

Capital value	Lands and properties
609,547	villas de behetría
112,045	Tudela de Duero
80,709	Sale of the Casa de la Ribera
802,301	

great political crisis in 1607 therefore added 802,301 ducats to the capital value
of his estate.

These extraordinary accretions to Lerma's wealth and *mayorazgo* provided
the need and formed the justification for a succession of agreements that he
made with his eldest son between July and September 1607. In effect these
amounted to his major testamentary provisions and he rounded them out when
on his feast day, 4 October, he made his will and testament.[46] These agreements
served two purposes; they established that the gains that Lerma had made could
not be taken from his family and they defined his relationship with his family –
and most especially, of course, with his elder son – for the foreseeable future.

Since Lerma had spent with abandon and had been exempted from a wide
range of legal restrictions that should have curtailed his ability to dispose of the
resources of his *mayorazgo*, he claimed that he was now uncertain whether the
amounts that he had already spent and those which he intended to spend in the
future exceeded the one-fifth of his *bienes libres* of which he could legally dispose.
He and Cristóbal therefore defined which *bienes libres* were to be reserved for
his testamentary provisions (20 July) and exempted his ecclesiastical and other
benefactions from inclusion in his *bienes libres* (8 August).

In the agreement of 20 July 1607 (which was signed in the Escorial) Cea
agreed that on Lerma's death he would as a priority reserve 20,000 ducats of
rent from his *bienes libres* to establish a *mayorazgo* for his brother. He would pay
all of Lerma's debts and provide 11,529 ducats of annual rent (capital value,
230,380 ducats) from the *bienes libres* to support selected religious and charitable commitments that his father had made and which were not important
enough to be incorporated into the *mayorazgo*. Father and son then allocated
152,400 ducats for the cost of Lerma's funeral, requiem masses and other testamentary expenditures and 40,000 ducats for charitable gifts. Cea promised to
have 20,000 masses said for the repose of his father's soul.

Cea also accepted Lerma's right to continue to support his ecclesiastical
foundations even if he made use of more than the fifth-part of his *bienes libres*.
Lerma agreed that all the *bienes libres* which remained to him after these obligations had been met should be incorporated into his *mayorazgo* when he died;

he could therefore enjoy the usufruct of his rents during his lifetime. Lerma promised not to seek royal permission to alter any of the conditions of the *mayorazgo* as it was now defined. However, he accepted that the proceeds from the *tratas de Sicilia*, the 'Lands of the Recompense' and the sale of the *Casa de la Ribera* could only be employed with the agreement of Cea: here at least there was a restriction on Lerma's freedom of action. Lerma agreed to have 20,000 masses celebrated for the salvation of his son's soul if Cristóbal predeceased him. In the agreement of 8 August, Cea undertook to maintain the major foundations that Lerma had established within the *mayorazgo*. Lerma justified his generosity in establishing these by claiming that he had made them 'in recognition of the great favours that God, our Lord, has bestowed upon us'.[47]

The King and the Council of Castile formally approved the agreements in September.[48] Even then, the King further extended the privileges that he had given to Lerma by adding what he called 'clarifications' in four areas: Philip solemnly waived the crown's right to the reversion of the dukedom of Lerma should any holder of the title commit a serious transgression against the majesty of the crown; he confirmed the three compensatory awards that he had given the duke when he renounced the right to the export concession on the 15,000 *salmas* of Sicilian wheat; he stated that there could be no other claimants to the increases in the *mayorazgo* since 1599; and he stipulated that, if Lerma or any of his successors committed a crime that justified their exclusion from the dukedom and *mayorazgo*, any punishment that was imposed could not be extended beyond the individual concerned since it was not right that a family that had served the crown 'so much, so well and with such love and faithfulness' should suffer because of the sins of any one individual.

The agreements with Cristóbal were in all probability rounded out by an understanding about how long Lerma would remain at court and how and when he would hand over power to his son. But on this most tantalising of subjects, the documents that Lerma and Cristóbal so carefully drew up say nothing. Over the following two years, Lerma made some amendments to the agreements, endowing a professorial chair at the University of Salamanca for the Dominican Order and making marginal alterations to his charitable provisions. He thereby added 3,542 ducats of rent or 70,840 ducats of capital to his commitments: this was taken from the 174,380 ducats.[49]

Bankruptcy, 9 November 1607

By the autumn of 1607 Villalonga appeared to be mad, and rumours circulated that he had been bewitched. When Carrillo visited him in September he claimed not to recognise him, denied ever having heard of the King of Spain or the Duke of Lerma and insisted that he knew nothing about the governmental business that he was alleged to have so mishandled. Carrillo had the Count bled twice; Villalonga's sanity and memory promptly returned.[50]

In the autumn of 1607 the Council of Finance drew up a budget for the financial year to October 1608. Unstated in the awful figures that the Council now laid before the King was its determination to re-establish its own authority after the struggle with the *Junta del Desempeño;* henceforth, the presentation of an annual budget in October became the central feature of the Council's management of financial affairs. The Council estimated that the crown's short-term capital debts came to nearly 23,000,000 ducats, of which 7,000,000 were owed to its own servants. Despite the truce in the Low Countries that had been negotiated in the spring of 1607, the military budget still came to over 4,000,000 ducats. Not the least dismal of the facts that the Council laid before the King was that the most important staple source of revenue was burning itself out; nearly 2,000,000 of the eighteen *millones* had not been collected.[51]

It therefore became imperative to summon another Cortes to seek a new *millones* grant. In order to make the new body more pliable, Lerma and Juan de Acuña were appointed as procurators for Madrid, while the Count of Alba de Liste sat for Zamora.[52] However, even their presence did not inhibit the procurators, and the stridency with which they criticised the crown's conduct marked the beginning of the sustained opposition of the Cortes of Castile to the crown's fiscal policy.[53] Vocal and critical though they were, the procurators could not resist the pressure brought by the crown, and on condition that Philip took an oath to observe the terms of the new grant, twenty-three of them agreed to prorogue the *millones* for seven years at 2,500,000 ducats a year, making a total grant of 17,500,000 ducats (6 February 1608).[54]

Since it would take several months to win the support of the urban oligarchies for the new grant, there was no resisting the logic of declaring a suspension of payments on the crown's commitments to its bankers. Philip duly issued the decree on 9 November, withholding 12,000,000 ducats that he had pledged to bankers and rescheduling payments over nineteen years. It took until 14 May 1608 to negotiate the details of the *medio general*, whereby the crown agreed to pay 1,000,000 ducats annually to its creditors for twelve years. The decree therefore added 16 per cent or so to the crown's annual repayments and burdened the Castilian taxpayers with a further 1,000,000 ducats annually at exactly the moment that they had shown themselves incapable of raising the eighteen *millones*. The settlement was rounded out on 28 January 1608 with a pragmatic which reduced the interest payable on all new *juros* and *censos*; this provided some temporary relief to the crown but was only of token relevance in view of the scale of its shortfall.[55]

The suspension of payments therefore provided only temporary relief to the exchequer. However, it did lasting damage to the reputation of the King's *valido*, who was now held responsible for a double humiliation – the ceasefire in the Low Countries and the suspension of payments to the crown's creditors. Worse still, Lerma also had to confront a haemorrhaging of his authority as Carrillo's investigation into Villalonga gathered momentum. In February 1608 Carrillo indicted Villalonga on 464 counts. The days of Lerma's unchallenged power were over.[56]

NOTES

1 *Relaciones*, pp. 276–9, 281–2, 284–5 (quotation), 291–2.
2 Jordán Vello de Acuña to Diego Sarmiento de Acuña, Madrid, 1 Apr. 1606, RB 11/2122, doc. 52.
3 *Relaciones*, pp. 281–5; *Gaçeta y Nuevas*, p. 27.
4 Indeed, as early as June 1603 he had been unable to walk in the funeral procession for the Duchess of Lerma because of his great weight ('que por su impedimento de ser tan gordo, á poco trecho se salió del acompanamiento, y en silla le llevaron á San Pablo'), *Relaciones*, pp. 179 (quotation), 310, 316, 317.
5 Parker, *Dutch Revolt*, p. 238.
6 Francisco de Toledo to Philip III, Havana, 1 Apr. 1606, AGI IG 749, no fol.; *Relaciones*, pp. 275, 278–9, 280–1, 283.
7 Pérez Bombín, *Monferrato*, p. 37; Parker, *Europe in Crisis*, p. 113.
8 'The *Marquis Spinola* (as I am informed) *was enforced to gage his own Estate to the* Gennoese *for the borrowing of this Year's Money for the Warrs. Poor Marques! dear shall he buy his Title, his Councellorship and his being a Grandee.* The Money must be repay'd within seven Months after the Receipt', Cornwallis to Salisbury, n. d. (1606), printed in Winwood, *Memorials*, ii, p. 225; *Relaciones*, p. 277; on remittances to the Low Countries, Juan Muñoz de Escobar, *Relación del dinero remitido a Flándes*, CODOIN, xxxvi, p. 543 and Allen, *Philip III*, pp. 31, 162.
9 Rodríguez Villa, *Spínola*, pp. 135–45; Parker, *Dutch Revolt*, pp. 237–8.
10 *Cntas*. Indies, 16 and 19 Oct. 1606, AGI IG 749, fol. 12 (?) and fol. ?; *Relaciones*, pp. 292, 294; P. Chaunu, *Séville et l'Atlantique, 1504–1650*, 8 vols., Paris, 1955–1959, iv, p. 218.
11 Lerma to Villalonga, Ventosilla, 27 Oct. 1606, quoted by García García, *La Pax Hispánica*, p. 292, n. 131. See also, Torras i Ribé, *Franquesa*, pp. 193–7.
12 C. Pérez Bustamante, *Felipe III. Semblanza de un monarca y perfiles de una privanza*, Madrid, 1950, p. 125.
13 The following account is drawn from Rodríguez Villa, 'Don Antonio de Mendoza', pp. 541–51.
14 Parker, *Dutch Revolt*, pp. 238–9 and J. Israel, *The Dutch Republic. Its Rise, Greatness and Fall, 1477–1806*, Oxford, 1998, pp. 399–401.
15 Parker, *Army of Flanders*, pp. 168, 213, 256.
16 *Cntas* Indies 22 Dec. 1606 and *Casa de la Contratación*, 30 Dec., AGI IG 749, fol. 34 and no fol.; Morineau, *Incroyables gazettes*, p. 75; *Relaciones*, pp. 295–6.
17 *Relaciones*, pp. 295–7.
18 'ha hecho tan buena diligencia, como si fuera de otra profesión', Albert to Lerma, Brussels, 3 Apr. 1600, CODOIN, xlii, p. 338; see also, pp. 322–3 and Isabella to Lerma, Brussels, 28 May 1600, BRAH, 1905, p. 279. Zúñiga observed that 'D(o)n fernando Carrillo no se puede negar sino q(ue) tiene alguna haspereza en el modo de proceder asi con los yguales y inferiores como en lo que trata con los superiores pero es hombre de … çelo en el seru(ici)o de su Mag(esta)d de retisima yntencion y de gran capaçidad y notiçia de cosas y yo le tengo por muy vtil aqui por algun t(iem)po', 'Relación de las Cosas de flandes y de las Personas de Ymportancia que siruen a su Mag(esta)d', unaddressed paper of 1602/03, a copy, BL Eg 2079, fol. 245.

19 On Carrillo's career, González Dávila, *Teatro de las Grandezas de ... Madrid*, p. 483, and the *Memorial* of his widow, Francisca Fajardo, 8 Jun. 1622 and *cnta*. Lic. Garcí Pérez de Araciel, 4 May 1622, printed by A. González Palencia, *La Junta de Reformación*, Valladolid, 1932, pp. 344–56 and 338–42.

20 'Escritvra de Mayorazgo que ottorgarón los Señores Don Pedro Franqueça y Doña Ana Grabiel ...', at fol. 14v.

21 *Relaciones*, pp. 297–8; Rodríguez Villa, 'Francisco de Mendoza', pp. 540–1.

22 Fernando de Vaca, Alcalde de Casa y Corte, 'Ynbentario de los Vienes del Conde de Villalonga ...', second of two copies of the document, AGS CMC 3a época, leg. 3079, no. 12; and 'Relaciones q[e] Hizo Domingo de la Torre sobre la Haz[ie]da del Conde de Villalonga', ibid., 986, no fol.

23 *Cnta. Junta de Tres*, 16 Jan. 1607, AGS E 2025, fol. 5. On the negotiations, some of them rather bizarrely conducted by a Franciscan, fray Jan Neyen, Tex, *Oldenbarnevelt*, ii, pp. 366–9.

24 Spínola to Philip III, Brussels, 18 April 1607, printed in Lonchay and Cuvelier, *Correspondance de la cour d'Espagne sur les affaires des Pays-Bas*, i, no. 567, p. 249; Parker, *Dutch Revolt*, p. 239.

25 *Relaciones*, pp. 301–4; García García, *La Pax Hispánica*, pp. 98–9. Fernández Duro, C., *Armada española desde la unión de los reinos de Castilla y de León*, 9 vols., Madrid, 1895–1903, iii, pp. 233–6.

26 'y pienso que el ejemplo de lo que ha pasado en 41 años que ha que durada esta guerra, es bastante prueba, pues tantos millones, y tantos gobernadores y capitanes generales y soldados tan afamados como se han gastado en ello, no han bastado para acabarla ni reducir los de Holanda á la debida obediencia? Pues cómo se debe esperar poderlo hacer agora con menos provisiones, teniendo los enemigos muchas mas fuerzas y asistencia que por lo pasado?', Albert to Lerma, Brussels, 21 Aug. 1607, *CODOIN*, xliii, p. 69.

27 Tex, *Oldenbarnevelt*, ii, pp. 381–4, at p. 381.

28 'The *Duke* of *Lerma* hath (as is reported) entred into a Resolution to abandon the World. For that Purpose he hath obtained a *Breve* of the *Pope* that he may enter the Monastery and the Profession both at one instant, and intreates to become of the Order of *St. Jerome*.' Cornwallis to Salisbury, Madrid, 17/27 Nov. 1606, in Winwood, *Memorials*, ii, 262.

29 Papal Nuncio to Secretary of State, Madrid, 17 Feb. 1607, ASV *Spagna*, 19, fol. 158; *Relaciones*, p. 299.

30 He instituted an enquiry into the size of the *tercios* in the Low Countries, the situation in the Mediterranean and Atlantic fleets and the *presidios* of Spain and Italy, letters to Andrés de Prada, Palace, 8 Mar. 1607 and San Lorenzo, 7 Jul. 1607, AGS E 2025, fols. 14 and 15. Among the reforms that came about as a result was the invention of a flotation line on the hulls of ships nearly three hundred years before the more celebrated 'Plimsoll Line'. For an analysis of the reforms, García García, *La Pax Hispánica*, pp. 107–82 and pp. 333–4, n. 22. See also, David Goodman, *Spanish naval power, 1589–1665. Reconstruction and defeat*, Cambridge, 1997, pp. 116–17.

31 A *hechura* of Juan de la Serna was sentenced to death by Carrillo for forging an order of Lerma's to the Council of Portugal, *Relaciones*, pp. 301.

32 Included in *cédula*, Buitrago, 7 Jun. 1607, AGS CJH 480, no. 22, copy.

33 See above, pp. 15–17.

34 *Cédula*, 7 Jun. 1607, op. cit.; the decree was drawn up by Juan de Amezqueta and counter-signed by Miranda, Idiáquez, Xavierre and Carrillo.

35 *Relaciones*, p. 317.

36 Ibid., pp. 322 and 324.

37 Lerma, 'Imbentario', ADL 53, fol. 21.

38 'Estado de Lerma. Bienes en Valladolid. Alcaydia de la Casa, Huerta y Ribera', ADL 8, no fol.

39 'Facultad Real original del s[eño]r d[o]n Felipe Tercero p[ara] q[u]e el s[eño]r Duque de Lerma pudiese funda uno, dos o mas Mayorazgos a favor del s[eño]r D[o]n Christóval de Sandoval y Rojas, Duque de Uceda, su hijo', Madrid, 31 Jan. 1607, ADL 12, no. 5; the document is the original but the title is a later copy – this explains why the title of 'Duke of Uceda' is used.

40 Lerma, 'Imbentario', ADL 53, pp. 3b–5.

41 The information in the following paragraphs is based upon Lerma, 'Imbentario', ADL 53, fols. 8b–11, 'Testamento … (1617)', ibid., 12, fols. 29r–v, 'Hacienda acrecentada por compras', ibid., 54, no. 9, no fol. and 'El estado q[ue] tiene el pleyto q[ue] llaman de la recompensa', AHN Consejos, leg. 7258; cnta. Fin. 28 Feb. 1608, AGS CJH 482–29–1 and CMC 3a época, leg. 1987, no. 19. On the seigneurial purchase of towns, N. Salomon, La vida rural castellana en tiempos de Felipe II, Barcelona, 1964, pp. 207–12.

42 See below, pp. 144–6.

43 Lerma, 'Imbentario', ADL 53, fols. 9–11b. A vecino was normally valued at 16,000 maravedís (42.6 ducats), AGS CMC 3a época, leg. 1978, no. 19.

44 Figures reworked from Lerma, 'Imbentario (1617)', ADL 53, fols. 6b–7 and 'Hacienda acrecentada', ibid., 54, no. 9, no fol. On Tudela, Bennassar, Valladolid, p. 171; on the transaction of 1607, Relaciones, pp. 306–7 and Cornwallis to Salisbury (May/July) 1607, Winwood, Memorials, ii, p. 324.

45 Anon., 'Estado de Lerma. Bienes en Valladolid. Alcaydia de la Casa, Huerta y Ribera en Valladolid', n.d., ADL 8.

46 Reference is made to Lerma's will in 'Codicilio de d. Francisco Gómez de Sandoval y Rojas (Duque de Lerma) (20 de Marzo de 1609), printed by Antonio Matilla Tascón, Testamentos de 43 personajes del Madrid de los Austrias, Madrid, 1983, pp. 111–14, at p. 111. I have been unable to find a copy of this will in the Lerma archive. The agreements between Lerma and Cea are printed in 'Testamento … (1617)', ADL 12, that of Madrid, 8 Aug. 1607, at fols. 5–8 and that of San Lorenzo, 20 Jul. 1607 are incorporated within it, at fols. 5v–7.

47 Chief among these were the monastery of San Pablo and the building of San Diego, Valladolid; his gifts to the monastery of Belén for building and houses; the building for the Trinitarios Descalzos in Madrid and those of the Franciscos Descalzos in Ampudia and Recoletas Agustinas in Denia; his colegial churches in Lerma and Ampudia.

48 Lerma, 'Testamento … (1617)', ADL 12, p. 9.

49 These are summarised in the 'Testamento … (1617)', ibid., pp. 16–18b. See also, 'Codicilio de D. Francisco Gómez de Sandoval y Rojas (Duque de Lerma)', in Matilla Tascón, Testamentos, pp. 111–14.

50 Relaciones, pp. 313, 315, 318.

51 'Relación Sumaria del Estado que tiene la real hacienda en 17 de Agosto de 1607 años', Madrid, 20 Oct. 1607, ACC, xxiii, pp. 543–59. See also I. Pulido Bueno, La Real Hacienda de Felipe III, Huelva, 1996, pp. 49–72.

52 ACC, xxiii, pp. 17–18.

53 Thompson, 'Crown and Cortes in Castile, 1590–1665', pp. 29–45.

54 ACC, xxiv, pp. 9–115.

55 Cntas. Fin. 19 Jul. 1608, AGS CJH 482, no fol. and fol. 34; García García, La Pax Hispánica, pp. 220–5.

56 'Visita y Cargos de Don Pedro Franqueza …', Escudero, Los Secretarios, iii, pp. 792–3; Relaciones, pp. 324, 332, 333.

7

Flight: the journeys of 1608–10 and the death of Henry IV of France

'They ... call him traitor'

The humiliations of 1607 emboldened Lerma's enemies but they also convinced Philip of the absolute need to reaffirm his commitment to the duke: the loving embrace that he gave Lerma in front of the whole of courtly society at the swearing of fealty to the heir in San Jerónimo on 13 January 1608 was a carefully-considered and stage-managed restatement of his affection for Lerma and of his confidence in him. When the Queen also embraced Lerma it must have appeared as if nothing had changed: the duke was still secure in the King's favour and pre-eminent at court.[1]

However, a very great deal had changed, for it soon became evident that Philip had made his stunning gesture as a whirlwind of criticism engulfed Lerma; it was almost as if he embraced Lerma to hold on to him, to prevent him from leaving court voluntarily or being driven away from it by his enemies. And those enemies were gathering in increasing numbers, not only at court but even in the lands belonging to the Sandoval family. In a memorable report in March 1608 Sir Charles Cornwallis, the English ambassador, recorded the wide range of criticisms that were being levelled against Lerma at court in the early months of 1608:

> They rail at him publicly for his engrossing the estate, and now lately are come to do it so confidently as, adjoining unto it the matter of this Low Country treaty, they in a sort call him traitor, saying that so dishonourable ... provisions of peace (whereof they hold him a principal contriver) cannot proceed out of other entrails than those of a traitor and a coward.

Nor was the King himself immune to criticism: he was, Cornwallis observed, confronted at the very heart of his palace by his own preachers and servants in a manner that was deeply embarrassing to him:

[The King's] preachers this Lent, in presence of the ambassadors of other princes and states, have been violent in telling him to his face of his extreme wants, unworthy of a King, and of his consumptions otherwise, in profuse giving where there has been no merit. The Ambassador of Venice, who sits where he may take full view of him, tells me he sits like an image, stricken but not moved. Divers of his guard in his way to his chapel have in like manner lately affronted him in troop of 6 or 7 at once, delivering petitions for their wages and accompanying them with exclamatory words, saying they have not been paid these 15 months, and are now come to such extremity as with difficulty they defend themselves from starving. The poor King takes their papers and follows his way; what he feels in his heart, God knows, but those that observe his countenance assure me that they find no change in it.[2]

Lerma had to confront these fulminating problems without the support of the Count of Miranda, who was finally given permission to retire from court in February 1608.[3] He left with the fullest honours; Philip raised him to the dukedom of Peñaranda de Duero (22 May) and allowed him to enjoy the salary as President of Castile for life.[4] Lerma needed to be completely certain of the loyalty of the new President of the Council of Castile and so in April he took one of the major risks of his *valimiento* by having Dr Juan Bautista de Acevedo appointed to replace Miranda with the retention of the Inquisitorship-general.[5] The message that Lerma now sent to his opponents was unambiguous: he would not give up his supremacy at court without a fight.

Once again, too, he took the King away; Philip was absent from his capital city for five months (18 May–3 October). So determined was Lerma to isolate the King from his opponents that he was even prepared to entertain him in his own houses; Philip visited Lerma three times, staying for thirty-one, nine and six days. Lerma also took Philip back to Valladolid, where for nearly seven weeks (2 August–25 September) he exercised his power as Governor of the royal palace to control access to him. This was much more than a summer progress: Philip was once again in quarantine, isolated from Lerma's opponents. The King was accompanied by the councillors of State upon whom Lerma could rely – Idiáquez, Velada, the Cardinal of Toledo and confessor Xavierre. The Constable of Castile remained in Madrid.

The *jornada* aroused even more widespread criticism of king and duke. Cornwallis wrote contemptuously of Lerma 'leading a King in such an unfitting sort after him with manifest Neglect of the important Affayrs of his Kingdom and disregard to what belongs unto his kingly Office'.[6] In June, in what appears to have been a carefully co-ordinated campaign, broadsheets appeared on the gates of the Alcázar in Madrid and in Lerma and Valladolid accusing Lerma of exploiting the King's grace for his own profit. A copy of one of them found its way into Philip's hands. It had pictures of Philip, Lerma and Cea, and under his arm the King carried a bag with the inscription 'King; Guard your doubloons because there are two thieves here'. The Admiral of Aragon handed a tract – it is not clear whether it was this one – to the King: for the second time he had directly challenged the legitimacy of Lerma's authority with Philip.[7] In doing so he provided a further rallying-point for the enemies of the duke at court.

Disaffection spread to Lerma's vassals in his newly-acquired *villas de behetría*. The Sandoval shield on the gates of Santa María del Campó was torn down and replaced with that of the King while the shield at Torquemada was also vandalised. Libels against Lerma also appeared in Tudela de Duero. *Alcaldes* were despatched to find the culprits but neither bribery nor the application of torture to a few unfortunates elicited any information on the authorship of the tracts.[8]

Lerma swayed before the storm. In mannered deference to his enemies, he let it be known that he was considering allowing the Marchioness del Valle to return to court.[9] More substantively, he began, very conspicuously, to hand over power to his son:

> The duke of Lerma is the same at Court that he hath beene and endeavors to make the duke of Sea his oldest sonne heir not to his landes and revenewes onlie but to his owne greatnes and privatye with the kinge, and for that ende never suffers him to be from the kinge's elbowe either in his sportes or exercises (whereto from the equalitie of their age he is fitter for his companion than the duke of Lerma, nor yet in matters of negotiation w[hi]ch for the most part he procures to be dispatched by his mediation, informing suitors unto him with these words *hablen con el duque de Sea mi hijo*, who now gives audience and dispatch in such manner as his father was accoustomed to do.[10]

In Lerma itself, Philip took one of the defining decisions of his reign. Isolated with Lerma and the councillors of State whom Lerma trusted, on 15 July Philip authorised the Archduke Albert to negotiate with the United Provinces for a truce for five or six years. He also undertook to recognise the United Provinces as a free and sovereign state if they permitted the exercise of Catholicism in their lands. Philip refused to give way over the right of navigation to the Indies but in his instructions to Spínola (who was given responsibility for the negotiations) he conceded that the Dutch could transport their goods to the Indies if they agreed to do so in Portuguese ships (18 July). The Estates-General rejected the offer (23 August), but pressure from Henry IV, who threatened to cut off his subsidies if they failed to open negotiations for a truce, forced them to change their minds.[11] The end of the war which had been pivotal to European relationships for a generation was now in sight.

Lerma's gamble in having Bautista de Acevedo serve the presidency of the Council of Castile and the Inquisitorship-general came to nothing for Bautista died suddenly on 9 July. The duke responded with ruthless clarity of purpose by securing the presidency of the Council of Castile for Pedro Manso

(6 September) and the Inquisitorship-general for the Cardinal-archbishop of Toledo (12 September). He further bolstered his position by having fray Luis de Aliaga, his own confessor, appointed to replace Xavierre as the custodian of the King's conscience (1 November).[12] These three appointments were designed to secure Lerma's control over the levers of power in court, Church and government and, once again, to make it evident that he would fight to protect himself.

Pedro Manso was a trusted member of Lerma's circle, well known to the duke himself and a friend of both Bautista de Acevedo and Sarmiento de Acuña.[13] However, his promotion to the senior judicial position in the kingdom of Castile was as scandalously inappropriate as it was spectacular. He was not yet forty years of age and had only two years' experience of significant office (President of the Chancellery of Valladolid, 1604–06) – and had been sentenced to death for murder. He was, reported the English ambassador,

> A Man meanly borne, and within these eight Years Condemned, and in great peryle to have receiv'd his End uppon the Gallowes, for cutting out the Tongue of a Man and after killing him, upon a particular Offence in words offered unto himself. The Duke that then was the Meane to save his Life, is now the Author to advance it, and lift him to a higher Stage than the Eyes of his former Age were able to look up to.[14]

The promotion of the Cardinal of Toledo to the Inquisitorship-general was not controversial in itself, for the two posts had often been combined. However, the appointment deepened Lerma's conflict with the Queen, for Philip had promised Margaret that the Countess of Harrach, one of her German courtiers, could nominate to the office when it became vacant, and she had decided to name Cardinal Zapata. The appointment of the Cardinal of Toledo therefore not only intensified Margaret's hostility to Lerma but encouraged Zapata (who had been loyal to Lerma and his family for many years) into beginning to move into opposition to the duke.[15]

Jerónimo de Xavierre had almost certainly displayed too much independence of Lerma. He was removed from influence at court by being raised to a cardinalate; it was axiomatic in Spain that cardinals – other, that is, than the cardinal-archbishop of Toledo or Inquisitor General – could not be involved in courtly politics. Fray Luis de Aliaga Martínez O. P. was a low-born Aragonese – his father had been a seller of cloth – who had come to court with Xavierre in 1604.[16] He was recommended to Lerma by the Count of Villalonga, and in 1606 the duke took him on as his own confessor. He had evidently been very satisfied with him and in passing him on to the King clearly anticipated that Aliaga would continue to serve his interests.[17] His confidence was shared within his *clientela*: Sarmiento de Acuña was assured that Aliaga would prove himself to be 'a very good friend'.[18] Cabrera de Córdoba welcomed Aliaga as 'a man of great virtue and education'.[19] No one, least of all Lerma himself, had any reason to suspect that the low-born friar would become the most determined of Lerma's opponents, the man who more than any other servant of the crown would undermine the King's confidence in his *valido* and in the very institution of the *valimiento*.[20]

The Twelve Years' Truce and the road back to war

In December 1608 Albert sent his confessor, fray Iñigo de Brizuela, to Madrid to bolster the King in his determination to agree to a truce with the United Provinces. Brizuela found his strongest ally in Lerma; in a series of four meetings of the Council of State between 17 and 25 January, Lerma took the lead in insisting that the King had to make a truce. The first of these meetings was called in the presence of the King himself to consider the momentous question of whether the Council should recommend that the war be continued or brought to a conclusion. In a magisterial opening *parecer*, Idiáquez argued that the condition of the royal finances meant that the war could not be sustained. He advised the King against making a peace or acknowledging the sovereignty of the Dutch for fear of undermining the legal basis for returning to war should that prove necessary. He therefore suggested that Philip should make a truce for a limited period. The Marquis of Velada fully supported him.

Lerma then presented one of the most incisive *pareceres* of his career, arguing forcefully that the truce had to be accepted. He assuaged the King's conscience over abandoning the Catholics living in the United Provinces by reminding him that the persecution of the Catholic minority in England had lessened with the peace of 1604, suggesting that the same would happen in the rebel provinces. Pointedly, he insisted that the great war effort of recent years had resulted in the capture of a mere five towns and hamlets (*lugares*) in eastern Spain, of which Rheinberg alone brought any advantage; the others could profitably be abandoned. It was, Lerma suggested, 'impossible' to find the 4,000,000 ducats that would be necessary to pursue the war for another year. Moreover, the kingdom of Castile could not be pressed for more money, and anyone who advised the King that it could yield another major grant was deceiving him. Lerma concluded with a powerful and moving statement: 'although God knows how much it weighs on him to say things of such gravity to Your Majesty, the obligation that he has towards his royal service obliges him to represent all the disadvantages'. Lerma left his hearers in no doubt about his policy: the King simply had to accept a truce. The other councillors present – the Constable of Castile, the Cardinal of Toledo, the Duke of Infantado and the Count of Alba de Liste all reluctantly agreed that the war could not be pursued.

Lerma then spoke again to drive home the need to make the truce. He urged Philip to 'pay attention' to financial realities and demanded that all of his colleagues should bind themselves to accept the decision: 'it would be good for the Council to meet every day to treat of this because the period of the armistice is so short that it is convenient not to lose an hour of time'. The King expressly agreed with Lerma's *parecer*.[21]

Five days after the great meeting of 17 January, Lerma placed two major financial documents in front of his colleagues on the Council to make explicit the very details of the financial realities that the King faced – a budget drawn up by the President and Council of Finance and the tabulation by *contador* Juan Muñoz de Escobar of all the monies that Philip had sent to the Low Countries since his accession.[22] The discussion of the documents took place on the following day, presumably after the councillors had pondered overnight on their implications. When the Council reassembled, Lerma insisted that there was no alternative to pursuing a truce. Once again, the other councillors concurred with his judgement.[23] Two days later, on 24 January 1609, the Council unanimously recommended that the King should concede sovereignty to the United Provinces for the duration of the truce and accepted that the truce could be converted into a lasting peace if the Provinces allowed the free practice of Catholicism in their lands. As was customary in Spanish peace settlements, the issue of navigation to the Indies was to remain unresolved.[24]

The Twelve Years' Truce was signed at Antwerp between Albert (on his own behalf and that of Philip III) and the United Provinces on 9 April 1609. The agreement stipulated that all hostilities were to cease on land and sea. Philip acknowledged the sovereign independence of the United Provinces and granted them the right to trade with Spain and Portugal and with the European states of the Spanish Monarchy. By not even mentioning the Dutch Catholics, Philip tacitly abandoned them. He maintained the principle that the Dutch could only trade in the Indies with his permission. It was a major gain for Spain that her ships could use the Channel without fear of attack from Dutch shipping and could even trade in the United Provinces. There was, however, no disguising that the Truce of 1609 was a historic defeat for Spain in psychological as well as in military and political terms. It was also a rebuke to a generation of Spanish statesmen, for the same terms could have been obtained at least twenty years earlier.[25] To his dying day, Philip III felt ashamed of having to come to terms with rebellious subjects: one of his last acts, two days before he died, would be to order that the war should be renewed.[26]

The Twelve Years' Truce brought to an end the era of major wars in western Europe which had opened in the 1560s. It also provided a precise framework before the war between Spain and the United Provinces which had been at the core of so many of those wars began again: the date of 9 April 1621 entered the consciousness of Europe's diplomats. Increasingly, the soldiers who sat in Madrid on the councils of State and War emphasised that the truce favoured the Dutch, freeing them to divert their energies overseas while obliging Spain to maintain a substantial (and expensive) military presence in the Low Countries and to guarantee the security of its military corridors against the time when the war was renewed.

The lead was taken by the Council of War, which was reinforced in the years after 1605 by the return to Madrid of many leading soldiers, including some of the senior commanders in the Army of Flanders: Agustín Mejía and the Marquis of San Germán took up councillorships in 1605, Enrique de Guzmán and Alonso de Sotomayor in 1607; Fernando Girón in 1608 and Antonio de Zúñiga and Rodrigo Niño Laso de la Vega in 1609. They formed an experienced and coherent group and attended to their duties with diligence; in 1606 the average attendance at the Council passed eight councillors per meeting for the first time. The driving insistence of this core of men that the war would have to be renewed began to shift the government as a whole towards a more aggressive stance in foreign affairs, and in doing so to undermine the influence of the *valido* whose policies were symbolised by the truce.

The years of the truce were also marked by a series of problems in central Europe which were created or aggravated by the degenerating mental condition of Rudolf II and by his feud with his brother Matthias. In April 1606 Matthias and three other archdukes agreed that while Rudolf was to be allowed to retain the imperial dignity Matthias was henceforth to be regarded as the head of the family. Rudolf retaliated in 1609 by undermining Matthias's hopes of succeeding him by granting freedom of conscience in Bohemia ('Letter of Majesty', 9 July 1609). Bohemia's vote was often decisive in the imperial College of Electors, and Rudolf's action was designed to swing the succession away from his brother even if that meant that the House of Habsburg lost its historic hold on the imperial title.[27]

Rudolf also involved himself in the crisis over the succession to the duchies of Jülich and Cleves, two small but strategically important states on the borders of the Low Countries. When Duke John William of Cleves, Jülich, Marck and Berg died without heirs (25 March 1609) Rudolf asserted his right to arbitrate between the candidates for the succession. He had the Archduke Leopold take possession of the fortress of Jülich (23 July) but Leopold then found himself blockaded by the two 'princes in possession'. War broke out in December.[28]

On 18 October the Council of State agreed with Baltasar de Zúñiga, ambassador at the imperial court, that the crisis in central Europe threatened the preservation of Catholicism in Germany and 'the succession to the imperial throne and the survival or decline of the House of Austria'. Zúñiga was instructed to try to secure the election of Matthias or, failing that, to ensure that an Austrian Habsburg succeeded Rudolf. However, from Spínola came advice that was even more forceful than Zúñiga's: Philip should declare that he himself was Rudolf's heir and seek to revive the Austro-Spanish empire of Charles V. For once, Philip was prepared to listen to his general, for this was a project worthy of his greatness: in December, Zúñiga was ordered to plan for Philip's succession to the imperial title.[29] Within months of making the Truce with the Dutch, Spain was being drawn deep into the conflicts of central Europe.

The attack of the Admiral of Aragon

Lerma's nerve held in the face of the attacks upon him at court, and he responded by throwing down the gauntlet to the Mendoza family in the most provocative manner: on 20 May 1609 Silva de Torres travelled to the Infantado palace at Guadalajara and arrested the Admiral of Aragon.[30] Lerma then established a bench of judges to try the Admiral that consisted exclusively of his own *hechuras:* Silva de Torres sat with Pedro de Tapia and Diego de Alderete.[31] To save himself, Lerma would go to war with the Mendozas and in doing so make it crystal clear to all his opponents that he would confront each and every one of them without flinching.

That, at least, was the public face that Lerma presented at court. In reality, he knew that he did not have to worry too much about the Admiral because he had been foolish enough to write contemptuously to the Archduke Albert of the immaturity and unreliability of the King himself:

> It was said that he said that he distrusted His Majesty because of the little experi-
> ence that he has and because he cannot keep a secret either as a man or as a king,
> and he should reform in these two matters and that he should not play games for
> so much of the time...[32]

The Admiral had also written that the King's pardon for Calderón in 1607 was against 'conscience and good government'. Lerma was safe – and so in all likelihood, at least in the short-term, was Calderón himself.

The Queen gave birth to a third son on 16 May 1609; he was named Ferdinand. Margaret's need to convalesce formed the justification for a royal progress to Segovia; she and Philip spent July and August there. Lerma, however, was given licence to visit Valladolid and Lerma, and with the exception of eight days in July, spent two months away from Philip in the longest separation of his *valimiento*. He must have been supremely confident of the King's enduring affection to risk such an extended absence from court. Cristóbal took over the management of his papers.[33] Lerma's absence was well-judged: he was in his ducal town when Philip, in Segovia, ratified the truce with the Dutch (7 July).

While Philip was prepared to tolerate Lerma's absence from the final discussion of the truce he did not allow him to evade responsibility for the expulsion of the *moriscos*. Philip II had determined as long ago as 1582 that the *moriscos* posed a security threat and would have to be expelled from Spain as soon as was practicable. For Philip III (who had been born at the moment when plans for a *morisco* rebellion had been uncovered) the expulsion was to be the chief glory of his reign and he summoned Lerma to Segovia to take part in the meetings which recommended that the *moriscos* be expelled. Lerma was much less enthusiastic; having taken part in the discussions, he returned to his ducal town, distancing himself as best he could from the decisions made in Segovia.[34]

About 130,000 *moriscos* were expelled from the kingdom of Valencia; this represented the loss of one-third of the population of the kingdom. By the end of March 1610 over 150,000 *moriscos* – one-half or so of those in Spain in the previous September – had left the country. The threat of war with France in the spring of 1610 brought a temporary halt to the expulsion in Aragon and Castile since the government dared not risk allowing Henry IV to use the services of thousands of embittered *moriscos*. However, the expulsion of large communities from Andalusia, Granada and Murcia went ahead, untouched by the threat of war on the northern frontiers.[35] For Philip, the expulsion was a historic victory against the infidel. His *valido* was at best ambivalent about the need to expel the *moriscos*. He had more pressing concerns.

The verdict on Villalonga

On 22 December 1609 Fernando Carrillo presented the King with his judgement in the Villalonga case.[36] He found that the three principals were guilty of most of the charges against them and sentenced each of them to life imprisonment, to the confiscation of all *mercedes* and titles and to fines totalling 2,477,101 ducats – Villalonga to 1,406,259 ducats; Ramírez de Prado to 358,671, and Núñez de Correa to 711,011. All office-holders in the Council of Finance and its *contadurías* were summoned to hear the verdicts read out. The gravamen of the judgement against Villalonga was that he had systematically betrayed the royal trust:

> He had come to hold so much grace and favour with me, that all matters of government, both of war and of finance and also of the grant of royal favours and other things of importance and consideration dealt with in my councils and juntas, justly passed through his hands. His opinion was greatly valued and esteemed and he was occupied in the gravest matters of my royal household and court and in so many different councils … He followed my royal person on all

... journeys, and by my command (was appointed) to so many different councils and juntas.[37]

Central to Villalonga's misuse of power had been his ability to use his 'special friendship and working relationship' with Ramírez de Prado to control the management of finances 'to the exclusion of others' and 'without any other minister participating in the decisions'. This was the crucial element in Carrillo's verdict – that it had been Villalonga and his close associates rather than the members of the *Junta del Desempeño* as a whole who had been responsible for mismanaging the crown's finances.[38] In particular, Carrillo uncovered the mechanics of the operation whereby in 1606 Villalonga and Ramírez de Prado had convinced Philip and his senior ministers that the *desempeño* had been accomplished and that the royal finances brought to 'a happy state', improved by a total of 14,728,890 ducats. He demonstrated, too, how Villalonga had worked closely with Núñez de Correa to commit large-scale frauds on every aspect of governmental financial business, in Portugal as in Spain. He established that Villalonga had also perverted the administration of justice: when, for instance, the *fiscales* of the councils of the Indies and Finance had accused Pedro Gómez Reynel of defrauding the exchequer of 700,000 ducats, Villalonga and Ramírez de Prado had sat as judges and had dismissed the case. Villalonga had also been involved in frauds with other *asentistas* from as early as 1603.[39] In passing, Carrillo drew attention to the malign influence that Villalonga's wife had exerted upon him.[40]

On the day after Philip received Carrillo's report he appointed him to the presidency of the Council of Finance and its tribunals: the significance of the appointment was unmistakeable, a clarion call to rid his government of corruption. Juan de Acuña was absolved of blame for the financial disaster and was honoured with the presidency of the Council of the Indies in succession to Lemos (who now became Viceroy of Naples at the age of thirty-six); there could be no doubt that Acuña retained the favour of the King and of Lerma.[41] However, in allowing Carrillo to enter the presidency of the Council of Finance Lerma had made one of the defining errors of his *valimiento*, for – exactly as he had done with Aliaga – Lerma had promoted a trusted confidant to a position which lay beyond the point at which he could control him.

The third dukedom: Uceda, 1609–10

Once again, as he fought desperately for survival at court, Lerma secured a stunning advancement for his family. On 16 February 1610 Philip granted the dukedom of Uceda to Bernardo Antonio, Cristóbal's second son. The dukedom of Cea now passed to Francisco Gómez II while Cristóbal himself would use the title of Uceda until he succeeded to the dukedom of Lerma; only then would it pass to Bernardo Antonio. On his father's death, therefore, Cristóbal would become duke of Lerma while Francisco Gómez II would become duke of Uceda and Bernardo Antonio, duke of Cea. On 16 February 1610, in other words, Philip assured Lerma that when he died his heir and both of his own sons would all hold dukedoms simultaneously. It may reasonably be doubted whether any Spanish aristocratic family had ever presumed to dream of enjoying such status. Certainly, in the next generation the family would enjoy even greater pre-eminence in courtly society than that during the years of Lerma's *valimiento.*[42]

Cea had bought the town of Uceda and its castle at the end of 1609. It was suitable as an aristocratic rural retreat; 60 kilometres north of Madrid in the mountains off the Burgos road, Uceda provided good hunting and riding lands and had a fast-running river for fishing. Its lands produced wheat and vines and were home to about 2,500 inhabitants. The *mayorazgo* of Uceda was centred on the town of Uceda and the villages of Torremocha and Galapagu-illos. Cristóbal also owned a town house in Madrid and held the treasuryship of the *casa de la moneda* in perpetuity and some modest rents in the city. He did not seek to build up a concentrated estate as his father had done. He bought the town of Belmonte del Tajo, 20 kilometres south-east of Arganda, and in 1613 Philip obligingly raised Bernardo Antonio to the marquisate of the town. He took advantage of the fall of Villalonga to acquire some towns and *lugares* in eastern Spain from the possessions confiscated from his estate. He was given the privilege by the King of enjoying the income from the *encomiendas* of Monreal (Santiago) until the end of 1628 and that of Bolaños (Calatrava) to the end of 1632. Uceda's ecclesiastical patronages were similar to those of his father but much more modest in scale. In his ducal town he spent 12,600 ducats in endowing the monastery of the barefoot Franciscans and its patronage to the *mayorazgo*. In Lerma he held the patronage of the monastery of the *Ascensión de Nuestro Señor* which his wife had founded.

Sadly for Lerma, it was already becoming evident that Cristóbal had not lived up to his early promise. In 1608 Luis Abarca de Bolea had written to Diego Sarmiento de Acuña that he was 'among the best and most intelli-gent men that I have known.'[43] But Cristóbal had not developed any interest in politics; he remained a courtier, and he remained – enduringly – little more than his father's son. His elevation to the dukedom of Uceda did not improve his abiding mediocrity. If anything, it seemed to confirm it; his chief characteristic was that he had neither the energy nor the determination to involve himself in courtly politics.

The journey of 1610 and the assassination of Henry IV of France

There was further good news for Lerma when Margaret let it be known that she intended to give birth in Lerma.[44] Eager to have the Queen travel north before she changed her mind, the duke took the royal couple away from the Escorial on 27 February 1610 for what proved to be the longest of all of Philip's absences from a capital city: they did not return until the first week of December. Never was Philip's kingship more escapist and more irresponsible than during this long *jornada*: never was Lerma's control of him more frivolous and self-indulgent. Faced with a grave crisis in foreign affairs as Henry IV prepared armies of 50,000 men to attack Habsburg power in the Low Countries and in Italy, and in the midst of the enormous military operation to expel the *moriscos*, the government collapsed into surreal chaos as King and *valido* roamed around Old Castile on a journey which was as devoid of political justification as it was of financial resources. [45] But a royal child would be born in Lerma.

Philip III did not even have the money with which to begin his *jornada;* at the outset of the progress, Lerma had to order the *corregidores* of Burgos and Valladolid to make monies available to the King that they were holding for the *encabezamiento* tax.[46] On 22 April Lerma expressed his concern to Carrillo that the *moriscos* of Aragon might rise in rebellion and provide Henry IV with the opportunity to intervene within Spain. He showed the importance that he attached to his fears by writing the letter to the President in his own hand; it is perhaps the most important of all of his extant holograph letters. He was anxious that 'we would lose much reputation, including even that which has been gained [with the expulsion of] the *moriscos* in Valencia and Castile and we would be placed in new and greater need of [resorting to] arms and greater financial expenditure'.[47] But the duke would not curtail the King's journey: a royal child would be born in Lerma.

Philip and his household reached Valladolid on 4 March and stayed there until 16 April. He attended the celebrations of Easter Saturday and Sunday (10–11 April) in *San Pablo* rather than in the city's cathedral and then went on to Lerma, where the royal couple took pleasure in attending masses in Lerma's churches and religious houses and enjoyed the new comforts of the *Casa del Duque*, which was now developing into a comfortable palace, if still a small one.

While Philip prayed in Lerma, Henry IV prepared in Paris to wage war. He mustered his armies and formed an offensive and defensive league against Spain with Charles-Emmanuel and agreed to marry his daughter Elizabeth to the Prince of Piedmont (Treaty of Bruzzolo, 25 April 1610).[48] On 13 May 1610 he had Marie de Medici crowned so that she could govern France while he was at the front and on the following day was leaving Paris for the front when a Catholic fanatic, François Ravaillac, leapt into his coach and stabbed him twice. He died within hours. On 15 May, the widowed queen was proclaimed as regent until Louis XIII attained his majority (which would be in 1614).[49]

The momentous news of the assassination reached the King of Spain in Lerma on 24 May, and Philip immediately convened the Council of State to advise him on the response that he should make. Idiáquez (who had always delighted in expressing his contempt for the King of France) recommended that an appropriate demonstration of mourning should be made 'not because of what [Henry IV] deserved, but only because the Queen has always shown herself anxious for friendship'. He considered that the assassination was a divine confirmation of Philip's status and a reward for the expulsion of the *moriscos*.

Lerma, more positive for once than Idiáquez, seized the moment. He was equally acerbic about Henry IV: 'if the King of France, now dead, could see the mourning that Your Majesty has ordered for him, he would moderate his vote, but since it is the Queen who has to witness this demonstration he is of the view that the mourning ought to be the greater'. Lerma appreciated that France would have to eschew adventures in foreign policy so as to avoid providing Spain with the opportunity to interfere in French domestic politics. He therefore looked toward the creation of an alliance with France in which the two great Catholic powers would 'become close partners'. This would demonstrate Philip's greatness 'to all the world' and have a domino effect on other powers. Lerma stressed that since James I had not dared to support Henry IV in breaking with Spain he would most certainly not risk doing so now. He suggested that the Dutch might extend the Truce 'seeing that they are without the protection of France' and that the crisis in Cleves and Jülich could be resolved without war. Lerma was optimistic that Philip could now restore his financial position and concluded that 'it seems highly appropriate to enjoy the opportunity sent by Our Lord' to achieve the King's ends 'by means of lasting agreements'.[50] Doubtless, Lerma reflected privately that Henry IV's death had come at an extraordinarily fortuitous moment for himself, reaffirming his own position at court as the King and his advisers pondered on the probability that France would remain weakened for many years.

At midnight, Queen Margaret was delivered of a daughter; she was named Margarita Francisca after her mother and the duke in whose town she had been born. The triumph of the Sandoval family seemed to be confirmed. On 8 and 9 June, the exequies for Henry IV were celebrated in the church of *San Pedro*, and on 10 June – the feast of Corpus Christi – the baptism of the princess took place: the Cardinal of Toledo officiated and Lerma served as godfather.[51] The identification of the Sandoval family with the triumphs of the crown was reinforced.

However, joy turned to dread when on a brief progress from Lerma Prince Philip fell gravely ill at Aranda de Duero. The King was forced to spend

July and August in the small provincial town as his son struggled for life and then began slowly to recover.[52]

This may have accounted for a mysterious and eccentric interlude in Lerma's life, for at the end of July he let it be known that he intended to marry the Countess of Valencia, a rich widow. The Countess was about Lerma's age and if he was at all serious about marrying her it was presumably for companionship rather than to have children. Probably it was a strategem to convince Philip that he no longer wished to abandon court for the religious life.[53] Certainly, Cristóbal opposed the marriage, presumably because he was fearful that if children did issue from it Lerma might try to create *mayorazgos* for them at the expense of his own inheritance. When Lerma called the wedding off in the late autumn the bride's wedding clothes had been made and she and her family were understandably furious. Whether Cristóbal expressed any gratitude to his father is not known. Lerma's disappointment, if such it was, was no doubt assuaged by the news that he had been left 60,000 ducats in the will of his uncle, Tomás de Borja, archbishop of Zaragoza.[54]

NOTES
1 See above, p. 45. Four anonymous accounts of the ceremony are printed by Simon Diaz, *Relaciones breves de … Madrid*, pp. 49–69 (quotation, p. 55); *Relaciones*, pp. 322–30.
2 Cornwallis to Salisbury, Madrid, 5/15 Mar. 1608, HH CP 125/39.
3 John Jude to T. Wilson, Madrid, 10/20 Feb. 1608, NA SP 94/15, fol. 26. See also, *Relaciones*, pp. 331–2.
4 *Cédula*, Honrrubio, 23 May 1608, AGS QC 30. He died on 4 September.
5 Title, Madrid, 13 Apr. 1608, AGS QC 24; González Dávila, *Teatro de las Grandezas de Madrid*, pp. 385–9; *Relaciones*, pp. 337–8.
6 Same to Lords of the Privy Council, Madrid, 12 May 1608 (OS – Old Style: Spain adopted the Gregorian Calendar in 1582, adding ten days to the date, and taking January 1 as the start of the year rather than 25 March, as in the Julian Calendar. During the period of this study there was therefore a ten-days's difference in dating), printed in Winwood, *Memorials*, ii, pp. 395–6, quotation at p. 395.
7 'the poore duke of Lerma is soe openlie and generallie assaulted with the exclamations and curses of the people, as were it not, that he houlds in his handes the best helpes and comandinge trumps he might runne the danger of loosinge the game if not the whole sett both of life and fortune', John Jude to Mr. (T.) Wilson, Madrid, 16/26 Jul. 1608, NA SP 94/15, fols. 83–83b, quotation at fol. 83. See also, *Relaciones*, pp. 344–5.
8 Rott, *Philippe III et le Duc de Lerme*, p. 368.
9 *Relaciones*, p. 338.
10 John Jude to T. Wilson, Madrid, 27 Jul./6 Aug. 1608, NA SP 94/15, fol. 89b.
11 Philip III to Albert, Lerma, 15 Jul. 1608, printed in Lonchay et Cuvelier, *Correspondance de la Cour d'Espagne sur les affaires des Pays-Bas*, 1 and 6 Mar. 1608, i, no. 661, pp. 284–5; Tex, *Oldenbarnevelt*, ii, pp. 386–96. See also, *CSPV*, xi, 1 and 3 Mar., 1608, nos. 184 and 186, pp. 101–2.
12 Manso's title, Valladolid, 6 Sep. 1608, AGS QC 37; the reaction at court, *Relaciones*, p. 346. Cardinal Sandoval y Rojas took possession of the inquisitorship on 8 Oct., AHN Inq lib. 361, fol. 58. On Aliaga's oath, Pedro de Paladiñas O. P. to Diego Sarmiento de Acuña, Valladolid, 1 Nov. 1608, RB 11/2117, doc. 116.
13 Manso to Sarmiento de Acuña, Valladolid, 16 Feb. and 16 Jul. 1608, RB 11/2126 doc.122 and 11/2127, doc. 16.

14 Cornwallis to the Lords of the Council, (Madrid), 7/17 Sep. 1608, Winwood, *Memorials*, ii, p. 432. Italics in original. John Jude noted that Manso's promotion to the presidency 'is not well relished with some, in regarde his life hath beene so various and skandalised with the death of one whom he killed as is saide not past 8 yeares since and cut out his tongue for hauinge offended', to Salisbury, Madrid, 24 Aug./3 Sep. 1608, NA SP 94/15, fols. 115–115b. On Manso's retirement in 1610 Francis Cottington noted that he 'was very meanly borne and not many years since condemned to be hanged for killing of a man. By favour of the Duke he was then pardoned, made Alcalde de Corte from thence Chancelor of Valladolid, the Patryarche of the Indies, and so President of Castile ...', to Salisbury, Madrid, 20/30 Oct. 1610, ibid., 94/17, fol. 228b.

15 *Relaciones*, p. 351; Rott, *Philippe III et le Duc de Lerme*, pp. 368–9.

16 Bernardo García García, 'El confesor fray Luis Aliaga y la conciencia del rey', in Flavio Rurale (ed.), *I religiosi a corte. Teologia, politica e diplomazia in Antico Regime*, Rome, 1998, pp. 159–94; on Xavierre, T. Echarte, 'El cardenal fray Jerónimo Xavierre (1546–1608)', *Cuadernos de Historia. Jerónimo Zúrita*, xxxix–xl, 1981, pp. 151–76; I am obliged to Bernardo García for bringing this article to my attention.

17 Aliaga's *prueba*, AHN Inq *Pruebas* 1306 (3); Lerma wrote to the Kingdom of Aragon that Aliaga's promotion was a favour towards the Kingdom, Madrid, 28 Dec. 1608, BN Mss 1492, fol. 339, copy.

18 Luis Abarca de Bolea to Sarmiento de Acuña, Valladolid, 13 Sep. 1608, RB 11/2117, doc. 88.

19 *Relaciones*, p. 350.

20 See below, pp. 168–9, 175–7.

21 Draft of *cnta.* St. 17 Jan. 1609, AGS E 626, fols. 1–3. On the negotiations, Allen, *Philip III and the Pax Hispánica*, pp. 203–33.

22 Draft of *cnta.* St. 22 Jan. 1609, AGS E 626, fol. 4.

23 Draft of *cnta.* St. 23 Jan. 1609, ibid., fol. 5.

24 Draft of *cnta.* St. 25 Jan. 1609, ibid., fol. 7.

25 Parker, *Dutch Revolt*, pp. 222–4 and 239–40.

26 See below, p. 246.

27 Herbert Haupt, 'From Feuding Brothers to a Nation at War with Itself', in E. Fučíkova (ed.), *Rudolf II and Prague. The Court and the City*, London, 1997, pp. 238–49. The complexities of the conflict are best summarised by G. Parker, *Europe in Crisis, 1598–1648*, 2nd edn., 2001, pp. 89–91.

28 On these crises, Parker, *Army of Flanders*, pp. 214–15.

29 *Cnta.* St. 18 Oct. 1609, AGS E 2638, fol. 38; B. Chudoba, *Spain and the Empire 1519–1634*, Chicago, 1952, pp. 198–202.

30 *Relaciones*, pp. 370–1, 376–7, 384; Rodríguez Villa, 'D. Francisco de Mendoza', pp. 541–58 and 601–8.

31 *Relaciones*, pp. 606–7.

32 Ibid., pp. 550–1.

33 See, for instance, his letter to Andrés de Prada, from Segovia, 5 Jul. 1609, in which he reported that Philip 'has ordered me to reply to you because my father is not here', AGS E 626, fol. 59.

34 *Relaciones*, p. 377; Diego de Colmenares, *Historia de la insigne ciudad de Segovia y compendio de las historias de Castilla*, 2 vols., Segovia, 1969–70, ii, pp. 382–3; P. Boronat, *Los moriscos españoles*, 2 vols., ed. R. García Cárcel, Granada 1992 reprint, ii, pp. 274–77; for modern perspectives, Domínguez Ortíz and Vincent, *Historia de los moriscos*, Madrid, 1978, pp. 178–9 and Rafael Benítez Sánchez-Blanco, 'The "Géographie de l'Espagne morisque" Forty Years On', *Spain and Sweden*, pp. 471–504.

35 *Relaciones*, pp. 375–7, 380–1, 383–6, 389–91, 393–4; H. Lapeyre, *Géographie de l'Espagne morisque*, Paris, 1959, pp. 65–87; Domínguez Ortíz and Vincent, *Historia de los moriscos*, Madrid, 1978), pp. 183, 186.

36 The verdicts of the *fiscales* of Inquisition and Aragon were published in 1611, Francisco de Monzón, 'Testimonio de las sentencias dadas en la visita y cargos de Don Pedro Franqueza ...', Madrid, 20 Oct. 1611, in Escudero, *Los secretarios*, iii, pp. 817–18.

37 'Visita y cargos de Don Pedro Franqueza ...', Madrid, 22 Dec. 1609, in Escudero, *Los secretarios*, p. 794.

38 Ibid., pp. 795–7.

39 Ibid., at pp. 798–802, 804, 806–11.

40 'Cargos ...', no. 212, BL Eg 2026, fol. 57.

41 Carrillo's title, 23 Dec. 1609, AGS QC 14; Acuña's, same date, ibid., 24.

42 'Fundación. De los mayorazgos y estado de la villa de uzeda ... Madrid, 18 de Febrero de 1610', the *cédulas* addressed to Cristóbal, Madrid 16 February, ADL 12, no. 16, fols. 4–13 and 14–19.

43 Valladolid, 7 May 1608, RB 11/2117, doc. 83.

44 *Relaciones*, p. 397.

45 R. Mousnier, *The Assassination of Henry IV. The Tyrannicide Problem and the Consolidation of the French Absolute Monarchy in the Early 17th Century*, London, 1964, pp. 116–83.

46 Lerma to Carrillo, Valladolid, 6 March 1610, and undated letter of same to same, AGS CJH 361, no fol. An important series of letters and papers from Lerma are printed by Boronat, *Los moriscos españoles*, pp. 576–83.

47 Lerma to Carrillo, Ventosilla, 22 Apr. 1610, ibid. 495, no fol.

48 Bombín Pérez, *Monferrato*, p. 18.

49 Antonio Foscarini, Venetian Ambassador in France, to the Doge and Senate, Paris, 14th May 1610 'at 24 of the clock', and postscript of 'the night of the 14th May, 1610', *CSPV*, xi, nos. 898 and 899, p. 483; Mousnier, *The Assassination of Henry IV*, pp. 21–6; Parker, *Europe in Crisis*, pp. 91–2.

50 *Cnta.* itinerant Council of State, Lerma, 24 May 1610, AGS K 1593, fol. 22; *cnta.* resident Council in Madrid, 26 May 1610, ibid., fol. 23. This second *consulta* was in turn considered by the itinerant Council on 29 May, ibid., fol. 34.

51 *Relaciones*, pp. 406–9.

52 Ibid., pp. 410, 411–12, 414.

53 On this curious episode, J. A. Martínez Barra, *La condesa de Valencia de Don Juan, el Marqués de Poza y el Duque de Lerma*, Madrid, 1978.

54 *Relaciones*, pp. 412, 415, 418. Cottington to Salisbury, Madrid, 29 Jun./9 Jul. and 19/29 Aug. 1610, NA SP 94/17, fols. 111 and 159b.

8

Survival: death of the Queen and Lerma's 'other course', 1611–13

Restoration of Spanish primacy in Europe?

Marie de' Medici had good reason to fear that the Bourbon dynasty in France might not long survive the assassination of Henry IV, and – in a remarkable admixture of bravery and foolhardiness – promptly decided that her best hope of securing some measure of stability during the hazardous years of her son's minority lay in seeking a *rapprochement* with the King of Spain. Where Henry IV had planned for war with Spain, Marie de' Medici committed herself to peace by proposing at the end of 1610 that France and Spain should secure their amity with a double marital alliance: Louis XIII would marry Anne while Elizabeth would marry Prince Philip. The double marriage would, Marie hoped, ensure that Spain did not exploit the aristocratic and religious tensions that were certain to arise in France during her regency.

Her proposal was well-received in Madrid. Philip and Lerma were both determined to take advantage of the death of Henry IV to create a grand Catholic alliance against the enemies of the faith and the Council of State strongly recommended that the King should accept Marie's offer, not least because it would help to reduce the assistance that France would give to the United Provinces. Convinced – wrongly, as it happened – that the succession to the Spanish thrones would never be placed at risk through the marriages, the Council advised the King to agree to the proposal. He did so with enthusiasm, and the treaty was agreed on 30 April 1611.[1]

The French lead was followed by other rulers, and in the years after 1610 a succession of diplomats trekked to Madrid to seek the hands of one or other of Philip's children. Notable among them were the representatives of James I of England, who was fearful that the alliance between the Catholic powers would unbalance European politics and leave England isolated. The pursuit of a Spanish marriage – proposed by Lerma to the Earl of Nottingham in 1605 – now became central to James's diplomacy.

Charles-Emmanuel of Savoy alone refused to fear Spanish power. Although he recognised that the alliance between Spain and France would restrict his ability to play the two crowns off against each other, Charles-Emmanuel emerged in the years after the assassination of Henry IV as the most determined and resourceful of Spain's opponents. He sought an English marriage for his eldest son and a French marriage for a daughter. However, the duke also took the precaution of sending his son Philibert back to Spain to beg pardon from Philip III for his alliance with Henry IV.[2]

It was far from apparent that, from a position of such humiliating weakness, Philibert would be able to mount a substantial challenge to the authority of the Duke of Lerma, that he would become another of the enemies who were mustering against the duke. However, so intense was Lerma's loathing of Charles-Emmanuel and his resentment of Philibert that he pursued a vendetta against the young Savoyard. In doing so, he further undermined his own relationship with the King: Philip III ignored many of the precepts of Habsburg kingship but he never allowed himself to forget the primacy of familial relationships. Lerma had intruded into Philip's relationship with his wife and now began to involve himself in a feud with the King's nephew. Worse even than this, Lerma compounded his misjudgement by beginning in 1611 to give some priority to his relationship with the King's heir, even at the expense of his commitment to the King himself. Philip took note. So, too, did Lerma's enemies at court – chief among them the Queen and Luis de Aliaga – who played on the fissures that now began to open up between Philip and Lerma.

The confessor's attack and the death of the Queen

On 21 January 1611 Lerma kissed the Prince's hand as his *ayo* and *mayordomo mayor*. It was an intriguing move by the *valido* to have himself appointed to the key positions in the household of the heir, for he clearly could not expect to outlive the King, who was now thirty-three years old while he was fifty-seven.[3] Lerma was subtly shifting the focus of his ambitions, beginning now to concentrate on his responsibilities towards the heir – sometimes even at the expense of his obligations to the King himself – while encouraging Cristóbal to undertake a greater role at the heart of the King's affairs. He was at last preparing actively to hand over his authority to his son, and in another deeply symbolic act, in February 1611 he resigned his post as *capitán general de la caballería de España*.[4]

The transference of power to Cristóbal could only be effected with the tacit consent of the leading nobility and it must have alarmed Lerma that a number of coded attacks on him by senior aristocrats began now to take place. He dealt with them firmly but with discretion. In July 1611, for instance, the

Duke of Sessa was ordered to retire to his estates because he was becoming too close to the heir.[5] Sessa was a peripheral figure at court and was probably sent away because he was a relative of the Countess of Valencia and might embarrass Lerma by raising the question of his intentions towards the Countess.

More serious (and more enduring) challenges to Lerma were mounted by two aristocrats who were figures of substance at court, the Marquis of Velada and the Duke of Infantado. Velada had hitherto been quiescent in Lerma's *valimiento*, content to retain his position as *mayordomo mayor* to the King while pressing his claims for *grandeza*. Santiago Martínez Hernández has authoritatively demonstrated that by the end of 1609 relations between Lerma and Velada 'barely existed' as the Marquis moved into open opposition to the Duke. Velada's resentment at the capricious manner in which Lerma had tantalised him over winning *grandeza* was compounded now by political differences over the expulsion of the *moriscos* and by the resentment which Velada shared with so many others at the behaviour of Rodrigo Calderón. An experienced and accomplished politician, Velada began now to wage a sophisticated campaign against Lerma. He brought with him the weight of the Toledo clan and he had, too, had the social rank to associate himself with the Queen in her drive against Calderón.[6]

The Duke of Infantado was not given to subtlety. Enraged by Lerma's vendetta against his brother, he demanded that the King should have the conduct of Silva de Torres placed under judicial review on the grounds that he had been prejudiced in his treatment of the Admiral's case. Philip capitulated: in November 1610, Silva de Torres was exiled from court and by June 1611, fifty-one charges were laid against him.[7] Infantado would wreak a first, satisfying, revenge on Lerma by breaking Silva de Torres.

At the beginning of 1611, Infantado provocatively entered the chamber of the judges in his brother's case without their permission and compounded his insult to the court by wearing his sword. Juan de Acuña, head of the judiciary as President of the Council of Castile, objected to the King about the outrage. Once again, Philip failed to discipline the duke; he offered a compromise whereby Infantado could attend the court if he left his sword at the door. Infantado treated the offer with the disdain for which his family had long been known: he subsequently arrived at the courtroom claiming that since he was suffering from gout he needed to retain his sword for use as a walking-stick. Lerma understood well enough that Infantado was challenging his authority as well as the King's and the court's. He hinted that he might have the case of the Admiral speeded up but made no effort to do so: the Admiral was too useful a hostage for the good behaviour of his brother.[8]

On 27 June 1611 Philip left Madrid to spend the summer in the Escorial. Lerma intended to join him four days later with the Prince and the other royal children. However, on 29 June, Carlos and Anne became ill and it was not until 7 July that Lerma travelled to the monastery. For ten days, therefore, Lerma was separated from the King. The Queen took advantage of Lerma's absence to undermine his authority with the King. She did so from a position of strength, for it is evident from the reports of Cabrera de Córdoba that Philip and Margaret had drawn ever closer to each other throughout recent months. Certainly, during the summer months of 1611 Philip barely separated himself from Margaret: they attended mass together, hunted at the Prado, enjoyed the gardens in Aranjuez and the Escorial and laid the foundation stone in Madrid for the great convent of the *Encarnación* that the Queen was establishing. In the summer of 1611 Philip and Margaret were inseparable.[9]

Margaret moved now into open and full opposition to Lerma, and she did so with the full support of Luis de Aliaga. Like Mardones before him, Aliaga was deeply offended by the behaviour of Rodrigo Calderón but it now became evident that his opposition to Lerma was founded in a principled hostility to the *valimiento* itself; from the summer of 1611, fray Luis set himself first to undermine and then to destroy Lerma's dominance of the King. Initially, he confined himself to supporting the Queen in her attack upon Calderón. It was perhaps his sudden realisation that he was in danger of losing control of the King that pushed Lerma once again into despair. On or about 11 July he returned to Madrid.

Aliaga also crumbled under the strain of conflict and left the Escorial for Madrid. There, on 17 July; he collapsed, becoming so ill that he was given the last sacraments. Lerma went at midnight to bid him farewell but the confessor hung on, and after a week began to rally. Perhaps it was disappointment at Aliaga's recovery that led Lerma also to collapse into a sickbed. However, he recovered his strength sufficiently to return to the Escorial and demand of the King that he dismiss Aliaga. When on the feast of the Assumption of the Virgin (15 August) Aliaga was unable to confess Philip, Lerma urged the King to avail himself of his own confessor, fray Jusepe González, Prior of *San Pablo.* Philip refused, and – in the first public rebuke that he had ever directed towards his favourite – allowed it to be known at court that he had done so: if he could not confess to Aliaga he would confess to no one. The King had drawn a line: even Lerma could not dictate to him on confessional matters. Slowly, Aliaga recovered and resumed his duties.[10] Lerma's physical and emotional collapse was so severe that sympathisers feared for his life. Among them was Lope de Vega, who wrote on 17 August to the Duke of Sessa:

> There is great confusion here about the illness of the Duke. A thousand things are being said with the fear that everyone has that we might lose him, for it is always the good ones whom we lose ... and those who do not deserve it who die ... How Spain would suffer through the loss of such a Christian and able man who is so accomplished in government, because since he has been at the side of the King our lord Spain has not suffered any adversity.[11]

Lope de Vega's testimony was undoubtedly partisan; two days later he wrote to Sessa that 'it is certain that the lord Duke is loved by everyone as the father of the nation'.[12] Less sympathetic to Lerma, but somewhat more fully informed than the playwright about the circumstances behind the conflict between the *valido* and the confessor was the new English ambassador, Sir John Digby, who in a report on 28 August brought together the personal and political elements that had crushed the duke:

> The Duke of Lerma hath lately bene exceedingly sick. And the voice goes, that yt grewe upon conceite. For that (as yt is rumoured) the kings Confessor in a greate late sicknes that hee had, writt planely Unto the king, the wrong he did himselfe by transferring all power and authoritie from himselfe. Whereupon, the King dispatched some businesses without the Dukes Councell or Consente, w[hi]che hee accustomed not to doe. Thereupon he tooke thought, & grewe discontented & so fell desperately sick at the Escuriall of an extreme Callenture. Where hea is now upon mending, though not yet recouered in his extreamitie of sicknes he grewe very charitable, & sent moneys for the freeing of moste of the poore prisoners, that were in for debte in Madrid, & some other places. All the Sacraments were heere discouered for him, & many Masses sayd. But whether the prayers of the people were more for him, or against him, is scarce a question to be asked, suche is the envye that attends his greatenes.[13]

Lerma's resilience must have further diminished when his daughter-in-law Mariana, Duchess of Uceda died suddenly at the Escorial from fever (26 August). Lerma was deeply fond of Mariana and it was significant of the closeness of his relationship with her (and with his own son) that she was interred in *San Pablo*.[14] His opponents refused to relent: Margaret and Aliaga remorselessly pressed home their attack with such force that on 14 September Digby reported that Lerma 'was much broken' and was sinking deeper into despair.[15]

As the drama unfolded, Margaret prepared for her delivery by adding a codicil to her will and testament of 1601. She retained Lerma as a testamentary but now added Uceda's name in tacit recognition that he would succeed his father in the *valimiento*.[16] On 22 September, ten years and one day after the birth of her first child, Margaret was delivered of her eighth child and fourth son. He was named Alonso. Shortly after the birth, Margaret toured the monastery in the company of her husband and the imperial ambassador. A few days later she sank into a delirium, induced in all probability by premature exertions after childbirth. By 30 September, her doctors realised that she was dying. On 1 October Philip summoned Lerma and Aliaga from Madrid. The duke arrived in time to be present with Uceda and the dowager countess of Lemos when the Queen was given the last rites: even in her final moments, Margaret was surrounded by Sandovals.

On 3 October 1611, at about nine-thirty in the morning, the Queen died, not yet twenty-seven years of age.[17] Philip was at prayer when the news was brought to him. He went to Margaret's deathbed and proclaimed 'How greatly the Lord tests us: He must be praised by everybody' before returning to his prayers. Stricken with grief, the King blamed himself for Margaret's death, believing that the scented gloves that he had worn when he visited her had sent her into paroxysms.[18] He isolated himself in his chambers and allowed only Lerma and Aliaga, Calderón and Bernabé de Bibanco to have access to him.[19] It was nearly two weeks before Philip could bring himself to sign the *cédulas* informing the world of the death of his 'very dear and beloved wife'.[20]

By contrast, Lerma could barely contain himself. At the very moment of Margaret's death he breathlessly reported the news to Fernando de Acevedo and contrived to report the reaction of the King and of himself without recording a word of respect for the Queen.[21] He then brought Prince Philip and Anne to kiss Philip's hand; once again, he was at the very heart of the royal family's most private affairs.

Lerma now moved with cold calculation to gather control over the royal children to himself. Alonso was baptised on the day after his mother's death. The child was sickly and it was feared that he would not live long, but that Lerma's own feast day was chosen for his baptism may well have been understood at court as an affirmation of the King's enduring confidence in his *valido*. Certainly, Lerma now insisted that as *mayordomo mayor* of the Prince he had responsibility for supervising the households of all the royal children and demanded that La Laguna should relinquish to him the duties towards the children that he had exercised as the Queen's *mayordomo mayor*. La Laguna was compensated with a councillorship of State. Lerma delegated responsibility for supervising the upbringing of the children to his sister Catalina, dowager duchess of Lemos. Since Leonor, Countess of Altamira, already served as *aya*, the duke now effectively controlled their households.[22] However, among the Queen's private papers a dossier was discovered which contained a range of allegations against Calderón: when they found their way into the King's posses-sion, Philip turned his anger at his bereavement on Calderón, believing that he had been involved in Margaret's death.[23] While the King needed Lerma more than ever, he was determined that he would no longer endure the presence of Calderón at court.

Inevitably, Lerma took Philip away. The little *jornada* on which they set out lasted for only five weeks but proved to be one of the turning-points in their relationship. They travelled to Segovia (9 October) and on to the Escorial (15 October) before returning to Segovia. They then went to Ventosilla and Lerma for nearly a fortnight, arriving back at the Pardo on 12 November in time for the funeral service for the Queen, which took place at San Jerónimo el Real on 17 November.[24] Lerma isolated Philip even more stringently than usual; for instance, Philibert of Savoy was peremptorily ordered back to Madrid, much to his disgust. Lerma tried once again to save Calderón but found Philip immovable.[25] It may have been frustration at Philip's refusal to reinstate Calderón that provoked the duke to broach once again the matter of his own retirement.

He did so at Segovia by showing the King some papers. The nature of these documents is unknown but they certainly related to Lerma's intention to enter the religious life. Clearly, Lerma was trying to force Philip to redeem Calderón, as he had done in 1607. But there was more to his letter than this. Lerma had always been easily dispirited by setbacks and difficulties. Now, demoralised and ill, weary of the struggle with Aliaga, he probably found the prospect of a future without the support of Calderón unendurable. Faced with Philip's refusal to let him retire, Lerma decided to pursue what he subsequently called 'another course'.[26] There can be little doubt that this was to seek the cardinalate that he acquired at the turn of 1617–18.

As Digby had predicted, Calderón's fall was heavily disguised. During the King's annual hunting sojourn in the Pardo in November it was announced that Philip had acceded to Calderón's request to leave the palace. In a piece of solemn theatre, don Rodrigo solemnly gave up his responsibilities for governmental and courtly work by formally handing over his papers to Lerma. It was announced that he was to go to Venice as ambassador and that the King was honouring him with the grant of *encomiendas* for himself and his second son and with a variety of other awards. For his part, Lerma proclaimed that he would not replace Calderón and would conduct all business by himself.[27] In December, 'the whole court' (in Cabrera de Córdoba's words) attended the ceremony in which Lerma himself presented don Rodrigo with the *encomienda* of Ocaña in the Order of Santiago so that he could travel with appropriate dignity. Lerma chose to make a very explicit display of his affection for Calderón: 'in the presence of everybody, the Duke gave him very tight embraces' which left no room for doubt of 'the affection that the Duke has for him'.[28] In the circumstances, the duke's actions could not but be seen as other than a public rebuke to the King himself.

Astonishingly, Philip did not take offence. Rather, on 12 January 1612 he assured the duke of his continuing favour with three deeply symbolic awards. He granted Lerma's heirs the right to enjoy the revenues of the *encomienda mayor de Castilla* for twelve years after his death; this would be worth 144,000 ducats to them.[29] On the same day he raised Rodrigo Calderón to the countship of la Oliva and promised that Diego Sarmiento de Acuña would be given the countship of Gondomar.[30] There could be no doubt at court that Lerma, his *parentela* and *clientela* remained firmly fixed in the King's favour.

But over the new Count of la Oliva, the King was utterly unyielding. In February 1612, Philip named him as ambassador extraordinary to the court of the Archdukes in Brussels, charged with exploring the possibility of negotiating a permanent peace with the United Provinces and with supervising a general reform of the Army of Flanders. Still, Lerma pushed the King, announcing that he would not replace la Oliva in his private office. Still, Philip refused to relent. In tacit recognition of his failure to win a reprieve for his favourite, Lerma gave responsibility for the management of the affairs of his private office to Juan de Ciriza. Philip's willpower had been greater than the duke's, and he held to his decision; la Oliva managed to secure some postponements of his departure but on 27 April 1612 he left court for the Low Countries.[31]

The dismissal of la Oliva was a shattering defeat for Lerma. He sank deeper into melancholy and abandoned his governmental duties, proclaiming that he was too tired to give audiences.[32] At the beginning of November Lope de Vega wrote of his growing concern at Lerma's physical and emotional collapse:

> The Duke does not have the health that so many (who know his generous spirit) desire for him and which is so important to the public and private good. They say that his melancholy is very deep and has developed out of this illness that afflicts him. May God cheer him with the health that so many desire for him.[33]

In the midst of his despair, Lerma decided that la Oliva might be able to redeem himself with a positive achievement in northern Europe.[34] He therefore emphasised at court how well la Oliva was doing in seeking a long-term peace with the United Provinces. It was an uphill struggle; Digby recorded that one senior aristocrat had angrily confronted Lerma to insist that if la Oliva returned he himself would leave court —'when that rogue enters the palace I will take myself out of it'.[35] Was it the Duke of Infantado? Certainly, Infantado was triumphant when in March Silva de Torres was found guilty of the charges against him and sentenced to be exiled from court for ten years and a fine of 10,000 ducats. It was of little consequence to Silva de Torres, who died in August, but the condemnation of such a prominent hechura was a very public setback for Lerma.[36] Lerma had suffered an even more direct attack when at the beginning of February the Marquis of Camarasa criticised him in an audience with the King. Camarasa was arrested and placed under house arrest (8 February 1612). But the damage had been done: the whole court knew the details of his allegations against the duke.[37]

Lerma never forgave Infantado or Camarasa, but as he had done in his crises in 1607 and 1611 he moved quickly to seek reconciliation with other leading opponents so that the revolt against him should not spread further. He announced that a junta was to be established to oversee the work of the councils as in the later years of Philip II and that he would henceforth play only a superintendent role in managing the affairs of state. Moreover, the Marquis of Castel Rodrigo and the Constable of Castile – the two men whom Lerma had been most determined to keep away from court in the early years of the reign – were summoned back to Madrid to take their places on the Council of State.[38] Neither could seriously threaten Lerma; both were old men with little time left to live. When the Constable arrived in the summer of 1612 it was evident that he was suffering serious mental decline. He announced that St Francis had appeared to him in a vision to inform him that he had secured a few days extension of his life so that he could repent of his sins, and he dressed himself in a Franciscan habit as he prepared for death. His life petered out until he died, a sad object of ridicule, on 23 March 1613.[39]

As the Constable donned his friar's garb, Lerma reiterated his own intention to end his life as a religious. On 17 July 1612 he set down in a letter which he wrote to Philip while they were together in Ventosilla his determination to retire into religious life. His letter was as precise as it was powerful:

> Sire. Your Majesty has known for seven years that I have wanted to be a religious, and finally [learned this] through the papers that I showed him a year ago in Segovia. I have asked many times for a licence from Your Majesty, [and] he was not pleased to give it to me, and because of this, and out of the love that I hold for him, when finally in Lerma all my insistence was of no avail, I decided to take another course.[40]

The letter allows a precise reconstruction to be made of the events to which it alludes. The request that Lerma had made 'in Segovia' for permission to retire into religious life can be dated with confidence to the three weeks after the death of the Queen, when Lerma and Philip had made two short visits to the city. They then spent a few days in Lerma early in November 1611 while Margaret's catafalque was prepared in the capital. It would have been now – at the time when Philip was at the lowest ebb of his life – that Lerma had made his plea to be allowed to retire and had been refused, as he must have known that he would be. No evidence survives to identify the 'other course' referred to by Lerma, but it may reasonably be inferred that it was to begin the process of securing a cardinalate. The reference to Lerma's acting 'out of love' for the King might imply that he was prepared to stay at court after retiring – thus reconciling his own wishes and those of Philip by withdrawing from his governmental responsibilities while remaining at court? Uceda would succeed to the *valimiento*: Lerma would guide him and reassure the King by his continued presence. Would Philip allow him to do so ?

On 26 January 1612, Louis XIII's council accepted the marriage agreements with Spain. Both governments now determined to push the marriages through rapidly. Louis sent Henry, Duke of Mayenne, to Madrid to negotiate the details of the marriage and Philip brought the year's mourning for Margaret to a precipitate end (after only four months) so that the ambassador could be received with full honours.[41]

Lerma identified his commitment to the marriages by welcoming Mayenne to Madrid and by lodging him in his palace. He then made a considered public statement about the changing roles of his son and himself by allowing Uceda to bring Mayenne to the Alcázar for his audience with Philip while he himself accompanied the heir to the throne (21 July). However, Lerma would not delegate the major business of the visit: as *caballerizo mayor* he commanded the guard of honour that accompanied Mayenne to the Alcázar for the ratification of the treaty, and it was he who signed the documents on behalf of Philip (22 August). Three days later – on the feast of St Louis, King of France – Lerma again commanded the troop of gentlemen who brought Mayenne to the palace. The King himself accompanied Lerma and Mayenne on the return to Lerma's *huerta* and stayed there for an hour. It was not only the ambassador whom Philip was honouring: once again, in a very measured and public manner, Philip was reaffirming his confidence in Lerma.[42]

It was not enough for the duke. Soon after Mayenne left court, he announced that he was so exhausted that he would henceforth give audiences only on a very restricted basis. Unfortunately, Cristóbal again proved unequal to the task that his father was setting him: he continued to sleep in, often until after midday, and did not schedule any specific hours during which he would deal with governmental work. The Duke of Uceda was, Cabrera de Córdoba wryly noted, 'not inclined to paperwork'. The business of government ground to a halt.[43]

Lerma's authority was, however, reaffirmed when on 2 September the Council of State met twice to discuss the agreements with France. The first meeting dealt with English affairs. James I had been so angry at the news of the marriages that he had dismissed the new Spanish ambassador (the Count of Floresdávila) from his presence and announced that he would marry his daughter Anne to Frederick, Count Palatine. This was a potent threat, for the Count held a vote in the imperial college while his territory stood astride part of the Spanish Road and could be used to obstruct the passage of reinforcements to the Army of Flanders. Lerma presented himself as a frustrated militarist: 'if the royal exchequer of Your Majesty was in better condition then he would invite [him] to break the peace with England and to help in Ireland because of the persecution that is inflicted upon the Catholics [there], but with affairs being in the condition that can be seen it is better to leave it for the time when we can properly send the help that is so just and necessary'. The other councillors acknowledged his leadership by declaring simply that 'they agreed with the Duke of Lerma'.

At the second meeting of 2 September, Lerma reported on his negotiations with Mayenne and made some quite unexceptional remarks about how the marriages could be pushed forward. His colleagues competed in obsequiousness to praise his *parecer* – Castel Rodrigo suggested that his actions were 'very Christian and prudent and [worthy of] such a great minister of Your Majesty'; Idiáquez noted that 'he had been greatly pleased to have heard what the Duke of Lerma said for it was so convenient for the service of God and to the good of Christianity and so worthy of such a great minister of Your Majesty'; the Cardinal-archbishop of Toledo 'was greatly pleased to have heard what the Duke of Lerma said because it was all so worthy of praise and accordingly he agrees with it'; the dukes of Infantado and Alburquerque, the Marquis of Villafranca and don Agustín Mejía also expressly agreed with Lerma. This carefully-staged show of admiration for the Duke marked the high-point of Lerma's influence at the Council of State but it may be that the stronger councillors were prepared to submit themselves to it because they appreciated that not only had Lerma said nothing of substance but that his position at the centre of government was now under serious threat.[44] The task of beguiling James into the hope that he really could have a Spanish bride for his heir (and to prevent him from making a French match) fell upon Diego Sarmiento de Acuña, who was appointed ambassador to England early in 1613. It was unclear to everybody, not least to don Diego himself, whether he was to be a resident or a temporary ambassador. He sailed for Portsmouth on 19 May 1613.[45]

Fray Luis de Aliaga, the decree of 23 October 1612 and the return of Calderón

Even Luis de Aliaga buckled before Lerma's renewed authority; he agreed to another public reconciliation with the duke and even went so far as to give Lerma a written pledge of his loyalty (5 April 1612).[46] However, he soon regained his nerve and continued to snipe at Lerma in public until, apparently in mid-September 1612, Lerma's patience snapped: he ordered the President of the Council of Castile instigate an enquiry into Aliaga's conduct. It was a foolish move by Lerma and when Philip heard of it he was again openly furious with him. He summoned Lerma and Aliaga to the Escorial and insisted that they make up their quarrel. Significantly, it was Lerma who was the supplicant: Cabrera de Córdoba noted that the duke 'made great demonstrations of friendship and love' with Aliaga. The new friends agreed to go to the monastery together on 21 September but Lerma backed out at the last moment, pleading illness. It was another crass error: Aliaga spent three days with Philip, unchallenged by Lerma.

The King evidently became alarmed at the breach between the two men who were closest to him, for on 24 September he hurriedly rode to Madrid to see Lerma in the hope of resolving the dispute with Aliaga. The nature of the disagreement between the two men now became known at court and it was exactly as Digby had reported a year earlier – that Aliaga had opposed Lerma over the return of la Oliva and had insisted that Philip govern by himself and with the aid of his councils because he could not otherwise meet the requirements of his conscience.[47] Aliaga held all the moral high ground. Moreover, in maintaining – and indeed in developing – the assault upon Lerma after the death of the Queen, Aliaga demonstrated a rare courage. Certainly, there could now be no doubting the seriousness of his determination to defeat his old patron, and it was central to his strategy that he let everyone at court know how uncompromising he intended to be.

Lerma, too, was unbending. He, too, was given to making very public statements of his resolve when he was in serious difficulties: he now took Philip on a short progress into Old Castile while Aliaga remained in Madrid. It was quite extraordinary – unheard of, almost – for the King to travel without his confessor, but Philip now did so, presumably in an effort to demonstrate to Lerma (and to the court) that the duke retained his affection. Lerma had bought the town of Melgar de Fernamental near Burgos (for 35,000 ducats) and he now travelled to take possession of it, with the King of Spain in tow.[48] Philip and Lerma then went on to Ventosilla. It had been in the hunting lodge in July that Lerma had written to the King on 17 July of his intention to retire and it was from there that Philip on 23 October 1612 issued the decree which ordered his councils to carry out whatever instructions Lerma gave them and reaffirmed his trust in him. It was the defining document of Philip's kingship and in it he addressed directly the criticisms that Aliaga was making of Lerma's role in government.[49] King and *valido* then travelled on to Valladolid, where on 30 October they were joined by Aliaga. On All Saints Day, 1 November, the friar then heard the King's confession. Once again, doubtless at the insistence of the King, Lerma and Aliaga publicly demonstrated their affection for each other, but it was Lerma who made the running – 'the Duke made great demonstrations of friendship' towards the friar, recorded Cabrera de Córdoba.[50]

By the time that Philip, Lerma and Aliaga returned to Madrid (18 November) the decree had become widely known and had created a scandal. One councillor compared it to the abdication of Charles V, and Digby wrote admiringly that Philip 'hath of late transferred so much power upon the Duke of Lerma, as I conceave hath scarcely been knowne that any king ever did to any subject'.[51] For once, the ambassador missed the point – that Lerma's position had been under such powerful and sustained challenge at the very heart of the King's court that it had become necessary for Philip to formally and publicly reaffirm his confidence in him, exactly as he had done in January 1608 in the ceremony of the swearing of the oath to the heir.[52] Cabrera de Córdoba understood this and explicitly drew a connection between the decree and the conflict between Lerma and Aliaga.[53] Digby did, however, notice that another point of tension was festering between Philip and his *valido* – that Philip was becoming determined to remarry while Lerma was insistently urging him not do so.[54] It was a portent of the significance that Philip attached to the issue that it was observed that he was speaking 'to others more freely' about his intentions than he was to the Duke.[55]

Despite this, the King gave further reassurance to Lerma by giving him the fullest support at the splendid ceremonies that marked the double marriage between the Sandoval and Enríquez families on 28–29 November 1612. Uceda's eldest son, Francisco Gómez II, Duke of Cea, married the Admiral's sister Feliche while Luisa, Uceda's eldest daughter, married Juan Alonso Enríquez de Cabrera, IX Admiral of Castile and V duke of Medina de Rioseco. Philip honoured Lerma and Uceda by allowing the marriages to take place in the royal chapel and by acting as *padrino*. The ceremonies were conducted by the Cardinal-archbishop of Toledo.[56] Once again, the Sandovals were – as appeared – supreme at court.

The marriages of 1612 brought Lerma's dynastic policy to a triumphant conclusion. In addition to the dukedoms of Lerma (1599), Cea (1604) and Uceda (1610) for himself and his heirs, Lerma's daughter Francisca had become duchess of Peñaranda (1608) and his grand-daughter Luisa now became duchess of Medina de Rioseco. When the Duke of Medina Sidonia died, Lerma's daughter Juana would become duchess of Medina Sidonia, and on the death of the Duke of Infantado, Diego Gómez would carry his title. Lerma's sisters were countess of Altamira (Leonor) and dowager-countess of Lemos (Catalina) while his daughter Catalina was Countess of Lemos. There remained one great marriage still to make, and it had been agreed as long ago as 1608: Lerma's grand-daughter Isabel would marry Juan Téllez-Girón, heir to the III duke of Osuna. When that marriage took place in 1617, Lerma and his immediate kin held or shared in the five richest aristocratic titles in Spain. The pre-eminence of the Sandovals within the highest and richest levels of the noble elite was a phenomenon for which there was no precedent (see Appendix I).

Defining confirmation of Lerma's recovery – indeed, of his triumph – came when on 13 January 1613 the Count of la Oliva returned to court and was embraced repeatedly by the King himself. The great men of court hastened to follow the royal lead and welcome la Oliva back.[57] He was taken into the very heart of government and within days was meeting with Idiáquez to discuss proposals that he had made on affairs in the Low Countries.[58] When in mid-February the Council of State considered a series of position papers that la Oliva had drawn up on northern Europe, Castel Rodrigo and Idiáquez fulsomely praised his diligence and zeal and suggested that he was worthy of further honours from the King. But more significant even than the plaudits of the venerable servants of Philip II was the astonishing encomium delivered by the Duke of Infantado, who had hated la Oliva so deeply and for so long:

> Many men have come here from Flanders ... but no one has ever given such a precise analysis of affairs there as the Count of la Oliva has done. The accounts that he has given are, in the view of the Duke, the best that have ever come into the Council. Through these accounts and through what we have heard reported by word of mouth we understand that his views are so perceptive, as can be expected from his great prudence and intelligence. With his great understanding he has known how to advance (affairs), so much so that it appears appropriate that Your Majesty should command that he be thanked for this great service ... and honoured by being occupied in a position which would be appropriate to his outstanding qualities. The zeal and care with which he has managed the affairs of Your Majesty and the integrity and authority with which he has treated of them are admirable.

The King noted that he was 'very satisfied' with la Oliva's work and undertook to take account of his advice in the future. The Admiral of Aragon was released from prison in an explicit recognition of the reconciliation between Lerma and Infantado.[59] On 13 July 1613 the Count of la Oliva was raised to the marquisate of Siete Iglesias.[60]

Stunning though Lerma's triumph was, it was much less complete than it appeared. At the turn of March/April, the Marquis of Camarasa was declared innocent of all charges and awarded costs against the crown, and when he returned to court he too was greeted with great warmth by Philip. The King's greeting was understood to be a public rebuke to Lerma.[61] It might have been no accident that Lerma was harassed by relatives of the Countess of Valencia seeking satisfaction for her honour. To placate them he announced that he would go ahead with the marriage if the King gave him permission to do so. Not too surprisingly, Philip did not do so.[62] But while Lerma had fought Aliaga, placated Velada and Infantado and hoped that he might be able to restrain Camarasa, he now had to contend with open and sustained opposition from within the royal family itself – and with further indications that the King was beginning to emancipate himself from him.

The sons of the Duke of Savoy

The opportunity to undermine Spain's position in northern Italy for which Charles-Emmanuel of Savoy had been waiting presented itself in December 1612 when Duke Francis Gonzaga II of Mantua died, leaving his duchies of Mantua and Montferrat without direct heirs. The succession to Mantua passed to Ferdinand, the elder of Francis's two brothers. However, the duchy of Montferrat could be transmitted through the female line and so Francis's widow Margaret, daughter of Charles-Emmanuel, claimed it in the name of her daughter Maria. Charles-Emmanuel acted decisively to enforce the claim; in April 1613, he invaded Montferrat, splitting the duchy into two. He expelled the Spanish ambassador and sent Victor Amadeo to Spain to negotiate directly with Philip to find a solution. The Duke of Mantua asked for Spanish support to defend his territories.[63] The King of Spain stood now at the point of war with his own brother-in-law.

It was an especially awkward time for Lerma to accept the presence of the Savoyard heir at court. He had long resented the pleasure that Philip took in the company of Philibert and feared that he would become a rival to Uceda for the succession to the *valimiento*, and the appearance of Victor Amadeo in Madrid to pursue a marital alliance to which he was profoundly hostile deepened his anxieties about the role of the princes at court. At the beginning of 1612, Lerma had engineered Philibert's appointment as Captain General of the Galleys of Spain, a position which conveniently required him to live in Denia.[64] Embarrassingly, the appointment had to be deferred for lack of money and when Philibert returned to court Lerma made no effort to disguise his chagrin at his reappearance. The money was promptly found to pay a salary for Philibert and he was hurriedly appointed as *general de la mar;* he took the oath on 4 October and left court again, now to take up residence in Puerto de Santa María.[65]

When the Prince of Piedmont arrived at the Escorial, he was welcomed with 'a great demonstration of love' by the King (3 August).[66] Victor Amadeo proposed on behalf of his father that Philip should marry one of his own sisters while he himself would wed the *infanta* María. It was a characteristically bold and imaginative offer by Charles-Emmanuel, for the idea of resolving the crisis in Italy and accommodating his own wish to remarry appealed to Philip's vanity as much as it alarmed Lerma's sense of self-interest.[67]

The autumn of 1613 was a miserable time for Lerma. Philip twice made a point of dispensing his favour against his wishes and let it be known that he had done so: Cabrera de Córdoba recorded that 'it is known that [these grants] have been made without the intervention of the Duke, merely from the pure will of His Majesty'.[68] When in September Lerma went to take possession of Arganda, a town of about 2,500 people 27 kilometres east of Madrid on the Valencia road, he travelled without the King. Lerma had paid 27,136 ducats for the town and 12,000 ducats for a splendid town house. Arganda was in fine hunting (and fishing) country and Lerma intended to use it – as he was doing with Valdemoro – as a stopping-off place for Philip on the return to Madrid. Unfortunately, the sale of the town was fiercely opposed by many inhabitants and Lerma's celebrations were marred by an altercation in which one of his coachmen slapped the *alcalde*, thinking (so he claimed) that the law officer was a drunkard. The *alcalde* refused Lerma's bribe to ignore the matter, saying that the offence had been committed against the dignity of his office. As was normal at times of difficulty, Lerma became ill. He recovered his strength, however, and left for Segovia to join Philip and the Prince of Savoy, appreciating that at this time he needed to be near the King.[69]

Lerma took Philip on a progress to Burgos, Lerma and Ventosilla that lasted for a month; they returned to the Escorial on 30 October. Once again, a short *jornada* was the occasion of significant tension between king and *valido*, and it focused on the futures of the Marquis of Siete Iglesias and the Prince of Savoy. Lerma tried to persuade Philip to send Victor Amadeo back to Madrid but the King refused, saying how much he enjoyed his company. Moreover, when Juan de Idiáquez – who was now seventy-three years' old – asked to be allowed to retire and suggested that Siete Iglesias should take over his papers, Philip pointedly instructed Lerma himself to tell Idiáquez that his request was refused. Soon the King went even further, letting it be known – in Lerma! – that he could not bear to have Siete Iglesias near him. By the end of the *jornada* Lerma was again sunk in despair. He abandoned his audiences and proclaimed that he was intent on enjoying himself rather than on conducting business.[70] His triumph in saving his favourite in 1611–12 was now comprehensively undone.

Philip took offence at Lerma's behaviour and again made no attempt to disguise his annoyance: when he returned to Madrid at the end of November he allocated some of Lerma's lodgings in the Alcázar to Victor Amadeo. Moreover, while Lerma continued to make no secret of his wish for Victor Amadeo to leave court, Philip proclaimed how congenial he found the Prince's company and refused even to leave the palace without him by his side – a prerogative that of course pertained by right to Lerma as *caballerizo mayor*.[71] The King had drawn a line, and he had done so explicitly and publicly: Lerma could not determine whether he himself would marry and he could not challenge a prince of the blood.[72] As 1613 drew to a close, Philip III was beginning to emancipate himself from his *valido*, and he was angry enough with Lerma not to be too concerned who knew it. But Lerma, too, was moving away from the King: on 1 May 1614 the papal nuncio reported to the Vatican that Gabriel Trejo de Paniagua had told him in 'the very strictest confidence' that Lerma was hoping to become a cardinal.[73] To become a prince of the Church, Lerma would have to leave the *valimiento*.

NOTES

1   *Cnta. St.* 7 Jan. 1611, AGS K 1611, fol. 15; F-T. Perrens, *Les Mariages Espagnols sous le règne de Henri IV et la régence de Marie de Médicis*, Paris, 1869, p. 350 and García García, *La Pax Hispánica*, p. 91.

2   Sir Henry Wotton to Salisbury, Venice, 1 Jul. 1610, printed in L. Pearsall Smith, *The Life and Letters of Sir Henry Wotton*, 2 vols., Oxford, 1907, i, pp. 492–3. See also Bombín Pérez, *Monferrato*, pp. 18–20.

3   *Relaciones*, p. 429.

4   Ibid., p. 433 and García García, *La Pax Hispánica*, p. 123.

5   *Relaciones*, p. 442.

6   Martínez Hernández, *El Marqués de Velada*, pp. 431–92.

7   *Relaciones*, pp. 426, 440.

8   Ibid., p. 430.

9   Ibid., pp. 429, 432, 434, 436, 438, 441, 442, 445.

10 Ibid., pp. 443–4, 446. See García García, 'El Confesor fray Luis Aliaga', pp. 184–9.

11 Felix Lope de Vega to Duke of Sessa, Madrid, 17 Aug. 1611, *Epistolario*, ed. Agustín G. Amezua y Mayo, 4 vols., Madrid, 1935–43, iii, pp. 51–2.

12 Same to same, Madrid, 19–20 Aug. 1611, ibid., p. 53.

13 Digby to Salisbury (?), Madrid, 17/27 Aug. 1611, NA SP 94/18, fol. 161.

14 Anon., 'Relación del entierro y funeral que la Ciudad de Vall[adol]id y monasterio de S. Pablo hizo a la ex[celentíssima] señora Duquesa de Uzeda, Doña Mariana de Padilla', n. d., BN Mss 18725/5; *Relaciones*, pp. 446, 448–9.

15 '[Lerma] is much broken with this fith of sickness, w[hi]ch hath been seconded w[i]th some other greifes; first by the death of his daughter in lawe the Dutches of Uceda, wife unto his eldest sonne, whome he much esteemed, and was a lady that had great power in this Court. He hath further beene troubled about Don Rodrigo Calderon his chiefe creature and instrument, who hath (by a Letter of the king's Confessor sent unto the king, and likewise by the yll will the Queene bearethe him) beene called into some question, and the generall [opinion ?] was, that he was to have forsaken the Court, w[hi]ch was rather that w[hi]ch men desired than what I suppose will be, for whilest the Duke lives, he is a Minister of such use unto him that he will uphold and maynteyne him ...', to Salisbury, Madrid, 14/24 Sep. 1611, NA SP 94/18, fol. 174. See also, same to same, 26 Sep./6 Oct., ibid., fols. 194–194b.

16 'Testamento y Codicilio de la Reyna D[oñ]a Margarita de Avstria...', 'Codicilio', AGS PR 31 D20, fol. 25v.

17 *Relaciones*, pp. 450–1; León Pinelo, *Anales de Madrid*, pp. 96–100; Diego de Guzmán, *Reyna católica. Vida y muerte de Doña Margarita de Austria, Reyna de Espanna*, Madrid (1617?), pp. 231b–38.

18 Digby to Salisbury, Madrid, 26 Sep./6 Oct. 1611, NA SP 94/18, fols. 194–194b.

19 *Relaciones*, p. 452.

20 For instance, the *cédula* to the city of Madrid was dated 14 October, AHM LA 29, 14 Oct. 1611, fol. 464.

21 'A la hora que esta escribo, que son las nueve y media de la mañana, ha sido Dios servido de llevar para sí á la Reyna nuestra Señora, de que queda el Rey (Dios le guarde) con la pena y dolor que pide perdida de compañia, que con tanta razon amaba y estimaba tanto, y es para dar gracias á su Divina Magestad la gran christiandad, valor y prudencia que ha mostrado y muestra en esta ocasion. Todos quedamos con la aflición y desconsuelo que se dexa considerar, de que he querido avisar á V. S. para que lo tenga entendido, y sepa de la manera que nos hallamos. Sea Dios bendito por todo y guarde á V. S. En San Lorenzo 3 de Octubre 1611. El Duque, Marqués de Denia', printed in J. Loperraez Corvalan, *Descripción histórica del obispado de Osma con el catálogo de sus prelados*, Madrid, 1978, 3 vols., iii, p. 402. A shorter version, González Dávila, *Teatro de las Grandezas de ... Madrid*, p. 394.

22 *Relaciones*, p. 453.

23 Digby to Salisbury, Madrid, 21/31 Oct. 1610, NA SP 94/18, fols. 215b–215.

24 Juan Gómez de Mora, 'Relación de las honras funerales que se hizieron por la Reyna doña Margarita de Austria...', and Anon., 'Relación verdadera de las honras que se hizieron a la Reyna ...', printed by Simon Diaz, *Relaciones Breves de ... Madrid*, pp. 72–80; *Relaciones*, pp. 453–6, 459.

25 'The king now, to passe his melancolie, is by the Duke of Lerma ledd to diuers places, and the Prince of Savoy hath been willed to retire himself from the king to Madrid, w[i]th w[hi]ch he and his friends are much distasted', Digby to Salisbury, Madrid, 21/31 Oct. 1611, op. cit., fol. 214b.

26 The chronology of this paragraph is based on the letter of Lerma to the King quoted above, p. 173.

27 *Relaciones*, pp. 456–7.

28 Ibid., p. 459 and Salazar y Castro, *Los Comendadores de ... Santiago*, pp. 246–7.

29 Salazar y Castro, *Los Comendadores de ... Santiago*, pp. 146–9.

30 *Gaçeta y Nuevas*, pp. 33–4. On 11 April, Philip raised the Marquis of San Germán from his Savoyard title to the Castilian nobility as Marquis of la Hinojosa, ibid. Sarmiento de Acuña's elevation was probably contingent upon him taking up the post of *Asistente de Sevilla* to which he had been nominated, but the appointment did not go through and he was not given the countship until 1617, by which time he was ambassador in England, see J. M. Castroviejo and F. de P. Fernández de Córdoba, *El Conde de Gondomar. Un azor entre ocasos*, Madrid, 1968, pp. 230–32 and 238–9.

31 *Cnta*. St. 13 Feb. 1613, AGS E 2027; *Relaciones*, pp. 462–3, 465, 473.

32 *Relaciones*, p. 478.

33 To Sessa, 'primeros de noviembre', 1612, *Epistolario*, iii, p. 73.

34 García García, *La Pax Hispánica*, pp. 72–4.

35 Digby to Carleton, Madrid, 18/28 Jul. 1612, NA SP 94/19, fols. 126–126b.

36 Juan de Monclús to Diego Sarmiento de Acuña, Madrid, 10 Feb. 1612, RB 11/2142, doc. 104; *Relaciones*, pp. 470, 491.

37 Digby to Carleton, Madrid, 2 Feb. 1611/12 Feb. 1612, NA SP 94/19, fols. 18b–19; *Relaciones*, pp. 463–4, 466, 470, 476, 479.

38 Same to same, Madrid, 24 Feb./4 Mar. 1612, ibid., fol. 43; on the Constable, *Relaciones*, pp. 479, 488, 496.

39 Digby to Salisbury, Madrid, 10/20 Apr. 1612, NA SP 94/19, fol. 67; same to Carleton, Madrid, 24 May/4 Jun. 1612, ibid., fol. 97; same to Carleton, Madrid, 22 Sep./2 Oct. 1612, ibid., fol. 158b; same to James I, Madrid, 5/15 Mar. 1613, ibid., fol. 294; *Relaciones*, p. 513. On Moura's intrigues against Lerma within the Council of Portugal, Gaillard, *Le Portugal sous Philippe III*, pp. 129–30.

40 Printed by González Dávila, *Felipe III*, p. 203; see Williams, 'Lerma 1618: Dismissal or Retirement?', pp. 313, 329, n. 29.

41 Lerma even allowed Mayenne and his entourage of 700 people (and 134 mules for the baggage train) to stay at Lerma for two days on their way to Madrid, Perrens, *Les Mariages Espagnols*, pp. 401–3.

42 Anon., '*Entrada suntuosa en la corte de Madrid el Duque de Umena ...*', Granada, 1612 and Anon., '*Relación verdadera en la qual se declara la embaxada que dio el Duque de Umena...*', Alonso Martín, 1612, and Anon., '*Relación verissima del efecto, y fin de los conciertos del felicissimo casamiento de la serenissima Infanta de Castilla doña Ana Mauricia de Austria, con el muy católico Ludouico Rey de Francia ...*', Malaga, 1612, printed by Simon Diaz, *Relaciones Breves de ... Madrid*, pp. 80–7; *Relaciones*, pp. 480–7. CSPV, xii, 26 Aug. 1612, no. 619, p. 414; Perrens, *Les Mariages Espagnols*, pp. 410–17.

43 *Relaciones*, p. 489.

44 *Cntas* St., 2 Sep. 1612, AGS E 2513 no fol. and K 1427, fol. 87.

45 Digby to James I, Madrid, 12/22 Jan. 1613, NA SP 94/19, fol. 247; *Relaciones*, p. 508.

46 See below, p. 252.

47 *Relaciones*, pp. 494–5; the letter is dated 20 Sep. 1612 but internal evidence makes it clear that it should be dated 20 Oct.

48 Lerma, 'Imbentario', ADL 53, fols. 8–8b and 'Hacienda acrecentada ...', ibid., 54, no. 9, no fol; *Relaciones*, p. 500.

49 See above, p. 42.

50 *Relaciones*, pp. 498–9.

51 Digby to James I, Madrid, 7/17 Dec. 1612, NA SP 94/19, fol. 187.

52 See above, p. 45.

53 'Los dias pasados envió S. M. billetes de su mano á los Consejos, mandándoles que todo lo

que el duque de Lerma les escribiese ó dijere en su nombre lo hiciesen y cumpliesen como si su misma persona se lo mandase, de que se han causado diversos discursos ó imaginaciones, paresciendo á todos mucha novedad; pues nunca antes han dejado los Consejos de cumplir todo lo que se les ha ordenado, si ya no ha sido menester esto por lo que S. M. hizo al presidente de Castilla, cuando dió lugar á inquirir por escrito sobre la vida y costumbres del padre Confesor, que escandalizó a todos, y causara mucho escándolo sino se remediara; y asimesmo ha mandado que cosas semejantes no se hagan de aquí adelante sin darle cuenta', *Relaciones*, p. 501.

54 See above, pp. 179–80.

55 Two letters of Digby to James 1, Madrid, 12/22 Nov. 1612, NA SP 94/19, fols. 168–9; quotation from the first, at fol. 169.

56 Anon., 'Memoria de las bodas del Almirante de Castilla y del duque de sea nieto del de Lerma', BN Mss 18722, no dates, *Relaciones*, pp. 500–3 and *Gaçeta y Nuevas*, pp. 35–6; Quintana, *Madrid*, p. 363. Lerma took the precaution of advancing a number of his leading *hechuras* to major offices at this time; Juan de Ciriza was raised to the secretaryship of the Council of State dealing with the Low Countries (1 Sep.) and Tomás de Ángulo to that of the *Junta de Obras y Bosques*, with retention of his secretaryship of the *Cámara y Estado de Castilla* (27 Oct.) In addition, Bernabé de Bibanco was appointed as a royal secretary (18 Oct.) and Tristán de Ciriza, brother of Juan, was raised to a secretaryship (31 Dec.). Juan de Ciriza's title, AGS QC 25; those of Ángulo and Tristán de Ciriza, both in ibid., 40 and Bibanco's, Ventosilla, ibid., 9; see also, *Relaciones*, pp. 495–6.

57 *Relaciones*, p. 506.

58 See, for example, *cntas* of la Oliva and Idiáquez, for example, 16 Jan., 16 Feb., 14 May 1613, AGS E 2027, no fols.

59 *Cnta*. St. 14 Feb. 1613, AGS E 2027, no fol.; *Relaciones*, p. 513. See García García, *La Pax Hispánica*, p. 155.

60 *Gaçetas y Nuevas*, p. 36.

61 Digby to Carleton, Madrid, 26 Mar./5 Apr. 1613 (OS), NA SP 94/19, fol. 309; *Relaciones*, pp. 514, 516.

62 Same to James I, 5/10 and 10/20 Mar. 1613, NA SP 94/19, fols. 293b–4 and 304.

63 Bombín Pérez, *Monferrato*, pp. 55–60.

64 'Título de Capitán General de la Mar en el S[eño]r Principe Emanuel Filiberto', Madrid, 1 Jan. 1612, copy, BN Mss 8850, fols. 1–3v; a copy of his instructions, ibid., fols. 4–16v.

65 Digby to Salisbury, Madrid, 18/28 Apr. 1612, NA SP 94/19, fol. 68b. On the return of Philibert to court ('the only cause whereof I understand to have beene, for that they wanted mony to dispatch him'), same to same, Madrid, 15/25 Jun. 1612, ibid., fol. 98b. See also, *Relaciones*, pp. 471, 474, 495, 504.

66 Pedro García Dovalle, '*Nuebas de Madrid del mes de agosto de 1613, 24 de agosto 1613*', BN Mss 18,419, fol. 29.

67 *Relaciones*, pp. 521–2, 523, 526–7.

68 Ibid., pp. 532–3.

69 On the purchase of Arganda and the house, 'Hacienda acrecentada ...', ADL 54, no. 9, no fol and Lerma, 'Imbentario ... (1617)', ibid. 53, pp. 5b–6b; on the royal travels and the altercation in Arganda, *Relaciones*, pp. 528–30.

70 *Relaciones*, pp. 530–2. Cabrera de Córdoba was incorrect in recording that Lerma entered Segovia with the King on 18 September; he was still in Madrid and arrived in Segovia on 24 September. He had also not noted that la Oliva had been raised to the marquisate of Siete Iglesias.

71 *Relaciones*, pp. 537, 541.

72 Digby to Carleton, Madrid, 10/20 Oct. 1613, NA SP 94/20, fol. 97.

73 C. Pérez Bustamante, *La España de Felipe III*, vol. xxiv of Ramón Menéndez Pidal (ed.), *Historia de España*, Madrid, 1979, pp. 150–2.

9

Retreat – and the erosion of authority

Ambition, 1613: a cardinal's robes and the great building programme in Madrid and Lerma

Only four Spaniards had been raised to the purple during Philip III's reign, and all of them were *lermistas* (at least at the time of their elevation): Bernardo de Sandoval y Rojas, Lerma's great-uncle (1599); Antonio Zapata, a member of his sister Catalina's circle (1605); Jerónimo de Xavierre, his confessor before he became the King's (1605) and Gaspar de Borja, his great-nephew (1611). Indeed, after 1606 (when Cardinal Francisco Dávila, who was unconnected to Lerma, died) these men comprised the entire Spanish cardinalate. In 1615 they were joined by Gabriel Trejo y Paniagua and Baltasar Moscoso y Sandoval. They, too, were *lermistas*; Trejo was a close friend of Siete Iglesias's while Moscoso y Sandoval was Lerma's nephew, the son of his sister Leonor. When Lerma himself was raised to the cardinalate in 1618, therefore, he joined a group of Spanish cardinals all of whom were closely connected to him and who may reasonably be presumed to have been obliged to him for their advancement. As might be observed, he had his own little college of cardinals.[1]

There were three categories of cardinals: episcopal, priestly and diaconal. The first of these was pre-eminent: thirty-three of the forty-four Spaniards who had been named as cardinals during the sixteenth century had been episcopal cardinals. The dignity did not come easily, even to the most senior churchmen, for the crown was extraordinarily reluctant to allow ecclesiastics to play a significant political role at court: only five of the ten archbishops of Toledo and seven of the ten archbishops of Seville during the sixteenth century were raised to the purple.[2] The Catholic Kings of Spain were innately suspicious of men who owed a primary loyalty to a foreign prince – even if it was to the sovereign pontiff – and, unlike the Most Christian Kings of France, they were not prepared as a rule to have churchmen filling important political positions at court. Accordingly, it was even more difficult for churchmen to achieve the cardinalate and maintain an important political role at the centre of government; surprisingly few of the men who were archbishops of Toledo and Inquisitors General managed to do so. The chief exceptions to this rule had been Cardinal Juan de Tavera under Charles V and cardinals Espinosa and Quiroga under Philip II, and it may not have been entirely coincidental that both Espinosa and Quiroga were dismissed from their governmental offices. Philip III had commissioned Cardinal Fernando Niño de Guevara as Inquisitor General in August 1599 in the wake of the embarrassment caused by the need to dismiss Pedro Portocarrero, but his tenure of the office was marked by uncertainty and he was ordered to resign in January 1602.[3] Otherwise, Philip III allowed only Bernardo de Sandoval y Rojas, cardinal-archbishop of Toledo from 1599 and Inquisitor-General from 1608 to serve in an administrative capacity at court, and he was of course Lerma's great-uncle.

The second category, of the priestly cardinal, tended to be confined to the king's confessors; Xavierre had achieved this in 1605, but on assuming the cardinalate he had left the royal confessorship. To all intents and purposes the third category, of diaconal cardinal, did not exist in sixteenth-century Spain: no lay Spaniard had been raised to the cardinalate in this period. That Lerma should have aspired to the cardinalate while still a layman was indicative of his vaulting ambition but it was also suggestive of his determination to withdraw from the *valimiento*. Lerma never wavered after 1614 in his determination to become a prince of the Church. Vanity no doubt played its part in this ambition: there was undeniably a symmetry in passing from his unique position as *valido* to the purple of the Church. Doubtless, too, Lerma took pride in not merely following in the family tradition of service to the Church of his revered ancestors, Cristóbal de Rojas and Francisco de Borja, but in surpassing what they had achieved.[4] Certainly, he fully understood that the papal curia required that any diaconal cardinal would take holy orders within a year.

There was, however, a deeper relevance, for to become a cardinal carried the clear implication that Lerma intended to withdraw from secular political life: as cardinal, he would no longer serve as a courtier in the service of the King. This was certainly how Philip himself understood it: when he dismissed Lerma from court in 1618, he observed that he found it easier to do so '*since ... ecclesiastical ministers are the more esteemed the less they deal in affairs*'.[5] Philip could have exercised the veto that Spanish monarchs had in practice over the nomination to a cardinalate but, much as he resented Lerma's decision to leave court, Philip chose not to do so. Instead, he insisted that on becoming a cardinal Lerma would have to leave the court. Lerma had made his decision: so, too, had the King.

In declaring his ambition to become a prince of the Church – in taking the 'other course' to which he had referred in his letter to Philip of 17 July 1612 – Lerma was preparing to force the King to release him from his obligations at court. He had stopped talking about retiring from life at court and was now actively engaged in doing so. But if Philip, who was, after all, the most devout of Spanish kings, could not object to his *valido's* intention to enter religious life, he could show his resentment at Lerma's decision by cutting off the favour that he had lavished on him since 1598. This, he now did: after May 1614, Philip gave Lerma no more major grants or offices until he presented him with a valedictory gift of money as he left court in October 1618. For both men, Lerma's decision to seek a cardinalate was a defining point in their relationship, opening a long drawn-out end to their closeness to each other.

While Lerma had finally resolved on the form in which he would enter religious life he was determined to achieve another ambition before leaving court – to create a monument in stone to his life's work and achievements. This he now did on the very grandest scale: the building programme to which he committed himself in 1613 was the greatest private building programme in Spain during the Habsburg period and it was designed in a carefully co-ordinated fashion to come to completion during the summer of 1617. Only then would Lerma be prepared to leave court. But in staying on at court merely so that he could bring his buildings to fruition and groom his son to succeed him in the *valimiento* Lerma gave profound offence to the King, and the anger that Philip had displayed towards Lerma during 1613 deepened and hardened in the years until 1617. Moreover, Lerma committed himself to the expenses of an enormous building programme at precisely the time when his income had ceased to increase: in 1612 his income reached its highest level.

Lerma's great building programme had two clearly differentiated purposes: his priorities in Lerma were essentially religious while those in Madrid were predominantly seigneurial. The core of the programme lay in the creation of four buildings in Lerma – the ducal palace, the collegial church of *San Pedro* and two Dominican houses, the monastery of *Santo Domingo* and the convent of *San Blas*. Moreover, while Lerma was building this great complex in his ducal town he was also completing his reconstruction of *San Pablo* in Valladolid and creating a palace in Madrid that not only dwarfed the palaces of all of his peers but which threatened even to outstrip the Alcázar itself – something which may also not have commended itself to Philip.

Lerma's programme in his ducal town was designed – the great palace apart – to create a perfect Christian community. The presence in a community of one thousand or so people of a collegial church and seven religious houses provided a degree of religious care for the people of the town that greatly enhanced their opportunities for salvation. As always, of course, there was a personal purpose; the creation of the church of *San Pedro* and the conventual houses would enable scores of churchmen and women to pray for Lerma's soul and thereby accelerate his eternal salvation. On the other hand, in Madrid, the great palace served Lerma's seigneurial purposes while his religious houses were small in scale, at least until he created the *Casa Profesa* for the Society of Jesus in 1617. In Valladolid, the monastery-church of *San Pablo* combined both purposes, religious and seigneurial.

Lerma's grandest buildings were planned in meticulous detail but – with the exception of *San Pablo* – were then constructed at an extraordinary pace: it was truly remarked of the building programme in Lerma that 'such was the speed with which his Excellency completed his buildings, that it was not as if he built them but that they came there from somewhere else, already built'.[6] However, this was no jerry-building programme undertaken for short-term purposes. Lerma's enormous programme was conceived and executed with the most fastidious care. Moreover, the processes and materials that he employed were of the highest quality and have stood the test of time; all of the buildings except the palace in Madrid (which was demolished at the beginning of the twentieth century to make way for the 'Palace Hotel') have survived to the present day and continue to be used, for the most part for their original purposes. Lerma built on the very grandest of scales – and he built to last.

The completion of the building programme was for Lerma the expression and the climax of his life's work, bringing him to the point from which he could retire into religious life. When, in June 1617 – exactly as his buildings were being completed – he drew up the final version of his Will and Testament he spoke revealingly, and indeed lovingly, of the inspiration that lay behind his religious endowments:

> It has been my principal purpose, and the inspiration of my [building] works, to place [them] into the service of God and the divine cult, so that His divine Majesty should be better served for His glory and honour. [I have done this] because everything that I have has come from His hand, and so that my descendants and successors should recognise this and continue with this same purpose of increasing and improving religious affairs, and creating charitable works, churches, religious foundations and convents in which works of piety and religion are conducted for the benefit and support of Christians and for the public good.[7]

But even as he brought his great programme to completion, Lerma could not limit his ambitions. During 1617 he also committed himself to creating another two buildings in Lerma – a convent for the discalced Carmelites and a Cistercian monastery – and a splendid Jesuit church in Madrid to house the bones of Francisco de Borja. In doing so, he broke his own finances – finances which, of course, the King had not supplemented since 1612.

The return of the court to Madrid led to an astonishing growth in the size of the city, as its population trebled from 50,000 in 1606 to 150,000 in 1617. In

that decade or so, Madrid became a city of extraordinary contrasts. A floating
population of about 20,000 people had no roots in the city, and so the contrast
between extreme wealth and abject poverty that marked Madrid formed the
subject for so much of the moralising and politico-social comment that characterised Spanish literary and artistic culture during the seventeenth century.[8]

Lerma and the royal couple led the way in the building boom that was the
expression of this growth. In 1606 Lerma owned three sets of properties in the
city: a small palace in the *Calle de Arenal* in front of the church of San Ginés; a
terrace of four town houses in the *Plaza de las Descalzas Reales*; and some land
off the *Prado de San Jerónimo* that was known as the *huerta* ('garden').[9] He did
not own any religious buildings in the city. The palace and the town houses were
both conveniently close to the Alcázar but neither was suitable for development
into a great palace – the palace because it was too small and the houses because
they were uncomfortably cramped. In 1613 Lerma sold the houses in the *Plaza
de las Descalzas Reales* to the King for 33,000 ducats, once again placing Philip in
his debt for making property available to him, as he had done in 1602 with his
palace in Valladolid and in 1606 with the *Casa de la Ribera*. It was only now that
he fully committed himself to creating a grand palace in the *huerta*.[10]

Lerma had begun buying up properties and lands to expand the *huerta*
as early as 1609, and by 1613 the building was grand enough to accommodate
Philip and his household no fewer than four times.[11] In front of what could now
properly be described as a palace, Lerma created the first purpose-built bull-
ring in Madrid so that he and the King could enjoy the bull-fights and courtly
spectacles.[12] Philip relished his visits to the *huerta*. For instance, at the end of
1613 he went there directly on his return from Old Castile:

> His Majesty and his children entered [Madrid] on the 3rd and went directly to the
> *huerta* of the Duke of Lerma, where they ate. They slept there that night and on
> the following day enjoyed *fiestas* of bulls and *juegos de cañas* in the square in front
> of the *huerta* … in which six squadrons of six gentlemen participated – grandees
> and lords – all of whom were dressed in the most splendid and expensive liveries.
> The *fiesta* was very well received and there were no unfortunate accidents. At His
> Majesty's command all the councils came to witness the spectacle.[13]

In June and July 1614 Lerma provided some especially memorable entertainments in the *huerta* for the Cardinal d'Este, who had been sent to Spain by the
Pope to help find a solution to the crisis in Montferrat. It seems certain that
Lerma took advantage of d'Este's presence to open negotiations for his elevation to the cardinalate. The first of these celebrations took place on the feast
of St John the Baptist (24 June), and was attended by all the major figures at
court. Bulls were run, but the highlight of the entertainments proved to be
somewhat disappointing, when the tiger, bear and horse who had been selected
to fight each other for the amusement of the court refused even to enter the

ring. On 9 July Lerma gave a splendid banquet for Cardinal d'Este and the papal nuncio; thirty courses were served and once again the leading men of Church and State were present. After the meal, Lerma led his guests in a splendid cavalcade in front of the *huerta*. Lerma presented Cardinal d'Este with an Indies chest, eighty pairs of gloves, thirty wallets and many other expensive presents. The following day, d'Este left for Rome; weighed down with Lerma's presents, he almost certainly carried the message to the Pope that the duke wished to become a cardinal.[14]

When the great palace was completed, its grounds extended from the *Paseo del Prado* to the *Calle de San Agustín* and from the *Carrera de San Jerónimo* to the *Calle de las Huertas*. Its limits were marked by two new ecclesiastical foundations of Lerma's, the *Trinitarios de Jesús* and the *Casa Profesa* of the Society of Jesus. Its walls were hung with the finest of Lerma's paintings. The grounds were spacious enough to house a hermitage, an orchard, a riding school and bird-houses, and were decorated by a splendid collection of statuary.[15] Lerma claimed to have spent over 200,000 ducats on the palace in the years 1606–17.[16]

By contrast, Lerma committed only 12,512 ducats to his ecclesiastical foundations in Madrid in the decade after 1606: his programme in Madrid therefore bore no comparison to what he had accomplished in Valladolid (where he had committed 175,335 ducats). In 1606 he took over the patronage of the monastery of the *Santísima Sacramento* for the discalced Trinitarians, rebuilt it and dedicated it as '*Nuestra Señora de la Encarnación*', but he spent only 7,000 ducats on the building and provided only 400 ducats of rent (capital value: 8,000 ducats) to support the religious.[17] He built a house for the Capuchin monastery of *San Antonio de Padua* adjacent to his palace at a cost of 5,512 ducats. In 1611 he bought the *Hospital General* to serve as a church for the Dominican nuns of *Santa Catalina de Siena* and then connected it to his palace with a *pasadizo* across the *Calle del Prado*; he provided only 600 ducats of rent (capital value: 12,000 ducats) to support the foundation.[18] Not until 1617 did he commit himself to a major ecclesiastical foundation in the capital when he undertook to spend 70,000 ducats on the *Casa Profesa* for the Society of Jesus to house the body of Francisco de Borja.[19]

Lerma's family followed his example. Uceda paid 42,000 ducats for a small palace that faced the Alcázar and had Gómez de Mora rebuild it into one of the most splendid palaces in the city (1613–18).[20] Across the street, facing his palace, Uceda built the convent of the *Santíssimo Sacramento* for discalced Bernardines (1615). Now he had an urban complex that was worthy of his status as *valido*-elect, and he had a *pasadizo* built to connect his palace to the Alcázar.[21] The Cardinal of Toledo bought the splendid estate of the *Casa de la Florida* facing across the river Manzanares to the *Casa de Campo* to use as his residence in the capital. This was a large walled estate which incorporated a church and palace, and its grounds were large enough to allow equestrian pursuits. In 1613 he presented it to Lerma, who now therefore owned great walled properties on the eastern and western extremities of the city.[22]

Lerma's senior *hechuras* also emphasised their status in the capital with new or enlarged buildings. Villalonga rebuilt the palace that he had forced Pedro de Medicis to sell to him for 30,000 ducats into what Fernando Carrillo described in 1611 as 'one of the best and most costly' in Spain and valued at 160,000 ducats.[23] Rodrigo Calderón bought a palace near the Alcázar and Alonso Muriel y Valdivielso owned a grand house by the *Plaza de las Descalzas*.[24]

The royal couple threw themselves enthusiastically into a building programme in Madrid. Philip rebuilt the façade of the Alcázar and developed the *Casa de Campo* on the edge of the city as an urban hunting lodge (and appointed Lerma as its first *alcaide*).[25] He and Margaret also made a substantial contribution to what has been described as 'the most sustained church-building programme in the history of Madrid between the eleventh and the eighteenth centuries', creating six of the sixteen religious houses that were built in Madrid in the years 1606–21.[26] Most notable among them was the convent of the *Encarnación*, which the Queen began a few months before her death in 1611, and which Philip completed in 1616 in tribute to his late wife. The *Encarnación* was built in the style of the Alcázar and combined a cloister, church and garden with fountains. Its walls were decorated with a fabled collection of pictures, chief among them an exquisite set of portraits of the children of Philip II and Philip III. The completion of the *Encarnación* not only rounded out the royal complex at the heart of Madrid: it also emphasised beyond any doubt that the King was committed to retaining the city as his capital.[27]

It will be recalled that Lerma had supported the foundation by relatives of three convents in Lerma while the court was resident in Valladolid – *La Ascensión de Nuestro Señor* (or *Convento de Santa Clara*), *La Madre de Dios* and *San Francisco de los Reyes*.[28] He secured permission from Pope Clement VIII to create a collegial college in Lerma in 1603 on the site of the parish church of *San Pedro*, but it was not until 1609 that he began to commit himself to the foundation; on 9 February 1609 he signed the contract for the *pasadizo* linking *San Pedro* to the *Ascensión*, and a week later the papal nuncio approved the statutes for the church, instituting the dignities of abbot, archdeacon, *chantre*, treasurer and *maestrescuela*.[29] Even then, it was another three years before Lerma began to prepare his building programme; in 1612 he persuaded the King to raise the town of Lerma to the status of a city even though it only had only one thousand or so inhabitants. For good measure, he also had the same privilege conferred upon Denia (which had a population of similar size) while the *lugar* of Javea, which was home to fewer than four hundred people, was given the dignity of a town.[30] Now he was ready: early in 1613 he contracted with fray Alberto de la Madre de Dios, a Carmelite and architect, for the creation of the two buildings which would symbolise his religious and seigneurial status, the church of *San Pedro* and a great palace on the site of the old castle.

A church dedicated to *San Pedro* had stood on the northern edge of Lerma for many decades and the duke's forebears had given serious consideration to using it as the family mausoleum; for instance, Diego de Sandoval, I Marquis of Denia, had been buried there in 1502.[31] However, Lerma's commitment to having *San Pablo* in Valladolid as the Sandoval pantheon meant that project was never brought to fruition. He decided instead – stimulated, it may be presumed, by the success of his collegial church in Ampudia – to build a collegial church in Lerma so that the town should become a centre of religious learning.

The construction of the church was a formidable engineering achievement, for the site stood on an escarpment nearly 50 metres high over the river Arlanza. Accordingly, it was very expensive: Lerma spent 93,467 ducats on building and furnishing the church. However, he provided only 2,000 ducats of the 12,000 ducats (capital value: 240,000 ducats) that the annual maintenance of the church required; the remaining 10,000 were made available by the generosity of Philip III and Paul V (who had succeeded to the papal throne in 1605), who allowed him to draw on the income of benefices for his church. On its completion, an admirer wrote of *San Pedro* that it was 'worthy of being a cathedral'.[32] It now had thirty-three dignitaries, all of whom were of course appointed by Lerma – the five dignities themselves, twelve canons, eight *racioneros* and eight chaplains.[33] Lerma testified to his love of ecclesiastical music by making provision for a resident choir and by having two splendid organs built for the church, one of them designed by the King's organ master, Diego Quijano. He also presented the church with ten books of masses by Tomás de Victoria and others by Francisco de Guerrero.[34]

Lerma built the ducal *plaza* in front of his palace before beginning the reconstruction of the palace itself. The *plaza* was constructed on a grand scale; it was 6,800 metres square and had seventy-five columns in the covered *pasadizo* on its northern side. On the eastern and southern extremities houses were built (at their own expense) by kinsmen and *hechuras* of Lerma. Rodrigo Calderón and Tomás de Ángulo were neighbours at the corner of the western parade of houses while the properties of the Count of Barajas and the Marquis of La Laguna completed what became known as 'the Street of Blood' in reference to the ties of kinship or interest that bound the householders to Lerma. The Count of Saldaña built his house on the southern size of the *plaza* but the Duke of Uceda, as Lerma's heir, lived in apartments in the palace itself.[35]

The contract of 1613 for the construction of the palace stipulated that it was to be completed in 1617 and was to be three storeys high, with a fourth

storey incorporated into the roof. It was to have two slated towers on the front
corners of its façade in recognition of its owner's status as a duke. It was built
in vast grounds and enjoyed grand panoramas – northward to the great park
that sloped down to the river Arlanza and eastward to a splendid woodland.
As he had done at the *Casa de la Ribera* in Valladolid, Lerma had extensive lands
adjacent to a river in which he could walk or ride, hunt and fish. Each level of
the palace had about thirty rooms and on the ground floor there was a grand
reception patio, a dining hall and a great picture gallery. The façade had two
rows of windows, the upper floor decorated with 195 windows corrugated in
iron. Lerma's own balcony sat grandly in the centre above the main entrance,
between the shields of the Sandoval and de la Cerda families; it was from here
that he (or the King when he was present) presided over *fiestas* in the *plaza ducal*.
A grand staircase led to the upper floor, where Lerma had his own quarters
facing out on to the convent of *San Blas*.

It was remarkable that it was not until early in 1616 that Lerma turned his
attention to the design for the completion of the great palace; only then did he
decide to unite the *Casa Principal* with the *Casa del Castillo* by adding a new wing
to face the convent of *San Blas*. No evidence survives in his private papers as to
why he left this crucial decision so late and it is reasonable to assume that only
now was he confident that he would have enough money to finish the project.
In May 1616 he contracted with Juan de Valle Rozadilla to finish the building
in five months, adding two more towers and building an arched *pasadizo* to
connect the palace to *San Blas*. Remarkably, the work was completed on time.
The palace now measured 68m × 43m.[36] A contemporary observed of it that
'classical and modern architecture were united (here) in a perfection of perfec-
tions'.[37] Lerma admitted to having spent 218,667 ducats on the palace, *plaza
mayor*, park and waterworks and the purchase of properties around the *plaza*.[38]
However, he took a serious risk in abrogating to himself the right to have four
towers, for by tradition that privilege belonged only to royal palaces.[39]

Fray Alberto de la Madre de Dios also designed the two Dominican houses
in Lerma. The monastery of *Santo Domingo* was outside the walls of the city on
the western side of the Madrid road and was subject to the authority of the
Prior of *San Pablo*. Lerma spent 39,950 ducats on the building and 6,000 ducats
on silver altar vessels for the divine services. The consecration took place in
the presence of the royal couple on 17 September 1610 and by 1615 work had
proceeded far enough for fourteen religious to be living in the house.

In April 1611 Lerma brought thirty-eight Dominican nuns from their
convent in Cifuentes to establish the house of *San Blas* next to his palace. This
was to be the most splendid of Lerma's conventual foundations other than
San Pablo, and he spent 93,877 ducats on the convent – 69,887 ducats on the
building; 4,000 ducats on ornaments and silverware; and 20,000 ducats of

capital in funding 1,000 ducats of rent so support the nuns. Lerma stipulated in the *patronazgo* that the nuns were to maintain a choir and presented the convent with precious musical scripts as well as with paintings by Titian, Tintorreto and Bassano. He endowed it with a reliquary which he valued at 30,000 ducats and some silver and gold ornaments of unspecified value. He provided lands for a substantial garden and built high walls around it to ensure that the nuns enjoyed their privacy.[40]

Lerma established the monastery of *Santa Teresa* on the riverbank next to *La Ascensión* to house the confessors of the Carmelite nuns in *La Madre de Dios*. Once again, he connected it to his palace by a *pasadizo*. He also brought some Bernardine nuns from their house in Villamayor to found the Cistercian convent of *Nuestra Señora de San Vicente* and spent 14,000 ducats on the purchase of a house for them to use until he could create a purpose-built convent for them. The over-extension of his resources meant that he was not able to build the convent and so he endowed the house with 600 ducats of rent (capital value: 12,000 ducats). He presented the house with silver and ornaments worth 2,000 ducats.[41]

In total, therefore, Lerma spent 427,877 ducats on his ecclesiastical endowments in Lerma and his total traceable expenditure within his ducal city came to 646,377 ducats. This did not include the substantial expenses that others incurred on their foundations.[42] By 1617, Lerma's city probably had more religious foundations and more people in religious orders in proportion to its size than anywhere in Spain – thirty-three priests, fifty-four nuns and fourteen friars. The city was the visual expression of the duke's ambition to be not only the greatest nobleman in Spain but also the greatest patron of the Church, and that the great building programme was brought to fruition only in the last years of his *valimiento* was the clearest expression of the carefully considered calculations that underpinned the exercise of the whole of that *valimiento*.[43]

The French marriage journey and the decision to retire from the *valimiento*, 1615–16

At the turn of 1613–14 both Philip III and Marie de' Medici found themselves forced to agree to postpone the marriages to which each of them had committed so much. Philip needed to deal with two crises in foreign affairs which had suddenly arisen at the turn of 1613–14. The truce with the United Provinces was placed under serious stress when the Duke of Neuburg seized Düsseldorf and the United Provinces responded by placing a small garrison in Jülich. Even more seriously, in the summer of 1614 the crisis in Montferrat drew Spain into a war in Italy for the first time since 1559. But for the King, a personal crisis was of even greater consequence; at the turn of 1613–14, the *infanta* Anne became so ill with smallpox and measles that she was given the last sacraments. Anne's illness provided Philip with the perfect pretext for postponing her departure for France. When illness spread to the other children, Lerma selflessly took the heir to live in his *huerta;* it was a revealing indication of his commitment to the prince.[44]

Marie de' Medici had even more pressing reasons to defer the marriages, for in February 1614 Henry II, Prince of Condé, led a cabal of noble supporters away from court, vowing not to return unless the Spanish marriages were abandoned. Since Condé was a prince of the blood who had a claim on the throne, this was virtually tantamount to a rebellion. The prince broadened his appeal for support by issuing a manifesto denouncing the government's fiscal and diplomatic policies and by calling upon all true Frenchmen to oppose the marriages (19 February). Condé further emphasised the patriotic nature of his appeal by denouncing the pre-eminence in the Queen Regent's counsels of Concino Concini, a Florentine favourite. His patriotism did not, however, prevent him seeking help from foreign powers – the United Provinces, the Duke of Savoy and the Republic of Venice. In his challenge to Marie de' Medici, Condé therefore raised the spectre of the renewal of civil war in France, war that would be at once aristocratic and patriotic. Moreover, since the Huguenots naturally feared that the marriages with Spain would presage a crusade by the two Catholic monarchs against them, it was possible that they would join the princes, giving any war against the Regent a religious character. Marie capitulated, deferring Louis XIII's marriage at least until he attained his majority and summoning a meeting of the Estates-General (Treaty of Sainte-Ménehould, 15 May 1614). The States-General opened on 27 May. Far from resolving Marie's difficulties with her rebellious subjects, it was at least probable that the meeting of the Estates-General would further complicate them by broadening the hostility to the marriages with Spain. Marie's commitment to the Spanish marriages therefore threatened to place the survival of her regime – perhaps even of the Bourbon dynasty itself – at risk.[45] But she calculated that she had more to fear from Spanish hostility even than from that of the Prince of Condé and his supporters, and so she determined to see the marriages through.

In June 1614 Charles-Emmanuel billeted his troops in Vercelli and Asti, both of which faced the Milanese. Hinojosa sent the Prince of Castiglione to urge Charles-Emmanuel to draw back from conflict but the duke insulted the envoy and flamboyantly thrust his collar of the *Toison de Oro* at him, symbolically renouncing his fealty to Spain. When Hinojosa sent a second ambassador to retrieve the collar, Charles-Emmanuel imprisoned him and threatened to have him executed. It was in all but name a declaration of war upon Spain.

Hinojosa led his army into Piedmont in August but when he found that

Charles-Emmanuel had laid waste to the land over which he was to march he meekly returned to the Milanese. On 7 September, Charles-Emmanuel reciprocated by sending a unit of his army to pillage in the Milanese. Once again, Hinojosa marched into Piedmont and once again he withdrew before confronting the enemy. He did, however, begin the construction of a fort in front of Vercelli so that he could maintain a presence in Montferrat. In an unsophisticated attempt to force Lerma to support him he named it 'Sandoval'. At the end of November he moved on Asti, but again withdrew, this time after only six days. Three times during the second half of 1614 Hinojosa had made the military power of the King of Spain a thing of contempt in his *plaza de armas* and he had allowed Charles-Emmanuel to escape unpunished for opposing the power of Spain in Italy. The campaign of 1614 had piled fiasco upon fiasco, and it had associated the Sandoval family with national humiliation in the most explicit way.[46]

Lerma found some distraction from the crises in foreign affairs when the Countess of Saldaña was delivered of a son, her first child after eleven years of marriage (1 April 1614). The child was named Rodrigo Francisco Hurtado de Mendoza and had bestowed upon him one of the most resonant of all Castilian titles, that of the Count of the Cid. Philip honoured both families – Lerma by attending a celebratory feast in his palace and Infantado by allowing his fractious brother to return to court.[47] However, the birth of the first male heir to be born to the Infantado family in thirty years proved to be a turning-point in the relations between the Mendozas and the Sandovals, for the confidence that Infantado now enjoyed in the succession to his house encouraged him to distance himself from Lerma: within two years of the birth of the child, his grandson, Infantado had moved into open enmity to Lerma.[48] For his part, Lerma marked his son's success in fathering the heir to the Infantado title by having Saldaña appointed as Anne's *caballerizo mayor* so that he could then assume the same position for the heir after the exchange of brides.[49]

   In the spring of 1614 Lerma tried once again to secure a role in government for the Count of la Oliva by proposing that he should take over the papers managed by Juan de Idiáquez. Once again, Philip adamantly refused, ordering that the papers be given to Uceda. La Oliva's fall was gentle enough and was subtly managed: in June 1614 he was raised to the marquisate of Siete Iglesias. The new title served, if anything, to aggravate Siete Iglesias's arrogance and in March 1615 he further irritated the King by provoking an unfortunate scene with the Marquis of Camarasa, Captain of the Spanish Guards; after a royal *fiesta* in the *Plaza Mayor*, Siete Iglesias angrily claimed that it was his right rather than Camarasa's to lead the King's procession back to the Alcázar. Philip was furious by the scene created by Siete Iglesias and Lerma was deeply embarrassed; he continued to allow Siete Iglesias to accompany him in public but appears never again to have allowed him any authority to act for him.[50]

As Siete Iglesias's decline gathered pace, his chief opponent stepped self-confidently into the spotlight; in July, Lerma informed the Inquisitor General that Philip had made an award of a supernumerary councillorship of Inquisition to fray Luis de Aliaga 'on account of his good qualities'. Moreover, Lerma wrote, the King had ordered that there was henceforth always to be a Dominican on the Council because the Order 'holds the first place in matters of faith'. Lerma's attempt to promote his beloved Order infuriated the Inquisitor General and Council, who protested angrily at what they regarded as an insult to the dignity of *la Suprema*. Philip and Lerma swept their objections aside.[51] It was a crass manoeuvre by Lerma to turn the fury of the Inquisitor General and the Council of Inquisition upon himself while providing his chief opponent with a position in government from which he could continue to embarrass him. His sureness of touch was deserting him.

It may not have been entirely coincidental that criticism of Lerma was rising dangerously within the court and that much of it was coming now from churchmen. In the royal chapel, the King's own preachers were mounting what looked suspiciously like a concerted attack upon the management of religious affairs and they were doing so in a tone which (as Cabrera de Córdoba recorded in the spring of 1614) was becoming increasingly acerbic:

> His Majesty has spent Lent in Madrid and listened to the sermons which have been preached in the royal chapel, both those on days of obligation ... and those which are preached daily ... In the sermons he has been warned about many things that need to be remedied, and among them are the abuse and disorder that applies in the appointment to offices, bishoprics, *encomiendas*, and other offices and benefices through the intercession of (interested parties) and favours which are won with interest and through the giving of gifts.[52]

A further opening for the opponents of Lerma became available when a new Cortes of Castile opened on 9 February 1615 to vote the *servicios ordinarios y extraordinarios*. From the outset the procurators complained angrily about the effects that the *repartimiento* of 1611 was having on the people of Castile. Lorenzo Ramírez de Prado, son of Alonso and procurator for Salamanca, spoke eloquently of the damage that was being done to small communities by the *repartimiento*. A flood of petitions from such places bore testimony to the growing conviction in urban Castile that the *repartimiento* was forcing many people to leave the countryside for the towns and was, in consequence, bringing about substantial demographic change within the kingdom. Having made their protest, the procurators voted the *servicios ordinarios y extraordinarios* on 7 and 10 April. On both occasions it was Lerma, as procurator for Burgos, who carried the good news to the King.[53] Much more important, however, than the voting of comparatively minor taxes was the realisation that King and duke had now to confront the open hostility to crown policies of the procurators of the Cortes of Castile – and that they were having to do so at a time when the *millones* would shortly be coming up for renewal.

The journey for the exchange of the brides with France at last began when on 30 May 1615 Philip left Madrid. He was away for seven months, returning on 15 December. Those months were notable for the deepening of tensions between Philip and Lerma and for a deterioration in Lerma's standing in court and government. Philip was determined that his beloved daughter would be married in Burgos and then leave for France in the greatest splendour that he could provide while Lerma was adamant that he would not accompany Anne to the border. At sixty-two years of age, Lerma had neither the energy nor the financial resources to undertake the journey. Accordingly – while letting it be known how enthusiastic he was to travel with Anne – he did everything that he could to escape from the obligation of doing so.[54] For the first time, Lerma was presuming to be less than honest with the King – and he was making no pretence at being discreet in doing so.[55]

As he had done over the Marquis of Siete Iglesias, so again Philip refused to give way to Lerma. When he was informed that Elizabeth's entourage was led by the Duke of Guise – the leading nobleman of France – the King seized the opportunity to demand that Lerma perform the same duty for his daughter.[56] Lerma was compelled to agree. The King was so grateful that (as Lerma recorded) he embraced him warmly and assured him that 'I always knew that no one other than you could resolve this for me.[57] Lerma had splendid liveries made for his household servants, and his own accoutrements included a urinal made of silver for his use in his coach: he would travel begrudgingly to Burgos but he would do so in his customary style. However, he was forced to borrow 400,000 ducats to cover his expenses; as far as is known, this was the only major loan that he took out during his *valimiento*, and so stretched were his resources that he was never able to repay more than half of it.[58] Lerma could not support his building programme and the expenses of the royal *jornada:* he preferred to pay for his buildings.

The royal exchequer was even less able to bear the expenses of the royal *jornada* than was Lerma, and Philip's need to fund the journey to the frontier at a time when he was fighting a war in Italy and having to prepare for the possibility of another war over Jülich-Cleves stretched his resources to breaking-point. Accordingly, he was forced to become increasingly dependant upon the President of Finance to provide the monies that he needed so desperately. In consequence, during the long summer of 1615 Carrillo's stature became truly ministerial. He used his enhanced authority to begin a systematic and sustained – and increasingly vitriolic – attack upon the profligacy of the King's *valido*.

As early as January 1615 Philip promised Carrillo that he would reduce his expenditure so that the money could be found for the journey.[59] However, within two days of receiving the King's letter, Carrillo was ordered by Lerma to provide a further 100,000 ducats for household expenses. Carrillo therefore demanded a meeting with the duke before the King departed from Madrid so that he could agree on the costs that the Council of Finance would be expected to meet. The President knew well enough that the resources did not exist for the great *jornada* and was covering himself against the storm that he knew was coming.[60]

The repeated delays which prevented the French party leaving for the frontier forced Philip and Lerma to stay in Valladolid for three months (3 June– 9 September).[61] It had been during the visit to Valladolid in 1600 that Lerma had laid the basis for the fullness of his power and it was during the visit of 1615 that the disintegration of his unique authority began. To all outward appearances, Lerma's power remained undiminished; indeed, he once again took over the *Casa de la Ribera* and entertained Philip there as if he still owned the property.[62] But in reality, politics began now to move against him. Lerma was even blamed for the collapse of the government of Portugal, when in June Philip dismissed the Council of Portugal and appointed the Count of Salinas as viceroy.[63] It was symptomatic of Lerma's decline that when a *pasquín* against his abuse of power was handed to Philip a suspect was put to the torture and died proclaiming not just his own innocence but his great love of the King. The scandal threw Lerma into depression.[64] As was his custom at such moments, he attempted to reconcile himself with leading opponents; the Count of Benavente and Luis de Aliaga were both sworn in as councillors of State in Valladolid in July, and they each now had another avenue through which to attack Lerma's standing with the King.[65] Lerma's enemies were gathering.

Worse was to follow, for on 22 June Hinojosa brought the war with Savoy to a conclusion with the 'Treaty of Asti'. He agreed to the settlement against the advice of his captains and jettisoned the few gains that he had made. He even allowed the French ambassador to mediate with Savoy, and in doing so gravely compromised the majesty of Philip III for it was axiomatic that Spain had no equal in Italy. The treaty has been described by Antonio Bombín as 'the lowest point' for Spain's reputation in Italy during Philip III's reign, and it posed a keen dilemma for the King: if he ratified the treaty, he would compound the damage inflicted on his prestige by Hinojosa while if he did not it would be taken that he had reneged upon a solemn commitment given in his name by his viceroy.[66] Charges were laid against the governor on 9 April, and at the Council of State on 11 July Lerma began to distance himself from him, suggesting that he should be replaced by the Marquis of Villafranca.[67] This duly happened; Villafranca left Madrid for Milan on 2 October, determined to win laurels for himself by restoring the power and prestige of the monarchy in its *plaza de armas*.[68]

Lerma's embarrassment at the conduct of Hinojosa was compounded by the sustained attack now mounted on him by the President of the Council of Finance. In mid-August, Carrillo sarcastically suggested to the King that it was 'not helpful' for him to have to call the *hombres de negocios* in three or four times a week to ask them to provide money for the latest royal need. Philip assured the President that he trusted his 'good zeal' but that expenses could not be deferred.[69] A few days later, Carrillo rebuked Lerma that he 'should not allow this disorder' but was again told that he had to find the monies for the expenses of the household.[70] Carrillo then rounded on the King, itemising the monies that he had raised for him and furiously rebuking him for his unremitting demands for more:

> It is not credible how much the orders that Your Majesty has made for payments comes to … and so I have upon me a weight of injuries and aggravations that if God Himself our Lord inflicted them would be tolerable since I could attribute them to my sins and above all to divine providence. Provisions [have been made] of more than 9,332,000 ducats but they are not sufficient. We have done not merely the possible but the impossible. There is no record in either religious or secular histories or traditions of such expenditure in one year.

Carrillo disclaimed responsibility for any further monies that Philip might order. Furious, Philip instructed the President to pay the monies that had been ordered without 'a moment's delay'.[71]

When news came in the third week of September that the French party had left Bordeaux for the frontier Philip and his court were at last able to leave Valladolid for Burgos.[72] They stopped off in Lerma for a few days, and it was while Philip was there that he issued his instructions to Lerma for his journey with Anne; once again he reaffirmed his confidence in the Duke in the most generous language (23 September).[73]

On 16 October, in Burgos, Anne renounced her rights and those of her descendants to the thrones of Spain. Two days later, her marriage was celebrated in the great cathedral. Lerma dressed in his splendid clothes of velvet and pearls and was accompanied by twenty-four servants and twelve pages as, in one of the highlights of his career, he took the oath on behalf of Louis XIII of France. But now, such were his infirmities that he did so from his sedan chair (which was covered in gold leaf).

Lerma's devotion to duty elicited much sympathy and he used the occasion to beg Philip once again to excuse him from the duty of accompanying Anne.[74] The King finally gave way and named Uceda in his place. In the powers that he signed for Uceda on 23 October he referred to him as the 'coadjutor with future succession to the offices that the Duke of Lerma, your father, has in my household and in that of the prince, my son, and his brothers'.[75] The Sandoval succession seemed to be secure. Moreover, when Anne left for the frontier she passed under banners bearing the shields not just of Spain and France but also those of the house of Sandoval (24 October).[76] It was the most explicit identification of the marriages as the work of the Duke of Lerma – but it is unlikely that the King approved of the association that Lerma had presumed to draw between the house of Sandoval and those of crowned kings.

Philip accompanied Anne for 15 kilometres to Nuestra Señora de Gamonal, where he bade her farewell. Lerma travelled with Anne only as far as Briviesca, a further 20 kilometres along the road, before returning to Burgos to await the arrival of Elizabeth. Philip then broke with all the conventions of majesty by impetuously chasing after his daughter. He overtook Anne at Vitoria and stayed with her for two days until she reached Fuenterrabía. There, he finally wrenched himself away from her. He was in tears, knowing that it was all but certain that he would never see his beloved daughter again.[77]

As Philip rode back to Burgos he may well have reflected that for the first time Lerma had let him down, that he had failed to perform a duty to which he attached the very highest importance. Certainly, when he issued his valedictory instructions to Anne, Philip urged his daughter to pay particular heed to the advice of her confessor and to take advice from a variety of counsellors, perhaps implying that he was reflecting upon his reliance on one man.[78]

The exchange of brides took place in archaic splendour at the River Bidassoa on 9 November. Philip at least had the satisfaction that the Spanish greatly outshone the French, prompting Guise to complain that he had led his men to the frontier as soldiers and not as courtiers. Guise then took Anne to Bordeaux where on 25 November her marriage with Louis XIII was solemnised and (as Louis XIII subsequently claimed) consummated.[79] Uceda now led Prince Philip and Elizabeth, the future Queen of Spain, back to Burgos; at every town on the road, Uceda entered in front of the Princess's canopy. When the procession reached Burgos, Philip and Lerma rode with the royal children a league outside the city to greet the Princess. Lerma used the opportunity to reclaim primacy at court from his son. Although he professed himself proud of the role that Uceda had played he now accompanied Philip, emphasising that he did so not merely as *caballerizo mayor* but also as *regidor* of the city of Burgos and castellan of its castle. He then took the royal party back to the royal monastery of *Las Huelgas*, where he had prepared a splendid meal. He was back in control.[80]

Since Prince Philip was now a married man – if only ten years old – a household was established for him while the King was in Burgos (22 November). Thus far, Lerma had served as the Prince's *ayo* while Don Galcerán Albanel, a Catalan widower, had been his *maestro*.[81] Now Uceda's son Francisco, Duke of Cea, was named as *sumiller de corps*, to serve alongside Saldaña, who was the Prince's *caballerizo mayor*. Lerma, his sons and his grandson therefore held every major position in the prince's household. Moreover, fray Jusepe González, formerly confessor of Lerma and Prior of *San Pablo*, was confirmed as confessor to the Prince. The gentlemen of the chamber included another relative of Lerma's in Fernando de Borja, and Gaspar de Guzmán, Count of Olivares, who was considered at this time to be a supporter of Lerma's.[82]

It was against this background that at the end of November the papal nuncio reported that Lerma was once again talking of retiring from affairs. Lerma seemed to have chosen his moment particularly well: in pushing through the marriages with France he had emphatically reasserted the power of Spain in Europe while he himself appeared to be at the very height of his influence and authority, the leading statesman of Europe. Moreover, it seemed likely that France would remain weakened for the foreseeable future; the dissident nobles had perhaps as many as 40,000 men available and it was probable that the Huguenots would join with them in a war against the crown. Indeed, it seemed certain that Spanish power had not yet reached the limits of its expansion; since Philip still had two daughters whom he could marry off, he could look to make further diplomatic advances in his dealings with Ferdinand of Styria and James of England, both of whom were eager for a Spanish match. If the imperial succession could be secured for Ferdinand the future would once again belong to the house of Habsburg and to Catholicism. Although the Treaty of Asti remained an embarrassment to Lerma, the *Pax Hispánica* seemed to be firmly established: it was as if the defeats of the years 1598–1609 had never happened.

Philip left Burgos for the city of Lerma on 12 December. In his ducal city, Lerma once again provided lavish hospitality for the royal family, and he continued to do so after the King returned to Madrid. Indeed, on 19 December, Princess Elizabeth entered the capital by passing under an arch at Lerma's *huerta*, as if to confirm that the Franco-Spanish marriages were the work of the Duke of Lerma. Two days later, the King took Elizabeth and the royal children back to Lerma's *huerta* for a banquet before the city of Madrid formally welcomed her. When the royal family watched Madrid's procession from the balconies of Lerma's palace it was further confirmation that the duke remained firmly in the King's grace.[83] On New Year's Day 1616, Philip again brought his children to the palace: the royal family ate in public and in the afternoon watched the gentlemen of the court display their equestrian skills. The King let it be known how much he and his children had enjoyed the occasion.[84]

It was from this eminence that Lerma now prepared to retire. Early in January 1616, Sir John Digby reported that:

> The duke of Lerma, whose absolutenes in this State your Honour beste knowethe, did lately, as I formerly aduertized, transferre all or most of the places hee held

> unto the duke of Uzeda his sonne. Now, hee hathe put on a Resolution to retire himselfe from the dispatche of all Busines, & hathe introduced his sonne into the same Course, which hee formerly helde. And all men that negociate haue now recourse unto him. The Kings pleasure being in all things declared by him. The duke only retainethe a kind of secret superintendencie & wholy imployethe his tyme, & takethe upon him as his only Charge, to look unto the Education of the young Prince, & the reste of the Kings children. So that hee is now in the Pallace as the father of the Familie, but for Businesses of State, whosoever speak-ethe unto him he remittethe him unto his sonne. Who, I must tell your Honour, I doubte will hardely inheritt his father's Talent.[85]

Towards the end of the month Digby confirmed Lerma's projected retire-ment:

> The duke of Lerma dothe yet continuewe so constantly in the Course of his retirednes, that yt is certainely beleeued, that hee will not now, as at other tymes, returne to the direction or dispatche of the Affaires of this State. But that hee will wholy & intirely investe his sonne in them. Taking unto himself only as his peculiar Charge, the Education of the Prince and the reste of the Kings children.[86]

A Spanish chronicler corroborated the details of Digby's report:

> The Duke of Lerma has wished to free himself of so much work that he had and so the Duke of Uceda gives all the audiences to claimants. The Duke of Lerma continues to deal with the consultas. God protect his Majesty for many years. It is a great thing to have vassals and servants of such care and trust to help him carry the weight of such a great monarchy.[87]

Government and policymaking: the erosion of Lerma's authority

Lerma's announcement that he intended to retire proved to be a gross error of judgement – perhaps the strategically most important mistake that he made during his *valimiento* – for, rather than facilitating the transfer of power to his son, it accelerated the loss of his own authority across court and government. In consequence, the criticisms that Lerma had endured during 1614–15 now became more concentrated and bitter. Aliaga, who of course knew all the details of the tensions between King and *valido*, began to construct an alliance with other friars within the court as he attacked Lerma. Moreover, the councils of State and Finance now systematically undermined Lerma's authority with the King; by 1615 the Council of State was fully under the dominance of Flanders veterans who demanded a more forward foreign policy, while Finance was led by a president, Fernando Carrillo, who was increasingly strident in his criti-cism of Lerma. Even the procurators of the Cortes of Castile now presumed to attack the policies of the government with almost unrestrained relish. A still more pronounced belligerence informed the actions of proconsuls in Italy, who rose enthusiastically to the challenge thrown down by Charles-Emmanuel. At home and abroad, Lerma's enemies were gathering, and they were forcing politics beyond his control. Having announced that he intended to retire, the duke now had little political strength with which to resist them – and he had to worry about how much support the King whom he was shortly to abandon would give him.

The soldiers on the Council of State. Don Pedro de Toledo and don Agustín Mejía

The renewal of the Council of State began in 1611. In 1611–13, the surviving servants of Philip II – Castel Rodrigo, Idiáquez and Velada – accounted for 23 per cent of the attendances at the Council (234 of 1,007) but by 1614 their contribution had declined to 11 per cent (45 of 403). Castel Rodrigo died on 28 November 1613 and Idiáquez on 12 October 1614. By 1615, only three men who had sat before 1610 remained in attendance while five new councillors accounted for 74 per cent of attendances.[88] The Council had been renewed and reinvigorated.

The Council was led jointly by don Pedro Álvarez de Toledo y Osorio, fifth marquis of Villafranca (b. 1556) and don Agustín Mejía (b. 1555). Both were soldiers of excellence who had achieved fame on sea as well as on land. Villafranca had served with distinction in the Low Countries before taking up a naval career as captain of galleys in Naples and in Spain. Mejía was the most experienced Spanish commander of his generation; he had won honours in the Mediterranean at Lepanto and at Tunis (1571, 1573), in the conquest of Portugal (1580), in the campaigns of Parma in the Low Countries and on the *empresa de Inglaterra* (1588) and in the invasion of Aragon (1591).[89] The careers of Villafranca and Mejía had come together in 1610 when they had worked on the expulsion of the *moriscos*, and in 1611 they had been rewarded with councillorships of State. Thereafter they had developed a joint influence on policymaking but one that was sharply differentiated by their contrasting temperaments – Villafranca, forceful, eloquent and imaginative; Mejía, dour, concise and practical. Villafranca never used one word where a score or more could be conjured up and his colleagues were forced to impose a time limit on him so that they could find the time to give their views.[90] By contrast, Mejía never used two words where one would suffice and his *pareceres* were distinguished by the pungent and precise authority with which he spoke. Villafranca and Mejía were a formidable combination and they set themselves to take Spain back to war with the Dutch, regarding the alienation of direct control over Flanders in 1598 as a profound error and the truce of 1609 as a national humiliation. Their opposition to Lerma's policies came from deep conviction but it was heavily-spiced with personal hostility towards the duke – Villafranca because he had been so long denied the *grandeza* that he regarded as his due, and Mejía because of his humiliation over the loss in 1605 to Ambrosio Spínola of the *maestrazgo general* of the Low Countries.[91] They attended to their duties on the Council so diligently that between them they accounted for no fewer than 27 per cent of attendances in the years 1611–20 (1,060 of 3,902).

A series of debates in the Council during the first half of 1614 provided Villafranca and Mejía with the opportunity to advocate a more aggressive foreign policy. Addressing himself in January 1614 to the implications of the crisis in Jülich-Cleves, Villafranca insisted that the loyalist provinces in the Low Countries had to be protected because 'the preservation of this Monarchy consists in the possession of those states'. He urged that the Army of Flanders should be reformed so as 'to introduce the old discipline' and blamed Albert for the decline of Spain's power in the Low Countries.[92] Like so many others, in the United Provinces as in Spain, Villafranca was looking forward to the renewal of war in 1621.

On 27 May 1614 the Council considered the progress of the French marriage negotiations and the news that the United Provinces were contemplating sending troops into Jülich. Lerma attended, and insisted that the marriages with France had to go ahead – 'the Catholic cause has to take precedence over everything'. He accepted that Philip should not ratify the agreement until the meeting of the Estates-General had been concluded, in case the deputies forced Marie de' Medici to renege on the marriage agreement. He suggested that the Army of Flanders should be substantially reinforced to discourage Marie from making a marital alliance with England, describing the Low Countries as 'the parade ground for northern Europe and for France'. Lerma's policy in northern Europe was clear: to make the marital commitment with France; to protect Spain's strategic interests in the Low Countries and to secure the neutrality of England. Villafranca, however, emphasised that the Truce of 1609 was the underlying cause of Spain's vulnerability in northern Europe – 'since the truces we have seen the bad way in which things have been going' – and insisted that Jülich had to be retained so that the war with the United Provinces could be properly fought when it was renewed.[93] At a second meeting on 27 May, Villafranca stressed that if the United Provinces were allowed to gain control of Jülich, they would be able to threaten the security of the loyalist south. Mejía agreed that if Jülich was lost Flanders could not be held and spoke what others were only daring to think: 'it would be better to break the truce than to lose it [sc. Jülich]'.[94]

From Prague, Baltasar de Zúñiga – ambassador to the imperial court since 1608 – stressed that every day that the Dutch stayed in Jülich represented a threat to Spain's strategic interests.[95] A consensus was emerging among Spain's senior policymakers: the truce had been a mistake and the Dutch would have to be fought again. Indeed, at a meeting in July Villafranca positively welcomed Dutch involvement in Jülich as 'a gift from heaven' that entitled Philip to re-arm in the Low Countries. Mejía supported Villafranca, noting that sending help to Jülich 'is the same thing as to defend the country of Flanders.'[96]

Spínola opened his campaign on 25 August 1614 and rapidly cut a swathe through Jülich, Berg and Cleves, taking fifty-five towns and fortresses. The capture of the Calvinist stronghold of Wesel on 7 September provided Spínola with the capacity to close the Rhine to the Dutch and to place an army on the borders of the United Provinces. Maurice of Nassau responded by occupying Jülich and a number of towns in Cleves. Both generals were determined to avoid provoking a general European war, and indeed to preserving the truce for as long as they could, and so they skilfully avoided coming into contact with each other. Having both won their immediate objectives, Spínola and Nassau again negotiated at a great banquet given by Spínola. They agreed that they would withdraw their armies and return the duchies to Neuburg and Brandenburg. The settlement was ratified in the Treaty of Xanten (14 November 1614). However, Wesel was too important to be surrendered, and Spínola found excuse after excuse for not giving it up. The countdown to the expiry of the truce was beginning in earnest.[97]

The King at last won his great naval victory when in August 1614 an armada under Luis de Fajardo captured the pirate port of La Mamora on the Atlantic coast of Africa after a ferocious battle. In the euphoria of its capture few noted that the cost of maintaining La Mamora would be a further drain on crown finances.[98] The President of Finance understood the problem, calculating that the crown's expenses for 1615 would reach 10,610,149 ducats, of which no less than one-third (3,740,000 ducats) would be for military expenses.[99] Peace was indeed proving as expensive as war.

'This crown is subject to ruin': Fernando Carrillo and the management of crown finances

Miguel de Cervantes published the 'Second Part' of *Don Quixote* as Philip and Lerma returned to Madrid in December 1615. The 'Second Part' was much more politically orientated than the 'First Part' had been ten years before, and it had at its heart (chapters 40–63) a long swathe of explicit comment on contemporary political and social problems – instructions on how to govern (43–53); the treatment of the *moriscos* (54, 64–5); an account of the breakdown of order on the road from Madrid to Catalonia (60–1); the ravages of piracy on the Mediterranean coast (63). At the heart of the book lay recurrent (and quite explicit) criticisms of the King himself. Sancho, for instance, observed of a ruler that 'it would be a fine thing if people came wearied out to look for [a ruler] on some business, and he was amusing himself in the forest. The government would go to the devil at that rate. Indeed, ... hunting and pastimes are better suited to idlers than to [rulers]'. No one could doubt who Sancho had in mind with this stricture. Similarly, there was little doubt that Cervantes was stating his own position when he had Ricote condemn the expulsion of the *moriscos* with rhetorical praise – 'What an heroic resolve of the great Philip the Third, and what unheard-of wisdom in entrusting its execution to this Don Bernardino de Velasco!'[100] There was no explicit criticism of the Sandoval family – Cervantes was far too closely tied to the family for that, and he judiciously dedicated the 'Second Part' to the Count of Lemos – but no reader could escape the conclusion that Don Quixote himself adumbrated, that Spain was in crisis and that the King himself had to be told 'the naked truth'.

> It is the duty of loyal vassals to tell their lords the truth in its proper shape and essence, without enlarging on it out of flattery or softening it for any idle reason. I would have you know, Sancho, that if the naked truth were to come to the ears of princes, unclothed in flattery, this would be a different age. Other ages would be held to be of iron in comparison with ours, for this in which we live now I reckon to be of gold.[101]

It is probable that the prodigious success that the 'Second Part' of *Don Quixote* enjoyed played a significant role in validating and encouraging this outpouring of criticism. Certainly, the welling criticism of government in the years after 1615 helped to further undermine Lerma's authority at court.[102]

A substantial part of this attack on governmental practice and morality was directed not at Lerma but at the methods used by the President of the Council of Finance to raise money. It was ironic that Fernando Carrillo should have drawn so much obloquy on to himself, for he made little effort to disguise the contempt in which he held Lerma. Beleaguered by the unremitting pressure for money placed on him by Philip and Lerma, Carrillo practised short-term financial management, juggling resources to produce cash, peremptorily turning down requests for money from Philip and Lerma and the councils. He made a succession of *asientos* of more than three million ducats but in doing so he pawned the crown's resources ever farther into the future and gave ever greater control over them to foreign bankers. He was allowed no attempt at forward planning, no financial strategy other than that of producing money for the immediate need. It was a sad waste of exceptional abilities and energy, and more than anyone Carrillo knew it. While he cherished his growing power and stature in government he resented with fury the pressures under which he worked and the blithe irresponsibility with which Philip and Lerma imposed those pressures on him.[103] Carrillo's manner was not always well judged; he tended to be contemptuous of men who were less able than himself and was prone to vent his anger on them; the Count of Revilla acknowledged that 'the

President of Finance ... is a great minister and very zealous in the service of the King but he might remember that there are others who are also [great ministers] and that he is not alone in being the zealous defender of the service of [the King].' The Council of War, bedraggled by Carrillo's relentless refusal to meet its requests for money, noted that 'everyone knows how the President of Finance conducts business.'[104]

In December 1615 the Council of Finance reached an agreement with a consortium of Genoese bankers for an *asiento* of 3,730,000 ducats and *escudos* for the current financial year.[105] Carrillo insisted that the increase in the crown's expenditure was sufficient 'to drown a monarchy': the President of the Council of Finance was speaking the language of the *arbitristas*.[106] To the King, however, the *asiento grande* seemed merely to prove that monies could be raised where the will existed; he had learned nothing from the crisis of 1615. Insistently, therefore, Philip continued to order Carrillo to find monies for foreign commitments as and when they arose.[107] By the autumn of 1616 Carrillo had had enough: on 4 August he despatched a lengthy paper to the King in which he effectively challenged Philip either to take responsibility for the management of crown finances out of his hands or to allow his council and himself to have real and effective control over them.[108]

Carrillo's paper was one of the landmark documents of the reign and played an important role in redefining the terms in which the government controlled its finances in the last years of the reign. Carrillo patiently explained to Philip that his territories beyond Spain could not be maintained without the use of *asientos*: 'what was once always acquired through war today is (maintained) by money, and the strength of Your Majesty consists now in money, and the day that this is lacking everything abroad will be lost ...' He therefore stressed the absolute importance of the *asentistas* in providing credit for the crown and emphasised the need to exercise close control over the councils who disposed of resources without having responsibility for them. In a mannered rebuke to the King he looked back to the reigns of Charles V and Philip II as a golden age when kings of Spain had not committed themselves to expenditures without having the resources with which to meet them – a somewhat revisionist view of the financial history of the Spanish monarchy in the sixteenth century, it must be admitted. Certainly, his observation that hell awaited the king who did not practice sound financial management would most certainly not have been lost on Philip III. Carrillo made it clear that his own position and that of his council were no longer tenable:

> The Council of Finance and its President are not serving our offices nor Your Majesty nor the public cause, because the true President of Finance in terms of everything that comes to these kingdoms from the Indies is the *Junta de Guerra* of the Council of the Indies ... As to the remainder of the revenue of these

kingdoms, the true President of Hacienda is the Council of State, the Council of War and other *juntas* which have more responsibility for expenditures and provisions [than does the Council of Finance].

Carrillo insisted that the failure of the exchequer to meet its payments was leading to a widespread belief both at home and abroad 'that this crown is subject to ruin', and he impressed upon Philip the damage that his profligacy was inflicting upon all sectors of national life:

> It results in damage to the people and the poor, churchmen and laymen alike, for they are the true guarantors and paymasters of all that is spent, because it comes from them and from their blood and money. Since these kingdoms are in the state of poverty and shortage of people that is well known it is right that if the burdens with which the people are afflicted are not being reduced through good counsel these burdens could be made proportionate to their resources and to that of Your Majesty.

From the King and his *reputación*, Carrillo turned to the quality of the advice that Philip was receiving, and he could only have Lerma in mind when he made a blunt attack on 'powerful people' who were themselves grievously sinning by their conduct:

> What is being done to the President of Finance over the payment of these orders is something that should be remedied for it does not seem possible that a human being should suffer these afflictions, especially from powerful people who, shutting their eyes to all reason and purpose, avail themselves of their power [in such a way that] there are great sins and complaints and evil consequences to justice and to the esteem in which public ministers are held.

Even Carrillo would surely not have dared speak thus of Lerma to the King before the duke had announced his intention to retire from political life. He then noted the condition of the royal finances that he had inherited in 1609 and the increases in expenditure that he had made possible. Challenging the King to replace him, he suggested that a *Junta de Provisiones* should be established to allocate monies. Its membership should be drawn from the councils of State, War and the Indies and have sole responsibility for distributing all the resources of the royal exchequer. The use of such a body would end the system whereby the councils of State, War and the Indies 'spend money without the requisite knowledge and the Council of Finance is further stretched by the day'.

As for himself: Carrillo insisted that he wanted to be rid of his burden and proposed that the President of the Council of Finance should not be a member of the *Junta*. He concluded with a not entirely modest evaluation of his own historical importance:

> I am satisfied that (thanks be to God who has given so many graces) no minister of letters since the time of the Catholic Kings [sc. Ferdinand and Isabella] until

present times in the royal service has filled the posts nor followed the campaigns nor been involved in negotiations beyond these kingdoms with so much work and demands on his person and finance and time as I have.

Despite his protestations, Carrillo was not the man to give up power voluntarily, and a very different perspective informed his conclusion as he suggested that Philip might prefer to restore the authority of his President and Council of Finance. But he had overplayed his hand: Philip ordered that the *Junta de Provisiones* be established.

It did not take long for the King to regret his decision. Overpowering as Carrillo was, he was the only man who could produce the amounts of money that Philip, Lerma and the councils of State and War in particular demanded so remorselessly. But the situation in northern Italy deteriorated alarmingly when in November 1616 the Council of State was informed that the United Provinces were raising thousands of men to help Venice in its dispute with the Archduke Ferdinand. The news marked a decisive staging-post on Spain's road back to war after the settlements of 1604 and 1609.

Determined as he was to preserve the peace of Italy, Lerma played a key role in the beginning of the process. As a first step, on 11 December he took Uceda to meet Carrillo to discuss what he chose to call Carrillo's 'responsibilities' as President of the Council of Finance. The two dukes carried the message that the *Junta de Provisiones* had failed so signally that it had been abolished after little more than forty days' existence, and they made it clear to Carrillo that he and his council were once again to be in charge of administering the royal exchequer.[109]

Confirmed not just in office but in power, Carrillo acted quickly: on 21 December the Council of Finance reported to the King that it had negotiated an *asiento* for 4,670,000 ducats and *escudos* with five Genoese bankers and with the deputies of the *medio general*. This was an enormous loan, one-quarter as large again as that made only ten months earlier, and no less than half of it was scheduled to go abroad — 1,560,000 *escudos* for the Low Countries and 800,000 ducats for Milan.[110] On the same day, the Council presented the King with a projection that free income for 1616–17 would total about 5,357,000 ducats while the crown was already committed to expenditures of 8,234,113 ducats. Even while the Council was drawing up the accounts Philip ordered that it find a further 1,930,000 ducats for various purposes. He had, therefore, a shortfall of 4,807,112 ducats on his current account.[111] He would need his rumbustious President of Finance more than ever in the months and years ahead — and Carrillo's continuance in office would have serious implications for the authority of the Duke of Lerma, the more so because the resources with which he had to manage the royal finances were crumbling while the demands on them were growing as Spain headed irresistibly back to war.

NOTES

1 IEF, 'Cardenales Españoles', in Quintín Aldea Vaquero et al., *Diccionario de historia eclesiástica de España* (DHEE), 5 vols., Madrid, 1972–89, i, pp. 347–51.

2 The archbishops of Toledo who were cardinals: Francisco Jiménez de Cisneros, Guillermo de Croy, Gaspar de Quiroga, Albert of Austria and Bernardo de Sandoval y Rojas; those of Seville: Diego Hurtado de Mendoza, Juan de Zúñiga, Alonso Manrique de Lara, Juan García de Loaysa, Gaspar de Zúñiga y Avellaneda, Rodrigo de Castro and Fernando Niño de Guevara.

3 Williams, 'A Jewish councillor of Inquisition?', pp. 261–2 and Lea, *Inquisition*, i, p. 306.

4 IEF, 'Cardenales Españoles', *DHEE*, i, pp. 347–51; I am obliged to the late Rev. George Talbot and the Rev. Canon Brian Scantlebury for advice on this matter.

5 See below, p. 232.

6 Francisco Fernández de Caso, *Discvrso en qve se refieren las solenidades, y fiestas, con que el excelentísimo Duque celebrò en su villa de Lerma*, Madrid, 1619, quotation at p. 6; and Pedro de Herrera, '*Translación del Santíssimo Sacramento a La Iglesia Colegial de San PEDRO de la Villa ...*', Madrid, 1618. On the festivities of 1617, see below, pp. 227–30.

7 Lerma, 'Testamento ... (1617)', ADL 12, p. 31.

8 *Relaciones*, p. 283. Alonso de Velasco, Count of la Revilla, wrote to Diego Sarmiento de Acuña that 'hallo a Madrid de manera que no le conozco con tantos edificios y tan buenos y no beo calle donde no se comienzen de bueno', Madrid, 13 Dec. 1613, RB 11/2173, doc. 19. See Domínguez Ortíz, *La sociedad española*, p. 140.

9 Anon., 'Relación de las Rentas y hazienda libre que Posee el Duque de Lerma adelantado Mayor de Castilla mi señor de la que El cardenal duque mi señor dejo acrezentada el dia de su fallescimiento', Madrid (?), 25 April 1628', ADL 54, no. 9, no fol.; it is recorded that the properties were worth 105,300 ducats.

10 Anon., 'Quenta de 12,375,000 q[ue] su m[agestad] le a de pagar por las casas .... en la placa de las descalcas franciscas ... Año de 1613', AGS DGT Inv. 24, leg. 1288. See also, 'Venta para la villa de Madrid de las casas del mayorazgo de don Ant[oni]o Gutierrez', 1609, AGS PR 34, no fol.; *Relaciones*, p. 359.

11 'Casa del prado en la V[ill]a de M[adri]d', AGS PR 36, no fol. On the facilities made available by the city of Madrid, Téllez-Girón, *Anales de Madrid*, p. 280, n. 147.

12 *Relaciones*, pp. 441–2, 508, 520–1, 528, 536. M. del Carmén Pescador del Hoy, 'La más antigua plaza de toros de Madrid', *AIEM*, 3, 1968, pp. 29–41 and Ricardo de Sepúlveda, *El Monasterio de San Jerónimo el Real de Madrid*, Madrid, 1883, pp. 128–9.

13 Pedro García Dovalle, '*Gaçeta, Madrid á 14 de Dec[iembre] 1613*', BN Mss 18419, fol. 39.

14 *Relaciones*, pp. 557 and 561–2.

15 R. de Mesonero Romanos, *El Antiguo Madrid*, reprint, Madrid, 2000, pp. 230–1. In 1803 Lady Holland wrote of it, 'the mansion is immense; it covers several acres of ground, stands in three parishes, and communicates by covered galleries with three churches. 3,000 persons (including 500 servants with their wives and children) lodge under the roof', quoted by Hugh Thomas, *Madrid. A Travellers' Companion*, New York, 1990, p. 240.

16 Anon., *Casa del Prado en la v[ill]a de Madrid*, n.d., ADL 8.

17 Anon., 'Relación General de los Patronazgos que tiene el Duque de Lerma mi señor', ADL 54/9. On Lerma's patronage of the Trinitarians, Ventura Ginarte González, *El Duque de Lerma. Protector de la Reforma Trinitaria*, Madrid, 1982. I am obliged to Prof. Xavier Gil Pujol for bringing this to my attention.

18 Anon., 'Relación General de los Patronazgos que tiene el Duque de Lerma mi señor', ADL 54, no. 9, no fol.; J. Álvarez y Baena, *Compendio histórico de las grandezas de la coronada villa de Madrid*, Madrid, 1786, pp. 109, 114; León Pinelo, *Anales de Madrid*, pp. 84–5, 101; González Dávila, *Teatro de las Grandezas de ... Madrid*, pp. 273–4.

19 See below, pp. 230–1.

20 *Relaciones*, p. 527; Álvarez y Baena noted that 'El edificio es magnifico y suntuoso, particular-mente en lo interior', *Compendio histórico*, pp. 248–9.

21 'Copia autentica del testamento cerrado del ex[celentísi]mo s[eño]r Duque de Uzeda', Alcalá de Henares, 31 May 1624, ADL 12, no. 26, no fol., copy. On the palace, R. Guerra de la Vega, *Madrid de los Austrias. Guía de arquitectura*, Madrid, 1999, pp. 88–9.

22 Lerma, 'Imbentario … 1617', ADL 53, fol. 17.

23 Escudero, *Los Secretarios*, 'Cargos', nos. 434–6; Torras i Ribé, *Franquesa*, p. 121.

24 Mesonero Romanos, *El Antiguo Madrid*, p. 99.

25 Lerma to Ángulo, Madrid, 5 April 1612, AGS CSR 302–1, fol. 196. See also, *Gaçeta y Nuevas*, pp. 37–8.

26 *Madrid. Atlas Histórico*, p. 316.

27 Anon., '*Relación de la fiesta solemnissima que uuo en Madrid, a la Traslacion del Conuento, y Monjas de la Encarnación …a dos de Iulio deste año*', printed by Simon Diaz, *Relaciones Breves de … Madrid*, pp. 101–3; Guerra de la Vega, *Madrid de los Austrias*, pp. 36–7.

28 See above, p. 86. Lerma coerced his cousin, the historian fray Prudencio de Sandoval, into pledging 44,000 ducats in 1610 to build a convent into which the nuns of a Bernardine house in Tórtoles could be moved. The foundation did not materialise – probably because the nuns refused to move to Lerma – but it is likely that fray Prudencio was forced to hand the money over and that it was used by the duke on his own buildings in Lerma, 'Relación General de los Patronazgos que tiene el Duque de Lerma mi señor', ADL 54, no. 9, no fol. and Lerma, 'Imbentario', ibid., 53, fol. 34b; Cervera Vera, *La Iglesia de San Pedro*, pp. 62–3.

29 'Estado de Lerma', ADL 15, no. 6, no fol.

30 The *cédulas* were dated 3 Mar., 4 Apr. and 2 Jul. 1612, Lerma, 'Imbentario', ADL 53, fol. 23b.

31 Payo Hernanz, *Lerma*, p. 74.

32 Fernández de Caso, *Discvrso*, p. 4b.

33 'Relación General de los Patronazgos que tiene el Duque de Lerma mi señor', ADL 54, no. 9, no fol., and Lerma, 'Testamento … (1617)', ibid., 12, p. 31. For a slightly different estimate, of 88,667 ducats, Cervera Vera, *La Iglesia de San Pedro*, p. 112 and p. 200, n. 67.

34 Cervera Vera, *La Iglesia de San Pedro*, pp. 60, 71–102 and 194–6.

35 *Relaciones*, p. 224; for a plan of the houses in 1610, Cervera Vera, *El conjunto palacial*, p. 336.

36 'Estado de Lerma: Villa de Lerma: Casas en la Villa de Lerma', ADL 23, no fol.; 'Hacienda acrecentada por compras y mercedes de su Mag[esta]d', ibid., 54, no. 9; 'Imbentario', fol. 1b; Cervera Vera, *El conjunto palacial*, p. 462.

37 Fernández de Caso, *Discvrso*, p. 18b; In 1725, the Duc de Saint-Simon visited Lerma in the entourage of Philip V and described the palace as being 'magnificent in its size, design and beauty and in the unity of its great rooms and in the landings and the ironwork of its staircase', 'Viaje a España', in García Mercadal, *Viajes de extranjeros por España y Portugal*, iii, at p. 330.

38 'Hacienda acrecentada', ADL 54, no. 9 no fol. On the contract, Cervera Vera, *El conjunto palacial*, p. 407–8.

39 Payo Hernanz, *Lerma*, pp. 37–44.

40 'Relación General de los Patronazgos que tiene el Duque de Lerma mi señor', ADL 54, no. 9, no fol.; Lerma, 'Testamento … (1617)', ibid. 12, pp. 12 and 34b; Cervera Vera, *La Iglesia de San Pedro*, pp. 63, 69 and idem, *El convento de Santo Domingo*, p. 19–20 and p. 119, n. 106 where he has the cost at 30,000 ducats.

41 'Relación General de los Patronazgos que tiene el Duque de Lerma mi señor', ADL 54, no. 9, no fol.

42 See above, p. 86.

43 It also had a printing press, granted by royal licence of 9 February 1618, 'Hacienda acrecentada', ADL 54, no. 9, no fol.

44 *Relaciones*, pp. 540, 543.

45 *CSPV*, xiii, 14 and 28 April 1614, nos. 232 and 242, pp. 112 and 117; J. M. Hayden, *France and the Estates-General of 1614*, Cambridge, UK, 1974, pp. 54–73. Bergin, *Rise of Richelieu*, pp. 128–34 and 147 and Mousnier, *Assassination of Henry IV*, pp. 260–1.

46 On the 'first war of Montferrat', Bombín Pérez, *Monferrato*, pp. 83–170.

47 Anon., '*Verdadera relación, en que se da cuenta del Nacimiento y Bautismo del Conde del Cid*', Seville, 1614, printed by Simon Diaz, *Relaciones Breves de ... Madrid*, p. 90; *Relacione*, pp. 551, 554–5.

48 See below, pp. 216–7. Conversely, the Admiral of Aragon used the occasion to move towards a reconciliation with Lerma, writing to him that he was lost for words with happiness at the birth of the heir, Guadalajara, 21 May 1614, RAH N-72, fol. 67, a copy.

49 Digby to James I, Madrid, 24 Dec. 1613/3 Jan. 1614 and 8 Jan./18 Jan. 1614 (OS), and to Sir Thomas Lake, Madrid, 12/22 Mar. 1614, NA SP 94/20, fols. 193–193b, 229, 252–252b; *Relaciones*, pp. 540–1, 543–5.

50 Sepúlveda, *El monasterio de San Jerónimo el Real de Madrid*, pp. 162–3.

51 Lerma to Inquisitor General, San Lorenzo, 8 and 24 Jul. 1614; *Auto* of Council of Inquisition, 10 Jul. 1614; *cnta* Inq, 27 Jul. 1614, AHN Inq lib. 271, fols. 158v–163.

52 *Relaciones*, Madrid, pp. 549–50.

53 *ACC* xxviii, pp. 224–6 and 256–9.

54 Anon., '*Relación de la iornada, y casamientos, y entregas de España, y Francia*', n. d., printed by Simon Diaz, *Relaciones Breves de ... Madrid*, pp. 94–8, at p. 94.

55 See the fascinating argument by Professor Feros that Lerma dissimulated over the *jornada*, in *Kingship and Favoritism*, pp. 235–6.

56 Perrens, *Les Mariages Espagnols*, pp. 546–7.

57 Lerma, 'Testamento ... (1617)', ADL 12, p. 35; Novoa, *Historia de Felipe III*, lx, pp. 534–5.

58 Anon., 'Deudos del Cardenal duque de Lerma ... (1625)', ADL 15, no 6, no fol.

59 *Cnta*. Fin. 6 Jan. 1615, AGS CJH 536–26–3.

60 *Cnta*. Fin. 24 March 1615, ibid., 536–26–4. Lerma had Juan de Ciriza write to Carrillo two days after the King's promise, demanding a further 100,000 ducats for household expenses, to Carrillo, de casa, 26 Mar. 1615, ibid., 536–24–9.

61 On the delays, Hayden, *France and the Estates-General of 1614*, pp. 149–73.

62 García Dovalle, *Gaçeta, en Madrid a 25 de Ag[os]to 1615*, BN Mss 18419, fol. 135.

63 Digby to Somerset, Madrid, 16/26 Jun. and 14/24 Jul. 1615, NA SP 94/21, fols. 118–18b and 140–140b; in the first of these letters, Digby observed that 'the true reason thereof is supposed to be that the Duke of Lerma who often had his Intentions crossed by this Councell may now dispose of all things more absolutely at his pleasure', at fol. 118b. The appointment of Salinas was not confirmed until August 1616, Dadson, 'The Duke of Lerma and the Count of Salinas', p. 18.

64 Digby to Winwood, Madrid, 16/26 Sep. 1615, NA SP 94/21, fol. 167b.

65 Digby recorded that there was discussion as to whether Benavente might take over responsibility for accompanying Anne to Bayonne: 'there hath lately beene some doubts made whether the Duke of Lerma would goe this journy or whether it would be transferred upon the Conde de Benauente, who since the kings going to Valladolid hath beene sworne of the Councell of State, and a perfect reconcilliation hath beene made of some distastes w[hi]ch were betwixt the Duke of Lerma and himself, whereupon ever since he came from being viceking of Naples he hath liued priuately from the Court ... of late the kings Confessor who hath for diuers yeares beene knowne to beare little affection either to the Duke or his proceedings, is made a Councellor of State', to Somerset, Madrid, 14/24 July 1615, ibid., fol. 140. On the oaths of Benavente and Aliaga on 28 July, García Dovalle, *Gaçeta, En Madrid a 25 de jullio 1615*, BN Mss 18419, fol. 125.

66 Bombín Pérez, *Monferrato*, pp. 134–7 and 153–70 and Parker, *Europe in Crisis*, pp. 113–14.

67 *Cnta*. St. 11 Jul. 1615, AGS E 1937, no fol.; on the charges levelled against him, García García, *La Pax Hispánica*, p. 308, n. 44.

68 Garçia Dovalle, *Gaçeta, En Madrid a 17 de ott. 1615*, BN Mss 18419, fol. 158.

69 *Cnta*. Carrillo, 18 Aug. 1615, AGS CJH 536–26–7.

70 Carrillo to Lerma, Madrid, 24 Aug. 1615, AGS CJH 536, no fol.; same to same, same place and date, and reply, Valladolid, 27 Aug., ibid., 536–24–10.

71 *Cnta*. Carrillo, 2 Sep. ibid., 536–26–5.

72 *CSPV*, xiii, 26 Aug. 1615, no. 994, p. 567; Hayden, *Estates-General*, p. 171.

73 See above, p. 44.

74 Novoa, *Historia de Felipe III*, lxi, pp. 2–3; Ruth Kleinman, *Anne of Austria Queen of France*, Columbus, OH, 1985, pp. 17–27.

75 The instructions given to Lerma and Uceda are copied in RAH G-29; 'Poder dado por el rey Felipe III a(l) ... duque de Lerma ... para tratar de las capitulaciones matrimoniales de su hija dona Ana de Austria', San Lorenzo, 30 Jul. 1612, fols. 1–1v; 'Poder de Phelipe III al Duque de Lerma para conducir a la frontera la Infanta D[oñ]a Ana', Burgos, 23 Oct. 1615, fols. 22–22v; and 33b–34; 'Instrucción al Duque de Lerma para el viage a la frontera', Burgos, 23 Oct. 1615, fols. 35–37v; 'Poder de Su M[agesta]d al Duque de Uzeda para llevar a la frontera la Infanta de España', Valladolid, 29 Oct. 1615, fols. 37v–38 and 'Instrucción del Rey al Duque de Uzeda para que por enfermedad de su padre execute el viage y las entregas', Miranda de Ebro, 28 Oct. 1615, fols. 39v–40.

76 Novoa, *Historia de Felipe III*, lxi, 6, 7–8, 33;

77 Novoa, *Historia de Felipe III*, lx, pp. 125–7, lxi, pp. 1–35; Pedro Mantuano, *Casamientos de España y Francia y viage del Duque de Lerma, llevando la Reyna Christianíssima Doña Ana de Austria al passo de Beobia, y trayendo la Princessa de Asturias*, Madrid, 1618, *passim*. Fernando de Acevedo observed , 'S. M. que tanto amava a la Señora Infanta quiso mostrar su amor, acompañandola de rebozo, y fue con su Corte y acompanamiento hasta donde fueron las entregas, y no se manifestó a los franceses', M. Escagedo Salmón, 'Los Acebedos', *BBMP*, v–ix, 1923–27, at vi, p. 235; Kleinman, *Anne of Austria*, pp. 2, 23, 24, 27.

78 González Dávila, *Teatro de las Grandezas de ... Madrid*, pp. 104–9.

79 Kleinmann, *Anne of Austria*, pp. 24, 27. Condé submitted to the King's Council (Treaty of Loudun, 3 May 1616). He was arrested in September 1616: Bergin, *Rise of Richelieu*, pp, 135–60 and Bercé, *Birth of Absolutism*, pp. 65–84.

80 García Dovalle, *Gaçeta, En Madrid a 19 de Xbre 1615*, BN Mss 18419, fol. 172; Mantuano, *Casamientos*, p. 55.

81 Albanel was a Catalan widower; he began instructing the Prince in March 1612, *Relaciones*, p. 469. See also Digby to Carleton, Madrid, 28 Mar./7 Apr. 1612, NA SP94/19, fol. 50.

82 Digby to Winwood, Madrid, 12/22 Nov. 1615, NA SP 94/21, fol. 189b; he noted that 'The Gentlemen of the Prince his Bedchamber are foure Noblemen, all neerely Allyed or deeply obliged unto the Duke of Lerma', Olivares being one of them, at fol. 189b; Novoa, *Historia de Felipe III*, lxi, p. 34; García Dovalle, *Gaçeta, En Madrid a xxi de Nouiembre de 1615*, BN Mss 18419, fol. 166b.

83 Anon., '*Relación de la iornada, y casamientos, y entregas de España, y Francia*', printed in *Relaciones Breves de ... Madrid*, pp. 94–8, at p. 96; León Pinelo, *Añales de Madrid*, pp. 110–11. On the reception by Madrid, AHM LA 33, fols. 454b–461, 23 Dec. 1615.

84 García Dovalle, *Gaçeta, En Madrid a 23 de hen[er]o 1616*, BN Mss 18419, fol. 181.

85 Digby to Winwood, Madrid, 29 Dec. 1615/8 Jan. 1616, NA SP 94/21, fol. 210b. The details are repeated in Digby to Sir William Trumbull, 23 Jan. 1616, *HMCT* v, no. 847, pp. 408–9.

86 Same to Secretary of State, Madrid, 14/24 Jan. 1616, ibid., 94/22, fol. 2.

87 García Dovalle, *Gaçeta, En Madrid a 23 de ebrero 1616*, BN Mss 18419, fol. 190.

88 Attendance Register, Council of State.

89 González Dávila, *Teatro de las Grandezas de .... Madrid*, pp. 88–99, 125–6; Diego de la Mota, *Libro del principio de la Orden de la Cavallería de S[an]Tiago del Espada*, Valencia, 1599, pp. 302–3 and López de Haro, *Nobiliario*, ii, 482.

90 *Cnta*. St. 27 May 1614, AGS E 2028, no fol.

91 Villafranca's determination to win *grandeza* had created one of the great scandals of the reign when in 1603 he renounced the appointment as Governor of Milan and stormed away from court because the King had refused him the honour. He was raised to the dignity in 1608 for his extraordinary embassy to Paris to negotiate the marriage agreement, *Relaciones*, pp. 168, 171, 173, 191, 195, 339–40. On Mejía, see above, pp. 126–7; On their appointment to the Council of State, *Relaciones*, pp. 423, 435.

92   *Cnta.* St. 16 Jan. 1614, AGS E 2027, no fol.

93   *Cnta.* St. 27 May 1614, AGS E 2028, no fol.

94   *Cnta.* St 11 Jun. 1614, ibid. On Villafranca's hostility towards Lerma, García García, *La Pax Hispánica*, p. 95.

95   *Cnta.* St. 30 Jun. 1614, AGS K 1615, no fol.

96   *Cnta.* St. 29 Jul. 1614, AGS E 2027.

97   Parker, in his *Army of Flanders*, pp. 214–15, 252 and his *Europe in Crisis*, p. 153; Tex, *Oldenbarneveldt*, ii, p. 475 and Israel, *Dutch Republic*, pp. 407–8. See also *CSPV*, xiii, 19, 22 and 30 Sep. 1614, xiii, nos. 381, 398, 403, 416.

98   González Dávila, *Teatro de las Grandezas de ... Madrid*, pp. 63–6.

99   *Cnta.* Carrillo, 28 Oct. 1614, AGS CJH 528, fol. 41.

100 *Don Quixote*, trans. J. M. Cohen, Harmondsworth, pp. 695 and 895.

101 Ibid., pp. 465–6 and 483.

102 See J. H. Elliott, 'Self-perception and Decline in Early Seventeenth-Century Spain', republished in *Spain and its World 1500–1700*, New Haven, 1989, pp. 241–61.

103 For an important discussion of the crown's financial policy, García García, *La Pax Hispánica*, pp. 205–38. See also, Pulido, *La Real Hacienda de Felipe III*, pp. 217–40.

104 Alonso de Velasco, Count of la Revilla, to Diego Sarmiento de Acuña, Madrid, 13 Dec. 1613, RB 11/2173, doc. 19 and *cnta* War, 16 Mar. 1616, AGS GA.

105 The costs of exchange brought the cost of the *asiento* to 4,040,000 ducats, *cnta.* Fin., 3 Jan. 1616, AGS CJH 542/7, fol. 3.

106 *Cnta.* Carrillo, 4 Jan. 1616, ibid., fol. 1.

107 See for example Philip's order to Carrillo that he find 500,000 ducats for Milan and 100,000 for Germany, *cnta.* Fin. 29 Apr. 1616, ibid., fol. 25.

108 *Cnta.* Carrillo, 4 Aug. 1616, ibid., no fol., a copy.

109 *Cnta.* Fin. 12 Dec. 1616, ibid., fol. 55. On Lerma's attitude to the involvement of the Dutch in Italy, see below, pp. 218–9.

110 Ibid., 21 Dec. 1616, ibid., fol. 58.

111 *RELACIÓN DE LA REAL HAZIENDA DE CADA AÑO Y DE LAS PROVISIONES Y GASTOS DEL DE 1617'*, presented to the Cortes on 3 Jul. 1617, *ACC*, xxx, pp. 15–32.

10

Cardinal-Duke

Disengagement: the collapse of Lerma's authority, 1616–17

Lerma continued to undermine his own authority during 1616 by failing to carry out his duties at court. Most revealing of all was his carelessness in performing his responsibilities towards the heir to the throne; in the spring Galcerán Albanell complained to Philip that Lerma was neglecting his duties as *ayo* of the prince.[1] Indeed, the duke could not even summon the energy to pay attention to the most important of his private affairs; in 1616, for the first time since 1600, he did not visit his ducal city, even though his great building programme was rapidly coming to completion.

One major decision could not be avoided; Juan de Acuña, Marquis del Valle and President of the Council of Castile, died in December 1615 and even in his decline Lerma dared not risk allowing the great presidency to fall into the hands of an opponent. He therefore ensured in February 1616 that Fernando de Acevedo was named to succeed del Valle: it was the last major appointment in court, government or Church that he influenced. Acevedo, who was forty-seven years old, owed all his advancement thus far to the exercise of favour. He had been appointed as Inquisitor of Seville (1603) and then *fiscal* (1605) and councillor (1608) of *la Suprema* by his brother, Juan Bautista, Inquisitor-General. Lerma then accelerated his progress to the bishopric of Osma (1610) and the archbishopric of Burgos (1613).[2] Fernando was an able and honest man who was well respected at court but he could never escape the reality of his past: he owed his career to the exercise of favour.

It is probable (although the evidence is ambiguous) that the Marquis of Siete Iglesias opposed Lerma over Acevedo's appointment and pushed the claims of Gabriel Trejo de Paniagua. Certainly, Lerma and Siete Iglesias now moved apart. Early in 1616 the court was filled with fevered speculation that the duke had taken García de Pareja, a young Sevillian courtier, as his 'new favourite' in place of the Marquis. When Lerma confirmed Siete Iglesias's decline by refusing to admit him into his chambers the Marquis furiously proclaimed for all to hear that 'when times were good I protected myself against a dark night', implying that he was wealthy enough now not to need the duke's favour. Enraged, Lerma had Siete Iglesias expelled from court and even threatened to institute a *visita* into the means through which he had accumulated his fortune. The Marquis promptly came to heel and the *visita* was cancelled.[3]

Siete Iglesias's decline was confirmed by the rise to favour with Lerma of Friedrich Gedler, a German Jesuit who became confessor to the duke in 1615. Lerma allowed Gedler to assume many of the functions that Siete Iglesias had performed. It was a poor choice by Lerma, for the disadvantages that Gedler had as a foreigner were compounded by the arrogance with which he conducted himself; it was shortly observed of him that 'happie was the Grandee or other who could gaine his good opinion'.[4] In particular, Gedler seems to have gone out of his way to make an especial enemy of Luis de Aliaga.

Lerma's reliance upon Pareja and Gedler represented a sad decline from the days of the plenitude of his power when he had an impressive cohort of widely experienced advisers available to him, notably the Cardinal of Toledo, the Count of Miranda, Juan de Borja, Diego Sarmiento de Acuña and the Count of Villalonga. Of that group, only the Cardinal now survived, and he was suffering a long physical decline that meant he was rarely at court. Among the lesser figures who remained available to the duke, only Tomás de Ángulo and Juan de Ciriza had significant political experience and both were socially junior figures who did not carry weight at court. In his decline, and in his growing demoralisation, Lerma had to rely upon advisers who were manifestly unequal to the responsibilities that he placed upon them.

The first of Lerma's opponents to move against him in 1616 was the Duke of Infantado.[5] Although Infantado's hostility to Lerma was familial and personal in character he cleverly chose to make the break over a matter of foreign policy. In January he presented a lengthy and exceptionally detailed paper to the Council of State supporting the proposal of Baltasar de Zúñiga that Philip should cede his claim to the throne of Bohemia to the Archduke Ferdinand in return for control over Alsace, thereby facilitating the movement of Spanish troops to the Low Countries. In the years after his appointment to the Council in 1603, Infantado had not performed his duties with any particular diligence or effectiveness but by 1611–12 – perhaps encouraged by the new belligerence being displayed by his colleagues on the Council – he had developed into a deeply serious councillor. Indeed, he attended the Council with such sustained diligence in the years after 1608 that by the end of Philip III's reign he had been present on more occasions than any other councillor (1,052). With his *parecer* of January 1616 he announced himself as a major figure on the Council, measuring himself against all of his colleagues as well as against

Lerma. As Infantado began to assert his importance at the Council of State (and to begin building an alliance with Zúñiga) he also won a major position at court: when the Marquis of Velada died (27 July 1616), Infantado succeeded him as the King's *mayordomo mayor*. Infantado now pursued his (and his brother's) vendetta against Lerma from a position of strength in both court and government.

Lerma's authority was further undermined by the growing assertiveness being displayed by a number of viceroys and ambassadors abroad. The command structure of Spanish Italy was transformed at the turn of 1615–16 by the appointment to its two most important positions – the governorship of Milan and the viceroyalty of Naples – of men who believed themselves destined to restore the prestige of Spanish arms, and to do so indeed even if it meant acting counter to the orders coming to them from Madrid. The Marquis of Villafranca arrived in Milan on 19 November 1615 and the Duke of Osuna in Naples on 27 July 1616.[6] Both announced themselves with grandiose declarations of intent: Villafranca boasted that he would destroy the power of Charles-Emmanuel and conquer Piedmont within a few days while Osuna was reported to have bragged that he would surpass 'all the captains who have ever been'.[7] The two men recognised each other as kindred spirits and co-operated closely; when Villafranca asked Osuna for some troops, he was sent twice as many as he had requested. Soon, Villafranca had an army of 22,000 soldiers and 3,000 cavalry.[8]

Villafranca and Osuna were far from alone in their disregard of the government in Madrid. In the key embassies in London, Prague and Venice the Counts of Gondomar and Oñate and the Marquis of Bedmar were also taking advantage of the collapse of Lerma's authority to pursue increasingly aggressive policies. The five men – Villafranca, Osuna, Gondomar, Oñate and Bedmar – have become known as 'the great proconsuls' but they did not form a party, save in that they were united in their lack of respect for the government in Madrid. Indeed, there were significant tensions between them; Gondomar, for instance, despised Villafranca and Osuna.[9] There were, however, two points on which the proconsuls were broadly agreed – that the truce with the United Provinces had demeaned Spanish greatness, creating more problems than it had solved, and that the government of the monarchy had become contemptible in its weakness. All took advantage of the disintegration of government but they had very different attitudes to it; for Gondomar, the collapse of Lerma's authority was a painful spectacle while for Osuna (who was about to unite his family to the Sandovals in marriage) it represented an opportunity to further his own ambitions abroad.

The Duke of Savoy responded to the challenge thrown down by Villafranca with a round of diplomatic and military activity that was energetic even by his standards. He proclaimed himself the talisman of anti-Spanish Europe and secured the promise of troops from the French Governor of Provence, Marshal

Lesdiguières. He also persuaded the United Provinces to allow troops to be raised for him in their territories and James I to promise to give him support if Spain broke the terms of the treaty of Asti. Charles-Emmanuel even presumed to involve himself in Venice's conflict with the Uskok pirates of the Adriatic (who were protected by the Archduke Ferdinand), offering to fight for the Republic in return for the payment of his expenses; Venice eagerly accepted his offer.[10]

Charles-Emmanuel raised his standard in Turin on 26 August 1616 and the second war of Monferrat began when Villafranca led his army into Piedmont on 14 September.[11] He was brilliantly successful; within a month he had taken more than fifty places, including the important town of San Germano. However, he did not have the resources with which to pursue the war and his campaign ground to a halt. Exactly as it did so, France gave a first indication that it would pursue a more active involvement in Italy, for in the autumn the aged ministers of Henry IV ('the Barbons') were replaced by new and vigorous men, among them the future Cardinal Richelieu, who became Minister of State for Foreign Affairs.[12] Spain could no longer assume that France would remain quiescent while she waged war in Italy.

It may have been the deepening seriousness of the crisis in Italy that obliged Lerma to stir himself into activity in the last weeks of the year. In November he engineered the acquittal of Hinojosa. Certainly, with war underway in Italy, Lerma appreciated that this was not the time to impeach a Spanish agent in Italy, however incompetent he had been. However, if Villafranca and Osuna needed any encouragement to disregard the policies of their government, Hinojosa's good fortune undoubtedly provided it.[13] In a meeting with the English Secretary at the turn of the month, Lerma once again insisted that Philip III had been forced into war by the contumacy of Charles-Emmanuel, whom he was reported to have described as an 'unquiet spirit' who was 'continually disturbing the world'.[14] But while Lerma gave vent to his hatred of the Duke of Savoy he fully appreciated that Spain did not have the financial resources to pursue the war; at the Council of State on 14 December he observed that it was a miracle that the troops in Italy had not mutinied for their backpay.[15]

Lerma's greatest concern at the end of 1616 was with the security of Italy. He was deeply anxious that the imminent arrival of 4,000 Dutch mercenaries to help Venice against Ferdinand might lead to the introduction of heresy into the Italian peninsula. On 26 December he therefore took the extraordinary step of attending a debate in the Council of War to consider whether the United Provinces were breaking the truce in sending help to Venice: it was the first time since 1599 that he had attended the Council. He declared himself fearful that a general conflagration was imminent in Italy and convinced that all the states of the peninsula were measuring the firmness of Spain's response. The *consulta* of the Council of War summarised his view:

Since Italy has so many provinces which have been preserved in (the Catholic) religion for so many years, if heresy is introduced there everything will be corrupted and one province after the other will be lost ... It is important to resist the help from the north-east and to suggest that it needs to be considered whether it is more important to maintain the faith and religion of Italy than to break the truce [with the United Provinces]. Although the troubled condition of the exchequer and the needs in which Your Majesty finds himself require remedy, in such an important cause he urges Your Majesty to find (the resources), for it is important that heretics should not enter into Italy because of the grave dangers that will result from their doing so.

The other councillors eagerly followed Lerma's lead. Infantado agreed that Philip should be prepared to risk breaking the truce to keep heresy out of Italy and Mejía reiterated his familiar theme that 'it would not be a bad thing for Your Majesty to break the truce because with very little extra expense than at present war could be made.[16]

On 29 December Philip ordered Osuna to sail into the Adriatic to force Venice (and by implication, Charles-Emmanuel) to the negotiating table. Osuna was full of his habitual self-confidence and on 12 January 1617 wrote to Uceda offering to join with Villafranca in putting an end to the war with Savoy within three months: the world, he assured Uceda, was laughing at Spain and was contemptuous of its inability to punish Charles-Emmanuel.[17] In addressing himself to Uceda rather than to Lerma, Osuna implicitly acknowledged that Lerma was withdrawing from power; he, too, was looking to a future which did not include Lerma.

Osuna's unbridled ambition provided Aliaga with the opportunity to distance himself from Uceda. In March 1617 the deputies of the Kingdom of Naples asked Philip for permission to make gifts of 40,000 ducats to Osuna 'for the good with which he governs the realm' and 50,000 ducats to Uceda. When the Council of State considered the proposal in October, Aliaga reminded his colleagues that it had been forbidden for viceroys to accept gifts since 1563. He noted that the King had allowed gifts of 80,000 ducats to be made to members of the Lemos family – 25,000 ducats to the dowager Countess of Lemos on the death of her husband in 1602 and 55,000 ducats to the seventh count and his wife in 1611. Aliaga's colleagues did not follow him in his tacit condemnation of the Lerma regime but Mejía spoke of the 'evil consequences' of allowing the gifts to be given, and Zúñiga pointedly agreed with him. Philip allowed the monies to be presented to Osuna and Uceda.[18] Aliaga had lost the encounter, but he had further identified the Sandovals, father and son, with a corruption of standards in government. Even as he lost the argument over the grants to Osuna, Aliaga continued to hold the moral high ground.

By the beginning of 1617 Lerma barely maintained any pretence of interest in governmental affairs. A meeting of the Cortes of Castile opened on 4 February 1617 to vote a new *millones* grant but Lerma did not deign to have himself elected as a procurator, and when the *servicios ordinarios y extraordinarios* were voted (6 March and 4 April) it was the President of the Council of Castile rather than Lerma who informed Philip of the award.[19] Indeed, so little interest did Lerma take in the work of the Cortes that its members had to urge Acevedo to persuade him to assign a day when he would be able to deal with their business (16 June 1617).[20]

Lerma's indifference may well have encouraged the procurators to extend their attacks on the policies of the government. Throughout the spring of 1617 the procurators insisted that Castile was enveloped in a crisis of depopulation which had gathered pace since the *repartimiento* of 1611. They urged that a census be organised to establish the extent of the demographic changes that had taken place and criticised the government for the burdens that it was imposing upon the kingdom. It was a measure of the weakness of the crown's authority that Fernando de Acevedo was obliged to present a budget of the crown's projected income and expenditure to the procurators to justify the request for a new *millones* grant (3 July). He spoke dispiritedly of the hostility to Spain throughout Europe – 'since almost the whole of the rest of the world is opposed to this crown and (are) enemies to its greatness, either publicly or in secret'.[21] He secured permission for the crown to mint 800,000 ducats of *vellón* as an interim measure until the *millones* were granted. On 1 August, Acevedo formally initiated negotiations for the new tax. He thereby opened the floodgates to debate on the condition of Castile and its ability to contribute yet another major grant; the debate inevitably took the form of a wide-ranging and unrestricted review of the policies of the government since 1598. This of course inflicted further damage upon Lerma's reputation as the leading minister of the King during exactly that period.[22]

In foreign affairs, too, the government was losing control of events. In particular, relations with England began to break down in the spring of 1617. Lerma reportedly made 'loud complaints' to the English ambassador when he heard that James had allowed Sir Walter Raleigh to sail for the Indies and he threatened that Spain would station a fleet at Gibraltar to prevent James sending any help to Charles-Emmanuel.[23] More serious still, the death of the *infanta* Margarita on 11 March meant that Philip would have to choose between the English and imperial marriages; James I's hopes of a Spanish match effectively ended with the death of Margarita, although in his desperation he quite failed to recognise the fact.[24]

On 20 March, in Prague, the Count of Oñate, who had succeeded Zúñiga as ambassador to the Emperor, agreed with the Archduke Ferdinand that Spain would recognise Ferdinand's right to the throne of Bohemia in return for the cession of Alsace and two imperial enclaves in Italy. Although the Council of State agreed to ratify the treaty Lerma was deeply offended by the independence that Oñate had shown and argued that Spain should not commit herself to actively supporting Ferdinand. He protested too, that forceful ambassadors were presuming to make policy and then to impose it on the government in Madrid:

> It is a great distress to see that those who are entrusted with such important affairs far away and who cannot be assisted do not see the difficulties that they are creating.

Lerma informed the Council that María would be married to an Austrian cousin. The English marriage was dead, but Lerma expressed the hope that negotiations could be spun out.[25]

In the spring of 1617, Osuna sent his fleet into the Gulf of Venice, and Villafranca once again led his army into Piedmont. Lerma spoke (as was reported) 'with great vehemence' to the English secretary about the help that James I had given to Savoy and asserted that Philip's cause 'was so just that he would have no fear even if all the world banded together against him'. He lambasted Charles-Emmanuel – 'such an unquiet prince, as was well known, that he had no other purpose but to throw the whole world into confusion'.[26] But still, Lerma struggled to bring about a peaceful solution. On 18 June he met with the Venetian ambassador, the papal nuncio and the French ambassador to insist that while Philip would stand by the treaty of Asti he would not permit the smallest alteration in it. Lerma held out the prospect of a settlement in the war between Ferdinand and Venice, it was reported, because of 'his desire to see peace established in Christendom and the heretics expelled who have been introduced into Italy.'[27] An understanding was reached which formed the basis of agreements between Savoy and Mantua and between Venice and the Archduke (Treaty of Madrid, 18–24 June).[28] It was Lerma's last major achievement in foreign affairs and it was born out of a determination to preserve Spanish hegemony in Italy and to maintain the religious orthodoxy of the Italian peninsular that had always marked his exercise of power. There was deep conviction on his part. But there was also calculation: his cardinalate, after all, depended upon it.

Lerma: the Testament, 12 June 1617

By the spring of 1617 Lerma had completed the plans for the celebrations in his ducal city that would mark the completion of his enormous building programme and preface his formal farewell to public life. He must therefore have been especially gratified when Philip let it be known how much he was looking forward to spending the summer in Lerma.[29] Lerma decided to travel a few days ahead of the King so that he could supervise the final arrangements for the celebrations. Before he did so, on 12 June in the royal palace Lerma signed a new version of his Will and Testament in front Francisco Testa, an *escribano*, and seven witnesses.[30]

The Testament was the most solemn document of Lerma's life. It incorporated all the major papers by which he had defined his wealth and estate, most notably the will and testament that he and Catalina had drawn up in 1603 and the agreements that he had made with Cristóbal in 1607 and 1610. It was a statement of what he had done with his inheritance and in effect with his life, and it justified his conduct to the Almighty and to the members of his own family, past, present and future. But it was also a highly political document in which Lerma defended his conduct during his *valimiento*. Intent on pre-empting any future attacks on his family's wealth, he ordered that a copy be given at his death to the King (whoever that might be).

Lerma drew his testamentaries and executors from family and political circles. Among his senior relatives, he nominated his sons, Uceda and Saldaña; his sister, the dowager Countess of Lemos; and the Cardinal of Toledo. From among his *hechuras*, he chose his most trusted confidants – Fernando de Acevedo, Archbishop of Burgos and President of the Council of Castile; Lic. Melchior de Molina, councillor of Castile; Juan de Ciriza, secretary of the Council of State; Friedrich Gedler, his confessor; and Juan Ladrón de Guevara, his secretary. In this most formal and considered document, Lerma also included the Marquis of Siete Iglesias: despite all that had separated them in recent years, the old spell lingered on.[31]

Lerma began by invoking the Most Holy Trinity; the Virgin Mary; his 'patrons and advocates', saints Francis, Dominic and Santiago; his guardian angel, and – significant of the cast of his mind, perhaps – 'all the celestial court'. He instructed his executors to compile an inventory of his possessions as soon as possible after his death, to fulfil the terms of the Testament (and of any subsequent codicils that he might draw up) and then to incorporate all other goods and incomes into the *mayorazgo* of Lerma, together with the yield from any property sales that he might yet undertake.[32] Lerma reminded his testamentaries that the Pope and Philip III had given him the right to dispose of the fruits of the *encomienda mayor de Castilla* for twelve years after his death and advised them that he would in time specify the purposes for which the revenues were to be used.[33]

Lerma recorded that it was his intention to die in Valladolid and ordered that if he did not do so his body was to be immediately taken there, accompanied by twelve Franciscan and Dominican friars, for interment in *San Pablo*. All mourning was to be circumspect, most notably in the eulogy at the funeral. No fewer than 20,000 masses were to be said for him in the churches and religious houses of which he was the patron. The first of these was to be celebrated, if time permitted, on the day of his death, and on the following day as many more were to be conducted as proved possible. In each of the next nine days, sung masses were to be held in the place of his death and in all of his religious foundations. On the first anniversary of his death, a novena was to be celebrated in *San Pablo*. He had committed himself to having 6,000 masses said for the souls of the King and Queen and their family, and half of these had already been celebrated; he ordered that the remaining 3,000 should be said after his death. Similarly, he had already had 20,000 out of 40,000 masses said for the souls of the people in his charge – by which he presumably meant his vassals and well as his family and his dependants – and he now stipulated that the remainder of these were to be celebrated after his death.

His charitable provisions were practical; one hundred 'of the most naked' poor of the city of Valladolid and the lands of his estates were to be clothed at his expense in the days following his death, and during the next fortnight 16,000 ducats were to be distributed as alms to the poor of his lands. Over an unstipulated longer period 4,000 *fanegas* of wheat were to be allocated to poor people living on his estates.[34]

Lerma now had very little freedom to dispose of any property; neither could he alienate the lands and possessions that were incorporated into the *mayorazgo* nor could he alter the details of the settlements that he had made for his children. He was further constrained by the commitments he had entered into when making his agreements with his 'very dear and beloved' wife and with Cristóbal.[35] He could dispose now only of the usufruct of his rents and of the sums which had been ring-fenced in the agreements that he had made with Cristóbal in 1607 – 147,380 ducats for the endowment of religious and charitable benefactions; 152,400 ducats for his funeral and testamentary expenses; and 40,000 ducats for his charitable bequests and legacies. These needs therefore required 339,780 ducats in cash, a staggering amount even by Lerma's standards. Moreover, he had now to find this money while continuing to meet the costs of running his estates and bringing his great building programme to fruition and maintaining his standing at court. Accordingly, he made no new provisions but juggled his resources, altering some details and bringing his affairs up to date as best he could. This was not the simple matter that it should have been, for not only were the sums themselves so substantial but after the agreements with Cristóbal in 1607 Lerma had continued to alienate his resources, confident that he could always bypass any agreement and persuade the King to circumvent any difficulty. In spending without thought of the morrow Lerma had hopelessly over-extended even his fabled resources. He had now to square the circle.

Lerma calculated that in the decade since 1607 he had spent 489,305 ducats on his buildings and on improving the lands and rents of his *mayorazgo*. Slightly more than half of this (272,964 ducats: 56 per cent) had been spent on his secular estate and the remainder (214,342 ducats: 44 per cent) on his ecclesiastical foundations. Nearly two-thirds of the money had been spent in the city of Lerma (309,344: 63 per cent). By his own account, therefore, the Duke had since 1607 spent on average just under 50,000 ducats a year in making improvements to his estate. This was an enormous amount – only twenty-seven aristocrats in Spain had annual incomes of 50,000 ducats or more in 1617 – but Lerma was deliberately understating the realities of his expenditure, for most of the 487,305 ducats (see Table 6)[36] had been spent since 1613. To take one example: while Lerma allowed that he had spent 1,496 ducats in Arganda it is a matter of record that he had spent over 40,000 ducats in the town.[37] The figures that he provided therefore have to be regarded as an underestimate of his expenditure in this period and it is reasonable to suppose that in the years 1613–17 he was spending something in the order of 80,000 ducats a year or more on his building programme – a figure that surpassed the annual income of all but fifteen aristocrats in 1617.

Already, Lerma had overspent the 147,380 ducats that he had reserved for the endowment of his religious and charitable benefactions by 460 ducats. He had bought 3,542 ducats of annual rent (capital value: 70,840 ducats) and now pledged himself to provide a further 3,850 ducats of annual rent (capital value: 77,000 ducats) from his current rents rather than from his *bienes libres*. He was quite entitled to do this, but his new endowments would expire on his death unless he transferred them to his *bienes libres*. However, if he did that he would then have no further room for manoeuvre since the 147,380 ducats reserved

Table 6 Lerma's expenditure on his properties, 1607–17 (ducats)

Expenditure	Location		%
309,344	Lerma		63.0
13,104	Ventosilla		2.6
92,412	Madrid		19.0
17,093	Denia castle		3.5
1,496	Arganda		0.3
33,667	Valdemoro		7.0
14,419	Valladolid –	9,965 – *San Pablo*	2.0
		1,241 – *San Diego*	0.2
		3,213 – *Nuestra Señora de Belén*	0.6
3,516	Ampudia		0.7
4,254	Cea		
489,305			98.9

for ecclesiastical endowments would be fully committed. He showed no signs of worrying about the dilemma, claiming once again that he was returning some of the divine munificence that had been showered upon him – 'I implore our Lord to be pleased to accept (this) for his divine Majesty, in recognition of the great favours that He has given me, and the charity that he has employed toward me, and for His honour and glory.'[38]

While Lerma begged for divine support what he needed most immediately was filial indulgence, and it was with this in view that he solemnly reaffirmed 'the great love that I have always had, and continue to have for [Cristóbal], for the great deal that I esteem him and hope for from him on account of his great courage and qualities.'[39] The florid piety of Lerma's language was designed to pressure Cristóbal into accepting his right to make the new endowments and then – more importantly – into maintaining them after his death. Even at this solemn moment Lerma could neither limit his ambitions nor refrain from blurring the edges of the agreements that he had made with his heir. He did not seem to worry that he was putting an unnecessary strain on his relationship with Cristóbal.

Indeed, Lerma continued even now to place burdens upon the *bienes libres* that they could not conceivably support if they were to carry any of the 3,850 ducats of income from the usufruct of his rents. He hoped to situate the 2,000 ducats of rent for the two Dominican houses in Lerma in his rents, but if he was not able to do so they were to come from the 76,540 ducats that were still reserved: that would take up 40,000 ducats of capital, virtually half of what he had reserved. Notwithstanding this, he stipulated that after his death 30,000 ducats were to be set aside from the 76,540 ducats to endow 500 ducats of income for a number of charitable purposes – to release needy people from prisons; to marry 'fallen women, so that they can be freed from their sin, or young women who are in clear danger of losing themselves', and for masses for the souls in purgatory.[40]

Lerma even had to cut into some of the 152,400 ducats that he had reserved for his burial costs. He doubled his commitment to ransoming captives from the infidel, taking 10,000 ducats from the 152,400 ducats with which to do so. Far more substantially, he acknowledged that there would almost certainly be a shortfall in the monies available for the *Casa Profesa* of the Society of Jesus and authorised his executors to take up to 70,000 ducats from his burial expenses to spend on this if he had not endowed that amount from his rents by the time of his death. This was against the spirit if not the letter of the agreement of 1607. However, Lerma was determined to build the church in honour of Francisco de Borja and of the Society that he had helped to bring to 'its present perfection'. In truth, he seems to have had no idea how he was going to do this.[41]

Lerma reminded Cristóbal that he had promised to employ all of his household servants reminded him of 'the grace and love that I have always held for him'.[42] He reserved the right to add in his own hand to the provisions of the Testament and declared Cristóbal to be his universal heir.[43]

While the details of Lerma's Testament were highly confidential, it must have been well known what he was doing: that a document had been sworn in front of seven witnesses would not have long remained a secret in the corridors of the royal palace. It is probable that Lerma chose to complete and sign the document in the royal palace rather than in the privacy that he could easily have had in his own palace across the city precisely *because* he wanted the King to know that he had made his Testament and put his affairs into order.

This is confirmed by a curious incident which seems to have taken place on the next day. On 13 June Lerma sent about seventy cartloads of possessions on their way to Lerma itself, each of them large enough to require five mules to pull them.[44] Tellingly, the convoy did not proceed on the convenient and direct route northwards out of Madrid but took a cumbersome and difficult detour across the heavily-populated heart of the capital to the royal palace. As it passed the palace it made a great deal of noise. Again, the conclusion seems inescapable: Lerma wanted to make the point to the King that he was preparing to leave court. Certainly, Philip was livid with the disorder created outside his palace and administered a public rebuke to Lerma. The duke made a show of disclaiming responsibility, dismissing a number of his servants. Unmoved, Philip announced that he would not now be going to Lerma. There was clearly more than a row about noise here. One observer thought that 'it may be the beginning of a greater inconvenience unto the Duke'.[45]

The conjuncture of the events of 12 and 13 June 1617 cannot have been coincidental. Two things may be observed of Lerma with some conviction – that he was punctilious in arranging and servicing his own interests and that while he took advantage of his relationship with Philip III to become fabulously wealthy he never took liberties with the majesty of the King. But in the last days of his *valimiento* he did so: in signing his Testament and having it witnessed in the royal palace and in then sending his enormous convoy across Madrid to create a disturbance outside the royal palace, he must have been acting with cold calculation. There seems only one conclusion: Lerma wanted the King to know that he was finally ready to force the issue of his retirement from the *valimiento*. He had passed the point of merely talking about retirement and was now actively preparing to go. If this was so, Philip's fury is readily understandable. For nearly two decades he had showered unimaginable favours upon Lerma in a way which he knew had demeaned his kingship in many people's eyes (and, perhaps increasingly, even in his own) and he was now personally and publicly rejected by him. Even Philip III could not take that affront to his majesty.

It was presumably to mollify the King that Lerma now spent three weeks with him in Madrid and in the Escorial. Certainly, by the time that the duke left the monastery to travel to Lerma, the King's anger had subsided. The duke arrived in Lerma on 5 August. On 11th August, Philip wrote to him: he was ill and complained that Lerma had not kept closely enough in touch with him. The King passed on news of the court and signed off, as was his practice, 'your friend'. Lerma replied on 27 August, taking care to state that 'I wish ... to see Your Majesty and serve him' and expressing his eagerness to meet the King and to kiss his hand once again: it must have been in doubt. He sent Philip a variety of news, personal, political and religious, and signed the letter as 'the most humble slave of Your Majesty'. Philip in turn affirmed that he was anxious to see Lerma, and that he would be jubilant when they met. He again signed himself 'your friend' and enclosed a letter from his heir which expressed a sentiment that a king could not have written – 'hurry back, for we cannot suffer so long a separation from you'. Despite the unfortunate contretemps of June, Lerma still held the king's favour and deep affection.[46] He left his ducal city on 27 August to return to Madrid. His life, and his life's work, were approaching their climax.

Lerma reached a capital city that was celebrating a military triumph in Italy; on 26 July the Marquis of Villafranca had redeemed Spain's military prestige by capturing Vercelli, the strongest fortified town in Piedmont. Although Charles-Emmanuel claimed a compensatory triumph when his troops burned Felizzano on 2 September it did not compare with Villafranca's success: Spain was victorious in the 'second War of Montferrat'.[47]

It was not a moment too soon, for 3,000 Dutchmen arrived in Venice in July and shortly afterwards twenty-two Dutch and English warships sailed into the Adriatic to prevent help from Osuna reaching Ferdinand.[48] Villafranca enjoyed his triumph; he laughed dismissively when it was suggested to him that he might restore Vercelli in order to reach a peaceful settlement to the dispute. The Venetian Senate informed its ambassadors that Villafranca 'does not seem to be disposed' to obey orders from Spain 'if they are not to his taste' and that 'in this attitude he is supported by the Duke of Osuna'.[49]

Climax, October 1617: 'the happiest, most famous and celebrated *fiestas* that the world has seen'[50]

Lerma rejoined Philip at the Escorial on 31 August and spent three weeks with him before returning again to Lerma. What passed between the two men in these weeks is not recorded. However, there can be little doubt that the King had reconciled himself to Lerma's departure from office, for there are clear indications that, despite the apparent warmth of his letters of August, Philip was now deliberately constructing an alliance of Lerma's enemies to give himself the strength of purpose to dispose of his *valido*'s services. Philip summoned the Count of Benavente back to court, and he returned, most reluctantly, on 20 May. On 1 July Baltasar de Zúñiga reached the capital after spending three months on his return from Prague.[51] Philibert of Savoy arrived on 26 August and Cardinal Zapata on 6 September.[52] Moreover, on 14 August Philip raised Lerma's chief opponent in government to exalted rank when he appointed Fernando Carrillo to the presidency of the Council of the Indies with retention of that of Finance. He expressly noted in Carrillo's title to office that he was promoting him because of the deep satisfaction that he had taken from his service as President of Finance.[53] Lerma's enemies were gathering, and it was the King who was bringing them together.

Lerma arrived back in Madrid by 8 September. The King himself wrote to his daughter Anne, Queen of France, of how well Lerma had been received on his return to the capital and of how much he himself was looking forward to the *fiestas* in Lerma.[54] On 13 September, the duke at last presented himself at the Cortes. He urged the procurators to vote the 18,000,000 ducats of a new *millones* grant; and, when they promised to look more urgently at ways of helping the King, it was Lerma who carried the message to Philip.[55] Ten days later, the Cortes approved the grant of 17,500,000 over nine years, insisting that the money be used only for royal expenses and that the *consignaciones* should be administered by the Kingdom itself: Lerma's *valimiento* was to end with a further deepening of the burden on the taxpayers of Castile.[56]

Lerma may have played some role in the treaties that brought the conflicts in Italy to an end during September–October 1617. On 12 September, the Treaty of Madrid brought the war between Venice and the Archduke Ferdinand and his Uskok allies to an end by allowing both sides to withdraw with honour. Spain's war with Savoy was brought to a conclusion by the 'Agreement at Pavia', in which both parties agreed to restore the towns they had taken and to observe the Treaty of Asti (9 October). Montferrat was restored to the Duke of Mantua but Charles-Emmanuel escaped once again from a war with Spain without punishment.[57]

On Madrid's feast day, 21 September, Lerma led a troop of horsemen in what proved to be a valedictory tour around the centre of the city.[58] He then left for Lerma, arriving on 1 October. The King and his household joined him on 3 October. Philip had clearly forgiven Lerma for the tensions between them that had taken place in June, for he stayed in Lerma for three weeks. Three times – in 1605, 1608 and 1610 – the duke had played host to Philip in Lerma for longer periods, but those visits had each been notable for the manner in which the duke had systematically isolated Philip for his own purposes.[59] The entertainments of 1614 had lasted for a fortnight and, spectacular though they were, took place in a city that was covered with building works. Those of 1617 lasted for three weeks and were celebrated against the magnificent backcloth of Lerma's completed buildings and in a city that was extravagantly dressed for the occasion; the streets were covered with bullrushes and the walls were decorated with richly brocaded cloth. The *fiestas* formed a solemn and generous farewell to public life. They also marked the climactic point in Lerma's relationship with the King, at once a celebration and an ending.[60]

It was central to the spirit of the great *fiesta* that Lerma unveiled the greatest of his paintings for viewing by his guests. It will be recalled that when the court left Valladolid Lerma had begun to break up his collection of paintings, chiefly because he no longer had the wall-space on which to hang them, and that only in *San Pablo* and Ventosilla did he maintain significant collections. While his great building programme was gathering pace he seems to have had most of his paintings in storage – in his palace in Madrid in 1611–12 he appears to have had fewer than two dozen paintings on display. During June–October of 1617 he sent most of the pictures that he held in Madrid to Lerma so that they could be displayed during the great celebrations of the summer. It is evident that there was a great deal of discussion about where individual pictures should be hung, for it was not until the celebrations were completed, in November and December, that inventories were drawn up listing where they were hung. Unfortunately, these documents do not normally identify the artist responsible for each picture.[61] In the two-story *pasadizo* to the north of the *plaza ducal*, Lerma displayed a collection which celebrated his years in power. The portrait of himself by Pedro Antonio Vidal was accompanied by a picture of his eldest son as a child by an unknown artist. He also had two portraits of Philip III as a prince, but again the inventory does not identify the artist. He displayed six large pictures of La Hinojosa's campaigns against Charles-Emmanuel and dozens of pictures of the great cities of Europe such as Rome, Paris and Venice; included here were pictures of Ostend and Rheinberg, presumably in celebration of the great military triumphs of Ambrosio Spínola. Fifty-one portraits 'of different people' completed the collection in the *pasadizo*. Naturally, the most celebrated pictures were on display within the palace itself. Here, for instance, the inventory records that in Lerma's own quarters, facing *San Blas*, hung an *Ecce Homo* by Titian, while in his cell in *San Blas* Titian's *Salome* was accompanied by a *St Francis* by El Greco. Intriguingly, the artists responsible for portraits of Pope Paul V, Philip II as a child and Lerma himself in the ducal quarters are not identified in the inventory.

The entertainments in the *plaza ducal* and on the riverbank were on the grandest scale: a procession of floats included a full-sized galley; bulls were run which were (on the whole) suitably ferocious; the gentlemen of the court showed themselves off to their best advantage in the *juegos de caña*, while court dwarfs and a company of sixteen giants provided comic relief. A comedy by Luis

Vélez de Guevara was performed (with the poet Antonio Hurtado de Mendoza as stage manager), while the counts of Saldaña and Lemos produced pieces that they had written: it was tacitly understood that their rivalry in the theatre mirrored their deep personal hostility and no winner was declared. The great triumphs of Philip III's reign were celebrated, most notably the expulsion of the *moriscos*. The *fiestas* at Lerma in 1617 became legendary; Pedro de Herrera described them as 'the happiest, most famous and most celebrated *fiestas* that the world has seen'.[62]

It was in keeping with Lerma's priorities that the chief celebrations were liturgical rather than secular. The masses for the anniversaries of Francisco de Borja and Queen Margaret on 1 and 3 October were followed on 6 October by a mass in *La Madre de Dios;* both of the latter were attended by the King and his children. On 7 October, the Church of *San Pedro* was formally opened with the procession of the Translation of the Blessed Sacrament and a pontifical high mass which was sung by five choirs, prominent among them those of *San Pedro* and *San Blas*.[63] Over the next few days, masses were said by the abbot, archdeacon and *chantre* (8–10 October); on 17 October, the Cistercian nuns were welcomed to their convent of *Nuestra Señora de San Vicente*, and on 25 October the Carmelite friars entered the house of *Santa Teresa*. Distinguished churchmen said mass or preached at these masses – the papal nuncio; the Cardinal-Archbishop of Toledo; fray Hortensio Felix Paravicino, the celebrated royal preacher (and friend of El Greco); Juan de Guzmán, the Patriarch of the Indies and fray Antonio Trejo de Paniagua, General of the Franciscans (and friend of Siete Iglesias). When the celebrations were concluded, Lerma solemnly presented his great church with a dazzling array of ornaments and sacred vessels. He then departed with the King on 20 October. When they stopped at Ventosilla to relax, Philip wrote to Anne, the Queen of France, about how impressed he had been by the celebrations in Lerma.[64]

It was now well known in Madrid that the duke was about to become a cardinal, and he did not deny the rumours when they were put to him.[65] This gave a special resonance to two further celebrations that he held during December. On 11 December, Philip honoured Uceda by allowing the marriage of his daughter Isabel to Juan Téllez-Girón, Marquis of Peñafiel, to take place in the royal chapel in the Alcázar. The King himself served as a *padrino* and allowed his children to dine at the bride's table.[66] Philip then rode with Isabel to the Duchess of Osuna's house. The splendour of the occasion led Francis Cottington to report admiringly that there could be no doubt 'how much this king doth styll endeuor to ho[nou]r the D[uke] of Lerma and his howse', while Jerónimo de Quintana, historian of Madrid, described the celebrations as 'one of the greatest *fiestas* that have been seen in the court'.[67]

On 17 December, the body of Francisco de Borja was handed over to

Lerma, and on the following day Cardinal Zapata celebrated the inaugural mass in the *Casa Profesa*. Once again, the King and his children attended, and they then stayed for a celebratory banquet. The sermon was preached by Jerónimo Florencia, SJ. The church was given the name of *Nuestra Señora del Prado*.[68] Lerma had achieved one of the defining ambitions of his life.

The year was brought to an end by a minor but significant award by the King, when on 20 December he gave Lerma the right to dismiss all the officials in the royal palaces in Valladolid with the exception of the *veedor* and *pagador;* Philip clearly accepted that Lerma was preparing to depart for Valladolid.[69] Lerma now effectively withdrew from public affairs.[70] He was ready to leave the court that he had dominated for nearly twenty years.

Cardinal-Duke, 1618

As Lerma prepared to abandon court, Europe rushed headlong towards what Bohdan Chudoba called in 1952 'the longest continuous war in the history of Christian civilization'.[71] In May 1618, two events took place within days of each other which convinced much of Europe that both branches of the House of Habsburg were intent on war: in Italy, the discovery of what became known as 'the Conspiracy of Venice' (18 May) seemed to prove that Osuna had indeed attempted to overthrow the Republic while in Bohemia 'the Defenestration of Prague' (23 May) confirmed that the Austrian Habsburgs were pursuing a religious crusade against their opponents. In reality, the importance of both events was greatly exaggerated; the chief conspirator in 'the Conspiracy of Venice' was probably the Doge of Venice rather than the Duke of Osuna, while the men thrown out of a window in Prague castle walked way with relatively insignificant injuries.[72] However, the widespread belief in Europe that Spain was behind the 'Conspiracy of Venice' damaged the reputation of Philip and – as had happened with the 'Gunpowder Plot' of 1605 in England – identified him with an attempt to overthrow a European government by violence. The Spanish government faced this complex series of enveloping crises in a state of suspended animation as Lerma spent six months dallying over his departure and as the King built up his determination to dismiss him. Lerma's prevarication therefore had substantial importance at one of the critical junctures in the history of Europe.

Aliaga did not wait for the final confirmation of the award of Lerma's cardinalate before spreading the news of his elevation. Indeed he even rather waspishly encouraged speculation that Lerma was hoping to succeed his dying uncle in the primatial see.[73] On 26 March the cardinalate was granted, and it was a mark of special favour from the pope that it carried the title of the parish of San Sisto, which lay within the city of Rome itself. On 5 April Lerma joyously told Acevedo 'I want to be a great cleric'. He withdrew now from the Alcázar to live in his own palace, dressed in priestly robes and assisted at the celebration of mass (although he was not yet a priest). Philip ordered that every window in Madrid should display lighted candles as a mark of public joy, and many nobles and religious held firework displays in celebration. On the night of 10–11 April the nomination as cardinal arrived at court and on the following morning Lerma kissed Philip's hands and went to the Church of the Theatines, where he again assisted at mass.[74] The King thereby associated himself in the closest fashion with the celebrations over Lerma's cardinalate. However, as Lerma enjoyed the symbols of his new dignity, his position at court finally disintegrated. At the turn of March–April, Philip gave him written instructions to organise his affairs so that he could retire from court to enjoy the grants that he had given him. The King had finally accepted that his *valido* was leaving him. It was perhaps for this reason that when Lerma received his biretta he did so in secret (10 May).[75]

The perception that Philip took pleasure in Lerma's elevation to the cardinalate was confirmed by a letter he wrote to his daughter Anne on 6 June in which he observed how well Lerma wore ecclesiastical dress: 'he has taken very well to the new habit, and I believe that if you saw him dressed in the [purple] you would not recognise him'. He then made it clear that he approved of Lerma's decision to become a cardinal: 'he has taken this decision with very good intentions and thus I believe that God will help him'.[76] There can be no doubt that Philip approved of Lerma's decision to become a cardinal.

The accounts of Acevedo and Novoa both emphasised that Philip had ceased to resist Lerma's attempt to retire. Acevedo recorded that

> The duke having changed from secular to ecclesiastical clothing, his cardinal's hat arrived. His Majesty wanted him to retire, because he had asked him many times to grant him the licence [to do so] and he had not obtained it – either because his Majesty wanted him to assist him or because it did not appear to]the King] to be the appropriate time. The King found it better after he had become a cardinal since ... ecclesiastical ministers are the more esteemed the less they deal in affairs.[77]

Novoa observed that Philip withdrew his favour from Lerma and noted, without giving any indication as to the exact time of which he was writing,

> He asked and begged him (as he had done on other occasions) to give him the licence to retire to Lerma, where he had constructed some buildings with this purpose and hope in mind. The delay had cost him no little heartache ... Many times he had the desire to become a discalced religious of the Order of St Francis ... Finally, he asked for a licence from his king to retire; he replied that he was agreeable, and that in his time he would give him it.[78]

The fullest account of Lerma's departure from court was written by an anonymous observer at court who recorded that Aliaga persuaded Philip to grant an extension so that Lerma could prepare to leave with his reputation intact.[79] This account does not confirm that Lerma had intended to become a discalced Franciscan but corroborates the assertions by Acevedo and Novoa that in satisfying his ambition to retire into religious life, Lerma had forced the King's hand. The evidence of the anonymous writer therefore corroborates the evidence provided by Acevedo and Novoa that it had been Philip who had insisted that Lerma had to leave – that he would not allow him to remain at court and to have the best of both worlds, secular and religious. Confronted by Lerma's elevation to the purple, the King had finally brought himself to the point at which he could dispense with the services of his *valido*.

Even the appearance of authority began now to fall away from Lerma. He wore the purple splendidly well and marked his new dignity by abandoning his practice of dyeing his beard. However, he had to give up the courtesy title of 'Excellency' that attached to his dukedom, for the cardinals at court would allow him only 'most illustrious lordship'. He was teased by the nuncio and others on this most sensitive matter. He claimed the dignity of 'Cardinal-duke' but since this, too, was contentious it was referred to the pope for arbitration. Lerma began to show some regrets at having given up power, and in the spring took on again the management of some affairs of state.[80]

On 2 June the King gave Lerma a grant of the income of the offices of *caballerizo mayor* and *sumiller de corps*, and expressly stated that he had done so 'by way of retirement' and that Uceda was henceforth to exercise the offices.[81] Philip was holding firm. As he did so, the authority of the Sandoval family at court began to disintegrate; when in June the heir to the throne was preparing to go hunting and found that Saldaña was not ready to accompany him, he rebuked him. The scene was witnessed by Fernando de Borja and the Count of Olivares: they did not disguise their pleasure at Saldaña's discomfiture.[82]

On 4 July 1618, Lerma held his last *fiesta* in the capital, a bullfight in his ring at the *huerta*.[83] He prevailed upon the Prior of the Escorial to secure a further two months' extension from the King before he departed.[84] When that licence expired at the end of August Lerma summoned his carriage to the Escorial, but still he did not depart.

Lerma's irresolution led to a final collapse of his authority at court. In July, Baltasar de Zúñiga won the arguments at the Council of State over supporting the Emperor, although Lerma's judgement in fearing that Spain was being committed to a long war in central Europe was to be vindicated by events; in this respect, he was wiser than his formidable opponent. It was perhaps in the hope of distracting Philip from the crisis in Germany that Lerma urged him to undertake an expedition against Algiers, but the time for such enterprises was now long past and the King and his Council of State were eager to engage in Germany.[85]

Now, at last, Lerma's son moved openly against him. No evidence has come to light over the breakdown of the relationship between Lerma and Uceda in the summer of 1618 but it seems evident that two issues divided them – Lerma's relentless extravagance with the family's resources and his continuing prevarication as to when he would hand over his role at court to his son. Uceda was forty-one years of age but he had not acquired the discipline to dominate the court: diffidence and laziness remained his determining characteristics. However, he undoubtedly resented his father's delay in departing from court because it undermined his authority and encouraged his enemies. Lerma realised too late that he had pushed his son too far; as Uceda moved into open opposition to him in July 1618, it was said that he rebuked his son for betraying him and ruining the family's hope of carrying on in power – 'I will go and you will be left with everything, and you will throw everything away'.[86]

It is likely that it was the friars to whom Philip listened most in the summer months of 1618 at the Escorial. Aliaga himself was of course constantly at the King's side and among those who also spent the summer at the monastery was fray Juan de Santamaría. Ominously for Lerma, Philip let it be known that he was reading Santamaría's book, which took as its central precept that kings should govern without the intercession of favourites.[87] It seems certain, too, that Philip listened to the advice of Prior Peralta; since the King chose him to instruct Lerma to leave court it seems reasonable to infer that he had been instrumental in helping him to reach his agonising decision.

The initial stage of the contest with Uceda reached its climax with the dismissal of Fernando de Borja and four *ayudas de cámara* on 1 September. When on the following day Lemos remonstrated with Philip about Borja's dismissal the King commanded him to leave court. On 12 September, Benavente was named to replace Lemos as President of the Council of Italy: the appointment of Lerma's longest-standing enemy to such a key position was a defining moment.[88] Now even lesser politicians joined the onslaught on Lerma; the Count of Olivares and the second Marquis of Castel Rodrigo, both of whom were resentful of Lerma's treatment of their fathers, committed themselves to supporting Uceda and Aliaga.[89]

Before Lemos left court on 22 September he joined in a family conference which was attended by Lerma, his two sons, his grandson (the Duke of Cea) and the old Countess of Lemos. The family feasted together and separated 'very mournfully.[90] On the same day Lerma sent his last major instruction to a council when he ordered the Council of War to reduce its expenditures, once again attempting to implement major reforms in the midst of a political crisis.[91] Lerma then bought a *censo* on a house for the Society of Jesus in Madrid; in his final days at court he could not afford to pay cash for it.[92] Two days after he had carried out this transaction, Philip presented him with a last *ayuda de costa*, of 50,000 ducats.[93]

It seems likely that in his discussions with Philip, Lerma complained about the treatment of Lemos and used this as the pretext for asking for permission to leave court. As the King himself told Acevedo, Lerma now wrote to Philip requesting authority to retire. In putting his request in writing Lerma was making the final break:

> they had long discussions during which the duke came to tell his Majesty that he too wished to leave because his nephew had done so. His Majesty, who was accustomed to the idea and willing to have the Cardinal-Duke leave, replied to him that he could go. This reply was not to (Lerma's) taste, because it appeared to him that the King was going to deny him the licence, as on other occasions, and so he had started preparations to go even though he tried to remain. But finally the King did not wish it, and it is difficult to preserve the *privanza* in perpetuity, however much kings love [someone] and show that they love [him].[94]

This interview seems to have taken place on 2 October: Lerma left in tears. On the following day he attended the anniversary mass for the Queen, and on 4 October Philip ordered Juan de Peralta to do what he did not have the strength to do himself:

> Go to the Duke and tell him how much I have always valued his house and himself, and the great confidence that I have had in him, assuring him that I will never forget his faithfulness and services. What he has asked for me for so many times with much loyalty and earnestness for his rest, quietness and composure, I now give him, and thus he can retire to Lerma or Valladolid when he wishes.

By Novoa's account, Lerma thanked the King; few preparations were necessary, since most of his possessions had already gone. Lerma spent the night at Guadarrama. As a courtesy, Philip sent him the day's documents and a venison that he had shot.[95] The two men never met again.

Lerma went on to his ducal city and then proceeded to Valladolid, where the cardinal's hat was brought to him; he received it in *San Pablo*. Uceda now took on the management of affairs, working from his father's rooms in the Alcázar; Cottington reported that he 'doth all things in dispatch of Businesses that his father was wont to do'.[96] But Uceda was not able to maintain the effort and soon abandoned even the pretence of exercising power; no record survives of his attending the Council of State or any *juntas*, and the handful of notes that he wrote to the councils contain no direction to the affairs of state, being distinguished only by their illegibility.

The realization that Lerma would not be returning to court percolated only slowly through the body politic. Lope de Vega recorded that Madrid was 'divided into two parts' between those who believed that Lerma was retiring and those who refused to do so.[97] Juan de Ciriza insisted that his master would shortly return to court. However, the truth could not long be obscured and a fortnight after Lerma had left, Cottington wrote that 'it is generally beleeued that the duke of Lerma is now gone from the Court with intention nott to return unto it, and that from henceforth he will only intend and attend the salvation of his soule.'[98]

When Lerma received his cardinal's hat in the church of *San Pablo* he brought his courtly life to a triumphant conclusion, finally achieving his wish to retire from secular into religious life. He had not managed his withdrawal with any elegance but at last he had dragged himself away from court. For his part, Philip III had finally emancipated himself from his *valido*; it had cost him a great deal of anguish to do so but he had finally asserted his pre-eminence; he *was* the King of Spain.

Lerma initially threw himself with relish into the pleasures of the hunt; early in November 1618, Siete Iglesias wrote to Gondomar that Lerma 'is well and is very much enjoying the hunt' in Ventosilla.[99] But as the implications of his dismissal sank in, Lerma's health collapsed and he endured a miserable few years while he adjusted to the life away from court that he claimed that he had always wanted to enjoy in his retirement.

However, if Lerma had failed to remain at court in a supervisory capacity (as he had tried to do from as early as 1612) he had the consolation that he retained the affection of the King and of leading members of the royal family – Isabella and Albert and the Queen of France – although it was to prove an anxiety to him that the heir to the throne soon forgot him and then turned against him: Philip III never did so. He had, too, the confidence that his son was the King's chief minister, his uncle was Cardinal-Archbishop of Toledo and Inquisitor General and his *hechuras* held major office in leading areas of government and Church. He had little to fear. Lerma retained his affection. And of course as a prince of the Church he had the enduring support of the papacy.

NOTES

1 On Lerma's decline, see the important discussion by Feros, *Kingship and Favoritism*, chap. 11, 'Fall from power', pp. 230–46. See also Williams, 'Lerma, 1618. Dismissal or Retirement?'
2 Title as President, Madrid, 15 Feb. 1616, AGS QC 14; his own account of his promotion, 'Los Acededos', xx, pp. 237–9; see also González Dávila, *Teatro de las Grandezas de ... Madrid*, pp. 392–7; titles, Inquisitor of Seville, 20 Oct. 1603, AHN Inq lib. 367, fol. 27b; fiscal of Inquisition, 5 Jul. 1605, ibid., fol. 123; councillorship, 24 Jan. 1608, ibid., lib. 1338, fol. 40b.
3 Cottington to Sir R. Winwood, Madrid, 22 May/2 Jun. 1616; García Oro, *Gondomar*, p. 227.
4 Cottington to Lake, Madrid, 20/30 Nov. 1617, NA SP 94/22, fol. 216b.
5 He did so even though the Admiral of Aragon was released from prison in the spring of 1616, Cottington to Sir R. Winwood, Madrid?, 12/22 May 1616, NA SP 94/22, fol. 36.

6 Bombín Pérez, *La cuestión de Monferrato*, p. 175.
7 *CSPV*, xv, 9 Jan. 1618, no. 165, p. 98.
8 Bombín Pérez, *La cuestión de Monferrato*, p. 192; see also García García, *La Pax Hispánica*, pp. 93–6.
9 *CSPV*, xv, 8 Jun. 1617, no. 785, pp. 515–17.
10 García García, *La Pax Hispánica*, pp. 94–6.
11 Bombín Pérez, *La cuestión de Monferrato*, pp. 171–234.
12 Bergin, *Rise of Richelieu*, pp. 137–40.
13 *CSPV*, xv, 20 Nov. 1617, no. 520, p. 354; Bombín Pérez, *La cuestión de Monferrato*, pp. 237–8.
14 *CSPV*, xiv, 4 Dec. 1616, no. 538, pp. 368–9.
15 Bombín Pérez, *La cuestión de Monferrato*, p. 203, n. 97.
16 *Cnta*. War, 26 Dec. 1616, AGS GA 808, no fol.
17 Fernández Duro, *Osuna*, pp. 323–6.
18 *Cnta*. St. 18 Oct. 1617, AGS E 1880, fol. 255.
19 *ACC* xxix, pp. 123 and 224.
20 Ibid., pp. 497–8.
21 Ibid., xxx, pp. 10–12, quotation at p. 11.
22 The argument that the *repartimiento* had inflicted structural demographic change on Castile was developed most fully by Hernando de Quiñones, procurator for León, *ACC* xxx, 23 Aug. 1617, pp. 230–2.
23 *CSPV*, xiv, 26 Jan. and 17 Feb. 1617, xiv, nos. 608 and 650 (quotation), pp. 418–19 and 444–5.
24 On Philip's distress ['dejandonos con la pena y soledad que podeis pensar'], Philip III to Anne, Madrid, 13 Mar. 1617, Felipe III, *Cartas de Felipe III a su hija Ana, reina de Francia, 1616–1618*, ed. R. Martorell Telléz-Girón, Madrid, 1929, pp. 21–3.
25 *Cnta*. St. 9 Apr. 1617; AGS E 2326, fol. 17 (quotation); and *CSPV*, xiv, 15 Jan. 1617, no. 827, pp. 544–5.
26 *CSPV*, xiv, 18 Jun. 1617, no. 800, pp. 526–7.
27 Ibid., 19 Jun. 1617, no. 803, p. 528.
28 Bombín Pérez, *La cuestión de Monferrato*, pp. 242–3.
29 Cottington to Winwood, Madrid, 3/13 Jun. 1617, NA SP 94/22, fol.151.
30 'Testamento' of the Duke of Lerma, included at pp. 2–34v in AVTOS QUE SE HIZIERON PARA ABRIR el testamento del Excel[entísimo] señor Cardenal Duque de Lerma, Madrid, 12 Jun. 1617, ADL 12, a printed copy. The dating of this document presents some difficulties; in the margin on p. 2 the date is written as '21 Jun. 1617' and on p. 34b it is stated that it was sealed 'en veynte y vno de Iunio'. I have concluded that both of these are mistaken; on p. 35 Testa clearly stated that he received the document and witnessed it on 'doze dias del mes de Iunio', and since this is repeated elsewhere in the document I have taken this as the actual date of the document and concluded that the dating of 21 June is a typographical error.
31 Ibid., p. 34.
32 Ibid., pp. 2–2b, 32b.
33 Ibid., at p. 33b.
34 Ibid., pp. 14b–16b.
35 Ibid., at p. 26b.
36 Ibid., at p. 32b.
37 See above, pp. 179–80.
38 'Testamento', at p. 18b.
39 Ibid., at p. 29b.
40 Ibid., at p. 16.
41 Ibid., at pp. 19b–20.
42 Ibid., at pp. 26–26b.
43 Ibid., at p. 34b.
44 Cottington to Winwood, Madrid, 3/13 Jun. 1617, NA SP 94/22, fol. 151.

45 Same to same, Madrid, 9/19 Jun. 1617, ibid., fols. 155–6.
46 Lerma to Philip III, Lerma, 5 and 27 Aug. 1617, and replies, San Lorenzo, 11 and 29 Aug., and Prince Philip to Lerma, San Lorenzo, 27 Aug. ('da os prisa a venir por q[ue] ya no podemos sufrir el estar tanto aqui sin vos, no allo mas que deciros sino q[ue] Dios os guarde'), BL Mss Add 28,425, fols. 478–85. On the context, Williams, 'Lerma 1618: Retirement or Dismissal', pp. 319–20 and Feros, *Kingship and Favoritism*, pp. 123–4. Lerma wrote a second letter to Philip on 27 August and concluded it more formally: 'dios guarde la muy real persona de V[uestra] M[a]g[esta]d como la cristiandad ha menester y sus vasallos deseamos'; curiously, he signed it, 'el duque marques de denia', AGS E 1880, fol. 121.
47 Bombín Pérez, *La cuestión de Monferrato*, pp. 218–19.
48 Sir Henry Wotton to Sir William Trumbull, Venice, 24 Apr./4 May 1617, *Papers of William Trumbull the elder, Sep. 1616–Dec. 1618*, HMC 75, vols v and vi, London, 1988 and 1995, no. 377, pp. 166–7.
49 *CSPV* xv, 7 Sep. 1617, no. 12, p. 4.
50 Pedro de Herrera, *Translación del santíssimo sacramento a la iglesia colegial de San Pedro de la villa de Lerma*, Madrid, p. 373b.
51 On Benavente, Cottington to Winwood, Madrid, 20/30 May 1617, NA SP 94/22, fol. 144. Zúñiga's return from Prague via the Low Countries and Italy took three months; *HMCT* vi, nos. 254, 289, 336, 353, pp. 110, 130–2, 152 and 157.
52 *Gaçeta y Nuevas*, p. 43.
53 Title, S. Lorenzo, 14 Aug. 1617, AGS QC 14. Carrillo retained the presidency of Finance until the Count of Salazar was given his title, Madrid, 8 Jan. 1618, AGS QC 9.
54 'no dire mas sino que vuestro compadre vino de Lerma, y fue muy bien recibido y quedamos aliviando para ir puesto alla, a donde dicen nos tienen muchas fiestas, harto quisiera lo pasarais alli', to Anne, Madrid, 9 Sep. 1617, Felipe III, *Cartas de Felipe III a ... Ana*', p. 36.
55 *ACC* xxx, pp. 325–8.
56 Ibid., pp. 363–82.
57 'News from Venice', 12/22 Sep. 1617 and 'News from Geneva', 6/16 Oct. 1617, *HMCT* vi, nos. 608 and 649, pp. 283–4 and 305; Bombín Pérez, *La cuestión de Monferrato*, pp. 244–5.
58 *Gaçeta y Nuevas*, p. 44.
59 On the celebrations of 1614, G. Davies, *A Poet at Court. Antonio Hurtado de Mendoza*, Oxford, 1971, p. 223.
60 Fernández de Caso, *Discvrso en qve se refieren las solenidades, y fiestas*', p. 7b; Herrera, *Translación del Santíssimo Sacramento*, and J. Varona, *Lerma Profano Sacra. Noticias de la antigüedad y fundación de esta villa*, BN Mss 10609. See also, Cervera Vera, *La Iglesia de San Pedro en Lerma*, pp. 103–17; Shergold, *A History of the Spanish Stage*, pp. 255–7.
61 The following is based upon the inventory drawn up in Lerma by Sebastián Rugier, *casero* of the duke, on 30 November 1617, ADL 53, no 15, no fol. A detailed analysis, L. Cervera Vera, *Bienes muebles en el palacio ducal de Lerma*, Madrid, 1967. I am grateful to Xanthe Brooke for her guidance on Lerma's collection.
62 Herrera, *Translación del Santíssimo Sacramento*, fol. 373b.
63 Douglas Kirk, 'Music to beguile a king', notes to Gabrieli Consort and Players, *Music for the Duke of Lerma*, Archiv Produktion, 2001.
64 'A nos festejado vuestro compadre alli bravamente y en acabandose la relacion de todas las fiestas que hubo, os la enbiare, y ya hemos dado la vuelta hacía Madrid, y entre tanto que viene el carruage nos hemos detenido aqui, donde yo he muerto algunos venados, y esta tarde he muerto dos, y está harto lindo este sitio', Ventosilla, 23 Oct. 1617, *Cartas de Felipe III a ... Ana*, p. 38.
65 Cottington to Lake, Madrid 4/14 Dec. 1618, NA SP 94/22, fols. 230–231b.
66 *Gaçeta y Nuevas*, pp. 45–6.
67 To Lake, 4/14 Dec. 1618, as at no. 66, and Quintana, *Madrid*, p. 363.
68 'Casa Profesa de la Compania de Jesus en Madrid', in 'Estado de Lerma', ADL leg. 8; González Dávila, *Teatro de las Grandezas de ... Madrid*, pp. 275–6; León Pinelo, *Anales de*

Madrid, pp. 218–19; Quintana, *Madrid*, pp. 439–40; *Gaçeta y Nuevas*, p. 46.

69   Anon., 'Bienes en Valladolid. Alcaydia de la Casa, Huerta y Rivera en Valladolid', in 'Estado de Lerma', ADL 8, no fol.

70   'The Duke of Lerma holds still the same place in his ma[jes]ties fauor, butt soe wysely retires himselfe from publike businesses as he hath allredy introduced ye Duke of Useda his sonne, who with ye assistance of the Confessor (being an actiue able man and free from ambition) manageth all things as his father did, and w[i]th no lyttle satisfaction to the king and his subjects', Cottington to Lake, Madrid, 10/20 Mar. 1618, NA SP 94/23, fol. 18b.

71   Chudoba, *Spain and the Empire*, p. 247.

72   Bombín Pérez, *La cuestión de Monferrato*, pp. 269–70.

73   Cottington to Lake, Madrid, 31 Mar./10 Apr. 1618, ibid., fol. 25.

74   Same to same, Madrid, 13/23 Apr. 1618, NA SP 94/23, fols. 27–27b.

75   Anon., 'Resolución que tomó Su Magestad acerca de algunas cosas que inportaban a la Monarchía por Septiembre del año de 1618', copy, BN Mss 1104, fols. 152–7 and see also, anon., 'Cómo fue apartado el Duque de Lerma del valimiento del rey don Felipe III', copy, ibid., 2348, fols. 401–4; *Gaçeta y Nuevas*, pp. 50–1.

76   'y a el le esta muy bien el habito nuevo, que yo creo, si le vierades no le conocierades vestido de colorado, y el ha tomado esta resolución con muy buenos deseos y asi creo que Dios le ayudará', Philip III to Anne, Madrid, 6 Jun., 1618, *Cartas de Felipe III a ...Ana*, p. 47

77   Escagedo Salmón, 'Los Acebedos', vii, p. 62.

78   Novoa, *Historia de Felipe III*, lxi, pp. 133–5.

79   Anon, 'Cómo fue apartado el Duque de Lerma del valimiento', BN Mss 2348, fols. 402v-403 and 'Resolución que tomo Su Magestad (Felipe III)', ibid., 1104, fols. 152–7.

80   Cottington to Lake, Madrid, 3/13 May 1618, NA SP 94/23, fols. 31b–32. Nine days later, Cottington reported to Lake that 'O[u]r Cardinall Duke (for soe he is caled) hath now put himselfe fullie againe into ye managing of all maner of Great businesses, nottwithstanding his Preesthood and is at this instant w[i]th the king at Aranjuez; he becomes his Cardenals weed excellent well, and forbeared nott to collor his beard as before', Madrid, 12/22 May 1618, ibid., fol. 37.

81   Lerma, 'Imbentario', ADL 53, fol. 24.

82   Novoa, *Historia de Felipe III*, lxi, pp. 145–6.

83   *Gaçeta y Nuevas*, p. 53.

84   'Resolución que tomó su Magestad', BN Mss 1104, fol. 182.

85   Chudoba, *Spain and the Empire*, pp. 218–19; Geoffrey Parker (ed.), *The Thirty Years War*, 2nd edn., London, 1997, pp. 44, 51; see also, Feros, *Kingship and Favoritism*, cap. 12, 'In search of culprits', pp. 247–61.

86   Novoa, *Historia de Felipe III*, lxi, p. 147.

87   'Su Mag[esta]d se ha entretenido este verano en S[an]t Lorenzo, en leer dos libros q[ue] compuso fray Juan de s[an]ta Maria descalço fran[ciscan]o intitulado Pulicia y Republica Christiana que trata de materia de estado y Gouierno hallandose presente el d[ic]ho religioso, muy gran sieruo de Dios', anonymous report, 'en Madrid, a postrero de Octubre 1618', inside anonymous letter of 14 Oct. 1618, ASV NS 440, no fol.

88   *Gaçeta y Nuevas*, p. 55.

89   Novoa, *Historia de Felipe III*, lxi, pp. 144–61.

90   Anonymous report, 'en Madrid, a postrero de Octubre 1618', inside letter of 14 Oct. 1618, ASV NS 440, no fol.

91   Lerma to Anaya, secretarial hand with Lerma's rúbrica, San Lorenzo, 22 Sep. 1618, AGS GA 1304, no fol.

92   Lerma, 'Imbentario', ADL 53, fol. 33.

93   Ibid. fol. 25b.

94   Escagedo Salmón, 'Los Acebedos', vii, p. 181.

95   'Resolución que tomó su Magestad', BN Mss 1104, fols. 182–3v; Novoa, *Historia de Felipe III*, lxi, pp. 154–6.

96 Cottington to Carleton, Madrid, 8/18 Oct. (quotation) and 29 Oct./8 Nov. 1618, NA SP 94/23, fols. 74–74b and 79–79b.

97 'Madrid está diuidido en dos partes: vnos, que hablan porque lo crehen; y otros, que callan porque no lo crehen. Yo ni soy de los vnos ni de los otros: amo al Cardena, y yo quisiera que nos faltara: mas si su Ex[celencia] se ha querido desocupar de la carga deste ymperio y prebenir el fin, discreto, dichoso, santo predestinado', Lope de Vega to Sessa, Madrid, ? Oct. 1618, *Epistolario de Lope de Vega Carpio*, iv, pp. 23–4.

98 Cottington to Lake, Madrid, 8/18 Oct. 1618, as n. 97.

99 6 Nov. 1618, RB 11/21904, doc. 50.

11

The end of the Sandoval hegemony and the deaths of Lerma and Uceda

Philip III and the abolition of the *valimiento*

Fray Luis de Aliaga, power-broker

For six weeks Philip made no public comment about Lerma's departure. This rendered all the more effective the stark simplicity of his announcement when on 15 November 1618 he informed the councils that the order of business which had obtained since the beginning of his reign was to cease with immediate effect. He conceded that Uceda had signed various orders in his name 'in the absence' of Lerma but ordered that henceforth only his conciliar secretaries were to communicate his orders to the councils. Moreover, he alone would now authorise commands which involved the exercise of the royal grace. Philip also announced that the right which he had given to Lerma to enquire into the details of any confidential matter that the councils dealt with was now rescinded and he called for the return to him of all documents which had conferred this authority on the duke.[1] The *valimiento* was abolished.

No indications were given as to who had advised the King on the contents of his decree but it clearly reflected the influence of the two friars in whom he trusted most, Luis de Aliaga and Juan de Santamaría, both of whom had for years been advising Philip to govern without a *valido*. Certainly, it was Aliaga who now seized the political initiative. Cardinal Sandoval y Rojas died on 7 December, and fray Luis consolidated his own authority by organising the succession to both of the Cardinal's great offices. The *infante* Ferdinand was raised to the cardinalate at the age of nine so that he could become Archbishop of Toledo and Primate of Spain. This was the most scandalous Church appointment that had been made in Spain in a century and breached every advance that the Catholic Church had made since the Council of Trent (1545–63) laid down strict guidelines covering episcopal appointments. Moreover, insult was added to injury by the elevation of the new archbishop to the cardinalate. Some senior men rather cravenly welcomed the appointment; for instance, from Brussels, fray Iñigo de Brizuela wrote to Gondomar that 'the Cardinal of Toledo has had a good successor'.[2] However, Lerma himself was among those who were outraged by Philip's decision. Indeed, he expressed himself so indiscreetly – 'with words that were not very moderate', as Góngora put it – that the King took offence.[3] Unabashed, Aliaga let it be known that he was the prime mover behind Ferdinand's nomination. He then dramatically re-emphasised his stature at court by having himself nominated to the inquisitorship-general, with retention of the confessorship to the King. The low-born friar was now unquestionably the most influential Churchman in Spain.[4]

Lerma's grief at the death of his great-uncle was deeply felt; despite all their disagreements the two men remained genuinely close to each other. Moreover, Bernardo's death deprived Lerma of 20,000 ducats of rents that were drawn from the archbishopric of Toledo and 6,000 ducats from the *adelantamiento* of Cazorla. In his reduced circumstances, this was a severe blow to him.[5] The last weeks of 1618 must have been an anxious time for the Cardinal-duke as he waited to see whether his enemies would be allowed to move against him. Aliaga trod carefully, aware of the affection that Philip felt for Lerma. Indeed, fray Luis betrayed his nervousness by having Philip instruct the duke not to leave his ducal city.[6]

At Christmastime, Siete Iglesias travelled to Lerma. What passed between him and Lerma is not known but their conversations must have been deeply uneasy.[7] The Marquis returned to Valladolid to await his fate; there, on 20 February 1619, he was arrested. Within a few days he was taken to the fortress of Montánchez in Extremadura to be interrogated.[8] Once again, Aliaga claimed the credit: Cottington reported to Sir John Digby that 'the confessor (who hath been the only worker in this residencia) willed me to wright it unto your lord'. It was, therefore, presumably Aliaga who suggested to Philip that he write to Lerma justifying his action. Philip did so, reassuring Lerma that he was writing to him 'out of the respect in which I hold you and will always have [for you]'.[9] He entrusted the delivery of the letter to Juan de Peralta and (as in October 1618) the details of what Peralta was doing were discreetly leaked: the Count of Gondomar was given a copy of the letter. Lerma was deeply resentful of the arrest of Siete Iglesias but made no protest, mollified by the King's assurance that he himself would remain safe.[10]

Three councillors of Castile were appointed to judge Siete Iglesias. Francisco de Contreras came eagerly out of retirement at the age of seventy-five to preside over the case and he was supported by Luis de Salcedo and Diego del Corral y Arellano.[11] Siete Iglesias's friends and supporters were deeply apprehensive: when Góngora and Villafranca discussed the case, the Marquis's prediction that a death sentence was inevitable put the poet off his food.[12]

The contest for the succession to Lerma: the journey to Portugal, 1619

Having spent most of his reign resolutely avoiding making a state visit to Portugal, Philip was now eager to visit the kingdom, and in doing so to escape from the turmoil that Lerma's retirement had created at court. He travelled against the advice of virtually all of his senior ministers. The Count of Salazar (who had taken over as President of the Council of Finance from Fernando Carrillo early in 1618 so that Carrillo could concentrate on his work on the Council of the Indies) argued in December 1618 that the exchequer could not afford to pay for the *jornada de Portugal*.[13] The Council of Castile pointedly included a request in its *consulta* of February 1619 that the royal travels should cease.[14] The Council of State was almost unanimous in its opposition to the journey. On 19 April, Mejía argued that the King should not proceed with his plans while Benavente, Aliaga, Villafranca and Zúñiga urged Philip to postpone the journey for the immediate future. Cardinal Zapata alone spoke clearly in favour of proceeding at once. Philip insisted that the journey was to go ahead and brusquely informed the councillors that if they wished to accompany him they could do so.[15] On 22 April Philip set out for Portugal.[16] No significant planning had taken place for the journey.

Of the active councillors of State only Villafranca, La Laguna, Aliaga and Zúñiga chose to travel, while Mejía, Benavente and Zapata remained behind in Madrid. Remarkably, the Duke of Infantado also stayed in the capital even though he was Philip's *mayordomo mayor;* like Benavente, he excused himself on grounds of illness and old age.[17] The absence of so many senior councillors made it easier for Zúñiga to establish his authority over the King and his heir during the journey. Indeed, it is probable that several of Zúñiga's senior colleagues already feared the extent of his ambition; in February, four of them – Infantado, Mejía, Aliaga and Benavente – suggested that he be sent back to Prague to carry Philip's condolences to the Emperor on the death of his wife. It was only with some difficulty that Zúñiga fought off the appointment. But having done so, he immediately reinforced his new authority by taking over from Uceda as *ayo* to the heir to the throne.[18]

Uceda passively accepted the loss of the position, perhaps because he did not consider Zúñiga to be a threat to his position. After all, he travelled to Portugal as *sumiller de corps* and *caballerizo mayor* of the King and *sumiller de corps* and *mayordomo mayor* of the heir while Saldaña journeyed as *caballerizo mayor* of the heir. Moreover, on the first night of the journey, Philip appeared to confirm the ascendancy of the Sandovals within his household by appointing three members of the *parentela* as *gentileshombres de la cámara* – the Duke of Cea, the Admiral of Castile and the Marquis of Peñafiel. These appointments surprised many but they proved to be valedictory, the last significant posts given to the Sandoval family in the reign.[19]

Philip crossed into Portugal on 9 May. On 18 May he attended a great *auto de fé* at Alamada with 124 penitents, 12 of whom were subsequently led to the stake as part of the celebrations to mark the arrival of their monarch: the jibe of Philip being the *Rex Judaeorum* was laid to rest with their deaths.[20] The King made his formal entry into Lisbon on 29 June but as he settled down in the city the Council of State learned that a Bohemian army had appeared at the gates of Vienna.[21] Villafranca was pessimistic: 'We may expect soon either the loss of everything or a disadvantageous and humiliating peace, or a war as long as that with the Dutch', he noted with prescience. When Zúñiga insisted that Philip should send troops to assist Ferdinand, the King agreed to do so.[22] Spain was being drawn into the conflicts of central Europe.

Philip took the oath to the kingdom of Portugal and his eldest son was sworn in as heir to the throne on 14 July. Four days later, he opened the Cortes of Portugal. The session – the first for thirty-six years – dragged on until the end of September. Events in Germany did not move at such a leisurely pace. The Bohemian Diet dethroned Ferdinand as King of Bohemia (19 August) and a week later elected Frederick, Elector Palatine, in his place. When Frederick accepted the throne of Bohemia (28 September) Ferdinand agreed to pay the expenses of Maximilian of Bavaria, the leading Catholic prince, to use the army of the Catholic League to occupy the Upper Palatinate (October 8).[23] The news from Germany convinced Philip that he had to return to Madrid. He dissolved the Cortes, and on 29 September he left Lisbon.

On 8 November Philip was struck down with a violent fever at the small hamlet of Casarrubios del Monte, only 35 kilometres from Madrid.[24] After three harrowing weeks, during which he hovered at the point of death, the King recovered sufficiently to be able to resume his journey. When he reached Madrid on 5 December, he had been away for seven months. It had been fourteen months since Lerma had left court, and Philip could no longer avoid establishing a new leadership for his government.

Stalking-horses: the Marquis of Siete Iglesias and the Duke of Osuna

As he headed back to Madrid, Philip was informed that the case against Siete Iglesias had made sufficient progress for him to be brought to the fortress of Santorcaz, 10 kilometres from Alcalá de Henares. Siete Iglesias was subject now to the most stringent security as his judges sought to break his spirit: chained by his legs for twenty-four hours a day, he was allowed to talk only to his confessor and his two legal advisers.[25] He refused to incriminate himself in the death of the Queen but admitted responsibility for the death of Francisco de Juara, a soldier of fortune who had insulted him. His judges therefore brought him to Madrid and imprisoned him in his own house (and at his own expense). He lived under round-the-clock surveillance, and with candles illuminating his room at night he was deprived of privacy and dignity. When he continued to deny involvement in the death of the Queen, the King authorised the use of torture. The first session began shortly before midnight on 7 January 1620 and lasted for three hours. So agonised were the Marquis's screams that a platoon of fifty guards was placed around the palace in case the populace of Madrid tried to free him. Ominously, it was reported to Gondomar that the judges had consulted with the Duke of Infantado about sentencing; the duke was unlikely to be charitable to his old enemy.[26]

The decision to intervene in Germany added urgency to the need to remove Osuna from the viceroyalty of Naples. Osuna had stepped up his attacks on Venetian shipping in 1619 and when the deputies of the city of Naples asked for permission to appeal to the King against his fiscal exactions, Osuna threw them into prison.[27] The authority of the crown was now in jeopardy in its richest province in Italy. Cardinal Gaspar de Borja y Aragón was named to replace Osuna and when he arrived in Naples in June Osuna fled so quickly that he left his wife behind him. Osuna then made a leisurely return to Spain and on arrival at the Escorial he was received with carefully contrived courtesy by the King.[28] No one doubted, however, that Osuna was now in disgrace and that proceedings would be initiated against him. Nor could anyone doubt that the cases that were being built against Osuna and Siete Iglesias would further discredit the regime of the Duke of Lerma.

Philip IV and the new *valimiento*

Death of Philip III and the change of regime

In December 1619 the Council of State recommended to Philip that he intervene in Germany, and it was agreed that an army of 35,000 men should be despatched into the Palatinate from Flanders. Ambrosio Spínola crossed the Rhine in September 1620 and within six months had secured the Lower Palatinate, and with it, a key part of the 'Spanish Road'. In Bohemia, the Catholic army crushed Frederick's forces outside Prague ('Battle of the White Mountain', 8 November 1620). Frederick fled from Prague on the day of the battle, thereby earning the derisory title of 'The Winter King'.[29]

While Spanish arms appeared to be demonstrating their invincibility in central Europe, the Cardinal-Duke of Lerma sank into despair. His health was not good; in February 1619 he complained of breathing difficulties and in September, when he decided to travel from Valladolid to Lerma he did not have the strength to do so.[30] In July 1620, news reached court that he had been 'dangerously' ill but that he had again been comforted by messages of enduring support from the King.[31] Luis de Góngora received a first-hand report:

> I believe that the Duke of Lerma is crumbling, both in judgement as in life, because he is impatient and disturbed. His melancholy is so profound that three times he has left Lerma for Valladolid and returned after two or three leagues. He tugs at his beard and says 'there is no comfort for the man who has done the damage to himself with his own hands'. This has been told to me by the Duke of Pastrana, who went to see him because he is his friend; he told me that (the Cardinal-Duke) received him in some anxiety and dismissed him in the same way.[32]

Philip was also in poor health. It is probable that he never recovered his strength after his illness at Casarrubios in 1619. Certainly, he did very little governmental work during 1620.[33] He did, however, stir himself to arrange the affairs of his children: on 30 January, Ferdinand was given his biretta as cardinal, and in November the marriage of the heir and Elizabeth was consummated.[34]

At the end of February 1621 Philip was taken ill with erysipelas, a form of scarlet fever.[35] His condition was worsened when he was bled three times by his doctors and was further aggravated by his continuing gluttony. But the greatest threat to his life was that he had lost the will to live. Convinced that he was in danger of being consigned to hell because of his failure to exercise his kingship responsibly, he rebuked his doctors when they told him that he would recover.[36] Góngora noted that Philip also blamed Aliaga for misleading him and thereby endangering his eternal salvation. He recorded that when the friar answered that he had always spoken truthfully to the King, Philip poignantly replied that 'this was true in the first years'.[37]

In his desolation, Philip agreed to Uceda's suggestion that he summon Lerma to comfort him. Lerma needed no second bidding and immediately left for court. However, on orders from the heir, the Cardinal-Duke was intercepted by Alonso de Cabrera, a senior councillor of Castile, at Villacastín, less than 80 kilometres from the capital. Góngora recorded that Lerma 'seemed to die' when he was ordered to turn back. He also noted that on returning to court, Cabrera went directly to Zúñiga to report to him.[38]

On 29 March 1621, Philip decided that he would not renew the truce in the Low Countries; it was the last decision that he took in foreign policy and it reflected his shame at his acceptance of the truce in 1609.[39] On the following day he signed the final version of his Testament. As executors and testamentaries, he named his children and senior figures in Church, Court and State – his confessor, *mayordomo mayor* and *capellán mayor*; the presidents of the councils of Castile, Indies, and Finance and the *vicecanciller* of Aragon. He included Juan de Peralta, Prior of the Escorial, and fray Antonio de Sotomayor, confessor of the Prince. Naturally, too, he named Uceda, who held two major positions in his own household and two in his son's. All of these men could have expected to be named as testamentaries by reason of their offices but Philip then added the name of the Cardinal-Duke of Lerma: doing so implied that Lerma might legitimately return to court to help administer the Testament.[40] On his deathbed, in the most solemn moment of his life, Philip showed yet again that the spell of his favourite still hung over him as it had hung over his whole reign.

When Philip summoned his children for his final blessing, Zúñiga and Olivares took the precaution of accompanying the Prince. The King urged his son to govern well, and several accounts recorded that he insisted that he retain the services of the Duke of Uceda. He passed the night in fitful sleep. Clutching the crucifix that Charles V and Philip II had held at their deaths, he begged God to forgive him for his failings as king and not to condemn him forever but to send him to purgatory for many years. He was comforted by the priests and friars in whom he had trusted so much: Fr Jerónimo de Florencia; fray Francisco de Jesús, fray Juan de Santamaría (who was reputedly told by the King that 'you spoke the truth to me') and Friar Peralta. At five o'clock, Aliaga said some last words to the King and then the great men of the land, led by the President of the Council of Castile, came to bid farewell. As Philip sank into unconsciousness, his last words were the traditional ones of a dying Catholic – 'In manus tuas Domine'. He died at about 9.30. He was two weeks short of his forty-fourth birthday.

The news was taken to his son, who was in bed: he did not arise. Philip III's body was dressed in a Franciscan habit, as his father's and grandfather's had been, and two days later was taken to the Escorial for interment.[41] The monks humiliated Aliaga by refusing to give him a room for the night and he was forced to accept a room provided by the doctor of the monastery. In an order that was redolent of Philip III's first act in 1598, Philip IV instructed all conciliar secretaries to obey the orders given to them by Zúñiga. On 2 April don Baltasar began to give audiences: he was now fulfilling the functions that Lerma himself had undertaken at the beginning of Philip III's reign.[42] However, Góngora noted that he was not alone in his exercise of power, commenting that 'everything' belonged now to don Baltasar and to the Count of Olivares.[43]

On the first day of the new reign, Tomás de Ángulo and Bernabé de Bibanco were dismissed from their secretaryships of the councils of Castile and Inquisition and Juan de Ciriza was deprived of his management of the consultas of the Council of State but allowed to retain his other papers. Pedro de Tapia and Antonio Bonal were removed from their councillorships of Castile.[44]

The hunt began in earnest on 7 April, when Osuna was imprisoned on charges of corruption and of misleading the king.[45] On the following day the King ordered that the 72,000 ducats'-worth of rent that Lerma enjoyed from the commutation of the tratas de Sicilia were to be returned to the royal exchequer and he established a junta to investigate the circumstances under which the award had been made.[46] Lerma had now lost 108,000 ducats of income since the death of his great-uncle in December 1618: 26,000 ducats that had been granted to him by the Cardinal; 10,000 ducats of salary as *caballerizo mayor* and *sumiller de corps* of the King and the 72,000 ducats of compensatory rents for the *tratas de Sicilia*. On 13 April, Lerma wrote to the King welcoming the decision to deprive him of the rents if it would benefit the royal patrimony and asserting that he would readily make his wealth available to the crown if Philip wished him to do so.[47] The King needed no encouragement: on 5 May he placed Lerma's estates in administration under the supervision of Alonso de Cabrera. In doing so, he symbolically reduced the Lerma *mayorazgo* to the condition that it had endured until the beginning of his father's reign, when it had been in administration in the hands of Sebastián de Pascual.

Lerma's sons were both now ordered to resign their chief offices – Uceda as *sumiller de corps* and Saldaña as *caballerizo mayor*. Saldaña was replaced by his father-in-law, the Duke of Infantado, who accepted the office on 12 April with barely-disguised pleasure.[48] On 23 April, Uceda was ordered to retire to his ducal town and Aliaga was given three days in which to leave court.[49]

On the same day, the King appointed Fernando Carrillo to lead a commission of investigation into all the grants made by Philip III to Lerma, his children and supporters.[50] No one at court could have mistaken the significance of Philip's choice. Certainly, Lerma himself did not do so; he wrote to the King, insisting that he could not be deprived of the income that originated in the award of the *tratas de Sicilia* because the grant was legally valid and protesting that he should not be judged by a man who was a proven enemy to him. When the contents of the letter became known many at court leapt to defend Carrillo. In the uproar, few noted that Lerma's letter demonstrated that he would fight for his wealth and that he would be a formidable opponent for anyone wishing to deprive him of it.[51]

Lerma took the precaution of writing to Pope Paul V on 29 July asking for permission to enter the Society of Jesus but 'without leaving the dignity of cardinal'.[52] He was no more successful than he had been in 1572, but nothing is known of the circumstances in which the Pope rejected his plea.

Although Baltasar de Zúñiga took the pre-eminent public position in the new government it soon became evident that the Sandovals had been replaced by a troika of apparently equal partners, the leading figures of the clan that had led the opposition to them throughout the reign of Philip III:

> They who are now most powerfull in this Court are Conde de Oliuares, a man generally noted for the fauorite and 6 days ago made a Grandee: Conde de Benauente, a man who hath ever borne himself very styffly against the family and faction of the howse of Lerma is lykewyse very gracefull with this yonge king and governes much. Don Baltasar de Cuniga, who was Ayo to the Prince, hath now in his hands the governm(en)t of all consultas and papers of that quality and

unto him all Amb(assador)s and forrayne Ministers haue recourse for dispatche of their businesses.[53]

What was interesting about Edward Wilson's description of the new leaders at court was that he described Olivares as the 'favourite' of the new king and listed him first among the three men even though he was manifestly the most junior of them in terms of experience.[54] Volatile and impetuous, Olivares was the very antithesis of his two colleagues; where Zúñiga and Benavente measured every action with cool calculation, Olivares tended to act without thought of the consequences. He had very nearly thrown away all hope of advancement when in 1619 he had stormed out of Lisbon and returned to Seville because of his frustration at not winning *grandeza;* he had committed the grave error of abandoning court to return to his house in Seville.[55] It was perhaps because he had learned to curb his impetuosity that in 1621–22 he acted with exemplary caution. He had been raised on 12 April to the *grandeza* that his family had so long pursued and five days later was named as *sumiller de corps* to the King.[56] He did not, however, take up the seat on the Council of State to which he had been appointed at the time of Calderón's death and it must have been by choice that he did not do so: very deliberately, Olivares presented himself as a courtier rather than a politician.[57]

Lic. Juan Chumacero de Sotomayor laid the charges against Uceda at the end of April. He confined himself to a general criticism about Uceda's misuse of the royal grace but emphasised his support for Osuna – 'reducing the affairs of Italy to the convenience of the Duke of Osuna and not to the service of his Majesty'.[58] In effect, Uceda was charged not with being Lerma's son but with being Osuna's protector. He defended himself by proudly claiming that he had resolved grave crises in Italy ('giving his time and energy to each'). He further commended himself for his role on the royal journeys of 1599, 1615 and 1619, on taking over the papers after Lerma's departure and on 'renouncing' the right that his father had enjoyed of giving orders to councils and tribunals. He therefore effectively claimed responsibility for the decree of November 1618 which deprived him of the right to issue orders as his father had done. He claimed, too, that he had intervened to ensure the election of Ferdinand as emperor and had supported the involvement in Germany – or, as he put it, he had come to the aid of Catholicism in Germany.[59] It was not much of a defence but it was sufficient; he was only sentenced to eight years' exile from court and to a fine of 20,000 ducats (22 November 1622).[60] It was a dismissive verdict, demonstrating the insignificance that his enemies attached to him.

The Council of State was reshaped during May to ensure that it pursued more belligerent policies. The Marquis of Villafranca had stormed away from court – yet again! – in June 1620 and was ordered to return.[61] Diego de Ibarra, who had been so hostile to the truce of 1607–09 was appointed to the Council;

he would certainly support the re-engagement in the Low Countries.[62] A few months later Ambrosio Spínola was raised to the noble rank that he had craved for so long, as Marquis of los Balbases. He, too, was a friend of Zúñiga's; there would be no resentment at the Council of State at the successes that the great general would surely have in Flanders.[63]

The kissing of hands by the councils took place in San Jerónimo on 2 May.[64] A week later, the last symbols of the pre-eminence of the Sandoval family in the Alcázar were removed; Lerma's *tribuna* in the royal chapel was taken away and the King ordered that the *pasadizo* from Uceda's palace to the Alcázar should be destroyed. On 23 May, Uceda was placed under house arrest in the fortress of Torrejón de Velasco.[65] But Lerma was safe: Philip was informed that the Pope would not allow the crown to institute proceedings against him.[66] The fate of Siete Iglesias came to lie at the very heart of the reform programme. It was said that when he heard the bells tolling for the death of Philip III, the Marquis had observed that they were tolling too for his own death.[67] Proving him correct was the first priority of the new regime. Siete Iglesias would die in expiation of the sins of the regime of which he had been such a prominent part.

Execution of don Rodrigo Calderón, 21 October 1621

Within a week of his accession, Philip IV consulted three times with the judges in the case of the Marquis of Siete Iglesias and then authorised the application of a further round of torture. Siete Iglesias's courage grew in adversity, and as news of his resilience leaked out sympathies began to edge in his rather unlikely direction. His lawyers fought skilfully, claiming that the prosecution was inspired by envy and political ambition and that the tortures used were disproportionate to the allegations against him. They pointed out, too, that when in 1607 Philip III acquitted him of the charges levelled against him he had expressly ordered that these matters were never to be raised again. They also argued that Siete Iglesias's ability to defend himself was handicapped by Lerma's refusal to give evidence on his behalf. They knew, as of course did Siete Iglesias, that he had no hope of acquittal, but their tactics served to heighten the unease that was held — sometimes by men in very senior positions — at the way in which he was being pursued.[68]

They were surprisingly successful. On 9 July, Siete Iglesias was informed that he had been found not guilty of murdering the Queen, of bewitching the King and of attempting to poison the Inquisitor-General. He was also acquitted of four charges of murder. In a verdict that was a remarkable tribute to the tenacity of his own lawyers — and perhaps even to the independence of the judges? — Siete Iglesias was cleared of every charge against him that had courtly or political implications. However, he was convicted of having imprisoned and murdered Agustín de Ávila, *alguacil* of the court, and of having Francisco de

Juara and others assassinated. Like many others, Siete Iglesias thought that these were trivial and rather personal matters which pertained to his private honour rather than to his public position.

The judges divided over sentencing. Contreras insisted on a death sentence but Corral y Arellano demanded a lesser punishment. The casting vote reverted to Salcedo: he supported Contreras. Siete Iglesias was stripped of his titles and of his offices – the captaincy of the Guards; the office of *contino* of the *Casa de Aragón*; all of his offices in Valladolid and the *patronazgo* of the monastery of Portaceli; his income from the bulls of Crusade and his other municipal offices. He was also sentenced to the loss of half of his possessions and to a fine of 1,250,000 ducats. For a man who had been cleared of the major charges against him it was a savage sentence. Rodrigo Calderón (as the prisoner now became known once again) heard the verdict with unchanging countenance: 'God be praised; blessed be the Virgin Our Lady', was his only reaction. His wife and children tearfully begged Zúñiga and Olivares to intercede, but they were deaf to their pleas.[69]

Lerma stayed conspicuously silent and only Cardinal Trejo de Paniagua risked showing any personal loyalty to Siete Iglesias. However, Corral y Arellano found support from the President of the Council of Castile.[70] Fernando de Acevedo had never disguised his loathing of Calderón but he fought for him now because he was outraged by the illegality of the measures used against him.[71] He was duly removed as President of the Council of Castile but was allowed to leave court for his archbishopric with full honours. Francisco de Contreras was named to take his place as President: Calderón had little time left now.[72]

Don Rodrigo composed himself to die bravely. On 19 October he made his Testament and was told that he would die two days later: he welcomed the news. On 20 October, he was formally stripped of his habit of Santiago; he felt this degradation very keenly since he had wished to wear the habit to his death. Calderón wrote to the King – who had left Madrid while the execution took place[73] – but left instructions that the letter was only to be delivered after his own death. It was not a plea for life that don Rodrigo was making: he urged the King to move against other ministers who had been as guilty as he. He suggested that while the crown could not institute proceedings against Lerma for what he called *raçon de estado*, Philip could invite the duke to satisfy his conscience over the great riches that he had acquired. He urged Philip to proceed against the Genoese bankers who had despoiled the country 'through the most devious and indirect ways that can be imagined'. He concluded with a wide-ranging and detailed condemnation of the regime of which he had been such a prominent member that his own prosecutors could not have bettered, and encouraged the King to investigate the wealth acquired by his ministers throughout his reign. Calderón estimated that king and kingdom had been

defrauded of some 50,000,000 ducats during Philip III's reign, with the consequence that levels of taxation had become intolerable.[74] He urged Philip either
to reform his kingdoms or to risk losing them: like so many others, Calderón
was using the language of the *arbitristas*.

On 21 October, Madrid was bursting with people straining for a view of
Calderón. He was carried to the *Plaza Mayor* seated backwards on a mule and
he conducted himself with such dignity that some in the crowd yelled their
support with shouts of 'God save you'. Immersed in his devotions, Calderón
ignored them, may even have been unaware of them. Strapped into a chair on
the scaffold in the *Plaza Mayor*, he maintained his dignity during the formali-
ties of his last moments. When these were completed, the executioner cut his
throat from the front: as the only mark of honour allowed him, don Rodrigo's
head therefore remained on his shoulders.

Even after death, Calderón was hounded by his enemies. Contreras
ordered that he was to be left in his chair all afternoon and that no bells were
to be tolled for him. When his body was taken away and prepared for burial it
was found that it was blood-red with scourging, and that his knees had been
worn down by his devotions in the last years of his life. Calderón became the
hero of Spain, courageous, devout – and a victim of political persecution. One
writer proclaimed that the day of his death, 21 October 1621, 'was the most
famous day that this century has seen'.[75] Indeed, so great was the impression that
Calderón made on those who watched him die that to this day Spanish people
measure manly courage by that shown 'by Don Rodrigo on the scaffold'.

The reaction of the Cardinal-Duke of Lerma to Calderón's death is not
recorded. There was never any danger that Lerma would follow Calderón to
the scaffold but he recognised well enough that he needed political support, and
during the summer of 1621 he sought it from powerful patrons. From Brussels,
the Archduchess Isabella assured him that he could 'be certain that I will not
forget the reasons that I have to support you' and from Rome the new Pope,
Gregory XV, promised that 'we will not forget your piety, nor is it just to desert
you (since) you hold such a distinguished place in the Church'.[76] Lerma's task
became significantly easier in November 1621 when Benavente died.[77]

Only Aliaga of the major *hechuras* of Lerma now remained in office.
Francisco de Contreras judged his case in company with Álvaro de Villegas,
administrator of the archdiocese of Toledo for the Cardinal-*infante* Fernando.
They found him guilty of using his positions at court to deflect the attack upon
Osuna and noted his written act of fealty to Lerma of 5 April 1612 – 'such an
unworthy deed in a man who ministers to the royal conscience'. They suggested
that Philip invite the Pope to remove him quickly, citing the precedent of the
dismissal of Portocarrero in 1599.[78] On 12 January, fray Andrés Pacheco was
commissioned as Inquisitor General.[79]

Lerma and Uceda: decline, testaments and death

Lerma's first defence: the Inventory of March 1622

Lerma was received into the priesthood early in March 1622, and he celebrated his first mass in *San Pablo* on 5 April. It was an emotional experience for him and before he was ordained he made his act of confession with many tears.[80]

At the turn of March–April he produced the inventory of his estates and possessions that Philip IV had demanded of him. Notwithstanding that he vouchsafed the integrity of the document with his oath as a priest, the inventory was designed to obfuscate rather than to clarify the nature of Lerma's wealth and how it had been acquired. He brazenly minimised the value of his possessions and put the most favourable gloss on the methods by which he had accumulated them, repeatedly stressing that they could not be confiscated because they had been given to him with legal title and were vested in his *mayorazgo*. He therefore omitted some major items such as the value of his buildings, the property that was held in pawn by others and his gambling debts. He stressed, too, that he had used much of his wealth on his ecclesiastical endowments, implying that building for the glory of God was a justifiable use of the wealth that Philip III had lavished upon him. He asserted that his services to Philip III had been 'for the good government and peace of his realms' and that he had spent lavishly on his buildings so that the King could be properly accommodated on his travels. Indeed, he argued that he had spent a great deal of his own money to maintain the royal greatness both at court and on journeys of state; he claimed that he had spent well over 300,000 ducats on the journey of 1599 and that he still owed 240,000 ducats from the loan of 400,000 ducats that he had taken out to cover his expenses on the marital journey of 1615. He had also spent in the royal service the bequests left to him by the archbishops of Toledo and Zaragoza. In consequence, he was now so impoverished that he would not be able to leave even 100,000 ducats in cash when he died. He calculated that his income was worth 119,027 ducats and that two-thirds of this came from rents that were held in perpetuity (see Table 7).

Table 7 Lerma's income, 1622: evidence of his Inventory

Value	Sources of income
82,658.7	rents and commercial concessions
20,000	*encomiendas* and palatine offices
6,368.6	municipal offices
10,000	rents from *juros* held for Saldaña's *mayorazgo*
119,027.3	

The Inventory was Lerma's first line of defence, a statement of the position that he would maintain against Carrillo's *visita*. He could have felt little confidence that it would withstand even cursory investigation by a judge whom he feared so much. However, his good fortune held, and in doubly spectacular fashion; the *recusación* that he entered against Carrillo was upheld and then on 23 April 1622 Carrillo collapsed and died. Lic. Juan Chumacero de Sotomayor, *fiscal* of the Council of Military Orders, was named to replace him. By comparison with Carrillo, Chumacero was a junior figure at court, and as he began to master the complexities of the case the day of judgement for the Cardinal-Duke receded into the distance.[81]

Lerma prepared now for death. Aware, as he put it, of the frailty of life and of the 'changed condition that my rents and income have', on 21 October 1622 – one year to the day after the execution of Calderón – he signed a codicil to his Will and Testament.[82] He insisted that he had always served the crown 'with much love and faithfulness' and that he had conducted himself 'with the conscientiousness and integrity that my obligations required'.[83] He had never knowingly committed an injustice in the administration of justice or the distribution of public offices and insisted that he had sought to carry out his responsibilities with impartiality in the service of God, king and kingdom. He affirmed that he had never accepted gifts that were intended as bribes and that he had returned some that had been offered to him, adding that if his testamentaries found that any had been given to him with this 'evil intention' they were to return them to their donors. As to the notorious grant of the right to export Sicilian wheat: he insisted that 'I acted, as far as I could judge and understand, with all good faith and with security of conscience '.[84] Somewhat optimistically, he asked Philip IV to allow his family to retain the *mercedes* that it had received from the crown in recognition of his services to him.

Lerma confirmed that the investment of monies to produce the 20,000 ducats of rent for the establishment of the *mayorazgo* for the Count of Saldaña were to have priority over all of his other obligations. He reminded Uceda that he had agreed in the *concordia* of 1607 to take on his household servants after his death. He particularly commended Pedro de Solórzano and his son and Benito de Salcedo to him. He noted that 'the shortages and inadequacies of my rents and the need to meet unavoidable expenses' had forced him to moderate the 'desire with which I was born' to endow the Church and asked his heir to fulfil the terms of his religious foundations and his charitable works.[85]

Much more substantially, Lerma was forced now to acknowledge that he could not afford to maintain the foundations to which he had committed himself, and which meant so much to him. Most painful of all the reductions that he was now forced to make was that for the *Casa Profesa* for the Society of Jesus in Madrid. He had pledged 70,000 ducats to this but since he could not find the cash to do so he ordered that a much reduced *Casa* was to be funded out of any monies available from the 12,000 ducats that he enjoyed annually from the *encomienda mayor de Castilla*. He was not able to make an estimate of how much could be freed from this revenue (which would of course only be available for twelve years after his death). Similarly, he could not fund the 1,000 ducats of rent for the monastery of *Santo Domingo* in Lerma and so the foundation was to be abolished; this must have been deeply painful to him. Lerma still hoped to be able to provide the 1,000 ducats of annual rent for the convent of *San Blas* but he could not specify how this could be done. In the last settlement of his affairs, Lerma found himself unable to be confident that he could fund some of the ecclesiastical projects that meant the most to him.

Other adjustments had to be made to accommodate changes in circumstances since Lerma had drawn up the Testament in 1617. Baltasar Gilimón de la Mota and Melchior de Molina were removed from the list of testamentaries, ostensibly because their commitments made them too busy to fulfil the task but in practice because they were now pillars of the new regime. Among the new testamentaries whom Lerma named were his grandson, the Duke of Cea; the Count of Paredes; Lic. José González and Dr Colmenares, his personal lawyers; and Juan de Arce. He declared that he had drawn up the codicil 'in difficult times when I have been abandoned by many'.[86]

Even as Lerma prepared for death, his good fortune at court continued: Baltasar de Zúñiga died on 7 October 1622. Only the Count of Olivares now remained of the troika that had come into power in the spring of 1621, and he had no choice but to move to the centre of the stage himself. At the end of September it had been recorded that Olivares 'is introducing himself' into public ceremonies and acts and when Zúñiga died it was observed that 'the Count of Olivares enters into the despatch (of business)'. Olivares had effectively, if reluctantly, assumed control of government.[87] On 20 October Philip perpetuated the *alcaidía* of the royal palaces in Seville in the Olivares family.[88] On 1 December Olivares sat for the first time on the Council of State, and on 20 December was formally appointed as *caballerizo mayor* to the King.[89] He now stood, formally and publicly, at the very centre of affairs in both court and government and it was no longer possible for him to pretend otherwise. During December 1622 he attended six of the twelve meetings of the Council of State.

Lerma might reasonably have doubted whether Olivares would survive for long; inexperienced in governmental affairs and given to huge mood swings, the Count did not inspire confidence. Indeed, his very reticence in assuming public responsibilities while Benavente and Zúñiga lived suggested that he himself may have shared some of these doubts. Lerma himself had once scathingly rebuked Olivares for having 'a nature not to be ruled'; he might well have felt confident that Olivares would have neither the resolution to pursue him for long nor the ability to build a governmental team which would work productively with him.[90]

If Lerma entertained such doubts, his judgement would have been confirmed by a number of conciliatory gestures that Olivares now made to seek a very public and explicit reconciliation with the members of his party and family. On 20 December 1622 the King quashed the sentence on Uceda and declared that he had not failed in his obligations as a minister of the crown. At Christmas Uceda returned to court and was offered the poisoned chalice of the viceroyalty of Catalonia; in an act informed by unaccustomed wisdom, he refused it. At the same time, Olivares began to rectify the errors of judgement made in the persecution of Rodrigo Calderón. The countship of La Oliva was returned to Calderón's son while his widow, doña Inés de Vargas, was allowed once again to use the title of Countess and was presented with an *ayuda de costa* of 10,000 ducats. In January 1623 the town of Siete Iglesias was restored to Francisco Calderón and when on 17 August the King granted the countship of la Oliva to Francisco, and it was explicitly recorded that 'everything was owed to the intervention of the Count of Olivares, who since he could no longer free the father honoured the son'. Don Rodrigo's posthumous triumph was complete.[91] When, in June 1623, the Duchess of Cea was delivered of a child, Olivares was prominent among the gentlemen of the court who called on the Duke of Cea to congratulate him.[92]

Further gestures were made towards *lermistas* over the course of the next year; in April 1623, Tomás de Ángulo was appointed to a councillorship of Finance and in 1624 Juan de Ciriza was promoted to the secretaryship of the Council of State dealing with Italian affairs. Juan Téllez-Girón, fourth duke of Osuna, was welcomed back to court.[93] That a line had been drawn under the past was further emphasised when, during the Prince of Wales's extraordinary visit to Madrid in 1623, Pedro de Tapia and Antonio Bonal were allowed to return to their councillorships of Castile, reputedly at the request of the royal visitor himself (who may well have been somewhat bemused at being invited to make it).[94]

The English party returned to Santander through Valladolid. It was there in 1605 in Lerma's garden by the river that English hopes had been raised of an English marriage and it was not inappropriate that Charles's party should have come across Lerma, the architect of the policy that had kept England quiescent for nearly twenty years. They admired the picture collection in the *Casa de la Ribera* and took advantage of Philip IV's generosity to remove Giambologna's alabaster fountain.[95] Charles himself did not tarry to meet the old man but one of his courtiers did so, and he mused upon his activities:

> The Cardinal-Duke of *Lerma* lives at *Valladolid*, he officiates and sings Mass, and passes his old Age in Devotion and Exercises of Piety. It is a common, and indeed

a commendable Custom among the *Spaniard*, when he has pass'd his *Grand Climacteric*, and is grown decrepit, to make a voluntary resignation of Offices, be they never so great and profitable (tho' I cannot say *Lerma* did so), and sequestring and weaning themselves, as it were, from all mundane Negotiations and Incumbrances, to retire to some place of Devotion and spend the residue of their days in Meditation, and in preparing themselves for another World. *Charles* the Emperor shew'd them the way.[96]

With Lerma content in his new life in *San Pablo* and with Calderón's family reinstated at court, the worst dangers for the *lermistas* were ebbing away.

At the end of 1623, Chumacero y Sotomayor presented his indictment of the old favourite. He charged that Lerma had been guilty of excess in receiving gifts and *mercedes*. He made no attempt to follow the byzantine complexities of Lerma's dealings but set himself to draw up a clear and specific list of what he had received. He listed every office that Lerma had held and the dates on which he had acquired them. He calculated that Lerma had received *ayudas de costa* totalling 568,000 ducats and gave the details of each award and the purpose for which it had been acquired. He also provided the identities of the people through whose hands each grant had passed: Juan de Ciriza, Tomás de Ángulo, García Mazo de la Vega, Juan Ladrón de Guevara and Jorge de Tovar now found themselves reminded uncomfortably of their dealings with Lerma. Chumacero made a valiant effort but a flawed one; his indictment ignored many awards and was confused about others. His conclusion was, however, simple: all the *mercedes* given to Lerma should be revoked so that he and his heirs should not be allowed to benefit from them. Less simple for the prosecutor was the central dilemma involved in levelling charges against Lerma – the active complicity of the late king of Spain in all that Lerma had done.[97] Olivares had little time to ponder the dilemma with which he was confronted for on 8 February 1624 Philip IV left Madrid for his first state visit, to Andalusia: as Lerma had taken Philip III to Valencia in 1599 so now Olivares took Philip IV to Andalusia, his own *patria*, in order to consolidate his relationship with him. He certainly appreciated that he could not leave behind him in Madrid a clutch of hostile and resentful Sandovals.[98]

Uceda: testament and death, 31 May 1624

In Alcalá de Henares on 16 May 1624, the Duke of Uceda made the final amendments to his Will and Testament, and on 31 May he died there from an illness of which no details have been recorded.[99] His passing occasioned little comment but Virgilio Malvezzi eventually reflected the benign way in which Uceda had come to be viewed by his opponents at court – 'few defects but no great talent unless it was a great defect to hold such a high position without the ability that was worthy of it.[100] On the following day, Uceda's body was taken for burial to his church of San Bernardo in Madrid.[101] He had stipulated that when the church was finished his wife and children were also to be brought there from *San Pablo* for burial alongside him; he and his family would lie separate from his father, and in death he would at last acquire his independence.

The provisions of Uceda's Will revealed a modest and decent personality. He paid for up to 100,000 masses to be said as soon as possible in the churches of Lerma and Uceda; they were mostly to be for his own soul, but the duke also remembered the royal family and the members of his own family. He founded masses for the souls of the dead *caballeros* of the order of Santiago and endowed charities in the towns where he had held his posts in the Order. He stipulated that his debts were to be promptly settled and that his servants were to be paid everything that was owed to them. As his testamentaries, he named his father and his surviving son and three priests, Gonzalo Chacón, Antonio de Portocarrero and Pedro de Alarcón. He left to his father 'all the contents of my chapel' in witness of 'the great love that I have always had and hold for him'. He bequeathed one of his best *oratorios* to Saldaña 'as a sign of love', and others to his sisters and the Admiral of Castile and the Marquis of Peñafiel. Some valuables that he had pawned were to be redeemed. An unspecified matter of conscience was to be resolved by his confessor. His rents were probably worth about 80,000 ducats annually.[102] The *alcaidía* of the Alhambra was returned by the King to the Mondéjar family; it had been taken from them when Cristóbal was raised to the dukedom of Cea in 1604 and its restoration was a powerful symbol of the change of régime.[103]

Lerma: the final codicil. His death, 17 May 1625

Nothing is known of Lerma's reaction to his son's death. In October 1624 he decided to replace the codicil that he had drawn up three years earlier and he signed it on 21 October: once again, it can have been no coincidence that he did so on the anniversary of Calderón's death. He confessed the fullness of his religious beliefs and entrusted himself once again to his 'patron saints and advocates', saints Francis, Dominic and Santiago, to his guardian angel and 'to all the celestial court'.

Lerma's final provisions displayed commendable humility. He recorded that he had left his confessor, Fr Juan Chacón SJ with the responsibility for seeing to certain matters on his behalf but did not specify what they were. He asked pardon from Philip IV, his Queen and family 'with all the humility and reverence that I can' for all the faults that he had shown in their service and that of the King's parents; he confessed that these faults 'weigh greatly on me'. He also asked for forgiveness from the servants of the royal households for the work that he had imposed on them and for the words that he had spoken to them in anger, even though these had been inspired, as he claimed, by his zeal that they should serve their offices well. He implored his vassals for forgiveness for his shortcomings in administering justice in both legal and financial matters; they were to be given satisfaction in everything that his confessor and his testamentaries judged to be appropriate. Lerma ordered that all his family, servants and vassals should pray for the royal family. He asked pardon from the servants of the royal households for the expenses that they had incurred on the royal journeys and for any illnesses caused to them during the journeys.

Since his eldest son had predeceased him, Lerma had to ask his grandson and namesake, the new duke of Uceda, to look after the welfare of his *criados* and to supervise the implementation of his charitable dispositions. He paid tribute once again to Pedro de Solórzano, who had managed his estates and who had even helped him financially from his own resources. Lerma charged his heirs to favour and honour Solórzano as much as they could, and named him as a new testamentary. Lerma's Testament of 1617 had been witnessed by, among others, Rodrigo Calderón; the codicil of 1624 was witnessed by Calderón's son, the new Count of La Oliva.[104]

There remained one outstanding piece of business, and Lerma conducted it on 23 March 1625 in Valladolid when he signed over to the crown the incomes that derived from the grant of the export licence on the Sicilian wheat. He formally bound himself and his successors to honour the new agreement.[105] Since the case against the Cardinal-Duke was reaching its climax in the Council of Castile it seems certain that the agreement was itself part an understanding that he had reached with the crown but there is no evidence on the matter.

On 16 May 1625, Lerma signed a last codicil to his Will. He reaffirmed that Fr Chacón had his authority to dispose of certain unspecified matters. He again charged his grandson to take care of his *criados* and ordered that the doctors who had treated him during his recent illnesses should be paid. He authorised the payment of some debts and ordered that investigations be made of some minor obligations to verify whether he had outstanding commitments. He donated some relics to his sister the Countess of Lemos, clocks to his grandson and heir and *escritorios*, statues and the like to other close relatives. The codicil was witnessed by his household servants and a number of them, notably Fr Chacón and Pedro Solórzano, were with him when at about 9.30 on the following morning, 17 May 1625, he died.

Lerma's body lay in the royal palace until Saldaña brought it to *San Pablo* for burial; he was laid to rest in his cardinal's robes and hat.[106] Later that day, Francisco de Garnica, *corregidor* of Valladolid, opened Lerma's testamentary documents and sent news of his death post haste to Madrid; it arrived within eighteen hours. Olivares no doubt received it with deep satisfaction.[107] On 2 June, a memorial service was held for Lerma in the Capuchin church in his *huerta*. The 'whole court' – other than the king? – attended. The sermon was preached by Fr Florencia SJ.[108]

NOTES

1 Copy, AGS E 4126, printed by Valiente, *Los Validos*, pp. 162 and 198, doc. 5. See also, *Gaçetas y Nuevas*, p. 57.

2 Brussels, 23 Jan. 1619, RB 11/2116 doc. 85.

3 Góngora to D. Francisco del Corral, Madrid, 19 March 1619, printed in Luis de Góngora y Argote, *Obras Completas*, eds. J. and I. Millé y Giménez, Madrid, 1961, p. 920 (henceforth, Góngora, *Obras Completas*) and IEF, 'Cardenales Españoles', *DHEE*, i, p. 349.

4 Cottington to Lake, Madrid, 7/17 Jan. 1619, NA SP 94/23, fol. 141. Aliaga took possession of the Inquisitorship-general on 28 Jan. 1619, AHN Inq *lib*. 1338, fo. 346. On the justification for the appointment, Gonzalez Dávila, *Felipe III*, pp. 236–7.

5 See above, p. 195.

6 Cottington to Buckingham, Madrid, 28 Jan./7 Feb. 1619, SP 94/23, fols. 152–4.

7 Escagedo Salmon, 'Los Acebedos', vii, pp. 186–7.

8 *Gaçeta y Nuevas*, p. 59.

9 Cottington informed Digby that Gondomar had shown him a copy of the letter in which Philip wrote (according to the transcription in Cottington's letter) 'Por lo que conuiene a my ser[vici]o he mandado prender la persona del marques de las Siete Iglesias de que he querido auisaros, por el respeto que os tengo, y de lo que siempre tiendre a v[uestr]a p[erson]a', Madrid, 21 Feb./3 Mar. 1619, NA SP 94/23, fols. 161–161b. See also Novoa, *Historia de Felipe III*, CODOIN lxi, pp. 163–9.

10 'He gaue him so much assurance of the continuance of his own affection unto the Dukes person, as he hath since forborne to stirr any more in the business.' Cottington to Carleton, 13/23 Mar. 1619, ibid., fols. 169b–170.

11 Góngora to Francisco del Corral, Madrid, 19 Mar. 1619, *Obras Completas*, pp. 920–1.

12 Góngora to same, Madrid, 26 Mar. 1619, ibid., p. 922.

13 Salazar to Philip III, 17 December 1618, AGS CJH 561, fol. 329; *CSPV*, xv, 27 Mar. 1619, no. 809, p. 509.

14 'Y tambien las jornadas, en las quales se gasta al doblo, y estando el patrimonio Real tan acabado, no conviene que V. M. las haga, no siendo muy forzosas, a costa del sudor de sus pobres vasallos, los quales padeçen infinitas molestias, speçialmente los labradores, quitandoles sus carros y sus mulas quando mas neçesidad tienen dellas', *cnta*. Castile, 1 Feb. 1619, printed in González Palencia (ed.), *La Junta de Reformación*, pp. 12–30, at p. 26; Escagedo Salmón, 'Los Acebedos', vii, pp. 218–21.

15 *Cnta*. St. 19 April 1619, E. 2327, fo. 65; Brightwell, 'Spain and Bohemia: the Decision to Intervene', *ESR*, 12, 1982, pp. 118–19; on Aliaga's role, Escagedo Salmón, 'Los Acebedos', vii, p. 218.

16 The account of the *jornada de Portugal* is based upon Novoa, *Historia de Felipe III*, lxi, pp. 188–243 and the following anonymous accounts: 'Coronación de la Magestad del Rey don Felipe tercero … juramento del … principe su hijo', Seville, 1619; 'Entrada en publico, y recibimiento grandioso de … don Felipe tercero en … Lisboa', Seville, 1619; 'La jornada que la magestad catholica del rey don Phelippe III … hizo a … Portugal', Lisbon, 1623. See also, González Dávila, *Felipe III*, pp. 229–36 and *Gaçeta y Nuevas*, pp. 67–73.

17 Attendance Register, Council of State; on Infantado, Góngora to Francisco del Corral, Madrid, 16 Apr. 1619, *Obras Completas*, p. 925.

18 Benavente suggested that if Zúñiga was not chosen the Count of Olivares would be suitable. Philip named Gondomar, but he also succeeded in fighting off the appointment, *cnta*. St., 28 Feb. 1619, AGS E 2327, fol. 150.

19 'La jornada que Phelippe II … hizo a … Portugal.'

20 Ibid., pp. 24.

21 A detailed discussion of the crisis, Brightwell, 'Spain and Bohemia', pp. 124–33.

22 Ibid., pp. 135–6.
23 Parker, *Europe in Crisis*, pp. 119–20.
24 Cottington to Naunton, Madrid, 20/30 Nov. and 12/22 Dec. 1619, PRO SP 94/23, fols. 252–252b and 260b.
25 León Pinelo, *Anales de Madrid*, pp. 128–9.
26 *Gaçeta y Nuevas*, p. 74. See also, Francisco Troncoso de Ulloa to Gondomar, Madrid, 15 Jan. 1620, RB 11/2180, doc. 56.
27 *CSPV* xvi, 26 Oct., 16, 30 Nov. and 7 and 14 Dec. 1619, nos. 59, 84, 112, 121 and 134, pp. 35, 48, 60, 64 and 71.
28 *Gaçeta y Nuevas*, p. 81; J. Raneo, *Los Vireyes Lugartenientes del Reino de Nápoles*, CODOIN, xxiii, pp. 339–41, 367–9.
29 Brightwell, 'Spain and Bohemia', pp. 385–7; Morineau, *Incroyables gazettes*, 'Tableau 6', p. 75; Parker, *Army of Flanders*, pp. 215–16.
30 Lerma to Caracena, Lerma (?) 2 Feb. 1619, BL Add 28,436, fol. 39. See also same to same, 28 Jul. 1619, ibid., fol. 56. Diego de Santana to Gondomar, Valladolid, 17 and 21 Sep. 1619, RB 11/2180, doc. 213 and 11/2115, doc. 217.
31 'The Duke of Lerma hath of late beene daungerously sicke, but hath now well recouered his health w[hi]ch is cheifely attributed to the gratious letters, messages, and visitts w[hi]ch the king sent him, during this tyme of his sickness and indeed the continuance of his ma[ges]ties affection towards him is very apparent', Sir Walter Aston to Sir Dudley Carleton, 9/19 Jul. 1620, NA SP 94/24, fol. 4.
32 Góngora to Francisco del Corral, Madrid, 21 Jul. 1620, *Obras Completas*, p. 966.
33 Same to same, Madrid, 30 Jun. 1620, ibid., pp. 962.
34 *Gaçeta y Nuevas*, pp. 74, 77, 81.
35 The account of Philip's illness and death is based upon the following sources: Andrés de Almansa y Mendoza, *Obra Periodística*, eds. Henry Ettinghausen and Manuel Borrego, Madrid, 2001, 'Carta I', 13 Apr. 1621, pp. 167–76; Escagedo Salmón (ed.), 'Los Acebedos', viii, pp. 245–58; González Dávila, *Teatro de las Grandezas de … Madrid*, pp. 127–36; Novoa, *Felipe III*, xli, pp. 327–43; M. Damonte, *Felipe IV el grande rey de las Españas. Manoscritto anónimo del XVII siglo*, Milan, 1980, pp. 89–93; Góngora to Corral, 6 and 13 Apr. 1621, *Obras Completas*, pp. 979–85; *Gaçeta y Nuevas*, pp. 85–9.
36 *Cnta Junta* of Francisco de Contreras and Álvaro de Villegas, 19 Aug. 1621, AHN Inq Lib 229, no fol. Philip's fears for his eternal salvation are confirmed in Damonte, *Felipe IV*, pp. 90–1.
37 Góngora to Corral, Madrid, 6 Apr. 1621, *Obras Completas*, p. 980.
38 Escagedo Salmón (ed.), 'Los Acebedos', viii, pp. 251–8; Damonte, *Felipe IV*, p. 100; Gongora to Corral, 6 Apr. 1621, *Obras Completas*, p. 980.
39 Juan de Ciriza to Martín de Arostegui, Madrid, 29 Mar. 1621, AGS GA 865, no fol.
40 Felipe III, *Testamento de Felipe III*, Madrid, 1983.
41 Novoa, *Historia de Felipe III*, xli, pp. 333–46; Edw. Wilson to (Sir T. Wilson ?), 'last of March 1621 (NS)', NA SP 94/24, fol. 134.
42 *Gaçeta y Nuevas*, p. 89.
43 Góngora to Corral, Madrid, 6 Apr. 1621, *Obras Completas*, p. 981.
44 Almansa y Mendoza, 'Carta I', 13 Apr. 1621, p. 175.
45 A graphic description, Góngora to Corral, Madrid, 13 Apr. 1621, *Obras Completas*, pp. 983–4.
46 *Gaçeta y Nuevas*, p. 91; Edw. Wilson to Sir T. Wilson, Madrid, 26 Apr. 1621 (NS), NA SP 94/24, fol. 154. I have not found a copy of the *cédula*; it is referred to in 'Hacienda acrecentada', ADL 54, no. 9, no fol.
47 Lerma to Philip IV, Valladolid, 13 Apr. 1621, BL Mss Eg 740, fol. 13b, a copy.
48 Saldaña was, however, allowed to remarry and when the *desposo* for his marriage to Mariana de Córdoba took place in April the King and his sister María acted as *padrinos*, *Gaçeta y Nuevas*, pp. 93–4; Góngora to Corral, Madrid, 13 Apr. 1621, *Obras Completas*, p. 984. Almansa y Mendoza, 'Carta 2', Madrid, 16 May 1621, pp. 179–80; Novoa, *Felipe III*, xli, pp. 358–9.
49 'Acusación de Don Juan de Chumacero y Sotomayor contra Don Cristóbal de Sandoval y

Rojas, Duque de Uceda, por haber convertido todo el poder que tuvo en beneficio suyo y de su deudos', BN Mss 2394, fols. 319–23, a copy.

50 'Traslado de la Cédula Real de la comisión que se dio al Presidente de Indias, D. Fernando Carrillo para el conoscimiento de las mercedes que Felipe le hiço al Duque de Lerma y a sus deudos y criados', Madrid, 23 Apr. 1621, copy, BN Mss 2352, fols. 450–1.

51 Edw. Wilson to Sir T. Wilson, Madrid, 26 Apr. 1621 (NS), NA SP 94/24, fol. 154. The anonymous gentleman writing from court to his friend reported Lerma's letter (which has not apparently survived) and defended Carrillo vehemently ('sabe el mundo ser uno de los más doctos christianos y rectos juezes de Europa'), letter of 22 Jul. 1621, BN Mss 11011, fol. 217, copy.

52 Cereceda, 'La vocación jesuítica del duque de Lerma', p. 522.

53 Edw. Wilson to Sir T. Wilson, Madrid, 26 Apr. 1621, (NS), NA SP 94/24, fol. 154.

54 Novoa, Felipe III, lxi, p. 229.

55 V. Malvezzi, Historia ... que comprehende sucessos de le reynado de Don Phelipe Tercero ..., in J. Yáñez, Memorias para la historia de Don Felipe II, Rey de España, Madrid, 1723, pp. 65–7.

56 Góngora to Corral, Madrid, 13 Apr. 1621, Obras Completas, pp. 984–5, and Gaçeta y Nuevas, p. 93; Elliott, Olivares, p. 45.

57 Attendance Register, Council of State. On his appointment, Almansa y Mendoza, 'Carta 9', Madrid, 16 Nov. 1622, pp. 243–4.

58 'Acusación de Don Juan de Chumacero y Sotomayor'; the indictment charged that 'ocupando el primer lugar en su gracia y en la resolucion de todos los negocios de esta corona, asi de justicia como de gracia y govierno por ser el primer ministro por cuya relacion y parecer corria el despacho de las consultas y lo mas secreto de las materias de estado, y guerra'; see also Benigno, La sombra del rey, pp. 225–34; Góngora to Corral, Madrid, 27 Apr. 1621, Obras Completas, pp. 985–7.

59 Undated memorial of Uceda to Philip IV, BN Mss 18724, fol. 6, copy.

60 Gaçeta y Nuevas, p. 138; Damonte, Felipe IV, p. 98.

61 Edw. Wilson (to Sir T. Wilson), Madrid, 22 May 1621 NS, SP 94/24, fol. 175.

62 J. H. Elliott, The Count-Duke of Olivares. The Statesman in an Age of Decline, New Haven and London, 1986, p. 73.

63 A. González Palencia (ed.), Noticias de Madrid, 1621–1627, Madrid, 1942, pp. 8, 14; and Walter Aston to Secretary Calvert, Madrid, 26 Jul./5 Aug. 1621, SP 94/24, fol. 255.

64 A detailed account, Gaçeta y Nuevas, pp. 95–7.

65 Ibid., p. 100.

66 Góngora to Corral, Madrid, ? Jun. 1621, Obras Completas, p. 991.

67 Novoa, Historia de Felipe III, xli, p. 346.

68 'Memorial que don Rodrigo Calderón dió a su magestad ... Felipe IIII ... en su abono', Madrid, 1621, pp. 3–7; Almansa y Mendoza, 'Carta 3', 22 Jul. 1621, pp. 195–7.

69 Gaçeta y Nuevas, pp. 103–4; Góngora to Corral, Madrid, 20 July 1621, Obras Completas, p. 994; Almansa y Mendoza, 'Carta 4', Madrid, 31 Aug. 1621, pp. 201–2; Novoa, Felipe III, lxi, pp. 371–3.

70 González Dávila, Teatro de las Grandezas de ... Madrid, p. 110.

71 Escagedo Salmón, 'Los Acebedos', ix, pp. 154–8.

72 On Acevedo's departure 'on so fayre and ho[noura]ble termes that he goes away well satiss- fied', Aston to Calvert, Madrid, 5/15 Sep. 1621, SP 94/24, fol. 301b; Almansa y Mendoza, 'Carta 5', Madrid, 14 Oct. 1621, p. 208. See also, Gaçetas y Nuevas, pp. 110–11, and González Dávila, Teatro de las Grandezas de ... Madrid, pp. 397–402.

73 Postscript, Aston to Calvert, Madrid, 30 Sep./10 Oct. 1621, SP 94/24, fo. 314b.

74 'Papel que D[on] Rodrigo Calderon remitio a Su M[a]g[esta]d el S[eno]r Ph[elip]e 4o. el dia antes que le sacassen a degollar encargandole al alcalde de su caussa no le diesse al rey asta que el quedasse en el suplicio muertto', BL Mss Eg 2081, fols. 118–21b, a copy.

75 The fullest account of his life, trial and death, Almansa y Mendoza, 'Carta 6', Madrid, 22 Oct.

1621, pp. 213–21; Elliott, *Olivares*, p. 108.

76 Isabella to Lerma, noting that she had received three letters from him, Brussels, 20 Sep. 1621, ADL 24 (Antiguo), no. 12; see also, same to same, Brussels, 24 Mar. 1623, assuring him that 'no tengo olbydado lo q[ue] os debo', ibid., no. 14. The pope's letter, Rome, 22 Aug. 1621, BN Mss 2352, fol. 509, a copy.

77 Almansa y Mendoza, '*Cartas 7, 8*', undated and 16 Nov. (?) 1621, pp. 222–9.

78 *Cnta.* Contreras and Villegas, 19 Aug. 1621, AHN Inq Lib 299, no fol.

79 *Auto de posesión* of Pacheco, Madrid, 26 Apr. 1622, AHN Inq lib 1338, fol. 275.

80 *Gaçeta y Nuevas*, p. 120; Castroviejo and Fernández de Córdoba, *Gondomar*, p. 194.

81 *Cédula* appointing Chumacero y Sotomayor, in 'Acusación de Don Juan de Chumacero y Sotomayor'.

82 'AUTOS QVE SE HIZIERON para abrir el Codicilio que se otogaron … con el testame[n]to del Excellentiss. Cardenal Duque de Lerma', appended to 'Testamento', ADL 12, with the 1621 codicil at pp. 3b–10.

83 Ibid., p. 3b.

84 Ibid., pp. 9b–10.

85 Ibid.

86 Ibid., p. 32v.

87 *Gaçeta y Nuevas*, pp. 133 and 135.

88 Ibid., p. 136.

89 Ibid., p. 139; *Noticias de Madrid*, p. 43; Elliott, *Olivares*, p. 131; Attendance register, Council of State.

90 Elliott, *Olivares*, p. 36.

91 *Gaçeta y Nuevas*, p. 141; On Uceda, Damonte, *Felipe IV*, pp. 98–9 and V. Malvezzi, *Historia de los primeros años del reinado de Felipe IV*, ed. D. L. Shaw, London, 1968, p. 35; on Calderón's family, *Noticias de Madrid*, pp. 44 and 71 (quotation). See also, Almansa y Mendoza, '*Carta 10*', Madrid, 12 Mar. 1623, p. 257.

92 'A 6 parió la duquesa de Cea un hijo, a quien fueron luego a dar el parabién todas las señoras de la corte, y al duque todos los señores y el conde de Olivares', Almansa y Mendoza, '*Carta 11*', Madrid, ? Jun. 1623, p. 265. The child died a week later.

93 Ángulo's title, 15 Apr. 1623, AGS QC 40; Ciriza's, 30 Apr. 1624, ibid. 25; on Osuna, Thompson, 'Philip IV', p. 5.

94 On the visit of Charles, Glyn Redworth, *The Prince and the Infanta. The Cultural Politics of the Spanish Match*, New Haven, 2003; see also Elliott, *Olivares*, pp. 207–14 and Henry Etting-hausen, 'Prince Charles and the King of Spain's Sister – What the Papers Said', University of Southampton, 1985.

95 *Gaçeta y Nuevas*, pp. 176–7.

96 James Howell, *Epistolae Ho-Elianae. Familiar Letters*, 11th edn, London, 1754, p. 158.

97 'Querella del fiscal del Consejo contra el señor Cardenal Duque de Lerma', n. d., BL Mss Eg 2081, fols. 128–30 and details included in 'Petición que se dió en el consexo, por el Duq[ue] mi s[eño]r, Adelantado Mayor, sobre el pleyto de las m[e]r[ce]des De su abuelo', 1626, ADL 14, no. 32.

98 Elliott, *Olivares*, p. 152.

99 *Noticias de Madrid*, p. 96 and 'Copia autentica del testamento cerrado del ex[celentisim]o senor Duque de Uzeda, Marques de Velmonte D[o]n Christobal Gomez de Sandobal', Alcalá de Henares, 31 May 1624, ADL 12, no. 26.

100 Malvezzi, *Historia de los primeros años del reinado de Felipe IV*, p. 36.

101 *Gaçeta y Nuevas*, p. 196 and *Noticias de Madrid*, p. 97.

102 'Copia autentica del testamento cerrado', ADL 12, no. 26, fols. 4–12.

103 *Gaçeta y Nuevas*, p. 197.

104 'Autos para abrir el codicilio de treynta y vno de Otubre de mil y seyscientos y veynte y quatro', appended to 'Testamento', pp. 1–4 of separate numeration.

105 I have not found the document; it is referred to in the *cédula*, Madrid, 20 Jul. 1626, copy,

detailing the agreement between the crown and Francisco Gomez II de Sandoval y Rojas, II duke of Lerma, ADL 53, no fol.

106 'Autos para el Codicilio y diez y seys de Mayo, deste año de mil y seyscientos y veynte y cinco', appended to 'Testamento', pp. 1–5; certifications of death of Lerma in 'AVTOS QVE SE HIZIERON PARA ABRIR el testamento del Excel[entisimo] señor Cardenal Duque de Lerma', Valladolid, 25 May 1625, prefatory to 'Testamento', pp. 1–2.

107 Novoa, *Felipe III*, xli, pp. 422–3; *Gaçeta y Nuevas*, p. 218; on Olivares's *annus mirabilis*, Elliott, *Olivares*, pp. 226–43.

108 Gaçeta y Nuevas, p. 219 and Noticias de Madrid, p. 120.

Conclusion

Lerma's exercise of the *valimiento* substantially changed the character of the Spanish Monarchy and many of the ethical values that operated in court and government. Commentators were of course extremely reluctant even to hint that the King of Spain was not equal to the task of governing but it was generally recognised that Philip III needed guidance in the early years of his reign; many observers would have agreed with friar Sepúlveda's forlorn comment that if the King had to have a favourite it should be someone of the qualities of the Duke of Lerma.[1] Part of the assessment of Lerma's role must concern the validity of his usefulness in providing real leadership for the Spanish monarchy at a time when the King was manifestly unequal to the tasks that destiny had imposed upon him. However, the voraciousness with which Lerma profited from his position to build his enormous fortune had profound implications for the standards of public life. Moreover, the support and protection that he gave to corrupt ministers such as Villalonga and Siete Iglesias helped to further diminish the levels of probity that operated in court and government. Service to the crown had always carried the possibility of self-enrichment but the rapacity with which Lerma profited from his power over the King established new parameters that gravely undermined the standards of integrity required of ministers.

If the years of Lerma's *valimiento* saw a decline in the quality of kingship and of ethical standards in government they also witnessed an expansion in the role played by the governmental councils and by the Cortes of Castile. The roots of this expansion can be traced to the last decade or so of Philip II's reign but it was only under Philip III that the councils and the Cortes of Castile reached the fulness of their new authority. The councils became more professionalised and – often at critically important moments – more independent of courtly authority. Certainly, it was during Philip III's reign that the Cortes of Castile came closest to imposing some measure of restriction upon the ability of the crown to tax its subjects without representation. It is probable that both developments would have taken place independently of Lerma's exercise of the *valimiento* but it is certain that the nature of the authority that he wielded substantially facilitated the growth in the authority of councils and Cortes. Moreover, the new vitality of councils and Cortes encouraged wider public discussion about the nature and values of government as the new levels of taxation led to new levels of debate; the reign of Philip III became something of a golden age of political discourse.

For all that his policies led to a growth in the fiscal burdens placed upon the King's subjects, Lerma was extraordinarily fortunate that his exercise of the *valimiento* coincided with the interlude between the end of the wars of Philip II and the beginning of the dreadful storm that marked the half-century after 1618. Indeed, his good fortune was characterised by the advantages that accrued to him as a result of the assassination of Henry IV in 1610. Unlike Olivares, Richelieu and Mazarin, Lerma did not find that his period of power was consumed by the dreadful demands that total war made upon the resources of the early seventeenth-century state. As a reflection of this he was not subject to the vicious attacks – personal and political – that the other great favourites of the first half of the seventeenth century had to endure. He was therefore able to be a much more suave and emollient figure in domestic politics than his successors.

Olivares and his colleagues sought to revive Spanish fortunes by harking back to the achievements of Philip II, contrasting the failures of Lerma (and by implication, of course, of Philip III) with the greatness of the *rey prudente*. But of course, Philip II was *not* the Prudent King in his last decade or so, when he committed Spain to one more gamble after another (exactly as Olivares was to do in the 1620s and 1630s). The 1590s were *not* a golden age in Spanish history; they were one of the darkest and most dreadful periods of political failure in the Spanish experience under the house of Habsburg. Moreover, they were rounded out by perhaps the most enormous natural disaster ever to befall the Spanish people, the plague of 1596–1602 which took away nearly one-tenth of the people of Castile. Lerma, therefore, for all his faults, lies not between the gigantic achievements of Philip II and those of the Count-Duke of Olivares but between the failures of two regimes which gambled without thought of the morrow.

We must remember, too, that Lerma's power developed and it declined. He was never again as secure as he had been in 1605. Rather, therefore, than remark – as has so often been done – about how Lerma exercised power for twenty years, we might usefully think of him exercising the plenitude of his power for five or six years and then having to develop strategies to survive in office. The same is true of other *validos*; Olivares, for instance, was never as secure after 1625–26 as he had been at that time of triumph, and he too had to develop strategies to remain in power, strategies which consisted partly of overwhelming his opponents, partly of accommodating himself to them. The acquisition of power was one thing, retaining it was quite another. Even a figure who was as overpowering as Lerma was in the years of his greatest power could still be opposed – in the court, by grandees and even lesser noblemen, by powerful women and by single-minded and self-confident individuals such as, for example, Fernando Carrillo, don Pedro de Toledo or don Agustín Mejía. Lerma was of course especially vulnerable to people holding strategically important positions, notably the Queen and the confessors of the King. Talk of a one-party state is therefore somewhat premature.

As part of this equation we should recall, too, that while Lerma packed court and government with his supporters, most of them were in position by 1604, and that thereafter he needed to place comparatively few men and women in office. The creation of his party or faction was therefore an achievement of those first years in power. Equally, those years were a time when he was surrounded by mature and able advisers – the cardinal-archbishop of Toledo, the Count of Miranda, Juan de Borja and the Count of Villalonga. But by the end of Lerma's first decade in power all but the cardinal-archbishop were gone; exactly as the duke entered his great crisis he was forced to rely upon men who were patently unequal to the task, such as the Marquis of Siete Iglesias, García de Pareja and Fr Friedrich Gedler. The collapse of his party encouraged the self-confidence and assertiveness of his opponents.

Nothing, however, so encouraged Lerma's opponents as his announcement at the turn of 1615–16 that he intended to leave power – except, that is, the failure of Cristóbal, Duke of Uceda, to develop into a credible and worthy successor to him. The collapse – rather, the slow disintegration – of Lerma's dazzling, historic exercise of power came about because he wanted to retire from political life to concentrate on his spiritual salvation and because he could neither bring himself to do so nor to trust the son who was so transparently incapable of taking on the reins of government that he intended to bestow upon him.

Lerma's *valimiento* becomes, therefore – like the man himself – much more interesting and complex a phenomenon than has sometimes appeared to be the case, and the development of the office of *valido* must be assessed within an institutional as well as a personal context. Certainly, Lerma's successor as *valido* learned a great deal from him. Olivares laid much of the basis of his authority in court and government by systematically criticising the Lerma regime. However, all his rhetoric and bombast could never quite obscure the extent to which he had based his methods upon those of Lerma: his great opponent was also his great teacher. Most obviously, like Lerma, Olivares had been appointed as *caballerizo mayor* of the King (1621) and raised to the dukedom so that he could deal with the leading figures at court on a basis of equality (1625). Moreover, he had a number of his kinsmen and supporters raised to new or improved titles of honour. He then consolidated his years of triumph in 1624 by taking Philip IV on a visit to his own *patria,* Andalusia, exactly as Lerma had taken Philip III to Valencia in 1599 and 1603–04.

Olivares rightly prided himself on his integrity and honesty but it was yet true that he sought to advance his family and his own financial interests as Lerma had done. Unfortunately for him, the last of his three children died in 1627 and he therefore never enjoyed the possibility – of which Lerma had made so much – of advancing his own family. However, like Lerma – and in this there is perhaps the closest point of similarity between them – Olivares sought to perpetuate the tenure of his family in power by endeavouring to ensure that his son-in-law, Ramiro de Guzmán, should succeed to the *valimiento.* To facilitate the young man's prospect of doing so he had him raised to the marquisate of Heliche in 1625 and to the dukedom of Medina de las Torres in 1626. That plan fell through but the *valimiento* in turn passed to Olivares's cousin, Luis de Haro. Olivares's family therefore managed the trick that had defeated the cardinal-duke, of ensuring that the *valimiento* passed into the next generation. Olivares, like Lerma, appreciated that the *valimiento* had, in order to succeed, to be multi-generational.

NOTE
1 See above, p. 87.

Appendices

Appendix I: Aristocratic income 1501-1624: an indicative table based upon contemporary estimates

Title and rank	Date of title	1501	1520	1539
No. of titles		54	53	78
Maximum income		50 400	50 000	60 000
Minimum income		2 800	6 000	4 000
Average income		10 627	14 561	18 769
Total rent-roll		573 900	830 000	1 464 000
Medina Sidonia (d)	1445	39 000 [2]	50 000 [1]	55 000 [6]
Denia (m)/ Lerma (d)	1484/1599	7 000 [30]	10 000 [28]	14 000 [35]
Frias (d)	1492	50 400 [1]	50 000 [1]	80 000 [14]
Medinaceli (d)	1492	28 000 [5]	24 000 [8]	30 000 [12]
Ureña(c)/Osuna (d)	1464/1562	16 800 [8]	22 000 [11]	20 000 [23]
Benavente (c)	1398	30 800 [4]	30 000 [4]	60 000 [1]
Alburquerque (d)	1464	16 400 [9]	20 000 [12]	25 000 [20]
Infantado (d)	1475	28 888 [5]	30 000 [4]	50,000 [7]
Fería (d)	1567	–	–	–
Santa Cruz (m)	1569	–	–	–
La Laguna (m)	1599	–	–	–
Lemos (c)	1456	2 800 [8]	10 000 [28]	12 000 [36]
Altamira (c)	1475/1608	2 800 [48]	6 000 [53]	*
Gandía (d)	1483	8 000 [29]	*	12 000 [36]
Miranda (c)/Peñaranda (d)	1457	7 000 [30]	16 000 [13]	20 000 [23]
Velada (m)	1557	–	–	–
Chinchon (c)	1520	–	6 000 [53]	8 000 [54]
Puñonrostro (c)	1523	–	–	8 000 [54]

* not listed

** entry is mistaken and not entered here

Note: A number of contemporary assessments of the incomes of noble families provide a valuable reference-point for comparing the changing fortunes of the aristocracy. They have to be treated with caution, not least because individual families often had good reason to exaggerate or to minimise their incomes. Equally, the reputation of a family often affected writers' calculations; this can be seen in the exaggeration of Lerma's income for 1616 and in the failure to take full account of the extent of the loss of his income in his later years. Nevertheless, they are useful in allowing us to form an estimate of how families' incomes developed over the period; for this reason, I have added in super-script a number indicating the place of the family in the league of incomes for that year.

1578	1595	1613	1616	1620	1624
105	118	148	174	169	182
150 000	170 000	160 000	300 000	170 000	200 000
4 000	4 000	4 000	4 000	2 000	3 000
26 952	34 732	31 676	28 158	27 982	27 549
2 830 000	4 272 000	4 688 000	4 984 000	4 617 000	5 014 000
150 000 [1]	170 000 [1]	160 000 [1]	200 000 [2]	170 000 [1]	160 000 [2]
14 000 [64]	20 000 [58]	150 000 [2]	300 000 [1]	165 000 [2]	200 000 [1]
42 000 [20]	65 000 [17]	90 000 [11]	70 000 [13]	80 000 [11]	70 000 [16]
28 000 [28]	60 000 [18]	55 000 [26]	40 000 [30]	80 000 [11]	50 000 [23]
112 000 [2]	150 000 [2]	140 000 [5]	126 000 [5]	150 000 [4]	150 000 [3]
74 000 [9]	120 000 [4]	100 000 [7]	100 000 [7]	60 000 [19]	110 000 [7]
50 000 [15]	50 000 [23]	50 000 [27]	50 000 [21]	50 000 [21]	40 000 [28]
100 000 [3]	120 000 [4]	100 000 [7]	130 000 [4]	120 000 [6]	120 000 [7]
30 000 [35]	50 000 [23]	65 000 [21]	50 000 [21]	70 000 [16]	50 000 [23]
15 000 [49]	35 000 [41]	26 000 [54]	20 000 [59]	25 000 [52]	30 000 [39]
–	–	12 000[116]	10 000[127]	**	80 000 [14]
48 000 [19]	40 000 [12]	30 000 [41]	60 000 [19]	30 000 [39]	35 000 [37]
12 000 [73]	12 000 [89]	12 000[116]	12 000[111]	12 000 [99]	14 000[100]
26 000 [29]	40 000 [29]	80 000 [13]	50 000 [22]	40 000 [26]	70 000 [16]
30 000 [25]	40 000 [29]	50 000 [27]	40 000 [30]	20 000 [58]	50 000 [23]
12 000 [73]	10 000[100]	45 000 [29]	45 000 [28]	40 000 [26]	40 000 [28]
17 000 [43]	30 000 [43]	60 000 [22]	40 000 [30]	30 000 [39]	30 000 [39]
15 000 [49]	25 000 [50]	26 000 [54]	20 000 [59]	20 000 [58]	20 000 [60]

Source: The list of aristocratic incomes is based upon the following documents. Only the 1624 document is formally dated; otherwise I have calculated the date from internal evidence.

1501 Antoine Lalaing, 'Relation du premier voyage de Philippe le Beau en Espagne, en 1501', *Collection des voyages des souverains des Pays-Bas*, Brussels, 1876, i, pp. 252–6

1520 Karl Otto Müller, 'Das Einkommen Kg. Karls von Spanien', *Quellen Zur Handelsgeschichte Der Paumgartner von Augsburg (1480-1570)*, Wiesbaden, 1957, pp. 113–15

1539 Lucas Marineo Sículo, *De las cosas memorables de España*, Alcalá de Henares, 1539

1578 Anon., 'Grandes y Nobleza de España', British Library Harleian Manuscripts 5275, fols. 61–4

1595 Pedro Núñez de Salcedo, 'Relación verdadera de todos los títulos que ai en España', ed. Vicente Castañeda, *Boletín de la Real Academia de Historia,* LXXIII (1918), pp. 468–91

1613 Anon., 'Curia Española, que contiene todos los Arçobispados ... Duques, Marqueses, Condes... que son en Castilla, y quienes fueron les Primeros, sus nombrres, Apellidos, rentas que cada uno tiene...', no date, BL Sl 1573, fols. 1–25.

1616 Printed by Eduardo Escartín Sánchez, ' La sociedad española del siglo XVII', *Historia General de España y America,* viii, 'La crisis de la hegemonía española', Madrid, 1986, pp. 276–80

1620 Francisco Pérez Carrillo, 'Dialogo de las virtudes Cardenales Prudencia y Justicia diuidido en dos Tratados ...', 1620, BN Mss 1254, fols. 185v-298.

1624 Anon., 'Relación de las rentas reales de arzobispados, obispados, duq[ue]s, marqu[ese]s y condes de España ..... doze de Febrero de 1624', BN MSS 3485. This corresponds to the list published by Francisco de Aguirre Vaca y Sotomayor, *Casas illvstres de España recogidas de diferentes autores en el anno 1624,* BN Mss 18355.

Dates of foundation of titles

Juan Moreño de Guerra y Alonso, *Guía de la grandeza historica genealógica y heráldica de todas las casas que gozan de esta dignidad,* Madrid, 1918?

Josef Berní y Catalá, *Creación, antigüedad, y privilegios de los títulos de Castilla,* Valencia, 1769

Antonio Ramos, *Aparato para la corección y adición de la obra que publicó en 1769 ... J. Berní y Catalá .. con el titulo : Creación, antigüedad, y privilegios de los títulos de Castilla,* Malága, 1777

Appendix II: The Duke of Lerma: religious foundations

Foundation	No. of clergy or religious	Expenditure	Lerma's	Others	Capital value
OLD CASTLE					
Valladolid					
Monastery of *San Pablo*					
patronazgo	28		2,000	2,000	80,000
Building and furnishings		73,443			
Gifts for divine services		32,747			
Choir stalls		24,200			
Statues of Lerma and wife		16,000			
Sunday memoria			1,000		20,000
Chapel of S. Miguel		2,150			
Convent of *Nuestra Señora*					
de Belén	6				
Building and furnishings		9,329	467		9,340
Monastery of *San Diego*					
Building	8	16,400			
Furnishings and gifts		1,066			
Ampudia					
Collegial church					
Buildings and furnishings	33	12,000	1,000	9,000	200,000
Monastery of *San Antonio*	5				
Buildings		500			
La Ventosilla					
Chaplaincies			350		7,000
	2				
Cea					
Monastery of *Nuestra Señora*		4,254	600		12,000
de Trianos	2				
Lerma					
Church of *San Pedro*					
Building, furnishings, gifts	33	93,467	2,000		240,000
Convent of *Madre de Dios*					
Buildings, furnishings	6	20,700		10,000	
Cash to buy rents		20,000			
Convent of *San Blas*					
Buildings	2	69,877	1,000		20,000
Ornaments for services		4,000			
Monastery of *Sto Domingo*	14				
Building		39,950	1,000		
Gifts for divine services		6,000			20,000
Convent of *Nuestra Señora*					
de Vicente	9				
Gifts for divine services		2,000	600		12,000

Foundation	No of religious	Expenditure	Rents :		
			Lerma's	Others	Capital value
MADRID					
City of Madrid					
Monastery of *Santísima Trinidad*					
Building and gifts	2	7,000	400		8000
Convent of *Santa Catalina*					
Buildings and gifts	6		600		12,000
Monastery of Carmelites					
Building and gifts	8	5,512			
Casa Profesa of Society of Jesus					
Building and gifts	15	71,000			
Valdemoro					
Convent of *Santa Clara*					
Building and gifts	6	36,667			
KINGDOM OF VALENCIA					
Convent of *Nuestra Señora de*					
Loreto, Denia	8				
Building and gifts		19,400	570		11,400
Monastery of *San Antonio*, Denia					
Furnishings and gifts	12	1,500			
Monastery of *S. Francisco de*					
Paula, Javea	4				
Building		1,000			
DOMINICAN PROFESSORSHIPS					
Salamanca (*visperas*)			273		5,460
Valladolid (*visperas*)	1	3,000	150		3,000
Alcalá de Henares (*visperas, prima*)	1		300		6,000
	2				
MEMORIAS FOR WIFE					
Chaplaincy, Buitrago			300		6,000
Memorial masses, Medinaceli		800			
CAPITULAR PATRONAZGOS					
Provincia de España, Dominicans			600		12,000
Provincia de San Pablo, Franciscans			100		2,000
TOTALS		593,962	13,310	21,000	686,200

Note: Lerma's private papers are remarkably precise in recording the amounts of money that he invested in his ecclesiastical buildings but tend not to give precise figures for the number of religious who lived in them, presumably because these changed considerably over the years. The numbers given for the members of these communities must therefore be regarded as tentative, and will be developed by ongoing research.

Source: Anon., 'Relación General de los Patronazgos que tiene el Duque de Lerma mi señor adelantado mayor de castilla perpetuos en los Reynos de Castilla, Aragón y Valencia y la Renta que per Raçon dellas les dejo situada El Cardenal Duque mi s[eñor] que aya gloria …', 22 Feb. 1623, ADL 54 no. 9

Appendix III: The Duke of Lerma: revenues, 1597–1625

	1597	1598	1599	1600	1601	1602
RENTS						
Castile	8,027	8,027	8,027	8,027	8,027	8,027
Rents of Ampudia				3,000	3,000	3,000
Rents of 'Lands of Recompense'				4,000	4,000	4,000
Rents, *villas de behetría*						
Royal taxes, *villas de behetría*						
Minor municipal offices, *villas de behetría*						
Regimientos & *escribanias*, *villas de behetría*						
Rent, Tudela de Duero						
Valencia	8,000	8,000	8,000	8,000	8,000	8,000
Protection for *almadrabas*			5,000	5,000	5,000	5,000
Peage y leuda, marquisate of Denia			1,000	1,000	1,000	1,000
Production of salt, marquisate of Denia			2,000	2,000	2,000	2,000
Sisas, Valencia						
Perpetuation of *almadraba* concession						
Kingdom of Aragon						
Town of Purroy, Aragon			500	500	500	500
Rents and *juros* in Crown of Aragon						
Military habits						
Encomienda, Merida	2,267					
Encomienda, Hornachos	400	400				
Comendador Mayor de Castilla				12,000	12,000	12,000	12,000
Court offices						
Captain of Guards	667					
Gentilhombre de la cámara, Philip II	1,500					
Caballerizo Mayor & *Sumiller de Corps*, Philip III				10,000	10,000	10,000	10,000
Capitán General de la Caballeriza de España						
Capitán General de la Caballeriza de Aragón						
Trading concessions						
Escribanía de sacas		9,000	9,000			
Escribanías of Alicante and Origuela, Valencia			3,500	3,500	3,500	3,500
Rents in Portugal				9,200	9,200	9,200
Export licence on *salmas* in Sicily					60,000	60,000
Governorship of royal palaces						
Governor of *Casa de Campo*						
Governorship of *cavallerizas of Madrid*						
Governorship of *Casa de la Ribera*						
Grants from Cardinal of Toledo						
Grant	600					
Grant to redeem debts				20,000	20,000	20,000	20,000
Rents on *adelantamiento* of Cazorla						
TOTAL	21,461	25,427	79,027	86,227	146,227	146,227

1603	1604	1605	1606	1607	1608	1609	1610	1611	1612	1613
8,027	8,027	8,027	8,027	8,027	8,027	8,027	8,027	8,027	8,027	8,027
3,000	3,000	3,000	3,000	3,000	3,000	3,000	3,000	3,000	3,000	3,000
4,000	4,000	4,000	4,000	4,000	4,000	4,000	4,000	4,000	4,000	4,000
				8,265	8,265	8,265	8,265	8,265	8265	8,265
									13,100	13,100
									4,000	4,000
									7,927	7,927
				3,595	3,595	3,595	3,595	3,595	3,595	3,595
8,000	8,000	8,000	8,000	8,000	8,000	8,000	8,000	8,000	8,000	8,000
5,000	5,000	5,000	5,000	5,000	5,000	5,000	5,000	5,000	5,000	5,000
1,000	1,000	1,000	1,000	1,000	1,000	1,000	1,000	1,000	1,000	1,000
2,000	2,000	2,000	2,000	2,000	2,000	2,000	2,000	2,000	2,000	2,000
1,500	1,500	1,500	1,500	1,500	1,500	1,500	1,500	1,500	1,500	1,500
1,500	1,500	1,500	1,500	1,500	1,500	1,500	1,500	1,500	1,500	1,500
500	500	500	500	500	500	500	500	500	500	500
72,000	72,000	72,000	72,000	72,000	72,000	72,000	72,000	72,000	72,000	72,000
12,000	12,000	12,000	12,000	12,000	12,000	12,000	12,000	12,000	12,000	12,000
10,000	10,000	10,000	10,000	10,000	10,000	10,000	10,000	10,000	10,000	10,000
12,000	12,000	12,000	12,000	12,000	12,000	12,000	12,000	12,000		
3,500	3,500	3,500	3,500	3,500	3,500	3,500	3,500	3,500	3,500	3,500
9,200	9,200	9,200	9,200	9,200	9,200	9,200	9,200	9,200	9,200	9,200
20,000	20,000	20,000	20,000	20,000	20,000	20,000	20,000	20,000	20,000	20,000
	6000	6000	6000	6000	6000	6000	6000	6000	6000	6000
170,227	179,227	179,227	179,227	191,087	191,087	191,087	191,087	191,087	204,114	204,114

1614	1615	1616	1617	1618	1619	1620	1621	1622	1623	1624	16
8,027	8,027	8,027	8,027	8,027	8,027	8,027	8,027	8,027	8,027	8,027	8,0
3,000	3,000	3,000	3,000	3,000	3,000	3,000	3,000	3,000	3,000	3,000	3,0(
4,000	4,000	4,000	4,000	4,000	4,000	4,000	4,000	4,000	4,000	4,000	4,0(
8,265	8,265	82,65	8,265	8,265	8,265	8,265	8265	8,265	8,265	8,265	8,2(
13,100	13,100	13,100	13,100	13,100	13,100	13,100	13,100	13,100	13,100	13,100	13,1(
4,000	4,000	4,000	4,000	4,000	4,000	4,000	4,000	4,000	4,000	4,000	4,0(
7,927	7,927	7,927	7,927	7,927	7,927	7,927	7,927	7,927	7,927	7,927	7,9.
3,595	3,595	3,595	3,595	3,595	3,595	3,595	3,595	3,595	3,595	3,595	3,5!
8,000	8,000	8,000	8,000	8,000	8,000	8,000	8,000	8,000	8,000	8,000	8,0(
5,000	5,000	5,000	5,000	5,000	5,000	5,000	5,000	5,000	5,000	5,000	5,0(
1,000	1,000	1,000	1,000	1,000	1,000	1,000	1,000	1,000	1,000	1,000	1,0(
1,000	1,000	1,000	1,000	1,000	1,000	1,000	1,000	1,000	1,000	1,000	1,0(
2,000	2,000	2,000	2,000	2,000	2,000	2,000	2,000	2,000	2,000	2,000	2,0(
1,500	1,500	1,500	1,500	1,500	1,500	1,500	1,500	1,500	1,500	1,500	1,5(
1,500	1,500	1,500	1,500	1,500	1,500	1,500	1,500	1,500	1,500	1,500	1,5(
500	500	500	500	500	500	500	500	500	500	500	5(
72,000	72,000	72,000	72,000	72,000	72,000	72,000	72,000				
12,000	12,000	12,000	12,000	12,000	12,000	12,000	12,000	12,000	12,000	12,000	12,0(
10,000	10,000	10,000	10,000	10,000							
3,500	3,500	3,500	3,500	3,500	3,500	3,500	3,500	3,500	3,500	3,500	3,5(
9,200	9,200	9,200	9,200	9,200	9,200	9,200	9,200	9,200	9,200	9,200	9,2(
20,000	20,000	20,000	20,000	20,000							
6000	6000	6000	6000	6000							
204,114	204,114	204,114	204,114	204,114	168,114	168,114	168,114	96,114	96,114	96,114	96,11

Select bibliography

Details of works referred to in the text and suggestions for further reading are presented here.

Archival sources

Archivo de la Corona de Aragón, Barcelona 650–9
Archivo del Duque de Lerma, Toledo 1–200
Archivo General de Indias, Seville
   Indiferente General, 789–851
Archivo General de Simancas, Valladolid
   Bulas y Breves Sueltas 5842
   Casas y Sitios Reales 301–2
   Consejo de Castilla, Cámara de Castilla, 807, 809, 815, 828, 845, 847, 898, 913, 918, 920
   Consejo y Junta de Hacienda 254–5, 263–4, 274, 284, 293, 308–11, 320–1, 332–4, 341, 345–6, 352–3, 356, 360–1, 366, 370–1, 376–7, 380, 383, 387, 391–2, 395, 397, 401–2, 405, 410, 414–15, 419, 432, 480, 482, 487, 495, 526, 528, 536, 542, 561
   Contadurías Generales 768, 886–8
   Contaduría Mayor de Cuentas, 3a época 986, 1978, 1987, 3079, 3532
   Dirección General del Tesoro, Inventario 24 508, 475, 1288
   Estado 183–4, 198, 201, 205, 621, 626, 840–1, 1226–7, 1288, 1880, 1885, 1937, 1945, 2023–35, 2327, 2511–15, 2636–45, 2763–9, 2771–83, 4126
   Guerra Antigua 80, 161, 175, 499, 552–3, 569–70, 579–80, 589–90, 604–6, 626–8, 640, 653–5, 667, 670–1, 688–90, 712–13, 728–30, 744–5, 762–4, 777–8, 789–90, 799–800, 808, 817–18, 826–8, 839–41, 853–4, 864–5 876–7, 1304
   K 1426–27, 1593, 1611, 1615
   Patronato Real 29, 31, 627
   Quitaciones de Corte 1–40
Archivo Histórico de Protocolos, Madrid 1847, 1849

Archivo Histórico Nacional, Madrid 33
  Consejos 7258
  Inquisición
    Libros 271, 359, 361–2, 366–7, 592, 1338
    Pruebas 1306
  Libros de Plaza 724
  Ordenes Militares 5089, 6278
Archivo Municipal de Valladolid, *Libros de Actas* 23–30
Archivo Secreto de Vaticano, Rome 440–449
Biblioteca Nacional, Madrid 904, 1104, 1167, 1429, 2058, 2079, 2081, 2346–9, 2352,
    2355, 2394, 2577, 3150, 3827, 3987, 4013, 5972, 6754, 7423, 8850, 10609,
    10857, 10923, 11011, 11085, 11250, 12179, 18419, 18633, 18722/7
British Library, London
  Additional Manuscripts 10,236, 28,337, 28,339, 28,341, 28,342, 28,344, 28,345,
    28,347, 28,349, 28,363, 28,374, 28,378, 28,422, 28,425, 28,426, 28,436,
    28,465, 28,701, 29,853
  Egerton 345, 2055, 2081
  Sloane 1573
  Stowe 71, 168, 170, 173–4
Hatfield House, Hertfordshire
  Cecil Papers, 125
Public Records Office, London SP 94/6–24
Real Biblioteca, Palacio Real, Madrid
    11/870, 1538, 1611, 1926, 1930, 1979, 2100, 2106–7, 2112–13, 2116–21,
    2123, 2129, 2132, 2136–8, 2140, 2142, 2146, 2154–6, 2164, 2166, 2173–80,
    2242, 2262, 2334, 2336, 2340–1, 2345, 2364, 2554, 2609, 2621, 2636, 2699,
    2856, 2882, 2996, 3096, 3309, 3312, 3333, 3405, 3434, 3436, 3563, 4050,
    4143, 4330, 4345, 4348, 4528, 4632, 4635, 4647, 4663
Real Academía de Historia, Madrid
  Salazar y Castro
    F-17–18, G-29, 31, K41, 58, M-71–3

Primary sources

Actas de las Cortes de Castilla, vols. xviii–xxxiv, Madrid, 1893–1909
Aguilar, Gaspar, *Fiestas nupciales que la ciudad y reino de Valencia han hecho al casamiento del
    Rey*, ed. Antonio Pérez y Gómez , Valencia, 1975
Alcocer y Martínez, M., *Consultas del Consejo de Estado*, Vols. III and IV of *Colección de
    Documentos Inéditos para la Historia de España y sus Indias. Archivo Histórico Español*,
    vol. III, años 1600–1603; vol. IV, años 1604–1606, Valladolid, 1930–32
Almansa y Mendoza, A., *Obra periodística*, ed. Henry Ettinghausen and Manuel Borrego,
    Madrid, 2001
Álvarez y Baena, J. A., *Compendio histórico, de las grandezas de la coronada villa de Madrid,*

corte de la monarquía de España, Madrid, 1786

Cabrera de Córdoba, Luis, *Relaciones de las cosas sucedidas en la corte de España desde 1599 hasta 1614*, Madrid, 1857

Cabrera de Córdoba, Luis, *Historia de Felipe Sigundo, Rey de España*, 4 vols., Madrid, 1876–77

Cervantes, M. de, *Exemplary Stories*, ed. C. A. Jones, Harmondsworth, 1972

Cervantes, M. de, *The Adventures of Don Quixote*, trans, J. M. Cohen, Harmondsworth, 1961

Ciscar Pallares, E., *Las corts valencianas de Felipe III*, Valencia, 1973 reprint

CODOIN (*Colección de Documentos Inéditos para la Historia de España*), Madrid, 1842–95:

Vol. xxiii, Raneo, José, *Libro donde se trata de los Vireyes Lugartenientes del Reino de Nápoles y de las cosas tocantes a su grandeza (1634)*, pp. 7–575

Vol. xxxvi, Muñoz de Escabar, Juan, *Relación del dinero remitido a Flándes*, p. 543

Vol. xli, *Correspondencia de don Francisco de Mendoza, Almirante de Aragón, con el Archiduque Alberto. Guerra de Flándes (1596–1602)*, pp. 421–555, and Vol. xlii, pp. 5–214

Vol. xlii, *Documentos del Archiduque Alberto (1598–1621)*, pp. 218–25 and *Correspondencia del Archiduque Alberto con don Francisco de Sandoval y Rojas, Marqués de Denia (1598–1611)*, pp. 276–572, and Vol. xliii, pp. 5–221

Vols. xlv–xlvii, *Documentos relativos a don Pedro Girón, III Duque de Osuna (1575–1621)*

Vols. lx, lxi, Matías de Novoa, *Historia de Felipe III*, pp. 3–555; 1–171

Colmenares, D. de, *Historia de la insigne ciudad de Segovia y compendio de las historias de Castilla*, 2 vols., Segovia, 1969–70

Damonte, M., *Felipe IV el grande rey de las Españas. Manoscritto anónimo de XVII siglo*, Milan, 1980

Escagedo Salmón, Mateo (ed.), 'Los Acebedos', *Boletín de la Biblioteca Menéndez y Pelayo*, Vols. v–ix, 1923–27

Escolano, Gaspar, *Decada primera de la historia de la insigne y coronada ciudad y reino de Valencia*, Valencia, 1972 reprint of 1610–11 edn

Felipe III, *Cartas de Felipe III a su hija Ana, reina de Francia, 1616–1618*, ed. R. Martorell Telléz-Girón, Madrid, 1929

Fernández Álvarez, M., *Corpus documental de Carlos V*, 4 vols., Salamanca, 1973–81

Fernández de Caso, *Discvrso en qve se refieren las solenidades y fiestas con que el excelentísimo Duque celebrò en su villa de Lerma*, Madrid, 1619?

Fernández Navarrete, P., *Conservación de monarquías*, Madrid, 1626

García Mercadal, J. (ed.), *Viajes de extranjeros por España y Portugal*, 3 vols., Madrid, 1952

Gascón de Torquemada, G., *Gaçeta y nuevas de la Corte de España, desde el año 1600 en adelante*, Madrid, 1991

Girón, Pedro, *Crónica del emperador Carlos V*, ed. J. Sánchez Montes, Madrid, 1964

Gondomar, Count of, *Correspondencia oficial de don Diego Sarmiento de Acuña, Conde de Gondomar*, in DIHE, 4 vols., Madrid, 1936–45

Góngora, Luis de, *Obras completas*, eds. J. Millé y Giménez and I. Millé y Giménez, Madrid, 1961

González Cellorigo, M., *Memorial de la política necesaria y util restauracion a la republica de España*, Valladolid, 1600.

González Dávila, G., *Teatro de las grandezas de la villa de Madrid. Corte de los Reyes Católicos de España*, Madrid, 1986, reprint of 1623 edn

González Dávila, G., *Historia de la vida y hechos del inclito monarca, amado y santo D. Felipe III*, in P. Salazar de Mendoza, *Monarquía de España*, Madrid, 1770–71

González Dávila, G., *Teatro eclesiastico de las yglesias metropolitanas y catedrales de los reinos de las dos Castillas*, 4 vols., Madrid, 1645–1700

González Palencia, A. (ed.), *La junta de reformación*, Valladolid, 1932

González Palencia, A. (ed.), *Noticias de Madrid, 1621–1627*, Madrid, 1942

Guzmán, Diego de, *Reyna católica. Vida y muerte de Doña Margarita de Austria, Reyna de Espanna*, Madrid, 1617?

Harleian Miscellany. Or, a Collection of Scarce Curious and Entertaining Pamphlets as well in Manuscript as in Print Found in the Late Earl of Oxford's Library, London, printed for Robert Dutton, 1808–11

Herrera, P. de, *Translación del santíssimo sacramento a la iglesia colegial de San Pedro de la villa de Lerma*, Madrid, 1618

Howell, J., *Epistolae Ho-Elianae*, 11th edn., London, 1754

Khevenhüller, Hans, *Diario de Hans Khevenhüller embajador imperial en la corte de Felipe II*, ed. F. Labrador Arroyo, SECCFC, Madrid, 2001

León Pinelo, A., *Anales de Madrid de León Pinelo. Reinado de Felipe III. Años 1598 a 1621*, ed. R. Martorell Téllez-Girón, Madrid, 1931

Lonchay, H. and Cuvelier, J., *Correspondance de la cour d'Espagne sur les affaires des Pays-Bas au XVIIe siècle*, 6 vols., Brussels, 1923–37

Lope de Vega, Felix, *Epistolario*, ed., Agustín G. de Amezua y Mayo, 4 vols., Madrid, 1935–43

Loperraez Corvalan, J., *Descripción histórica del obispado de Osma con el catálogo de sus prelados*, 3 vols., Madrid, 1978

López, Juan, *Tercera parte de la historia general de Sancto Domingo y de su orden de predicadores,* Valladolid, 1613

López de Haro, A., *Nobiliario genealógico de los reyes y titvlos de España*, 2 vols., Madrid, 1622

Malvezzi, V., *Historia de los primeros años del reinado de Felipe IV*, ed. D. L. Shaw, London, 1968

Malvezzi, V., *Historia ... que comprehende sucessos de el reynado de Don Phelipe Tercero ...*, in J. Yáñez, *Memorias para la historia de Don Felipe III, Rey de Espana*, Madrid, 1723

Mantuano, Pedro, *Casamientos de España y Francia y viage del Duque de Lerma, llevando la Reyna Christianíssima doña Ana de Austria al passo de Beobia, y trayendo la Princessa de Asturias,* Madrid, 1618

Matilla Tascón, Antonio, *Testamentos de 43 personajes del Madrid de los Austrias*, Madrid, 1983

Moncada, S. de, *Restauración política de España*, 1619 edn., ed. J. Vilar, Madrid, 1974

Mota, Diego de la, *Libro del principio de la orden de la Cavalleria de S. Tiago del Espada*, Valencia, 1599

Núñez de Salcedo, P., 'Relación de los títulos que hay en España', *Boletín de la Real Academía de la Historia*, Vol. lxxiii, 1918, pp. 468–92

Pearsall Smith, L., *The Life and Letters of Sir Henry Wotton*, 2 vols., Oxford, 1907

Pinheiro da Veiga, T., *Fastigiana vida cotidiana en la corte de Valladolid*, Valladolid, 1989 reprint

Quintana, Jerónimo de, *A la muy antigua, noble y coronada villa de Madrid. Historia de su antigüedad, nobleza y grandeza*, Madrid, 1629

Riba García, C. (ed.), *Correspondencia privada de Felipe II con su secretario Mateo Vázquez de Leca 1567–1591*, Madrid, 1959

Roco de Campofrio, Juan, *España en Flándes. Trece años de gobierno del Archiduque Alberto (1595–1608)*, Madrid, 1973

Sandoval, Prudencio de, *Chrónica del inclito Emperador de España, don Alonso VII*, Madrid, 1600

Sangrador, Matias, *Historia de la muy noble y leal ciudad de Valladolid*, 2 vols., Valladolid, 1854

Sepúlveda, Jerónimo de, *Sucessos de Reinado de Felipe III*, published by P. Fr. Julián Zarco Cuevas, *Ciudad de Dios. Revista Augustiniana religiosa, científica y literaria*, vols. cxxiii–cxxix, Madrid, 1924

Simon Diaz, José, *Relaciones breves de actos públicos celebrados en Madrid de 1541 a 1650*, Madrid, 1982

Teresa de Ávila, *Obras completas*, ed. Efren de la Madre de Dios and Otger Steggink, Madrid, 1962

Tresswell, R., 'A RELATION Of such Things as were observed to happen in the Journey of THE RIGHT HONOURABLE CHARLES, EARL OF NOTTINGHAM, Lord High Admiral of England', *Harleian Miscellany*, ii, London, 1809, pp. 535–66

Valle de la Cerda, Luis, *Avisos en materia de estado y guerra*, Madrid, 1599

Viciana, Martín de, *Crónica de la inclita y coronada ciudad de Valencia*, ed. Sebastian García Martínez, Valencia, 1972

Winwood, Sir Ralph, *Memorials of Affairs of State in the Reigns of Queen Elizabeth and King James I*, 3 vols., London, 1725

Yáñez, J., *Memorias para la historia de Don Felipe III, Rey de España*, Madrid, 1723

Secondary sources

Adamson, J. (ed.), *The Princely Courts of Europe 1500–1750. Ritual, Politics and Culture under the Ancien Régime 1500–1750*, London, 1999

Allen, P. C., *Philip III and the Pax Hispánica, 1598–1621. The Failure of Grand Strategy*, New Haven and London, 2000

Alvar Ezquerra, A., *El nacimiento de una capital europea. Madrid entre 1561 y 1606*, Madrid, 1989

Aram, Bethany, *La reina Juana. Gobierno, piedad y dinastía*, Madrid, 2001

Artola, Miguel, *La monarquía de España*, Madrid, 1999

Atienza Hernández, I., *Aristocracía, poder y riqueza en la España moderna. La Casa de Osuna, siglos XV–XIX*, Madrid, 1987

Aymard, M. and Romani, M. (eds), *La cour comme institution économique*, Paris, 1998

Baltar Rodríguez, J. F., *Las juntas de gobierno en la monarquía hispánica (siglos XVI–XVII)*, Madrid, 1998

Barrios, F., *El Consejo de Estado de la monarquía española, 1526–1812*, Madrid, 1984

Benigno, F. *La sombra del rey.Validos y lucha política en la España del siglo XVII*, Madrid, 1994

Benítez Sánchez-Blanco, R., 'The "Géographie d l'Espagne morisque" FortyYears On', in E. Martínez Ruiz and M. Pazzis Pi Corrales (ed.), *Spain and Sweden in the Baroque Era (1600–1660)*, Madrid, 2000

Benito Ruano, E., 'Recepción madrileña de la reina Margarita de Austria', *AIEM*, i, 1996, pp. 85–98

Bennassar, B., *Recherches sur les grandes épidémies dans le nord de l'Espagne à la fin du XVIe siècle*, Paris, 1969

Bennassar, B., *Valladolid en el Siglo de Oro. Una ciudad de Castilla y su entorno agrario en el siglo XVI*, Valladolid, 1983

Bergin, Joseph, *Cardinal Richelieu. Power and the Pursuit ofWealth*, New Haven, 1985

Bergin, Joseph, *The Rise of Richelieu*, New Haven, 1997

Bombín Pérez, A., *La cuestión de Monferrato 1613–1618*, Valladolid, 1975

Boronat y Barrachina, P., *Los moriscos españoles y su expulsión*, 2 vols., ed. R. García Cárcel, Granada, 1992

Boyden, J. M., *The Courtier and the King. Ruy Gómez de Silva, Philip II and the Court of Spain*, Berkeley, 1995

Braudel, F., *The Mediterranean and the MediterraneanWorld in the Age of Philip II*, 2 vols., London, 1973

Brightwell, Peter, 'The Spanish System and the TwelveYears Truce', *English Historical Review*, 89, 1974, pp. 270–92

Brightwell, Peter, 'The Spanish Origins of the Thirty Years War', *European Studies Review*, 9, 1979, pp. 409–31

Brightwell, Peter, 'Spain and Bohemia. The Decision to Intervene', *European Studies Review*, 12, 1982, pp. 117–41

Brightwell, Peter, 'Spain, Bohemia and Europe, 1619–1621', *European Studies Review*, 12, 1982, pp. 371–99

Brooke, Xanthe, 'The Patronage and Art Collection of the Duke of Lerma', unpublished M. Phil. thesis, Courtauld Institute, London University, 1983

Brown, J., *The Golden Age of Spanish Painting*, New Haven, 1991

Brown, J. and Elliott, J. H., *A palace for a king.The Buen Retiro and the Court of Philip IV*, New Haven and London, 1980

Bryant, L. M., *The King and the City in the Parisian Royal Entry Ceremony. Politics, Ritual and Art in the Renaissance*, Geneva, 1986

Bustamante García, A., *La Arquitectura clasicista del foco vallisoletano (1560–1641)*, Valladolid, 1983

Bustamante García, A., *La octava maravilla del mundo. Estudio histórico sobre el Escorial de Felipe II*, Madrid, 1994

Cabeza Rodríguez, A., Torremocha Hernández, M. and Martín de la Guardia, R., 'Fiesta y política en Valladolid. La entrada de Felipe III en el año 1600', *IH*, 16, 1996, pp. 77–87

Cámera Muñoz, A., 'El poder de la imagen y la imagen del poder. La fiesta en Madrid en el Renacimiento', in *Madrid en el Renacimiento*, Madrid, 1986

Campos y Fernández de Sevilla, F. Javier (ed.), *Felipe II y su época. Actas del Simposium (1) 1/5-ix-1998*, Madrid, 1998

Carbajo Isla, M. F., *La población de la villa de Madrid. Desde finales del siglo XVI hasta mediados del siglo XIX*, Madrid, 1987

Carlos Morales, C. J. de, *El Consejo de Hacienda de Castilla, 1523–1602*, Ávila, 1996

Carmén Pescador del Hoyo, M. del, 'La más antigua plaza de toros de Madrid', *AIEM*, 3, 1968, pp. 29–41

Carter, C. H., *The Secret Diplomacy of the Habsburgs, 1598–1625*, New York and London, 1964

Casey, James, *The Kingdom of Valencia in the Seventeenth Century*, Cambridge, UK, 1979

Casey, James, 'Spain: a Failed Transition', in P. Clark (ed.), *The European Crisis of the 1590s*, London, 1985

Castroviejo, J. M. and Fernández de Córdoba, F. de P., *El Conde de Gondomar. Un azor entre ocasos*, Madrid, 1968

Cayetano Martín, C. and Guerrero, P. Flores, 'Nuevas aportaciones al recibimiento en Madrid de la reina doña Margarita de Austria (24 de octubre de 1599), *AIEM* xxii, 1988, pp. 387–400

Cereceda, F., 'La vocación jesuítica del duque de Lerma', *Razon y Fé*, 605, June 1948, pp. 512–23

Cervera Vera, L., *El conjunto palacial de la villa de Lerma*, 2-vol. reprint, Lerma, 1996 of 1-vol. original, Madrid, 1967

Cervera Vera, L., *Bienes muebles en el palacio ducal de Lerma*, Madrid, 1967

Cervera Vera, L., *El convento de Santo Domingo en la villa de Lerma*, Madrid, 1969

Cervera Vera, L., *La iglesia colegial de San Pedro en Lerma*, Burgos, 1981

Chabas, Roque, *Historia de la ciudad de Denia*, 3 parts, Denia, 1874–6

Chaunu, P., *Séville et l'Atlantique, 1504–1650*, 8 vols, Paris, 1955–9

Checa Cremades, Fernando, *Felipe II Mecenas de las Artes*, Madrid, 1992

Checa Cremades, Fernando (ed.), *El real alcázar de Madrid. Dos siglos de arquitectura y coleccionismo en la corte de los reyes de España*, Madrid, 1994

Chudoba, B., *Spain and the Empire, 1519–1634*, Chicago, 1952

Clark, P. (ed.), *The European Crisis of the 1590s*, London, 1985

Clavero, B. *Mayorazgo. Propiedad feudal en Castilla (1369–1836)*, Madrid, 1974

Cochrane, E. (ed. J. Kirshner), *Italy 1530–1630*, Longman History of Italy, London and New York, 1988

Corral y Maestro, L., *Don Diego del Corral y Arellano y los Corrales de Valladolid*, Valladolid, 1905

Croft, Pauline (ed.), *Patronage, Culture and Power. The Early Cecils*, New Haven, 2002

Dadson, Trevor, 'The Duke of Lerma and the Count of Salinas: Politics and Friendship in Early Seventeenth-Century Spain', *European History Quarterly*, 25, 1995, pp. 5–38

Dalmases, Cándido de, *Padre Francisco de Borja*, Madrid, 1983

Danvila y Burguero, A., *Diplomáticos españoles. Don Cristóbal de Moura*, Madrid, 1900

Davies, Gareth, *A Poet at Court. Antonio Hurtado de Mendoza*, Oxford, 1971

Diccionario de historia eclesiástica de España, 5 vols., ed. Q. Aldea Vaquero et al., Madrid, 1972–89

Dickens, A. G. (ed.), *The Courts of Europe. Politics, Patronage and Royalty 1400–1800*, London, 1977

Domínguez Ortíz, A., *Política y hacienda de Felipe IV*, Madrid, 1960

Domínguez Ortíz, A., *La sociedad española en el siglo XVII*, 2 vols., Madrid, 1963–70

Domínguez Ortíz, A. and Vincent, B., *Historia de los moriscos*, Madrid, 1978

Echarte, T., 'El cardenal fray Jerónimo Xavierre (1546–1608)', *Cuadernos de Historia. Jeronimo Zúrita*, xxxix–xl, 1981, pp. 151–76

Eire, C. M. N., *From Madrid to Purgatory. The Art and Craft of Dying in Sixteenth-Century Spain*, Cambridge, UK, 1995

Elliott, J. H., *The Revolt of the Catalans. A Study in the Decline of Spain (1598–1640)*, Cambridge, UK, 1963

Elliott, J. H., *The Count-Duke of Olivares. The Statesman in an Age of Decline*, New Haven and London, 1986

Elliott, J. H., *Spain and its World 1500–1700. Selected Essays*, New Haven and London, 1989

Elliott, J. H., and Brockliss, L. W. B. (eds.), *The World of the Favourite*, New Haven and London, 1999

Entrambasaguas, J. de, *Una familia de ingenios. Los Ramírez de Prado*, Madrid, 1943

Escudero, J. A., *Los Secretarios de Estado y del Despacho*, 4 vols., Madrid, 1976

Ettinghausen, H., 'The News in Spain; *Relaciones de sucesos* in the Reigns of Philip III and IV', *European History Quarterly*, 14, 1984, pp. 1–20

Ettinghausen, H., 'Prince Charles and the King of Spain's sister – What the Papers Said', University of Southampton, 1985

Evans, R. J. W., *Rudolf II and his World. A Study in Intellectual History 1576–1612*, Oxford, 1973, pp. 43–83

Evans, R. J. W., *The Making of the Habsburg Monarchy, 1500–1700*, Oxford, 1979

Ezquerra Revilla, I., *El Consejo Real de Castilla bajo Felipe II. Grupos de poder y luchos faccionales*, Madrid, 2000

Fayard, J., *Les membres du Conseil de Castille à l'époque moderne (1621–1746)*, Geneva, 1979

Fernández de Béthencourt, F., *Historia genealógica y heráldica de la Monarquía Española, Casa Real, y Grandes de España*, ten vols., Madrid, 1897–1920

Fernández Conti, S., *Los consejos de estado y guerra de la monarquía hispana en tiempos de Felipe II, 1548–1598*, Valladolid, 1998

Fernández Duro, C., *Don Pedro Enríquez de Acevedo, Conde de Fuentes. Bosquejo encomiástico*, Madrid, 1884

Fernández Duro, C., *El Gran Duque de Osuna y su marina*, Madrid, 1885

Fernández Duro, C., *Armada española desde la unión de los reinos de Castilla y León*, 9 vols., Madrid, 1895–1903

Fernández Martín, L., 'La Marquesa del Valle: Una vida dramática en la corte de los Austrias', *Hispania*, 143, 1979, pp. 559–638

Feros, Antonio, 'Lerma y Olivares: la práctica del valimiento en la primera mitad del Seiscientos', in *La España del Conde Duque de Olivares. Encuentro Internacional sobre la España del Conde Duque de Olivares*, Toro, 15–18 September 1987, Valladolid, 1990, pp. 195–224

Feros, Antonio, *Kingship and Favoritism in the Spain of Philip III, 1598–1621*, Cambridge, UK, 2000

Feros, Antonio, *El Duque de Lerma. Realeza y favoritismo en la España de Felipe III*, Madrid, 2002

Ferrer Valls, T., *La práctica escénica cortesana. De la época del emperador a la de Felipe III*, London, 1991

Fuentes, J., *El conde de Fuentes y su tiempo. Estudios de historia militar. Siglos XVI a XVII*, Madrid, 1908

Gachard, L. P. (ed.), *Collection des voyages des souverains des Pays-Bas*, Brussels, 1974–82

Gachard, L. P., *Don Carlos y Felipe II*, Madrid, 1984

Gaillard, Claude, *Le Portugal sous Philippe III d'Espagne. L'action de Diego de Silva y Mendoza*, Grenoble, 1983

García-España, E. and Molinié-Bertrand, A. (eds.), *Censo de Castilla de 1591*, Madrid, 1986

García García, B. J., *La Pax Hispánica. Política exterior del Duque de Lerma*, Leuven, 1996

García García, B. J., 'Honra, desengaño y condena de una privanza. La retirada de la corte del Cardenal Duque de Lerma', iv reunión Científica de la Asociación Española de Historia, Alicante, 1997, pp. 679–95

García García, B. J., 'Los marqueses de Denia en la corte de Felipe II. Linaje, servicio y virtud', in J. Martínez Millán (ed.), *Europa dividida. La Monarquía Católica de Felipe II*, vol. ii, Madrid, 1998, pp. 305–31

García García, B. J., 'El confesor fray Luis Aliaga y la conciencia del rey', in Flavio Rurale (ed.), *I Religiosi a corte. Teologia, politica e diplomazia in Antico Regime*, Rome, 1998, pp. 159–94

García Martínez, S., *Bandolerismo, piratería y control de Moriscos en Valencia durante el reinado de Felipe II*, Valencia, 1977

García Oro, José, *Don Diego Sarmiento de Acuña, conde de Gondomar y embajador de España (1567–1626)*, La Coruña, 1997

García Pinacho, M. del Pilar (ed.), *Los Álvarez de Toledo. Nobleza viva*, Segovia, 1998

Ginarte González, Ventura, *El Duque de Lerma. Protector de la Reforma Trinitaria (1599–1613)*, Madrid, 1982

Goldberg, Edward L., 'Artistic Relations between the Medici and the Spanish Courts, 1587–1621', *The Burlington Magazine*, London, part. 1, no. 1.115, Feb. 1996, pp. 105–14, part 2, no. 1121, August 1996, pp. 529–40

González Pablos, E. (ed.), *El palacio ducal de Lerma de ayer a hoy*, Segovia, 2003

Goodman, David, *Spanish Naval Power, 1589–1665. Reconstruction and Defeat*, Cambridge, UK, 1997

Guerra de la Vega, R., *Madrid de los Austrias. Guía de arquitectura*, Madrid, 1999 (?)

Guerrero Mayllo, Ana, *Familia y vida cotidiana de una elite de poder. Los regidores madrileños en tiempos de Felipe II*, Madrid, 1993

Guerrero Mayllo, Ana, 'Don Pedro de Franqueza y Esteve. De regidor madrileño a Secretario de Estado', *Pedralbes*, no. 11, 1991, pp. 79–89'

Gutiérrez Alonso, A., Martín González, J. J., Urrea, J., Rubio González, L. and Virgili Blanquet, *Valladolid en el siglo XVII*, Historia de Valladolid, IV, Valladolid, 1982

Haupt, H., 'From Feuding Brothers to a Nation at War with Itself', in E. Fučíkova (ed.), *Rudolph II and Prague, The Court and the City*, London, 1997

Hayden, J. M., *France and the Estates-General of 1614*, Cambridge, UK, 1974

Herrera García, Antonio, *El estado de Olivares. Origen, formación y desarrollo con los tres primeros condes (1535–1645)*, Seville, 1990

Highfield, J. R. L., 'The De la Cerda, the Pimentel and the So-called "Price Revolution"', *EHR*, 1972, 87, pp. 495–512

Hollingsworth, M., *Patronage in Sixteenth Century Italy*, London, 1996

Howarth, D., *Images of Rule. Art and Politics in the English Renaissance, 1485–1649*, Basingstoke, 1997

Huemer, Frances, *Corpus Rubenianum*, London, 1977

Israel, Jonathan, *The Dutch Republic. Its Rise, Greatness and Fall, 1477–1806*, Oxford, 1998

Jago, C., 'The Influence of Debt on the Relations between Crown and Aristocracy in Seventeenth-century Castile', *Economic History Review*, 26, 1973, pp. 218–36

Jago, Charles, 'The "Crisis of the Aristocracy" in Seventeenth-century Castile', *Past and Present*, 84, 1979, pp. 60–90

Jago, Charles, 'Habsburg Absolutism and the Cortes of Castile', *American Historical Review*, 96, 1981, pp. 307–26

Juderias, Julián, 'Un proceso político en tiempo de Felipe III. Don Rodrigo Calderón, Marqués de Siete Iglesias. Su vida, su proceso y su muerte', *Revista de Archivos, Bibliotecas y Museos*, 3a época, v, May 1905, pp. 334–65; ix, Dec. 1905, 349–63; x, Jan. 1906, pp. 1–31

Juderias, Julián, 'Los favoritos de Felipe III. Don Pedro Franqueza, Conde de Villalonga, secretario de estado', *Revista de Archivos, Bibliotecas y Museos*, xx, Jan.–Jun. 1909, pp. 16–27 and 223–40

Kamen, H., *Philip of Spain*, New Haven, 1997

Keniston, H., *Francisco de los Cobos, Secretary of the Emperor Charles V*, Pittsburgh, 1960

Kirk, Douglas, 'Music to Beguile a King', Notes to Gabrieli Consort and Players, *Music for the Duke of Lerma*, Archiv Produktion, 2001

Kleinman, R., *Anne of Austria. Queen of France*, Columbus, Ohio, 1985

Lapeyre, H., *Géographie de l'Espagne morisque*, Paris, 1959

Lario Ramírez, D. de, *El Comte-Duc d'Olivares i el Regne de València*, Valencia, 1986

Lea, H. C., *A History of the Inquisition of Spain*, 4 vols., New York, 1906–07

Levy Peck, L., *Court Patronage and Corruption in Early Stuart England*, Boston, 1990

Lockyer, R., *Buckingham. The Life and Political Career of George Villiers, First Duke of Buckingham, 1592–1628*, London, 1981

Loomie, A. J., 'Guy Fawkes in Spain. The "Spanish treason" in Spanish documents', *Bulletin of the Institute of Historical Research, Special Supplement*, no. 9, London, 1971

López García, J. M. (ed.), *El impacto de la Corte en Castilla. Madrid y su territorio en la época moderna*, Madrid, 1998

Lovett, A. W., 'A Cardinal's Papers. The Rise of Mateo Vázquez de Leca', *EHR*, 88, 1973, pp. 241–61

Lovett, A. W., *Philip II and Mateo Vázquez de Leca. The Government of Spain 1572–1592*, Geneva, 1977

Mackay, R., *The Limits of Royal Authority. Resistance and Obedience in Seventeenth-century Castile*, Cambridge, UK, 1999

Madrid. Atlas Histórico de la ciudad, siglos IX–XIX, eds. V. Pinto Crespo and S. Madrazo Madrazo, Madrid and Barcelona 1995

Madrid en el Renacimiento, Madrid, 1986

Magurn, R. (trans. and ed.), *The Letters of Peter Paul Rubens*, Cambridge, MA, 1955

Márquez de la Plata, V. M. and Valero de Bernabé, L., *El Libro de Oro de los duques*, Madrid, 1994

Martí y Monsó, J., *Estudios histórico-artísticos relativos principalmente a Valladolid*, Valladolid-Madrid, 1898–1901

Martín González, J., *La arquitectura doméstica del renacimiento en Valladolid*, Valladolid, 1948

Martínez Barra, J. A., *La condesa de Valencia de Don Juan, el Marqués de Poza y el Duque de Lerma*, Madrid, 1978

Martínez Hernández, S., *El marqués de Velada y la corte en los reinados de Felipe II y Felipe III. Nobleza cortesana y cultura política en la España del Siglo de Oro*, JCL, 2004

Martínez Medina, Africa, *Palacios madrileños*, Madrid, 1997

Martínez Millán, J. (ed.), *La Corte de Felipe II*, Madrid, 1994

Martínez Ruiz, E. and Pazzis Pi Corrales, M. (eds.), *Spain and Sweden in the Baroque Era (1600–1660)*, Madrid, 2000

Mateu Ibars, J., *Los virreyes de Valencia. Fuentes para su estudio*, Valencia, 1963

Medina Encina, P. 'El Consejo de Indias', in P. González García (ed.), *Archivo General de Indias*, Madrid, 1995, pp. 196–248

Mesonero Romanos, R. de, *El antiguo Madrid*, Madrid, 2000

Mitchell, B., *1598. A Year of Pageantry in Late Renaissance Ferrara*, New York, 1990

Moffitt, J. F., 'Rubens's *Duke of Lerma*, Equestrian Amongst "Imperial Horsemen"', *Artibus et Historiae (Austria)*, 1994, 15(29), pp. 99–110

Molinié-Bertrand, A., 'El Adelantamiento de Cazorla en el siglo XVI', *Cuadernos de Investigaciones Españoles*, i, 1977, pp. 7–21

Molinié-Bertrand, A., *Au Siècle d'Or. L'Espagne et ses hommes. La population du Royaume de Castille au XVIe siècle*, Paris, 1985

Morineau, M., *Incroyables gazettes et fabuleux métaux. Les retours des trésors américains d'après les gazettes hollondaises, XVI–XVIIIe siècles*, Cambridge, UK, 1985

Mousnier, R. *The Assassination of Henry IV. The Tyrranicide Problem and the Consolidation of the French Absolute Monarchy in the Early 17th Century*, London, 1964

Nader, H., 'Noble Income in Sixteenth-Century Castile. The Case of the Marquises of Mondéjar, 1480–1580', *EHR*, 1997

O'Callaghan, J. F., *A History of Medieval Spain*, Ithaca, NY, 1975

Ossorio y Gallardo, A., *Los hombres de toga en el proceso de D. Rodrigo Calderón*, Madrid, 1918

Palacio Real, Biblioteca, *Las trazas de Juan de Herrera y sus seguidores*, Patrimonio Nacional, Santander, 2001

Palomares Ibáñez, J. M., *El patronato del Duque de Lerma sobre el convento de San Pablo de Valladolid*, Valladolid, 1970

Pardo de Guevara y Valdés, Eduardo, *Don Pedro Fernández de Castro VII Conde de Lemos (1576–1622)*, 2 vols., La Coruña, 1977

Parker, G. (ed.), *The Thirty Years War*, 2nd edn., London, 1997

Parker, G., *The Grand Strategy of Philip II*, New Haven, 1998

Parker, G., *Europe in Crisis, 1598–1648*, 2nd edn, London, 2001

Parker, G., *The Dutch Revolt*, London, 2002

Parker, G., *The Army of Flanders and the Spanish Road 1567–1659. The Logistics of Spanish Victory and Defeat in the Low Countries' Wars*, 2nd edn., Cambridge, UK, 2004

Payo Hernanz, R. J., *Lerma*, Centro de Iniciativas Turísticas de Lerma, 2004(?)

Pelorson, J.-M. 'Para una   reinterpretación de la Junta del Desempeño General (1603–1606) a la luz de la "visita" de Alonso Ramírez de Prado y de don Pedro Franqueza, Conde de Villalonga', *Actas del IV Symposium de Historia de la Administración*, Alcalá de Henares, 1983, pp. 613–17

Pelorson, J-M., *Les Letrados juristes castillans sous Philippe III. Recherches sur leur place dans la societé, la culture et l'état*, Poitiers, 1980

Pérez, Joseph, *La Revolución de las comunidades de Castilla (1520–1521)*, Madrid, 1977

Pérez, Bustamante, C., *Felipe III. Semblanza de un monarca y perfiles de una privanza*, Madrid, 1950,

Pérez, Bustamante, C., *La España de Felipe III*, Vol. xxiv of Ramon Menéndez Pidal (ed.), *Historia de España*, Madrid, 1979

Pérez Gil, J., *El palacio de la Ribera. Recreo y boato en el Valladolid cortesano*, Valladolid, 2002

Pérez Martín, M. J., *Margarita de Austria, reina de España*, Madrid, 1961

Pérez Mínguez, F., *D. Juan de Idiáquez, embajador y consejero de Felipe II*, San Sebastián, 1934–35

Perrens, F-T., *Les Mariages espagnols sous le règne de Henri IV et la régence de Marie de Médicis*, Paris, 1869

Proske, B. Gilman, *Pompeo Leoni. Work in Marble and Alabaster in Relation to Spanish Sculpture*, New York, 1956

Pulido Bueno, I., *La Real Hacienda de Felipe III*, Huelva, 1996

Ranke, L. von, *The Ottoman and Spanish Empires in the Sixteenth and Seventeenth Centuries*, London, 1848

Redworth, Glyn, *The Prince and the Infanta.The Cultural Politics of the Spanish Match*, New Haven, 2003

Redworth, G. and Checa Cremades, F., 'The Courts of the Spanish Habsburgs', in J. Adamson (ed.), *The Princely Courts of Europe 1500–1750*, London, 1999, pp. 43–65

Rennert, H. A., *The Life of Lope de Vega*, NewYork, 1968

Ribot García, L. A., Bennassar, B., Martín González, J. J., Parrado del Olmo, J. M., Rubio González, L. and Rodríguez Martínez, L., *Valladolid, corazón del mundo hispánico. Siglo XVI*, Historia de Valladolid, III, Valladolid, 1981

Río Barredo, M. J. del, *Madrid. Urbs Regia. La capital ceremonial de la monarquía católica*, Madrid, 2000

Rivera Blanco, J. J., *El palacio real de Valladolid*, Valladolid, 1981

Rizzo, M., Ruiz Ibáñez, J. J. and Sabatini, G. (eds), *Le Forze del Principe. Recursos, instrumentos y límites en la práctica del poder soberano en los territorios de la monarquía hispánica*, 2 vols., Murcia, 2003

Robledo, Luis, 'Questions of Performance Practice in Philip III's Chapel', *Early Music*, May 1994, pp. 199–218

Rodríguez-Salgado, 'Honour and Profit in the Court of Philip II of Spain', in Aymard, M. and Romani, M. (eds), *La cour comme institution économique*, Paris, 1998

Rodríguez Villa, A., 'D. Francisco de Mendoza, Almirante de Aragón', in *Homenaje a Menéndez y Pelayo*, ii, 1899, pp. 487–610

Rodríguez Villa, A., *Ambrosio Spínola, primer marqués de los Balbases*, Madrid, 1905

Rott, Edouard, *Philippe III et le Duc de Lerme (1598–1621). Étude historique d'après des documents inédits*, Paris, 1887

Salazar y Castro, Luis, *Los comendadores de la Orden de Santiago*, Madrid, 1949

Salomon, N., *La vida rural castellana en tiempos de Felipe II*, Barcelona, 1973

Sánchez, M. S., *The Empress, the Queen, and the Nun.Women and Power at the Court of Philip III of Spain*, Baltimore, 1998

Sánchez Alonso, M. C., 'Juramentos de príncipes herederos en Madrid (1561–1598), in F. Checa (ed.), *El Real Alcázar de Madrid. Dos siglos de arquitectura y coleccionismo en la corte de los reyes de España*, Madrid, 1994, pp. 29–41

Santiago Fernández, J. de, *Política monetaria en Castilla durante el siglo XVII*, Valladolid, 2000

Sanz Ayán, C. and García García, B. J., *Teatro y comediantes en el Madrid de Felipe II*, Madrid, 2000

Schroth, Sara, 'The Private Collection of the Duke of Lerma', PhD dissertation, New York University, 1990

Scott, H. M. (ed.), *European Nobilities in the Seventeenth and Eighteenth Centuries*, 2 vols., London, 1994–95

Seco Serrano, C., 'Los comienzos de la privanza de Lerma según los embajadores florentinos', *Boletín de la Real Academia de Historia*, 144, 1959, pp. 75–101

Sepúlveda, Ricardo de, *El monasterio de San Jerónimo el Real de Madrid*, Madrid, 1883

Shergold, N. D., *A History of the Spanish Stage, from Medieval Times until the End of the Seventeenth Century*, Oxford, 1967

Sieber, Harry, 'The Magnificent Fountain. Literary Patronage in the Court of Philip

III', *Cervantes: Bulletin of the Cervantes Society of America*, 18(2), 1998, pp. 85–116

Stirling-Maxwell, Sir W., *The Cloister Life of Emperor Charles V*, London, 1891

Suárez Fernández, L., *Historia de España. Edad Media*, Madrid, 1970

Terry, Arthur, *Seventeenth-Century Spanish Poetry*, Cambridge, UK 1993

Tex, Jan den, *Oldenbarnevelt*, Cambridge, UK, 2 vols., 1973

Thomas, H., *Madrid. A Travellers' Companion*, New York, 1990

Thomas, W. and Duerloo, Luc (eds.), *Albert and Isabella 1598–1621*, Brussels, 1998

Thompson, I. A. A., 'The Armada and Administrative Reform: the Spanish Council of war in the Reign of Philip II', *English Historical Review*, 82, 1967, pp. 712–14

Thompson, I. A. A., *War and Government in Habsburg Spain 1560–1620*, London, 1976

Thompson, I. A. A., 'Crown and Cortes in Castile, 1590–1665', *Parliaments, Estates and Representation*, 2, London, 1982, pp. 29–45

Thompson, I. A. A., *War and Society in Habsburg Spain. Selected Essays*, Aldershot, 1992

Thompson, I. A. A., *Crown and Cortes. Government, Institutions and Representation in Early-Modern Castile*, Aldershot, 1993

Thompson, I. A. A., 'The Nobility of Spain, 1600–1800', in H. M. Scott, *The European Nobilities in the Seventeenth and Eighteenth Centuries*, 2 vols., London, 1994–95, Vol. i, *Western Europe*, pp. 174–236

Thompson, I. A. A., 'L'Audit de la guerre et de la paix. Avant et après Vervins', in J.-F. Labourdette et al. (eds.), *Le Traité de Vervins*, Paris, 2000, pp. 391–413

Tobío, Luis, *Gondomar y su triunfo sobre Raleigh*, Santiago de Compostela, 1974

Torras i Ribé, J., *Poders i relacions clientelars a la Catalunya dels Àustria Pere Franquesa (1547–1614)*, Vic, 1998

Tovar Martín, V., 'La entrada triunfal en Madrid de doña Margarita de Austria (24 de octubre de 1599)', *Archivo Español de Arte*, no. 244, 1988, pp. 385–403

Trewinnard, Richard, 'The Household of the Spanish Monarch. Structure, Cost and Personnel 1606–65', unpublished doctoral thesis, University of Wales, Cardiff, 1991

Valiente, F. T., *Los validos en la monarquía española del siglo XVII. Estudio Institucional*, Madrid, 1963

Varela, J., *La muerte del Rey. El ceremonial funerario de la monarquía española (1500–1885)*, Madrid, Turner, 1990

Veríssimo Serrão, J., *História de Portugal*, 4 vols., Lisbon, 1977–94

White, C., *Peter Paul Rubens. Man and Artist*, New Haven, 1987

Williams, Patrick, 'Philip III and the Restoration of Spanish Government, 1598–1603', *English Historical Review*, 88, no. 349, October 1973, pp. 751–69

Williams, Patrick, 'Política interior', in *Historia General de España y América*, vol. viii: *La crisis de la hegemonía española. Siglo XVII*, Madrid, 1986, pp. 419–43

Williams, Patrick, 'Lerma, Old Castile and the Travels of Philip III of Spain', *History*, 73 (239), October 1988, pp. 379–97

Williams, Patrick, 'Lerma, 1618. Dismissal or Retirement?', *European History Quarterly*, 19, no. 3, Jul. 1989, pp. 307–32

Williams, Patrick, 'A Jewish Councillor of Inquisition? Luis de Mercado, the Statutes of *limpieza de sangre* and the Politics of Vendetta (1598–1601), *Bulletin of Hispanic Studies*, lxvii, 1990, pp. 253–64

Williams, Patrick, *Philip II*, Basingstoke, 2001

Williams, Phillip, *Piracy and Naval Conflict in the Mediterranean, 1590–1610/20*, unpublished D.Phil., University of Oxford, 2001

Williams, Phillip, 'Past and Present: the Forms and Limits of Spanish Naval Power in the Mediterranean, 1590–1620', in M. Rizzo et al., *Le forze del principe*, i, pp. 237–78

Wright, Elizabeth R., *Pilgrimage to Patronage. Lope de Vega and the Court of Philip III, 1598–1621*, Lewisburg and London, 2001

Index

EU authorised representative for GPSR:
Easy Access System Europe, Mustamäe tee 50,
10621 Tallinn, Estonia
gpsr.requests@easproject.com